PROTECTING THE WILD

PROTECTING THE WILD

PARKS AND WILDERNESS,
THE FOUNDATION FOR CONSERVATION

Edited by George Wuerthner, Eileen Crist, and Tom Butler

WASHINGTON | COVELO | LONDON

Published by the Foundation for Deep Ecology in collaboration with Island Press.

Foundation for Deep Ecology
1606 Union Street, San Francisco, CA 94123
www.deepecology.org

Island Press
2000 M Street, NW, Suite 650, Washington, DC 20036
www. islandpress.org

ISBN 978-1-61091-548-9
Library of Congress Control Number: 2014959302

Grateful acknowledgment is made to the following authors and publishers: Harvey Locke's
"Nature Needs (at least) Half" was originally published as "Nature Needs Half: A Necessary and
Hopeful New Agenda for Protected Areas," in *PARKS: The International Journal of Protected Areas
and Conservation* (2013) 19.2 and is reprinted here in slightly modified form with permission of
IUCN and the author. "Bolder Thinking for Conservation" by Reed Noss et al. is adapted from
its original publication in *Conservation Biology* and is reprinted courtesy of the lead author
and used by permission of John Wiley and Sons. "What Is the Future of Conservation?" by
Daniel F. Doak et al.was published originally in *Trends in Ecology & Evolution* and is adapted
here by permission of the lead author and reprinted by permission of Elsevier. George Monbiot's
"The British Thermopylae and the Return of the Lynx" appeared originally under a slightly
different title in the *New Statesman* and is reprinted by permission of that magazine and the
author. In Spencer R. Phillips's essay, "The Humbling Power of Wilderness," various passages of
scripture are taken from THE MESSAGE, copyright © 1993, 1994, 1995, 1996, 2000, 2001, 2002;
used by permission of NavPress Publishing Group. "Another Inconvenient Truth: The Failure
of Enforcement Systems to Save Charismatic Species" by Elizabeth L. Bennett was published
originally in *Oryx* and is reprinted by permission of Cambridge University Press and the author.

Book design by Kevin Cross

Printed in Canada on recycled paper (100% post-consumer waste) certified
by the Forest Stewardship Council

For Dave Foreman—
Undaunted defender of the wild.

CONTENTS

PART TWO:
REWILDING EARTH, REWILDING OURSELVES

PART THREE:
PROTECTED AREAS: THE FOUNDATION FOR CONSERVATION

FOREWORD

JOHN TERBORGH

BIOPHILIA—AN INHERENT LOVE of nature and its creatures—is manifested in the fact that nearly all 200 or so nation-states on this planet have formally designated areas for nature protection, the most iconic of them being classified as national parks. In their hearts most people believe this is the right thing to do—that nature and the wild animals, plants, and other organisms it has produced have a right to exist, though the exact meaning of "right" is seldom spelled out. As of today, nations around the world have established more than 130,000 protected areas in the name of conserving nature. Collectively, protected areas encompass roughly 13 percent of Earth's terrestrial realm. (The marine realm, unfortunately, is lagging behind at around 2 percent protected.) This is a significant accomplishment, most of which has accrued during the last fifty years. From the perspective of one who loves nature, this is intrinsically good. It is also tangible evidence that love of nature is a high value shared by virtually all nations and cultures, a value that transcends our differences and rivalries. If this isn't good, what is?

This is the positive side. But recently, a group of contrarian "environmentalists" has promulgated a radically different set of views. A leading claim of this group is that conservation is failing. The claim is based on the undeniable fact that species are still going extinct. Instead of seeing this unfortunate fact as testimony to the relentlessness of human pressures, and to the need to enlarge the scope of nature protection, the contrarians draw a different inference—namely, that continuing extinctions demonstrate that parks and other protected areas are not the answer. But humans have never before presided over an extinction crisis of our own making.

Even after there was widespread awareness that a global extinction crisis was under way, the fact remained that we did not know how to contain it. The science of biodiversity conservation simply did not exist, leading to many false starts being made in ignorance of the natural processes that maintain diversity. It is fair to say that the science of biodiversity conservation did not mature until around the year 2000. Only a single generation of conservationists has been aware of the science behind landscape-scale networks of protected areas based on a core-buffer-connectivity model and specifically designed to sustain large carnivores and other ecological keystone species and processes. How can one claim with a straight face that conservation is failing and that protected areas are not the answer in light of these realities? The fact that 13 percent of the Earth's land area has been designated for nature conservation speaks to a widespread recognition that protected areas *are* the answer. Is this a failure? To me it represents an unprecedented global success. How can one account for such a blatant discrepancy in viewpoints?

If the expectation is for immediate and unblemished success, then yes, conservation has fallen short. Species are still going extinct. But is that the point? The question to consider is how many more species *would* have perished in the absence of protected areas. No one knows the exact answer, but it would surely be a large number compared with the number known to have gone extinct over the last fifty years. The creation of protected areas has slowed but not stopped the global pace of anthropogenic extinction. For all its indispensable work in saving species, neither has the U.S. Endangered Species Act. The (greatly simplified) reason that extinctions continue, despite large areas devoted to nature protection, goes beyond the simple insufficiency of protected habitat to—more importantly—the fact that many existing protected areas are too small, isolated, and lacking in management resources to safeguard them. Much could be gained by consolidating smaller protected areas and restoring habitat continuity between them. Mismatches between the locations of protected areas and those of endangered species amount to another widespread problem in the implementation of conservation worldwide. Despite these shortcomings, there is universal recognition that protected areas are essential not only to preserving nature but to slowing the pace of extinction. Conservation efforts may not have resulted in perfect success, but falling short of perfection does not imply failure. The conservation movement could be given an A-, but certainly not an F.

If not a conservation strategy based on protected areas intended to sustain native biodiversity, then what? Some of the contrarians who question the value of protected areas propose that the overarching goal of conservation should not be preventing extinctions or preserving biodiversity but instead should be the maintenance of "ecosystem services." Here we run headlong into a collision of values and the ability of words to deceive. Don't get me wrong. I am not against ecosystem services. They are vital, indeed indispensable, to human welfare. Areas managed or conserved with an objective of providing ecosystem services may capture carbon from the atmosphere; protect watersheds from erosion and landslides; provide clean, potable water; restore degraded ecosystems; cleanse contaminants and return oxygen to the atmosphere; and offer aesthetic and recreational benefits. Like nature itself, the ecosystem services that nature provides are good. We could not survive without them.

But please do not confuse ecosystem services with biodiversity conservation, for they are very different things. For example, a plantation of nonnative tree species can provide some ecosystem services almost as well as a native forest, but the biodiversity value of the former is near zero. This is a crucial point that is lost on the contrarians, and unfortunately on much of the public as well. One of the great challenges to be faced by conservationists in the future will be that of clarifying in the public mind the distinction between ecosystem services and biodiversity protection. The two are not necessarily distinct, as when a natural environment provides "services," but they can be completely unconnected, as in the example of the tree plantation, so understanding the distinction requires a level of sophistication that most nonbiologists do not possess. The danger inherent in the contrarians' arguments is that they mislead by appearing to offer a win-win solution, namely that the protection of ecosystem services amounts to nature protection.

As a professor, I always defined conservation science to my classes as the quest to understand how to prevent extinctions. When I began my career fifty years ago, the science of extinction was in a rudimentary state. Populations that were reduced to very small numbers—fewer than 100 individuals—were at risk to the vagaries of fluctuating numbers, skewed sex ratios, and inbreeding. That is about all we could say about extinction and its causality except for a sketchy knowledge that mass extinction events had occurred in the distant past, for example, when the dinosaurs vanished. But at that time we knew almost nothing about mass extinctions as revealed in the fossil record. It was not until two decades later that the father-and-son team of Luis and Walter Alvarez discovered that the dinosaurs perished when the Earth was hit by a meteorite 10 kilometers in diameter.

The extinctions occurring today are not attributable to anything so dramatic as a meteorite impact. Instead, species are dying out piecemeal at scattered places around the globe, often with no obvious direct cause that we can discern. That is not to say that there are no consistent patterns. Island species are more vulnerable than their counterparts living on the continents, and freshwater species are more vulnerable than marine species. Jared Diamond summarized the most prominent overarching causes of extinctions, likening them to the four horsemen of the Apocalypse: habitat loss, habitat fragmentation, overexploitation, and alien-species invasions. All of these are clearly important drivers of the contemporary human-driven extinction crisis. So, the critical question is: How can all of these drivers be avoided so that extinctions are prevented? The answer is obvious: Protect and reconnect habitat, exclude poachers, and combat invasion by nonnative species. This is exactly what national parks and other protected areas are intended to do. There is no alternative. Parks and other strictly protected areas *are* the answer.

But not all parks are equal in protecting against extinction, and herein lies a further complication. The conservation world was thrown into a state of shock in 1985 when William Newmark, then a graduate student at the University of Michigan, published an article stating that some famous national parks in western North America had lost as many as a quarter of their mammal species since the time of their establishment. Newmark's data implied that parks were failing to protect against extinction, but such a facile conclusion would be a dangerous oversimplification. There was a telltale pattern in the data, and it showed that the parks that had suffered the greatest number of extinctions were the smaller ones. The largest protected area in Newmark's sample was the complex of Banff-Jasper-Kootenay-Yoho in the Canadian Rockies. Amounting to a contiguous area of more than 20,000 square kilometers, that complex had experienced no mammal extinctions.

Newmark's results, along with subsequent confirmations, cemented the idea that extinctions could be minimized in large protected areas— very large protected areas. Unfortunately, there are very few protected areas as large as 20,000 square kilometers anywhere in the world (and none in the 48 contiguous United States). So does this mean that we have to accept a continuing trickle of extinctions as inevitable? No—we need large protected areas, especially as we now understand, much better than we did in 1985, why small parks fail to maintain their native species.

The science of conservation biology was roughly seven years old in 1985 and still in its infancy. (The birth of a formal science of conservation biology dates to a conference organized in 1978 by Michael Soulé in San Diego.) Since then, we have learned a great deal about the natural forces that stabilize ecosystems and why these forces are disrupted in small areas, be they protected or unprotected.

Among the first species to go extinct in restricted areas are the top carnivores—the wolves, great cats, and bears. Although rare compared to other animals with which they share habitat, such animals have a disproportionate impact on the entire system by regulating the density of prey. Strong regulation maintains the populations of prey species at densities far below those at which they begin to adversely impact the vegetation and each other. In the absence of predation, two broad types of prey become superabundant: herbivores and mesopredators. Although the latter terms may be unfamiliar (especially, that of *mesopredator*), the phenomena are well known to rural and suburban Americans who nowadays must build fences to protect their gardens from superabundant deer. At the same time, an overabundance of raccoons, opossums, foxes, and feral cats (all mesopredators) is decimating their prey, including songbirds, lizards, frogs, and other small vertebrates and invertebrates.

Here we have two engines of extinction operating simultaneously. Overabundant herbivores are driving changes in the composition of natural plant communities by favoring certain species over others. Trilliums, for example, are a favorite of deer and have decreased precipitously over much of the eastern United States. Meanwhile, an abundance of mesopredators has greatly reduced the number of ground-nesting birds, including such favorites as bobwhite quail, ruffed grouse, and whip-poor-will. Thus, the loss of top predators unleashes a chain of ecological reactions that cascade from one level of the ecosystem to another. Do away with wolves and cougars, and deer overpopulation is an absolutely predictable consequence. The plants at the bottom of the food chain then bear the brunt of the loss of predators. In technical jargon, the chain reaction is called the "trophic cascade." Conservation biologists now understand that the natural state of the trophic cascade with top carnivores present is what stabilizes ecosystems. Interfere with the interaction chain, predator-herbivore-plant or predator-mesopredator-small prey animal, and ecological impoverishment is certain to ensue.

Now we are able to understand why only the largest protected areas resist extinction. It is because only the largest areas retain their top predators. The statement applies everywhere around the globe. Lion populations in Africa, having disappeared from many smaller parks and game reserves, are an example. The same is true of tigers in India. This forebodes serious management issues in parks that have lost top predators as prey populations increase and begin to compete strongly with one another for dwindling resources. The problem of predator loss also affects a major portion of North America. Wolves once inhabited the entire continent, but they have been relentlessly persecuted and pushed back to the farthest, wildest corners of the land. Cougars, being supremely secretive, have fared better in the West although they have become all but extinct in the East for over a hundred years; hence, the East's deer and mesopredator woes.

All this sounds very discouraging. What gives me hope for a better future is the situation in Europe. Surprisingly, there are wolves in almost every European country except the Benelux nations. And maybe even that qualification is breaking down, as a wolf recently strayed across the border from Germany into the Netherlands. If wolves can coexist with humans in densely crowded Europe, there is no reason other than obstinacy or prejudice that wolves cannot be restored in much larger parts of their native range in North America. If the wolf and cougar were reinstated across the continent, the health of ecosystems could be greatly improved and the threat of extinction would recede. Similar salutary results for the natural world would occur around the world by protecting and reintroducing top predators.

Regarding the U.S. situation, some argue that there is no room in the East, or even in the less populated West, for cougars and wolves, but that argument is a smoke screen promulgated by people who have other reasons for lobbying against the return of predators to American wildlands. Europe proves the argument is wrong. The North American continent can be consolidated and interconnected. Parks along with wilderness areas are the cornerstone of any strategy to restore ecological integrity to North America as well as the rest of the world. However, parks alone cannot restore the normal functioning of ecosystems and prevent extinctions in the areas of the world that are not protected—the vast majority. If there are a few parks where top predators are safe and can breed unmolested, these can serve as population nuclei out of which individual animals can disperse to establish other breeding nuclei in unprotected portions of the land.

Wolves and cougars don't require pristine conditions to thrive; they require freedom from persecution. They routinely roam through agricultural lands, forests, and prairie, even suburbs. So long as the habitat remains in large pieces and is not crisscrossed by high-speed highways, it can be used by large predators that are far more interested in prey than in the details of habitat quality. The need for predator restoration across North America is abundantly apparent and conditions are suitable, at least in many parts of both the East and West. Globally, the same "rewilding" lessons apply. We need to build the safety nets for large carnivores, expanding and interconnecting protected areas around the world. While the political will is still lagging, enthusiasm for rewilding is everywhere on the rise.

The Earth is currently in the throes of the sixth global extinction crisis, of that there is little doubt. But this sixth crisis differs from the five that preceded it, in that it is self-inflicted. Species are going extinct a thousand times faster than they would in the absence of human impact, and life scientists warn that the biosphere could lose 50 percent of its species by the end of this century if we fail to protect the natural world and chart a new relationship with it. We—and we alone—are responsible, as we are responsible for global climate change and environmental abuses of many kinds. I am old enough to remember the sudden decline of bald eagles in the 1960s, the impact of Rachael Carson's *Silent Spring*, and the ensuing environmental fervor that lead to the first Earth Day in 1970 and to a subsequent global surge of enthusiasm for "sustainability." Yet it seems to me that we are further from achieving ecological sustainability today than we were several decades ago. As a global society, we are distracted by too many other issues—wars, epidemics, unemployment, a struggling economy. In the cacophony of daily events, we appear to have lost sight of the fundamental importance of a healthy biosphere to the well-being of both humans and nature. Restoring confidence in the future can come about only through a renewed commitment to ecological sustainability inspired by a vision of a beautiful, secure, and equitable future. Such a future must be grounded in an enlightened relationship with the Earth in which the needs of nature are recognized as commensurate with those of humanity. For that, the global strategy must be to expand the number and size of protected areas, interconnect them, and rewild them. All other roads lead to an intensification of the sixth extinction crisis and to an impoverished future for humanity.

Protected Areas and the Long Arc Toward Justice

TOM BUTLER

CRAYFISH ARE CRUNCHY. And, it appears, tasty. Sound travels easily over water, and we can hear each distinct bite as an otter devours a crustacean across the pond from where our canoes float. Curious about the passing travelers, the pair of otters has retreated to a mudflat; they gambol about for a while, then sit, partially submerged and attentive. They watch us, unperturbed, while one finishes his snack. We enjoy their company for a time, and paddle on.

Where are we? First and foremost, we are uninvited but seemingly welcome guests in the home of otters. Three canoeing buddies and I are exploring an expansive wetlands complex in New York's Adirondack Park, the largest park in the contiguous United States, a 125-year-old patchwork of private and public land, the latter of which comprises the Adirondack Forest Preserve. The Forest Preserve is protected as "forever wild"; in perpetuity there can be no logging or development on these public lands. In the lexicon of conservation, we are in a "protected area."

On this brilliant late summer day, we have witnessed the aforementioned otters crunching, kingfishers cavorting, a northern goshawk plying the skies, and a gray jay, so typical of this boreal forest country, perched upon a larch at water's edge. Black bears, fishers, coyotes, deer, and moose are here, too, unseen today, but undoubtedly preparing for the long winter in this northern realm, not far from the Canadian border. And indeed, the landscape looks like much of eastern Canada, with spruce and fir interspersed with some species more typical of the northern hardwood forest to the south, sugar maple and yellow birch in particular.

Everywhere one looks the sights are pleasing to the eye—water and tree-clad hills stretching to the distance. The smells are earthy, piney and sprucey with a dollop of Christmastime (balsam) that will mix with our campfire smoke this evening. The sounds are also noteworthy—the occasional chattering of chickadees and wail of a loon wafting over the water, and between these natural noises a background sound track of . . . nothing. No traffic. No chain saws. No motors of any kind. Silence, the rarest of privileges in a world of 7-plus billion humans transforming the world in our image.

These are the gifts of the wilderness for those of us lucky enough to have time and the inclination to seek them out. The effort to reach what I'll call "Otter Pond" was modest—some hours of paddling and portaging, with one quick dunk in cold water when I lost my footing while dragging the canoe upstream over rocky shallows. The return on this muscular investment was extraordinary—the opportunity to experience beauty, spiritual refreshment, and the companionship of old friends, to reminisce with them about previous wilderness adventures and to contemplate future ones. Another gift was solitude. In a park that is within a day's drive of 60 million people, during the height of tourist season, we spent four days in the woods and saw no one else.

Our trip was not epic. No grizzlies charged us. No mist-shrouded summits were conquered. The scenery, while lovely, was commonplace to the region.

What is remarkable is the resurgence of wildness across the landscape. For more than a century, the area we canoed had been subject to intensive exploitation and manipulation at the hands of men (gender exclusivity intended). A moldering wooden dam at the pond outlet and an old railroad bed through the wetlands were some of the infrastructure that supported past logging operations. Not far from our campsite we found the remains of a former settlement along that long-defunct railroad; in the 1910s it had included a depot, sawmill, post office, etc. Now it is barely visible, just some crumbling foundations covered with moss, trees growing skyward where a roof once shed rain. In 1923 a forest fire swept through the area and *rewilding* commenced. Today the land is more wild than it was a century ago, and because of its conservation, in another century it is likely to be wilder still, and therefore more resilient to climate change effects.

Otter Pond is representative of the Adirondacks and so many other places where nineteenth-century timber barons scalped the land and moved on. Reacting to that rapacious logging, conservationists who were concerned about deforestation, associated watershed degradation, and collapse of wildlife populations succeeded in having New York establish a "Forest Preserve" including lands in the Adirondacks and the Catskills in 1885. At a constitutional convention the following decade, the clause ensuring that the public lands comprising the Adirondack and Catskill Forest Preserves would remain "forever wild" was incorporated into New York's state constitution.[1] (That conservation landmark celebrates its 120th anniversary this year.)

The pioneering conservationists who were responsible—among them the civil rights lawyer Louis Marshall, who was father of Wilderness Society cofounder Robert Marshall—blazed a path that still leads toward expanding beauty and health. Indeed, the Adirondack Park may be the greatest example of rewilding on Earth, the fullest expression of the incremental reforestation of the northeastern United States following the first wave of logging associated with European colonization of North America. Those otters at home in the Adirondack Forest Preserve, we visitors enjoying a sojourn in the forest, and future generations of wild residents and human recreationists owe earlier conservationists an immense debt of gratitude. Because of conservation action, the Adirondacks are more ecologically vibrant, provide more secure wildlife habitat, and are a more intact canvas for natural processes to create, shape, and sustain biodiversity than other parts of the Northeast[2] outside protected areas. That the Adirondack Park also provides tremendous social and economic values including watershed protection, the initial reason for its creation, is equally clear.

The landscape here is not pristine. It is not virginal, a place where, in the marvelous mixed metaphor attributed to the late David Brower, "the hand of man never set foot." The designated "wilderness" and "wild forest" units that make up the Adirondack Forest Preserve are *free*, consistent with the etymological roots of the word "wilderness," to follow their own course. They are self-willed lands, home to self-willed creatures.

The Adirondack Park is part of an amazing legacy of protected areas that now cover approximately 13 percent of Earth's land surface. (That percentage includes all categories of conserved land, from strictly protected natural areas to places managed for "sustainable" resource production.)

Across the planet, every national and state park, wilderness area, wildlife refuge, nature sanctuary, or other permanently conserved habitat exists today for one reason only: because an individual or group of individuals worked to have them protected. There is a grand history here; it is global in scope, and that historical narrative helps inform current discussions and debates about the future role of protected areas.

During the few months bracketing my Adirondack canoe trip, conservationists in the United States noted several landmarks:

The first is that 2014 marked the 150th anniversary of the Yosemite land grant when President Abraham Lincoln signed legislation giving Yosemite Valley to the state of California for its permanent protection with the condition that the land "be held for public use, resort, and recreation." That action put the federal government in the conservation business, setting the stage for the creation of Yellowstone, the world's first national park, the following decade.[3] (Yosemite Valley would come back into the federal domain several decades later after Yosemite National Park was established.)

A second landmark was the hundred-year anniversary of the death of the last passenger pigeon,[4] a captive bird named Martha. Formerly the most abundant bird species in North America (and perhaps anywhere on Earth), passenger pigeons entered the dark night of extinction in 1914. Martha died alone in the Cincinnati Zoo, a testament to the shattered myth that nature was inexhaustible and endlessly resilient.

Landmark three was the 50th anniversary of the Wilderness Act of 1964, which created America's national wilderness preservation system. The result of years of grassroots organizing and advocacy, the law is surely one of the most eloquent statutes ever passed, its language largely the work of Howard Zahniser, then executive secretary of the Wilderness Society.[5] Zahniser's pen was well used, inscribing more than 60 drafts before the final version became law. Not incidentally, Zahniser was a part-time resident of the Adirondacks, his family having a vacation cabin there, where he sometimes worked on those many drafts of the wilderness bill.[6] "Zahnie," as his friends called him, had been introduced to the region by conservationist Paul Schaefer, a tireless defender of the park's wild rivers during the midcentury era when dam building was all the rage. Schaefer's activism had been influenced, in part, by the Adirondacks' preeminent family of wilderness advocates, the Marshalls. Schaefer first met Robert Marshall atop Mt. Marcy, New York's highest peak, in 1932, and was a longtime conservation colleague of his brother, George Marshall, following Bob's untimely death.[7]

These three anniversaries reveal something about the evolution of arguments for protected areas. It's interesting to me that as the arguments for conserving protected areas morphed from aesthetic and recreational to scientific and ecological values—"from scenery to nature" in Dave Foreman's concise summation[8]—previous rationales were not abandoned, but built upon. To apply a geological metaphor, there has been deposition and accretion, but not erosion.

The suite of reasons undergirding advocacy for parks and wilderness areas deepened with the insights emerging from the fields of landscape ecology and conservation biology in the latter decades of the twentieth century. This did not, however, make moot the earlier, experiential arguments for conservation. Millions of us who visit national parks each year still are motivated by the scenic beauty of wild nature. We who seek to enjoy the freedom of the wilderness with family and friends still treasure the experience of muscle-powered recreation in a primitive setting and the challenge of developing appropriate skills for travel in wild country. Some 168 years after Henry David Thoreau was buffeted by howling winds atop Mount Katahdin—later describing the "Titanic" scenery he encountered there and averring that the "mossy and *moosey*" Maine woods were "no man's garden"—we feel exactly the same awe at natural forces in a wilderness setting. But there are now far fewer places on Earth one could describe as intact, primeval, wild, or ungardened, far fewer places where wildlife is secure from the pressures, direct and indirect, of a burgeoning humanity.

Which is why, of course, flocks of passenger pigeons no longer darken the skies and vast herds of bison no longer rumble across the Great Plains of North America. And why modern conservationists have viewed protected areas and wildlife protection laws as the key tools for combating the human-caused extinctions of our fellow members in the community of life. The conservation movement in the United States arose as a counterpoint to the loss of wilderness and wildlife as Euro-American culture swept across the continent. Conservation ideas, and particularly the national park concept, spread quickly across the globe and were widely embraced in diverse cultures.

When American conservationists succeeded in passing the Wilderness Act in 1964, the law didn't just codify the notion that some places should remain off-limits to resource exploitation; it also reflected a century's worth of intellectual development in conservation philosophy and practice. Implicitly, the law acknowledged that wild places have intrinsic value, regardless of their utility to people. In a notable bit of historical congruence, Congress also enacted a major piece of civil rights legislation in 1964.[9] It extended rights to a marginalized category of people whose skin had more melanin than that of the country's ethnic majority. That law did not magically abrogate racial prejudice but helped expand justice.

The Wilderness Act did the same, moving society toward a more equitable relationship between people and nonhuman nature. In effect, the law suggested that humanity's sphere of ethical concern should expand to embrace all members of the biotic community, including traditionally marginalized members such as large carnivores. This is a remarkable idea to emerge in an extraction- and use-focused culture, which has viewed the landscape almost exclusively through the lens of economic possibility: "How can I profit from this place? Can I log it, or mine it, or graze it? How can I make it my garden?"

A century and a half of conservation experience tells us that protected areas are popular, effective,[10] and broadly supported—but almost always controversial before establishment and sometimes long after. Land conservation stimulates strong feelings, particularly on the wilderness end of the spectrum but even sometimes when sustainable resource production is the objective. Land use is deeply personal. It is no surprise when communities with economic and cultural ties to particular extractive industries—industrial forestry and paper production in Maine, for example, or ranching and wool production in Patagonia—are skeptical about proposed protected areas. While there are exceptions to this norm, parks and wilderness areas very often have been the targets of such hostility from "traditional" resource users.

What is perhaps more surprising is when protected areas are attacked from the left for being the colonialist residue of Western imperialism. In truth, the modern conservation movement arose as a counterrevolutionary force in response to the land degradation and wildlife holocaust associated with the expansion of industrial civilization, a wave that extirpated indigenous cultures as well as native species. The movement's foremost tool—protected areas—rejects a colonialist, imperialist attitude toward the living Earth. The designation of protected areas is an expression of humility about the limits of human knowledge and a gesture of respect toward our fellow creatures, allowing them to flourish in their homes without fear of persecution.

PERHAPS NOT SURPRISING but discouraging is when it becomes trendy to attack parks and wilderness using strawman arguments. This seems to occur periodically and, unfortunately, the latest rhetorical dustup is under way. Indeed, it is the reason for this book, and for its companion volume, *Keeping the Wild: Against the Domestication of Earth,*[11] which constructively critiques a nexus of ideas being advanced by so-called new environmentalists or social conservationists. These ideas include:

▶ The Anthropocene has arrived, and humans are now de facto planetary managers;

▶ If "pristine wilderness" ever existed, it is all gone now; moreover, focusing on wilderness preservation has poorly served the environmental movement;

▶ Nature is highly resilient, not fragile;

▶ To succeed, conservation must serve human aspirations, primarily regarding economic growth and development;

▶ Maintaining "ecosystem services," not preventing human-caused extinction, should be conservation's primary goal;

▶ Conservationists should not critique capitalism but rather should partner with corporations to achieve better results;

▶ Conservation should focus on better management of the domesticated, "working landscape" rather than efforts to establish new, strictly protected natural areas.

This last point regarding the future role of protected areas is of such crucial importance that we have developed *Protecting the Wild* to consider it. Should the primary goal of conservation be to establish systems of interconnected conservation reserves across the globe—anchored by strictly protected areas such as national parks and wilderness areas—intended to halt the extinction crisis and sustain the evolutionary flourishing of all Earth's biota?

Or is such a goal of planetary rewilding a naive dream in a time of ballooning human numbers, with the demographic trajectory headed toward 10 billion or more people, the majority of whom will live in poverty? Given this context, should conservation give up on its core commitment of stopping anthropogenic extinctions and instead focus on humanized, managed landscapes intended to produce "ecological services" for people?

These questions are addressed in *Protecting the Wild* by a prominent cast of scientists, academics, and conservation practitioners from multiple continents. After a foreword by tropical ecologist John Terborgh, the book is organized into three sections—"Bold Thinking About Protecting the Wild"; "Rewilding Earth, Rewilding Ourselves"; and "Protected Areas, the Foundation for Conservation." The volume concludes with an afterword by Douglas Tompkins, the businessman-turned-conservation philanthropist. With his wife Kristine McDivitt Tompkins—former CEO of Patagonia Inc.—and colleagues, Tompkins has helped conserve well over 2 million acres, creating or expanding five national parks in Chile and Argentina.

The latest of these, the 130,000-hectare El Impenetrable National Park in the Chaco Province of northern Argentina, was formally established as Argentina's 32nd national park with a unanimous vote in Congress just before this volume went to press. As with most contemporary, large-scale conservation initiatives, it was a public–private collaboration. Argentine conservationists worked tenaciously to develop political support and raise funds to support the project.[12] The positive outcome for wildlife and local communities was made possible by broad-based fundraising and a major gift from a family foundation established by Tompkins.

This is not an isolated victory. Using science, passion, and ethical persuasion, conservationists are striving and succeeding to expand protected areas around the globe. In November of 2014, thousands of advocates from some 160 countries gathered at the World Parks Congress to chart the future direction of the parks movement. There was tremendous excitement and energy for a global commitment to protected areas that is commensurate with the ecological and social challenges we face.

The days of protecting wild nature are not, and should not, be in the past. A bolder, resurgent conservation movement need not settle for an agenda based on trying to ameliorate the effects of humanity's numbers and overconsumption. Rather, it might sound a clarion call for a peace treaty between humans and nature, a cease-fire in industrial humanity's war on wild nature. The most tangible sign of that rapprochement would be the encircling ribbons of green and blue, strongholds of terrestrial and marine[13] wildness, around the globe. It would be a profoundly pro-*life* movement, articulating the value of protecting nature for biodiversity, for humanity, for climate stability, for peace, and for future generations—of otters and people.

While he did not originate the aphorism, Martin Luther King Jr., the American civil rights leader, famously said, "The arc of the moral universe is long but it bends toward justice." That long arc bends fitfully in our diverse human tribe and, if we open our eyes to the natural world, we see that it also bends toward justice—and diversity, and beauty, and wildness—in the whole community of life.

The fundamental choice for our species is whether we will continue striving to be the planetary manager, the gardener-in-chief, or become a respectful member in the community of life. With every action to reassert the dominion of beauty, diversity, and wildness over the Earth—each hectare protected, each habitat secured—we tug the universe a bit more toward justice. That is the overarching story of conservation—past, present, and future.

ONE

BOLD THINKING ABOUT PROTECTING THE WILD

Nature Needs (at least) Half: A Necessary New Agenda for Protected Areas

HARVEY LOCKE

I ARGUE THAT CONSERVATION TARGETS should be based on what is necessary to protect nature in all its expressions. When in 1987 the Brundtland Report called for tripling the world's protected area estate (which was then at 3–4 percent of the land area) there was a strong belief that sustainable development would ensure the proper care for nature on the rest of the unprotected Earth. This has proven wrong. We therefore must materially shift our protected areas target to protect at least half of the world—land and seas—in an interconnected way to conform with what conservation biologists have learned about the needs of nature. Instead, we have set goals that are politically determined, with arbitrary percentages that rest on an unarticulated hope that such nonscientific goals are a good first step toward some undefined, better, future outcome. This has been a destructive form of self-censorship. It is time for conservationists to reset the debate based on scientific findings and assert nature's needs fearlessly.

It is well-settled scientifically that humanity's relationship with the natural world is in trouble. The Intergovernmental Panel on Climate Change stated bluntly: "The resilience of many ecosystems is likely to be exceeded this century by an unprecedented combination of climate change, associated disturbances (e.g., flooding, drought, wildfire, insects, ocean acidification), and other global change drivers (e.g., land use change, pollution, overexploitation of resources)."[1] The human species has become so dominant that some argue we have entered a new geological age dominated not by the chemical and physical workings of the Earth as they exist under their own motion from time to time but by us humans and they propose we call this new period "the Anthropocene."[2]

This is not new. Our species' troubled relationship with nature has been widely understood for twenty-five years. In 1987 the United Nations published *Our Common Future*, known widely as the Brundtland Report. It stated: "As the century closes, not only do vastly increased human numbers and their activities have that power [to alter planetary systems], but major unintended changes are occurring in the atmosphere, in soils, in waters, among plants and animals and in the relationships among all these."[3] A few years later the "World Scientists' Warning to Humanity," which was signed by the majority of the living Nobel Prize winners in science at the time, said starkly: "Human beings and the natural world are on a collision course. Human activities inflict harsh and often irreversible damage on the environment and on critical resources. If not checked, many of our current practices put at serious risk the future that we wish for human society and the plant and animal kingdoms, and may so alter the living world that it will be unable to sustain life in the manner that we know. Fundamental changes are urgent if we are to avoid the collision our present course will bring about."[4]

The concerned scientists identified the need to bring environmentally damaging activities under control in order "to restore and protect the integrity of the earth's systems we depend on" and stated that "we must halt deforestation, injury to and loss of agricultural land, and the loss of terrestrial and marine plant and animal species."[5]

The first global conservation targets for protected areas: 10 or 12 percent

Protected areas were identified by the authors of the Brundtland Report as a critical response to the troubled relationship between humanity and the rest of nature. They called them "areas managed explicitly to conserve species and ecosystems" and stated: "Conservation of living natural resources—plants, animals, and micro-organisms, and the non-living elements of the environment on which they depend—is crucial for development. Today the conservation of wild living resources is on the agenda of governments: Nearly 4 percent of the Earth's land area is managed explicitly to conserve species and ecosystems, and all but a small handful of countries have national parks." The chapter concluded, "a consensus of professional opinion suggests that the total expanse of protected areas needs to be at least tripled if it is to constitute a representative sample of Earth's ecosystems."[6] This led to the first widely accepted goals for protected areas. Depending on who did the math it became the 10 percent goal or the 12 percent goal for global protected areas. Note that the goal spoke to representation of ecosystems.

A global target emerges from the Convention on Biological Diversity

The urgency of the scientific declarations in the late 1980s and early 1990s about humanity's failing relationship with nature led to the Earth Summit in Rio di Janeiro in 1992. Many of the world's political leaders attended. They signed two conventions intended to confront the integrated problems: the Framework Convention on Climate Change and the Convention on Biological Diversity.[7] The objective of the Convention on Biological Diversity (CBD) is "the conservation of biological diversity, the sustainable use of its components and the fair and equitable sharing of the benefits arising out of the utilization of genetic resources." Biological diversity was defined as "the variability among living organisms from all sources including, inter alia, terrestrial, marine and other aquatic ecosystems and the ecological complexes of which they are part; this includes diversity within species, between species and of ecosystems."[8]

The CBD's provisions institutionalized protected areas as a key strategy to protect biodiversity. The CBD defines a protected area as "a geographically defined area which is designated or regulated and managed to achieve specific conservation objectives." It provides at Article 8 for "In-situ Conservation," and the first five items speak directly to protected areas:

Each Contracting Party shall, as far as possible and as appropriate:

a) Establish a system of protected areas or areas where special measures need to be taken to conserve biological diversity;

b) Develop, where necessary, guidelines for the selection, establishment and management of protected areas or areas where special measures need to be taken to conserve biological diversity;

c) Regulate or manage biological resources important for the conservation of biological diversity whether within or outside protected areas, with a view to ensuring their conservation and sustainable use;

d) Promote the protection of ecosystems, natural habitats and the maintenance of viable populations of species in natural surroundings;

e) Promote environmentally sound and sustainable development in areas adjacent to protected areas with a view to furthering protection of these areas.[9]

In 2002 the parties to the CBD did a strange thing. They set a nonnumerical goal that was designed to slow down the bleeding of life from the Earth but did not seek expressly to conserve biodiversity. The goal was "to achieve by 2010 a significant reduction of the current rate of biodiversity loss at the global, regional and national level as a contribution to poverty alleviation and to the benefit of all life on Earth."[10]

In the Foreword to the *2010 Global Biodiversity Outlook 3*, an assessment of the state and trends of biodiversity in the world, UN Secretary General Ban-Ki Moon summarizes how ineffective this "slow-the-bleeding" approach was: "In 2002, the world's leaders agreed to achieve a significant reduction in the rate of biodiversity loss by 2010. Having reviewed all available evidence, including national reports submitted by Parties, this third edition of the Global Biodiversity Outlook concludes that the target has not been met."[11]

In 2012, at Nagoya, Japan, the failure of this approach was recognized by the parties to the CBD and a more specific Target 11 for protected areas was set: "By 2020, at least 17 percent of terrestrial and inland water, and 10 per cent of coastal and marine areas, especially areas of particular importance for biodiversity and ecosystem services, are conserved through effectively and equitably managed, ecologically representative and well connected [sic] systems of protected areas and other effective area-based conservation measures, and integrated into the wider landscapes and seascapes."[12]

While these references to protected areas in the broader landscape and connectivity are important new developments, no scientific rationale is given for the protected area targets of 17 percent land and 10 percent marine. Nor was a longer-term target set against which these might be considered mileposts. In 1998, one of the fathers of conservation biology, Michael Soulé, and his then student, M. A. Sanjayan, published a provocative article "Conservation Targets: Do They Help?," in which they demonstrated that protecting only 10 percent of the Earth would not protect biodiversity.[13] No other publication has scientifically defended such low numerical targets.

What scientific analysis suggests protected area targets ought to be

In a world where humans were just one species interacting among many we would not need protected areas. This was the case for most of human history. Now we need them.

It is clear from a plain reading of its text that the goal of the CBD (and by extension of the 193 state parties to it) is to preserve nature, defined as biodiversity, with protected areas as an essential tool. It should follow that all the work done in furtherance of that Convention should be based on the best scientific answer to the question: "What does nature need in order to conserve biodiversity and how do we get there given the desires of humans?" Strangely that is not what has happened. Instead, the focus has been: "What are humans willing to spare?" This is, of course, political, not scientific, and suffers from the basic flaw that it does not seek an effective solution to the problem the CBD was created to address. So what is the best scientific information on how much we should protect?

Reed Noss and Allen Cooperrider concluded that in most regions 25–75 percent (or on average 50 percent) of an area will need protection to maintain biodiversity and ecological processes.[14] A poetic suggestion for the amount of protected areas needed came from biologist and author E. O. Wilson who called for "half the world for humanity, half for the rest of life, to make a planet both self-sustaining and pleasant."[15] Tropical ecologist John Terborgh noted that half the world was degraded and called for the protection of the other half.[16] Robert Pressey and colleagues noted that "recent comprehensive conservation plans have delineated around 50% or more of regions for nature conservation."[17] Leona Svancara and coauthors reviewed 159 articles reporting or proposing 222 conservation targets and assessed differences between policy-driven and evidence-based approaches.[18] By "evidence-based approaches" they meant an adequate understanding and mapping of the distribution and viability of the conservation requirements of individual biodiversity features, such as species and vegetation types, and found that the average percentages of area recommended for evidence-based targets were nearly three times as high as those recommended in policy-driven approaches.

Coordinated by the Canadian Boreal Initiative, 1500 scientists, from more than 50 countries around the world, came together to write to Canadian governments to urge protection of "in the range of half" of that country's vast boreal forests. Their letter included the following succinct summary of the widely known conservation science:

The relatively intact state of Canada's northern Boreal region provides an opportunity to implement conservation strategies to protect the region's ecological integrity. The field of conservation biology identifies four objectives that must be achieved to ensure the long-term viability of an ecosystem: 1) all native ecosystem types must be represented in protected areas; 2) populations of all native species must be maintained in natural patterns of abundance and distribution; 3) ecological processes such as hydrological processes must be maintained; and 4) the resilience to short-term and long-term environmental change must be maintained. Achieving these objectives requires an extensive interconnected network of protected areas and sustainable management of the surrounding areas. Reviews of previous conservation planning initiatives provide further direction by indicating that protected areas should cover in the range of half of the landscape to achieve the objectives listed above.[19]

Note that representation, the basis of the 10 percent or 12 percent goal that began with the Brundtland Report, remains fundamentally important but is only one of four elements needed to sustain ecosystems over time.

Ana Rodrigues and Kevin Gaston considered the needs of species and found the minimum percentage of area needed to represent all species within a region increases with the number of targeted species, the size of selection units, and the level of species' endemism and stated that "the 10% target proposed by the International Union for Conservation of Nature (IUCN) is likely to be wholly insufficient, and that much larger fractions of area are estimated to be needed, especially in tropical regions."[20] In 2004 The Nature Conservancy, The Nature Conservancy of Canada and other partners concluded their multi-expert-driven assessment of an area of mountains and valleys that straddles the Canada-U.S. border. The goal of the conservation assessment was to identify the suite of conservation sites and strategies that ensure the long-term survival of all native plant and animal species and natural communities in the region. They assessed with a coarse filter 40 terrestrial systems and 77 aquatic systems, and with a fine filter 75 rare plant communities, 95 rare plants, and 56 animals. They combined target plant and mammal species (both terrestrial and aquatic) in a SITES optimization model. They concluded that 49.7 percent of the region should be in conservation areas but noted this did not address connectivity needs for wide-ranging mammals.[21]

Traditional ecological knowledge combined with Western science has reached the same conclusion on at least one occasion. Grand Chief Herb Norwegian described a process in which elders were consulted about their traditional use of the boreal forests and mountains along the Mackenzie River in Canada's Northwest Territories and developed a land use plan that called for the conservation of more than half of the Dehcho Region in an interconnected network of protected areas.[22]

In a 2012 editorial in *Conservation Biology*, Reed Noss, I, and our coauthors surveyed several studies of the percentage of area needed and compared those results with politically derived targets. They noted that current political and convention targets tended to be much lower than those based on scientific assessment, review, and expert opinion where the midpoint of the range of evidence-based assessments was slightly below 50 percent and called for a precautionary target of 50 percent. They concluded: "Nature needs at least 50% and it is time we said so."[23]

The meaning of protected area

The CBD definition of *protected area* noted above is "a geographically defined area which is designated or regulated and managed to achieve specific conservation objectives."[24] This definition does not provide specific guidance about the range of protected area types that could be adapted to different situations. In the mid-2000s IUCN's World Commission on Protected Areas engaged in a multi-national expert consultation process to update its guidelines for protected areas that culminated in a summit in Almería, Spain, in 2007.[25] That process came up with a useful definition of *protected area* that is adopted for the purposes of this essay: "A specifically delineated area designated and managed to achieve the conservation of nature and the maintenance of associated ecosystem services and cultural values through legal or other effective means."[26] This includes the six categories of protected area recognized by IUCN for some time:

Ia/Ib. Strict Nature Reserve/Wilderness Area;
II. National Park;
III. Natural Monument or Feature;
IV. Habitat/Species Management Area;
V. Protected Landscape/Seascape; and
VI. Protected Area with Sustainable Use of Natural Resources.[27]

While some of these categories allow some resource extraction for local use, industrial activity is not included. This can be described as the difference between tapping sap from a maple or rubber tree and cutting trees down to feed to a pulp mill. Notably, the governance framework of these protected areas can range from international, national, provincial, regional, or municipal to indigenous, community, NGO (nongovernmental organization) or individual as long as the area is managed and dedicated by legal or other effective means.

Protecting half of the Earth's lands and waters

Conservation targets expressed in percentages can be misleading and will not be effective in protecting the full range of life on Earth if they are rotely numerical or area-based. In other words, protecting all of Antarctica is an excellent idea and would materially enhance the percentage of the world protected and do great things for life there but would do nothing for tigers, toucans, lions, or grizzly bears. To halt and eventually reverse the terrible trend demonstrated in IUCN's Red List of Threatened Species we ought to apply across all ecoregions of the world the four broadly accepted conservation planning principles adopted by the 1500 signatories to the Boreal Scientists' Letter. To recap, those are: to represent all native ecosystem types in protected areas as well as to protect sufficient area to maintain populations of all native species in natural patterns of abundance and distribution, ecological processes such as fire and flooding, and resilience to short-term and long-term environmental change.

The idea of *protecting half* conveys a better sense of the order of magnitude of protected areas required than stating "50 percent," which might imply a mathematical formula of universal application. What is required is principled study and conservation planning based on each ecoregion's unique characteristics followed by determined implementation of the results. When such rigorous study occurs it usually results in a finding that we should protect about half of any given ecoregion. Some noted conservation biologists have expressed private opinions to the author that that may well be too low a figure. Thus it would be most accurate and precautionary to say nature needs *at least* half.

Connectivity among protected areas

In addition to the question of how much is needed in protected areas is the now widespread scientific understanding that these areas must be not only protected but also connected to each other to allow for gene flow and to adapt to climate change.[28] Jenny Hodgson and colleagues issued an important reminder that connectivity is a supplement to and not a substitute for core protected areas.[29]

Nature on the other half

Lands outside of protected areas can be valuable for some species and are worthy of attention. They can provide connectivity between habitat patches and support migratory processes for birds and insects. Some species even thrive in landscapes fragmented by humans—the white-tailed deer (*Odocoileus virginianus*), for example—and a few even thrive in high urban concentrations of humans—such as Norwegian rats (*Rattus norvegicus*) and rock doves (*Columba livia*). But many species are habitat specialists and human-altered habitats do not support them. Intensely cultivated lands on which chemically supported agriculture is practiced have very low value for biodiversity. Humans on pasture lands outside of protected areas tend to have very low tolerance for species that compete with us for meat or forage for domestic animals. Thus we either kill competitor species or erect impermeable fences to exclude them, which in turn have the effect of fragmenting the landscape, which can terminate critically important seasonal migrations of large mammals. Humans outside protected areas often make large efforts to suppress inconvenient natural processes like fire and flooding that are vital to the ecosystem dynamics on which many species depend. So while lands intensely used by humans support some threads of nature (and more nature-friendly practices should be encouraged on them) they cannot support the full tapestry of life. Simply put, we need to share the world with nature.

Self-censorship in the conservation community when it comes to targets

The closing session at the World Wilderness Congress, WILD 9, in Merida, Mexico, called for the protection of at least half the world in an interconnected way.[30] Many delegates from many countries were wildly enthused as reflected in news stories that emanated from the event. Of particular note, the late Kenton Miller, father of the 10 to 12 percent target in the Brundtland Report, agreed that this new level of protection was required given how things have unfolded since 1987.[31] Some delegates sought to carry that idea into the negotiations at the CBD. When those enthusiasts returned to other settings censorship set in along the lines of: "Of course that is correct, but we will not be taken seriously," or "We must be realistic about what is politically achievable and that is not." This self-censorship raises important questions about the role and function of ideas in society and of park professionals as social participants.

Ideas clearly expressed have the most power. We in the parks community have the best product in the world to sell—intact nature with its myriad benefits for our species. We have a rational foundation for our passions. The science is that nature needs about half. Some of our caution no doubt can be explained by the fact that many park professionals work for governments who set the policy context for their work. There is no mandate to state one's own preferences and goals in such an institutional setting. That is entirely true and right. But this rationale does not apply to nongovernmental organizations whose role in civil society is to say the things that governments ought to do and to help find ways to bring that about.

The explanation for NGO caution could be found in the concern that the expression of ideas too radical will result in exclusion from participating in certain forums to the detriment of one's institution's work or one's own career. The concern is that it is better to be there in a less-than-perfect process than it is to be excluded or humiliated. Fear of the loss of such status or access is the motivation for self-censorship. This is a loser's game.

A different but cynical explanation for self-censorship could be that NGOs are very invested in their programs and priorities and fear that their donor relations require them to keep inconvenient new ideas away. This would be shameful conduct and requires no further comment than that.

The basic problem with self-censorship in an NGO setting is that it focuses on the actors not the outcome. The agreed outcome sought by the CBD should drive behavior. Its purpose is "the conservation of biodiversity." If no one brings forward the best scientific knowledge of what is needed to achieve the CBD's central goal then we are doomed to fail. AIDS advocates cannot back down when sexual transmission of disease is denied by politicians nor can doctors back down when the health effects of tobacco are denied, for to do so would fundamentally impair their cause. So it is with advocates for nature conservation: We should insist on that which is necessary to keep nature healthy. We can do it politely and thoughtfully but do it we must.

Another possible explanation that does not involve self-censorship is that, after assessment, NGOs conclude that there is no possible way that such a goal as "nature needs half" could be met and therefore it should be discarded. The thinking could be that in some places with huge human populations and vast intensive agriculture such a goal seems so fanciful as to be absurd. Though lower targets are known to be insufficient they are better than nothing and their deficiencies are better left unsaid. This approach is rooted in pessimism but is called "realism" by its proponents. The problem is that such so-called realism denies possibilities that are real without first taking the chance to bring them about. Hope is suspended and a dark future guaranteed.

Protecting at least half of the Earth is a viable goal

There are several examples from around the world in which the nature-needs-half goal has already been realized through public policy. In western North America, there are several examples of governmental action to protect at least half of a region. On Haida Gwaii, British Columbia (previously known as the Queen Charlotte Islands), a mix of national park, provincial park, and First Nations conservation has resulted in over 50 percent protection of the terrestrial system and an initial marine conservation area. In Boulder County, Colorado, located in that state's heavily populated Front Range, a combination of national park, federal wilderness areas, city and county parks, and private land conservation has protected over 50 percent of the county.[32] The Capital Regional District of Victoria, British Columbia, has set a goal of protecting at least 50 percent of its lands and waters after a public process that saw it explicitly "subscribing to the idea that nature needs half."[33] Note the varied forms of governance types that have achieved the nature-needs-half goal.

On the Indian subcontinent, the ancient Kingdom of Bhutan announced that it has achieved 50 percent protection by putting over 42 percent of its land in protected areas and over 8 percent in biological corridors.[34] The Seychelles archipelago is over 50 percent protected "as a contribution to fulfilling its obligations under the Convention on Biological Diversity."[35] The Galapagos Islands of Ecuador are much more than 50 percent protected.

The Serengeti ecosystem in Tanzania and Kenya is over 50 percent protected. The Canadian Rockies biome in Alberta, Canada, is about 65 percent protected through a mix of national parks, provincial parks, and wilderness areas. The American portion of the Crown of the Continent Ecosystem in Montana is over 50 percent protected by national park and wilderness designation and a similarly high percentage of park and wilderness areas is present in the core of the Greater Yellowstone Ecosystem. It is no coincidence that these areas in the Yellowstone to Yukon region and East Africa still support all their native species.

An obvious retort to these examples is that they are areas that have received special attention and are far away from large population centers. As to receiving special attention, yes, they have, and they should be taken as examples of how we should treat the whole world. As to their distance from population centers, this raises a different concern. Is it impossible to do something like this in the crowded areas of places like Europe, India, China, or the east coast of North America?

We are unlikely ever to protect half of the best agricultural land that has been in production for centuries. We may not even want to because we like the food it produces. But so much marginal land has been brought into cultivation in the last 250 years that we could make enormous inroads in restoring it.

In eastern North America, most of western Massachusetts, Vermont, New Hampshire, and Quebec's Eastern Townships were denuded of forests by farmers, sheep grazers, loggers, and charcoal makers. But the land was marginal and largely abandoned as other lands became available. Today there is extensive forest cover across the region and significant species recovery. In upstate New York the 6-million-acre (2-million-hectare) Adirondack Park was created in 1892 to recover cut-over lands whose degradation threatened downstream water quality. Today nearly half of it is managed as Forever Wild under the New York State constitution.

The rewilding of Europe has occurred at a remarkable rate as marginal hill and mountain farms are being abandoned by a declining population. The corresponding recovery of large mammals, including brown bears (*Ursus arctos*), in Western Europe is remarkable. Natura 2000 was a deliberate pan-European policy that increased Europe's protected areas to 20 percent and some jurisdictions like Germany are seeking formally to protect wilderness.[36]

The short-term feasibility of an idea does not invalidate the idea. It simply shifts it to becoming an aspirational goal.

A philosophical moment for the protected areas movement

We in the nature conservation community are at a philosophical crossroads. No one who studies the global state of nature could be satisfied.

Indeed things are bad and getting worse with a few happy exceptions.[37] We are not meeting the goals of the CBD.

At moments of philosophical crisis there are two ways one can turn. One is in the direction of deeper determination, higher aspiration, and courageous commitment to clear ideals. This is what the persecuted Christians did during the Roman Empire and ultimately converted its rulers to their way. This is what the Civil Rights Movement in the United States has done and continues to do, and that country now has a second-term black president. This is what the Nature Needs Half movement seeks to do: collectively assert a vision in which humanity returns to being one species among many that is humble enough to understand that we must protect all life and the processes it depends on for our own well-being and because it is ethically the right thing to do. It is about fixing the human relationship with nature by recognizing that any relationship needs mutuality to be healthy.[38] This is called "radical hope" because, though the idea is clear, the course of action that will make it possible is not yet fully clear.[39]

The other road to follow is to decide that the goal of biodiversity conservation as set out in the CBD is impossible and to set a new agenda. Thus some postmodern conservationists consider this a time of defeat and that now is the moment to abandon traditional conservation goals based on parks and wilderness areas. Instead the Green Postmodernists would have us embrace the idea that we should convert the Earth to a garden that serves the interests of local people and urban dwellers.[40] This of course would mean the end of inconvenient and difficult-to-conserve species like grizzly bears, tigers, lions, and elephants. It would also mean concerted efforts to prevent the natural and necessary but deeply disruptive process of renewal such as fire and flooding.[41]

The death of the wild in favor of the garden with *Homo sapiens* triumphant is no vision for those who proclaim to love nature. It will also inevitably be disastrous for the human species. We do not know how to run the world. It is time for our species to become humble and wise and to stop being greedy and clever.[42]

Philosopher Immanuel Kant summed up the human dilemma with two questions: *What can I know?* and *What ought I to do?* These are appropriate questions for conservationists in the twenty-first century. And we can answer them. We know that nature needs at least half. We ought to assert it even if it is not clear that we will succeed. Our failure to do so will likely guarantee failure of the conditions that support life on Earth.

Bolder Thinking for Conservation

REED F. NOSS, ANDREW P. DOBSON, ROBERT BALDWIN,
PAUL BEIER, CORY R. DAVIS, DOMINICK A. DELLASALA,
JOHN FRANCIS, HARVEY LOCKE, KATARZYNA NOWAK,
ROEL LOPEZ, CONRAD REINING, STEPHEN C. TROMBULAK,
AND GARY TABOR

SHOULD CONSERVATION TARGETS, such as the proportion of a region to be placed in protected areas, be socially acceptable from the start? Or should they be based unapologetically on the best available science and expert opinion, then address issues of practicality later? Such questions strike to the philosophical core of conservation. Ambitious targets are often considered radical and value laden, whereas modest targets are ostensibly more objective and reasonable. The personal values of experts are impossible to escape in either case. Conservation professionals of a biocentric bent might indeed err on the side of protecting too much. Anthropocentric bias, however, more commonly affects target setting. The pro-growth norms of global society foster timidity among conservation professionals, steering them toward conformity with the global economic agenda and away from acknowledging what is ultimately needed to sustain life on Earth.

The 2010 Nagoya Conference of the Convention on Biological Diversity demonstrates the pitfalls of timidity. M. R. W. Rands and colleagues summarized the calamitous global decline of biodiversity (which they defined as "the variety of genes, species, and ecosystems that constitute life on Earth") and challenged participants at the Nagoya Conference to develop a strategy to confront this crisis.[1] Unfortunately, the biodiversity targets for the year 2020 developed at Nagoya fall short of what is needed to maintain the "ecosystem services" upon which Charles Perrings and coauthors suggest human welfare and economic well-being depend.[2] These targets are even less likely to maintain the full breadth of biodiversity. Targets for 2020 set at the Nagoya Conference include protected areas covering 17 percent of terrestrial areas and inland waters, 10 percent of marine and coastal areas, and restoration of at least 15 percent of degraded ecosystems.[3] These targets are woefully below what the results of most scientific studies show are necessary to meet widespread conservation goals such as maintaining viable populations of native species, representing ecosystems across their range of variation, and promoting resilience of ecosystems to environmental change.[4]

Set targets designed to achieve goals

Biodiversity is on a downward slide, and those best equipped to say why and how this must be stopped are not being assertive. Conservation scientists and practitioners were not always so shy about developing conservation strategies. In the early twentieth century Victor Shelford and colleagues in the Ecological Society of America proposed a continent-wide network of protected areas that would establish "a nature sanctuary with its original wild animals for each biotic formation."[5] In the 1980s, when the promise of sustainable development seemed real, the Brundtland Commission set a target of tripling the amount of Earth's surface then protected (approximately 4 percent).[6] Such progress was followed in 1992 by global treaties signed in Rio de Janeiro at the Convention on Biological Diversity's Earth Summit, which promised to address human-caused climate change and halt biodiversity loss. The goals were commendable, but their implementation faltered.

By 2005 it was clear that these conventions and commissions were not meeting their stated goals.[7] Shortly thereafter, the Intergovernmental Panel on Climate Change stated bluntly: "The resilience of many ecosystems is likely to be exceeded this century by an unprecedented combination of climate change, associated disturbances (e.g., flooding, drought, wildfire, insects, ocean acidification), and other drivers of global change (e.g., land-use change, pollution, overexploitation of resources)."[8] According to the 2010 IUCN Red List, an estimated 20 percent of Earth's vertebrates are now threatened with extinction.[9] We suggest these profound failures to

achieve conservation goals are partly due to the reluctance of conservation professionals to articulate a bolder and more honest vision.

Protect at least 50 percent globally

Empirical data, models, and prioritization algorithms can be used to set
quantitative and transparent conservation targets. The proportion of a
region needed to meet a given set of conservation goals will vary widely
depending on physical heterogeneity, degree of endemism, past land-use
decisions, and many other factors.[10] Almost universally, when conservation targets are based on the research and expert opinion of scientists they
far exceed targets set to meet political or policy goals.[11] In contrast to policy-
driven targets, scientific studies and reviews suggest that some 25–75 percent of a typical region must be managed with conservation of nature as a
primary objective to meet goals for conserving biodiversity. These results
echo earlier models of habitat loss and fragmentation, in which the transition from one continuous patch to multiple patches of decreasing size and
increasing isolation begins after around 40 percent loss of original habitat.[12]

From a strict scientific point of view, the only defensible targets are those
derived from empirical data and rigorous analyses. The people who develop
conservation strategies and global treaties prefer to set targets a priori. When
establishing global targets, as at Nagoya, it would be prudent to consider the
range of evidence-based estimates of "how much is enough" from many regions and set a target on the high side of the median as a buffer against uncertainty. From this precautionary perspective, 50 percent—slightly above the
mid-point of recent evidence-based estimates—is scientifically defensible as
a global target. We suggest that conservation targets and plans be regularly
updated and synthesized into country- and continent-wide strategies, accompanied by specific steps and a timetable for implementation.

Maintain or restore connectivity across large landscapes

Large contiguous reserves should be functionally connected to allow movement of organisms and genes, for example the migratory and dispersal
movements of large animals[13] and distributional shifts of multiple species in
response to climate change. Although a well-managed landscape matrix may
provide connectivity and other conservation benefits,[14] it cannot be assumed
to conserve biodiversity unless legally binding and enforced regulations keep

land use compatible with conservation objectives. This is usually not the case.

To date, only three countries—Bhutan, India, and Tanzania—have identified major corridors at national extents. In Australia a national conversation about connectivity includes a proposed 2800-kilometer corridor from Queensland to Victoria,[15] mirroring the Yellowstone to Yukon corridor (3200 kilometers) in the United States and Canada.[16] We recommend that other countries carry out similar transboundary assessments and develop implementation plans that transcend political demarcations.

Focus attention on the greatest threat

An exclusive focus on global climate change, the current rage, may obscure other pressing conservation problems and divert funding from combating them. As a direct global threat to species and ecosystems, climate change is currently dwarfed by land-use change in response to human population growth and conversion of wild lands to agricultural use.[17] Current rates of land-use change will make adaptation of species to climate change virtually impossible. Conversely, protecting native ecosystems can increase their resilience and their ability to store carbon.[18]

Demonstrate the value of nature to humans

Biodiversity should be managed as a public good,[19] but it is narrow-minded to dwell exclusively on its material benefits to people. Discussions about human development and ecosystem services need to delve deeper and communicate more effectively. The broader values of nature to humans are exemplified by the Transition Towns movement in the United Kingdom, the practice of Shinrin-yoku ("forest bathing") in Japan, and the weak relation between material wealth and happiness.[20] Conservation professionals should not assume that only economic and utilitarian values determine people's attitudes toward conservation. Many people value nature for its own sake.

Natural history and conservation education must be expanded at all levels from preschool children to political leaders. Educators must explicitly recognize the importance of teaching people of all ages about basic ecological and evolutionary concepts—and of getting them outdoors. The focus of education must be on whole organisms and ecosystems; otherwise, conservation professionals risk losing the interest in the living world of generations of students of all ages worldwide.

Popularize the idea that conservation can be achieved

When continental-level conservation was proposed in the 1990s,[21] it was viewed by many as unrealistic, just as Victor Shelford's ambitious proposals were seen as inappropriate by some of his peers.[22] This view is changing. The United States Department of the Interior has initiated 21 Landscape Conservation Cooperatives that cover the entire nation, and the Obama Administration has launched the America's Great Outdoors Initiative to encourage public use and appreciation of natural areas. Such efforts have the potential to rescue conservation professionals from their defeatist mentality and draw out the interest and enthusiasm of citizens.

The conservation science community, as well as the broader circle of conservation professionals, must do a much better job of communicating a compelling vision across traditional disciplinary and societal boundaries. The media, in turn, has a role in promoting biodiversity as an indispensable public value. The BBC's *Planet Earth* and National Geographic's *Great Migrations* series show the promise of this approach. Conservation professionals of all varieties should invest more effort in explaining and marketing biodiversity conservation in compelling ways. When people understand and appreciate the value of biodiversity, they will be more likely to think about conservation when they vote, make purchases, or decide about uses of land and natural resources.

Reasonable targets

If the conservation community sets protection targets based on preconceived notions of what is socially or politically acceptable or on assumptions of inevitable population and economic growth, we will make very limited headway in stemming extinction. We suggest that strategies for conservation be passed first through a biological filter. Those options with a high probability of sustaining biodiversity are retained, whereas those with a lower probability are seen as incremental. The next step, however, is not to pass the remaining strategies through a political filter because most would fail to pass in the current political climate. Rather, conservation professionals must become part of the constituency that promotes life on Earth. Our task is not to be beaten down by political reality, but to help change it. Nature needs at least 50 percent, and it is time we said so.

Caring for People and Valuing Forests in Africa

JANE GOODALL

SO OFTEN, AS I TRAVEL around the world, I pay homage to those forward-thinking individuals who in the 1800s had the foresight, because of their love of the natural world, to urge governments to set aside areas of wilderness for protection. The first national park in the world was Yellowstone, created in 1872, and gradually other areas in North America and around the world were given protected status. If we did not have networks of conservation areas the natural world would be even more devastated than it already is.

I have spent a good deal of time in East Africa's national parks and reserves, and I briefly visited quite a number in the United States, Canada, Australia, and various Asian and Latin American countries. I am most familiar with habitats set aside to protect areas of forest. A central part of the mission of the Jane Goodall Institute (JGI) is to conserve the great apes and other primates. And this, of course, means conserving the forests where they live.

Forests are the habitat of a great wealth of diverse animal and plant species. For example, the forest of the Congo Basin, the world's second-largest tropical rainforest, is home to over 10,000 species of plants, 1,000 species of birds, 400 species of mammals, and three of the world's four species of great apes. The situation is similar in the Amazon Basin and in the great rainforests of Asia. It is shocking to realize that the destruction of these habitats, as the chain saws move into one area after another, is leading to the local or total extinction of species *every day*. And so those areas that have been set aside to protect forests and their biodiversity are critically important.

My own work has been in the Gombe National Park on the eastern shores of Lake Tanganyika in Tanzania. When I arrived in 1960 there was all but unbroken forest surrounding the lake and the chimpanzees of Gombe could move in and out of their tiny 23-square-mile (37-square-kilometer) national park. But by the mid-1980s the trees outside the park were almost all gone. The land had been overfarmed and the soil was losing its fertility. Farmers, looking for new land for their crops, turned to ever-steeper and more unsuitable hillsides. Without tree cover, more and more of the thin layer of topsoil would wash away with every heavy rain, causing terrible erosion and silting up the streams. There were more people living in the villages around the park than the land could support—the result not only of the population growth we have seen around the world since 1960 but also of an influx of refugees from the Democratic Republic of Congo (DRC) and Burundi. It was clear that these people, economically very poor, were struggling to survive and cutting down the last of their forests in their desperate efforts to grow crops to feed their families or earn a livelihood through charcoal production. The situation was desperate. Surely, only if we helped the people would it be possible to protect the chimpanzees and their habitat.

And so, in 1994, with a small grant from the European Union, JGI initiated TACARE (or "TakeCare," the Lake Tanganyika Catchment Reforestation and Education project), a program to improve the lives of the people in the villages surrounding the park. From the start it was a holistic program, and over the years we have proved that an integrated approach to poverty alleviation is what works. We selected a team of local Tanzanians who gained the cooperation of the villagers by respecting and addressing their needs and priorities. These were: increased food production (accomplished through restoration of fertility to the overused farmland—without the use of chemical fertilizers), improved health facilities, and better education for their children (accomplished with the support of the local Tanzanian government). We encouraged the establishment of wood lots comprised of fast-growing species close to the villages, and we introduced fuel-efficient stoves. We started micro-credit programs (especially for women) for environmentally sustainable projects of their choice, such as tree nurseries, and we provide scholarships for girls to stay in school through puberty. We also introduced hygienic latrines that afford privacy, and we provide sanitary supplies. All around the world, family size has dropped as women have become empowered and better educated. In each village we have trained volunteers who provide family planning information.

In 2008 we helped the villagers to draw up land use management plans (required by the government) using cutting-edge geospatial mapping technologies (with support from Esri, DigitalGlobe, and Google Earth) to create high-resolution maps. And, because of the good relations we had built up with the villagers, they agreed to set aside, for forest regeneration, a buffer zone surrounding Gombe National Park. Within this buffer zone—a designated village forest reserve—there can be no hunting or tree felling, although limited access does allow for foraging for medicinal plants and mushrooms, beekeeping, and gathering dead wood. Stretching along the peaks of the Rift Escarpment, this buffer zone also protects the watershed and thus the water supply to the villages. Over the past ten years new trees have grown from seeds and from the stumps left in the ground, and many of these have reached heights of over 20 feet so that the chimpanzees of Gombe can, once again, move out of the park when certain fruits ripen in the buffer zone.

It is not enough to conserve a forest and its wildlife when, as happens increasingly, it is disconnected from other forested areas. It is necessary to develop corridors of habitat to link areas of forest so that animals can move between protected areas and thus maintain genetic diversity. Because of the success of TACARE—and with support from the United Nations Development Programme (UNDP), the Pritzker Foundation, and the United States Agency for International Development (USAID)—we have been able to extend our work to other villages, some of which have set aside land for reforestation that will form contiguous corridors of forest reserves.

Most recently, with grants from USAID and Norad, we have been able to work with villages close to a large area of intact forest in the Ugala Region to the south, home to more than 600 (possibly as many as 1,000) chimpanzees. At present there is no legal protection for this important (and very beautiful) habitat, but JGI is hoping that, with the cooperation of the local government, the area can be officially gazetted as Local Authority Forest Reserve, managed by the district authorities. Additional contiguous patches of forest within village boundaries will become Village Forest Reserves.

Meanwhile, we have been training volunteer forest monitors, at least one from each of the 52 villages where JGI now works. Collecting data using android smartphones and tablets donated by Google Earth Outreach, these monitors patrol the newly restored forest areas, recording illegal activities and documenting the progress of reforestation. They report their findings to their village governments, and all information is sent immediately to Google Cloud Storage, from which it can be downloaded for analysis by JGI and our partners. The important thing is that these forest monitors have been empowered—it is they who have selected what should be recorded based on their indigenous knowledge. They have chosen 30 different types of human activity which they believe can threaten the forest. And these volunteers monitor 20 species of animals. Of course they note each time they either see or hear a chimpanzee or see a chimpanzee nest. It is in this way that we know there are almost as many chimpanzees outside as within protected forest areas—vital information for us as we—along with the villagers—devise plans to protect these endangered apes. Thus today these villagers have become effective stewards of the land, helping to restore not only their own environment, but also the forest habitat of the chimpanzees.

JGI has initiated similar programs in Uganda, the Democratic Republic of the Congo (DRC), the Republic of Congo, and Senegal. In all these programs there is an emphasis on creating and protecting corridors to link areas of protected forest. In Senegal we are hoping to create a cross-border national park to include the forests, rich in biodiversity, of Guinea. And we are just beginning to develop a similar project to protect the forest reserves and national parks of Burundi.

The days in Africa when wilderness areas could receive total protection from national legislation alone are vanishing. In most areas, ranger forces are underpaid and poorly equipped, making them vulnerable to bribes from poachers. And corruption within the government is often widespread. The horrific increase in poaching of elephants and rhinos, for their tusks and horns, is often the result of international criminal cartels. Even in a well-financed national park like Kruger in South Africa, heavily armed poachers fly in by helicopter, kill a rhino, dig out its horn, and fly away. This is driven by the high price fetched by rhino horn, principally for the Vietnamese market. The biggest importer of illegal ivory is China. The second-largest is the United States.

In some countries, including developed countries, even when an area is designated a national park, the government may permit road-building or the exploitation of natural resources, such as oil, gas, minerals, or timber. Forest reserves have been sacrificed for agricultural developments. National budgets seldom place the protection of wilderness high on their list of priorities, so it is often necessary for conservationists to provide financial incentives. Ecotourism can bring in foreign exchange but, especially in forested areas, this will not immediately deliver large payments comparable to selling or leasing concession for commercial development. And tourism itself can be destructive if not properly controlled.

Another way to show that protecting rather than destroying forests can be economically beneficial is by assigning a "monetary" value to living trees and compensating governments, landowners, and villagers for conserving. Forests are the lungs of the world: They take in carbon dioxide (CO_2) from the air and release oxygen. The CO_2 is stored as carbon not only in the trees but also in forest soils. As forests are cut down and burned, thousands of tons of CO_2 are released, and it is this, along with the burning of fossil fuels, that is a major component of the greenhouse gases that are causing the rise in global temperatures. Thus protecting and restoring forests is one of the most efficient and least expensive ways to slow down global warming.

Lengthy deliberations in many countries resulted in the United Nations program for Reducing Emissions from Deforestation and Forest Degradation (REDD+) in developing countries. The REDD+ program recognizes the importance of poverty alleviation, sustainable forest management, and the conservation of biodiversity, as well as protection of the forest for carbon sequestration. REDD+ assigns a value for the carbon stored in different kinds of forests and forest soils, so that appropriate compensation can be paid to those who protect their forests. And compliance can be verified through high-tech satellite imagery. It is money from a pilot REDD+ program in Tanzania which is enabling us to work in the Ugala Region, as we try to establish a protected forest to save the chimpanzees there.

It is increasingly being realized how extremely important it is for the preservation of national parks and reserves to have the goodwill and support of villagers in the vicinity. Legal protected status for such areas is essential, but it is not always enough: In some cases, the buy-in of the local people is key. Sharing some percentage of the revenue from tourism and providing jobs as guides, drivers, and employees of visitor facilities is one way, and many programs similar to our TACARE have been introduced to help local communities. But I believe that the most crucial aspect is for the local people to develop a sense of pride in their park, and a sense of ownership. In Uganda a planned deal by the government to sell a forest reserve that would have become a sugar cane plantation was halted as a result of successful demonstrations by the people.

Finally, we must try to ensure that new generations grow up to become better stewards than we have been. JGI's Roots & Shoots program, founded in Tanzania in 1991, aims to help young people understand the problems facing them and to empower them to take action. As of 2014, the Roots & Shoots program has a presence in more than 130 countries—with about 150,000 groups (a group is anything from two members to a whole school). Roots & Shoots empowers young people of all ages (ranging from preschool-aged through university and beyond) to play an active role in addressing ecological and social challenges. Each group chooses for itself three projects to make this a better world: one to help people, one to help other animals, and one to help the environment. Everywhere young people are learning respect for animals and the natural world. Some are lucky enough to be able to visit national parks and reserves to see and experience for themselves the wilderness. Of course, this is not always possible, but there are other ways for children to spend time in nature, even if it is only a city park. Botanical gardens are great places to experience the wonders of the plant kingdom and zoos are getting better and better at educating visitors of all ages about the importance of conservation. When people acquire a deeper understanding of the natural world, and of the ways their future is being destroyed, they are more likely to care and to want to help to save what is left.

The wilderness is under increasing threat: National parks, wilderness reserves, and other conservation areas are more important than ever before. Each of us must do what we can both to ensure that those existing, already-protected areas remain so and to encourage the creation and future protection of new ones whenever possible.

What Is the Future of Conservation?

DANIEL F. DOAK, VICTORIA J. BAKKER,
BRUCE EVAN GOLDSTEIN, AND BENJAMIN HALE

A RECENT MOVEMENT SEEKS to refocus the field of conservation biology and the practical work of conservation organizations by de-emphasizing the goal of protecting nature for its intrinsic values in favor of protecting the environment for its benefits to humans. This "new conservation science" (NCS) has inspired debate among academics and conservationists and motivated fundamental changes in the world's largest conservation groups. Despite claims that NCS approaches are supported by the biological and social sciences, we argue NCS has limited support from either. Rather, the shift in motivations and goals associated with NCS appear to arise largely from a belief system holding that the needs and wants of humans must be prioritized over any intrinsic rights and values of nature.

Shaking up the motives and practices of conservation

Throughout its history, and across the globe, environmental conservation has been motivated by a wide range of ethical, utilitarian, aesthetic, and economic concerns. However, a recent and much-publicized campaign, originating within the conservation community, marginalizes nature's intrinsic value in favor of a primarily human-centered conservation ethic. Spearheaded by prominent advocates, this campaign has been advanced in both popular and scholarly outlets[1] and has received considerable news coverage (for example, recent articles in *Time, Slate,* and the *New York Times*). The message—that the moral imperative of environmental conservation (henceforth, "conservation") should be to maximize the welfare of humans[2]—is increasingly popular among academics and policy makers and dovetails with tactical shifts in the mission statements of many conservation organizations.[3] This movement seeks not a subtle shift in the methods of conservation, but a stark change in its fundamental goals and methods: "Instead of pursuing the protection of biodiversity for biodiversity's sake, a new conservation should seek to enhance those natural systems that benefit the widest number of people."[4]

Here, we examine the claims and assumptions of those advocating for a "new conservation science," or NCS, a term we use because it has been adopted by some of the leading advocates of this position.[5] This analysis is important because NCS proponents have asserted that most current and past conservation is poorly done, wrongly motivated, and scientifically unsupportable. Given that this movement is directly affecting conservation practices, both the claimed failures of past efforts and the promises concerning their alternatives warrant careful scrutiny.

Central premises of the NCS argument

NCS advocates begin by suggesting that there are many flaws in traditional approaches to conservation: (1) Conservation emphasizes protection of biodiversity without regard for human welfare, resulting in regular harm to disadvantaged peoples and impediments to business and development;[6] (2) Conservation rests on the myth of a pristine nature and its core purpose is to conserve and restore this state, which in fact never existed—"We create parks that are no less human constructions than Disneyland";[7] (3) Conservationists wrongly assume that nature is inherently fragile and will sustain irreparable damage from human activities—"Nature is so resilient that it can recover rapidly from even the most powerful human disturbances";[8] (4) Conservation has failed to protect biodiversity; although we have created many protected areas, extinctions and ecosystem degradation continue—"Protecting biodiversity for its own sake has failed";[9] and (5) Conservation is also failing socially, with dwindling support from a mostly affluent white minority—"Conservationists are losing the battle to protect nature because they are failing to connect with the hearts, anxieties, and minds of a large segment of the American public."[10]

Given these perceived ills, NCS advocates call for the following remedies: (1) The primary objective of conservation should be to protect, restore, and enhance the services that nature provides to people—"The ultimate goal is better management of nature for human benefit";[11] (2) To succeed, conservationists need to ally with corporations and other significant economic actors—"21st century conservation tries to maximize biodiversity without compromising development goals";[12] (3) Conservationists should increase their focus on urban areas and on landscapes and species most useful to humans, since human benefits should drive conservation efforts—"Forward-looking conservation protects natural habitats where people live and extract resources and works with corporations to find mixes of economic and conservation activities that blend development with a concern for nature."[13]

What's wrong with these claims and remedies?

Although we focus here on the principal shortcomings in NCS's central claims and remedies, we also note that many specific examples and points of evidence offered to bolster NCS positions are poorly supported or misleading.[14]

Human well-being is already one of the core features of conservation policy and planning. Conservation's concern for biodiversity has always been accompanied by concern for human well-being and ecosystem services: these human-centered goals form one pillar of a diverse mix of motivations and strategies dating back at least a century to Gifford Pinchot and his predecessors.[15] Hearkening back to Pinchot (for example, "The first principle of conservation is development, the use of the natural resources now existing on this continent for the benefit of the people who live here"[16]), efforts to understand and protect ecosystem services have long been a plank in the conservationist's platform. More quantitatively, most federal lands in the United States that are in some sense managed for conservation are primarily devoted to the generation of ecosystem services. The U.S. Forest Service and Bureau of Land Management control more than 2.5 times the land area of the U.S. National Park Service and Fish and Wildlife Service, and only 17 percent of federal lands are designated as wilderness. Emphasis on human use of natural areas is also typical of other countries: In the European Union and the Russian Federation, less than 2 percent of all protected forest areas receive the most restrictive status of no active intervention.[17] Consideration of human well-being in conservation decisions does not require a radical departure from current practices. The NCS position, however, restricts the focus of conservation to the advancement of human well-being, which it frequently conflates with narrow definitions of economic development,[18] and thereby marginalizes efforts to preserve diverse and natural ecosystems or to protect nature for aesthetic or other noneconomic benefits to humans.

Conservation already takes a realistic view of nature's purity and fragility. The NCS argument caricatures the views of conservationists about pristine nature, while making the scientifically unsupportable claim that natural systems are almost infinitely resilient. There are still many relatively undisturbed areas across the globe,[19] and while conservationists have long recognized that these areas are not pristine,[20] they also recognize that such areas usually harbor far more biodiversity than do urban parks and plantations, a point NCS advocates only sometimes acknowledge.[21] Moreover, conservation scientists have focused at least as much on nature's resilience as its fragility.[22] Although many environmental harms can indeed be ameliorated or reversed, others are virtually irreversible (such as extinction, climate change, mountaintop removal).

Past conservation has not been a failure. The NCS claim that contemporary conservation has failed is overly simplistic, if not directly misleading. First, it ignores how the creation of parks, innovative resource-management regimes, and other conservation works have slowed the pace of biodiversity decline. Although it is difficult to quantify averted declines and extinctions, several recent studies have concluded that if the conservation community had not been trying for decades to protect land and water resources, biodiversity losses would have been far greater than they have been to date.[23] Second, it ignores the creation of legislation and public support for nature conservation that set the stage for arguments over conservation and development;[24] the very need to make arguments about conservation impacts versus economic gains is a central legacy of the conservation movement.

NCS approaches are a dubious fix for conservation's shortcomings. NCS advocates argue that the conservation movement's failure to halt biodiversity decline and resource degradation supports a shift toward markedly more human-centered approaches to conservation. But there is little basis for the assertion that a more narrow, anthropocentric conservation strategy would deliver better results, especially given the track record of poor management of natural resources in the past, including management of the parts of nature we economically value the most.[25] In addition, the NCS assertion that focusing on ecosystem services will save biodiversity as well ("the fate of nature and that of humans are deeply intertwined....many of the activities that harm biodiversity also harm human well-being"[26]) has essentially no rigorous scientific support.[27] Finally, the claim that NCS will be more effective than contemporary conservation relies on altering the primary goal of conservation from saving species and ecosystems to that of saving only those components of nature that directly benefit people: "Some human-caused extinctions are inevitable, and we must be realistic about what we can and cannot accomplish. We must be sure to first conserve ecosystems in places where biodiversity delivers services to people in need."[28]

The priorities of NCS rest on ethical values, not science. Although NCS advocates contend that their approach is science-based and aimed at more efficient conservation outcomes, their remedies appear to be primarily grounded in an assumption that human welfare should be granted a higher moral priority than the protection of species and ecological processes.[29] Therefore, they argue that conservation *should* be done for the sake of human well-being, which NCS often equates with business interests and economic prosperity.[30] Thus, these advocates urge the substitution of a human-centered ethical commitment for the one that has long motivated much of the conservation movement—that other species and nature as a whole have a right to exist—and do so under the guise of scientific objectivity.

Most worrying, NCS's rationale that to be effective and forward-thinking conservation should more directly and narrowly serve human interests is based on dubious evidence. First, NCS advocates argue that conservationists have sacrificed indigenous groups to form parks. While the establishment of protected areas has sometimes hampered local livelihoods and created conservation refugees,[31] widespread efforts have been under way to address this for three decades.[32] Indigenous groups and conservationists have also frequently formed alliances to protect lands and counter extractive industries.[33] Further, local and indigenous peoples often receive multiple, tangible benefits from well-designed protected areas.[34] Finally, a recent, extensive survey of development and conservation professionals revealed a broad consensus that biodiversity conservation and poverty alleviation are generally positively linked, even while countervailing minority positions have polarized the debate.[35] Altogether, the evidence shows that biodiversity-motivated conservation can be compatible with rights of indigenous groups, and that the motivation of preserving nature for its own sake does not need to be thrown aside to achieve both goals.

Advocates of NCS also argue—both as a matter of efficacy and as a matter of principle—that conservation should partner with, rather than impede, business. While groups with competing interests can negotiate agreements—and should certainly do so when it is truly beneficial—it is rarely possible to identify solutions that literally maximize both economic and ecological benefits, as NCS advocates propose.[36] Nor is it clear that giving up on conservation's core goals is the best way to reach compromise with those who might have legitimate, but mostly noncongruent, objectives. We cannot speak effectively on behalf of the natural world if at the outset we prioritize corporate and other human interests. NCS proponents also downplay evidence that corporations have done vast harm to lands and people through resource extraction,[37] that recent efforts to "green" business through environmentally responsible practices have often failed to reduce pollution or biodiversity losses,[38] and that indigenous rights groups view the "green economy" as a cultural and ecological threat (for example, the Statement of 500 indigenous groups at Rio+20 UN Conference on Sustainable Development: "The 'Green Economy' promises to eradicate poverty but in fact will only favor and respond to multinational enterprises and capitalism."[39]

Economic motivations are not always dominant, nor are moral values always weak or immutable. NCS proponents implicitly assume that people's core motivations are deeply self-serving and thus that economic self-interest is the most potent motivator, but a great deal of research shows that social and moral factors strongly shape behavior and support for policies, often outweighing direct economic self-interest.[40] This conclusion is borne out by even a cursory look at the long history of conservation successes. The majority of both national and international conservation laws (such as The Migratory Bird Act, U.S. Endangered Species Act, Canadian Species at Risk Act, CITES, Wilderness Act, and the Clean Water Act) have garnered strong support at least in part by appeals to noneconomic, ethical principles. Moral arguments are also the way to build alliances across broad coalitions of different constituencies, including those motivated by both social and ecological issues.[41] The stance that conservation progress should be driven by transient economic preferences rather than enduring values also hampers recognition of the possibility or even the need for structural and institutional changes in order to achieve and sustain conservation objectives. Finally, the assumption, and hence reinforcement, of only economic motivations for conservation ignores and may thus diminish the importance of political, scientific, philosophical, and religious motivations for conservation found across different nations and cultures.[42]

Recent polling in the United States also shows evidence that the public's concern for nature is not weakening, nor is support limited to the wealthy white population. Polls find that there is equal or greater support for moral versus human-use arguments for conservation[43] and that Hispanics, women, and young voters are currently among those most concerned with various conservation goals, which include protecting America's air and water, wildlife, and other natural resources, as well as confronting climate change.[44]

NCS proponents also implicitly assume that ethical stances are resistant to change, and thus conservation must refashion its message to better appeal to those who are apathetic or opposed to the goals of protecting species and ecosystems. However, innumerable social and environmental justice campaigns have shown that ethical views can be swayed, often very rapidly. Indeed, most successful efforts to win public support for a cause have focused on influencing notions of right and wrong, even if they also are combined with multiple other motivations. Slavery was not outlawed in the United States solely because abolition favored the interests of northern manufacturers over southern plantation owners.[45] Nor is the lack of complete success in eliminating slavery worldwide—to this day—a reason to conclude that the moral justification against this practice has "failed" or should be replaced with an economic efficiency argument. Recent campaigns over other human rights issues (same-sex marriage, for instance), animal welfare, and, yes, conservation, all show that beliefs and priorities are powerful motivators and that they can be altered, often with great speed.

Conclusions

Conservation policies and strategies can't stand still or dwell in the past. The profound and increasing pressures on our natural systems demand that conservationists critically review their goals and approaches, and seek ever-more effective ways of improving the outlook for all natural ecosystems. Likewise, we have no argument with the goal of meeting human needs, especially those of the poor. And, in some settings, joint economic development and conservation programs might be an important and cost-effective means to meet the dual goals of human betterment and environmental conservation. But the congruence of these different goals in some cases does not mean that conservation of biodiversity has to perpetually take a backseat to the betterment of human welfare.

The remedies that follow from NCS's critique of contemporary conservation's track record rest on the assumptions and the values of its authors, not analysis and facts. Conservation has long been concerned both with sustaining human resource needs and with conserving nature's intrinsic value. Rather than adding to the conservation toolbox, NCS seeks to shrink the range of conservation activities, and especially motivations, that are considered legitimate. That advocates of NCS denigrate much past and contemporary conservation work is of real concern, especially given evidence that broad coalitions are most effective at bringing about social change.[46] By the logic of NCS, conservationists should abandon many of the objectives that have motivated generations of activists and scientists. Faithfully following NCS prescriptions would also suggest conservationists withdraw their support for environmental legislation that seeks to protect rare species, and biodiversity in general, and that they dramatically transform the practices of conservation NGOs.

We believe it is neither quixotic, nor misanthropic, nor shortsighted to protect nature based on its intrinsic value. Moreover, we acknowledge that this position is a statement of values, and we hope that as the NCS debate continues, all parties will be clear about where the "science" of their arguments stop and start. If the mission of conservation becomes, first and foremost, the promotion of human welfare, who will work for the protection and restoration of the rest of nature—for desert tortoises, Delta smelts, Hawaiian monk seals, vernal pool invertebrates—and the many other parts of the natural world that do not directly benefit humans, and in some cases do demonstrable harm to immediate, economic welfare? Also, we wonder why donors should be generous to such NCS-motivated groups. For those who care about preserving and restoring ecologically rich natural areas, the NCS agenda has little appeal. For donors whose foremost concern is human welfare, groups like Save the Children, Oxfam, and Water for People already, and more explicitly and effectively, embrace the same values of human betterment, including environmental efforts that serve these goals.

While NCS advocates argue that traditional conservation is despairing and negative,[47] pared down to its essence, their solution seems far more so: Give up your original goals and focus only on a single species—humans.[48] There are now unprecedented demands on natural resources across the globe, and there will never be a shortage of advocates for the human needs for these resources. The question is whether conservation scientists and practitioners should make promoting economic prosperity their primary mission as well. As conservationists are already acutely aware, the effects of human industry are felt throughout the world, and we must plan conservation strategies that address coupled human and ecological dynamics. But refashioning conservation into a set of goals that primarily advance human interests means selling nature down the river, serving neither the long-term interests of people nor the rest of the species with which we share this planet.

Fool's Gold in the Catskill Mountains: Thinking Critically about the Ecosystem Services Paradigm

DOUGLAS J. McCAULEY

PERHAPS THE MOST IMPORTANT TREND in conservation science this decade is "ecosystem services," typically defined as economic benefits derived from species and ecosystems.[1] Ecosystem services form the basis of new market-centric mechanisms for conservation sometimes referred to as the "new conservation." The logic underlying this movement is that if we could properly quantify the economic value of nature, decision makers would suddenly recognize the folly of environmental destruction. In the words of key proponents of this so-called new conservation, conservationists must "jettison their idealized notions of nature, parks, and wilderness" and "partner with corporations in a science-based effort to integrate the value of nature's benefits into their operations and cultures."[2]

Market-based mechanisms for conservation are not, unfortunately, the panacea that they have been made out to be. If we mean to make significant and long-lasting gains in conservation, we must strongly assert the primacy of ethics and aesthetics in conservation. We must redirect much of the effort now being devoted to the commodification of nature back toward instilling in more people a love for nature.

The proponents of market-based mechanisms for conservation bolster their argument by repeatedly citing one example: the Catskill/Delaware Watershed. Through this project, New York City opted to conserve a watershed that filters its water as effectively as a filtration plant, and more cheaply. A growing number of ecologists, economists, and environmental scientists hold this shining example aloft and proclaim that where there is one golden nugget, there must be others. They describe, mostly in hypothetical terms, a world of win-win scenarios: We can save ecosystems and species and in the process make more money. It is a message with broad appeal: for the public, which is notoriously averse to bad news; for business-oriented politicians, who see an opportunity to further liberalize markets while appeasing the environmentally anxious; for philanthropists, who wish to do good without straying too far from their economic comfort zones; and for foundations that want to use the familiar capitalist rhetoric of ecosystem services to draw out new or wary donors.

It is both true and obvious that "ecosystems," in some sense of the word, are necessary for human survival. It is also true that there will be cases in which it will be lucrative to protect nature, and people will derive benefits from such conservation efforts. However, advocates of new conservation put an emphasis on ecosystem services that dangerously overstates its role in conservation. As a conservation tool, "ecosystem services" is limited in four fundamental ways.

First, although most conservationists would argue that nature should be conserved in perpetuity, the strength and direction of market forces that are now being called upon to motivate nature conservation are anything but perpetual. The often illusory and ephemeral relationship of the market to conservation is well illustrated by the case of a former coffee plantation, Finca Santa Fe, in the Valle del General of Costa Rica.[3] A recent study found that native bees from two forest fragments adjacent to Finca Santa Fe yielded approximately US$60,000 a year in pollination services to the coffee plants. This was hailed as an example of how conservation can yield "double benefits" for biodiversity and agriculture. Shortly after the conclusion of the study, however, Finca Santa Fe, probably affected by a severe dip in coffee prices, cleared its coffee trees and planted pineapple instead. Pollinators are irrelevant to pineapple production. Simple logic suggests that over a period of several years the monetary value of the pollinators in forest fragments around Finca Santa Fe dropped from $60,000 per year to zero.

The same phenomenon is observable at the global scale. In 1997, Robert Costanza and colleagues assigned dollar values to the worth of the planet's ecosystems in what served as the first financial statement for global nature.[4] This year, the group updated and revised these values.[5] They concluded that in the intervening seventeen years many of the world's ecosystems had increased in value, but a few ecosystems, like estuaries and floodplains, are today worth less than they used to be. To make ecosystem services the foundation of our conservation strategies is to imply—intentionally or otherwise—that nature is worth conserving only when it is, or can be made, profitable. The risk in advocating this position is that we might be taken at our word. Then, when these cases of ecosystem "devaluation" crop up, what are we to tell stakeholders who believed us when we promised nature would turn a profit for them? What right will we have to argue against those who wish to liquidate these poorly performing ecosystems (and the birds, and the fish, and the plants within them) like any other bad asset?

Second, the logic of ecosystem-service-based conservation rests on the implicit assumption that the biosphere is benevolent—that it provides us with useful services and protects us from malevolent abiotic forces such as hurricanes, floods, and rising temperatures. This reasoning ignores basic ecology: Environments don't act for the benefit of any single species. There are myriad examples of what might be labelled "ecosystem disservices." Trees take water out of watersheds;[6] wild animals kill people and destroy property;[7] and wetlands can increase the risk of disease.[8] Market-based conservation strategies, as currently articulated, offer little guidance on how we are to protect the chunks of nature that conflict with our interests or preserve the perhaps far more numerous pieces of nature that neither help nor harm us.

Third, conservation based on ecosystem services commits the folly of betting against human ingenuity. The entire history of technology and human "progress" is one of producing artificial substitutes for what we once obtained from nature, or domesticating once-natural services. One of the primary selling points for protecting the Catskill/Delaware Watershed was that the costs associated with constructing and operating a filtration plant would have driven up water prices in New York City. However, the city just recently decided to construct a filtration plant to clean the water in the Croton Watershed, its oldest and next-largest water source. While it is difficult to imagine that technology will soon produce a cheaper artificial alternative to the Catskill/Delaware Watershed, it was once unfathomable to consider filtering the Croton Watershed. For that matter, it was also unfathomable to imagine cost-effective manufactured alternatives to other natural products like rubber and timber. Although we will never replicate all of the "services" offered by nature, I would argue that conservation plans that underestimate the technological prowess of humans are ultimately bound to have short life spans.

Lastly, although it has been suggested that in most cases the services that come from nature are valuable enough to make conservation profitable, making money and protecting nature are all too often mutually exclusive goals. Take the case of Africa's Lake Victoria, where the introduction of the invasive Nile perch (*Lates niloticus*) contributed significantly to the decimation of local biodiversity while dramatically boosting the economic value of the lake. Local people profiting from trade in the fish hail its introduction as a success, whereas biologists have condemned the event as "the most catastrophic extinction episode of recent history."[9] John Terborgh,[10] discussing similar issues in tropical-forest conservation, remarked that these forests are "worth more dead than alive." If Terborgh's assessment is not always true, it is true all too often. So we must directly confront the reality that conservation may be expensive and stop deceiving ourselves and partners in conservation with hopes that win-win solutions can always be found.

Are there other viable paths for conservationists besides the commodification of nature? Yes. Nature has an intrinsic value that gives it great worth, and this is reason enough to protect it. The idea is not new. We view many historical artifacts and pieces of art as priceless. Nature embodies the same kind of values we cherish in these man-made objects: it has great aesthetic beauty, immense cultural importance, and deep historical value. Most species are older than the oldest artifacts in our museums. Most ecosystems not only are fundamental parts of our own cultures, but they tell part of the story of our own common biological origin. We can and do put dollar values on art. But just as it would seem wrong to teach New Yorkers to first and foremost value the paintings hanging in the Museum of Modern Art because they are expensive, shouldn't it also strike us as odd to teach them to principally value the wildlife and habitats of the Catskills because they can generate profit?

Some will argue that this view is simply too optimistic. They may believe that the best way to meaningfully engage policy makers driven by the financial bottom line is to translate the intrinsic worth of nature into the language of economics. But this is patently untrue—akin to saying that early civil rights advocates would have been more effective if they had provided economic justifications for racial integration. Nature conservation must be framed as a moral issue and argued as such to policy makers, who are just as accustomed to making decisions based on morality as on finances.

All of this is not to deny a role for ecosystem services in our general efforts to protect nature. Individual ecosystem services will occasionally prove to be useful bargaining chips in specific conservation plans and, as such, can meaningfully support programs aimed at protecting nature for nature's sake. Ecosystem services have certainly proven to be a lucrative platform for conservation fundraising. Major conservation nongovernmental organizations that have adopted ecosystem service rhetoric are now luring in wealthy supporters like Dow Chemical, Shell Oil, and the mining giant Rio Tinto. Profitable and productive conservation, however, may not be one and the same. To generally avoid trading in significant long-term conservation successes for marginal short-term gains, philosophical clarity is essential and caution is needed. When we employ the aid of ecosystem services to help pay the bills of conservation, we must make it abundantly clear that our overall mission is to protect nature, not to make it turn a profit.

The track record of achievements by conservationists motivated by a moral imperative to protect nature for nature's sake is impressive: Consider the international ban on commercial whaling, the national parks of the United States, and the CITES ivory-trade ban. Meanwhile, the only successful truly large-scale ecosystem-service-based conservation project yet achieved is the Catskill Watershed. But this nugget may ultimately turn out to be fool's gold. Most would agree that we are not making sufficient progress in nature conservation. In the long run, however, we are likely to do more for conservation by redoubling our efforts to teach people that nature's greatest values are those that cannot be expressed in dollars.

Parks, People, and Perspectives: Historicizing Conservation in Latin America

EMILY WAKILD

HISTORIANS MAKE A LIVING pointing out that few things are actually "new" despite the continual repackaging of ideas. The perspective of the past can provide vital context for changing social norms. For instance, consider that in 1940 Mexico had more national parks than any country in the world. Nestled among pine and fir forests, sprawling across volcanoes in the shadow of Mexico City, these parks bore the mark of a particular kind of conservation.[1] Linked to the nation's vibrant and widespread battle for social justice during the Mexican Revolution (1910–1940), the most representative government in Mexico's history created the parks. These parks formed one of many components of a pervasive policy transformation that sought to elevate and empower poor and working Mexicans by providing labor protections, redistributing land, invigorating education, and implementing meaningful political reforms. While the parks protected natural scenery and had some wild components (forests, lakes, glaciers), they were emphatically parks designed for people—places for rural and urban workers to relax or to find new livelihoods in tourism. At their creation, no wilderness whispered in these woods and no wildlife ran these ecosystems; this was conservation in service of the poor and vulnerable, conservation with social objectives, conservation with people at the center.

Today, nearly every remaining swath of greenery gasping for air in the Valley of Mexico is one of these emblems of the revolutionary movement—social justice stitched into the landscape as conservation. These early and often overlooked parks set important precedents showing that not all conservation comes from the United States. They reveal how social justice and environmental policy have been paired. And, they provide a blueprint for what happens to nonhuman nature when conservation places people at the center.

Mexican poet and environmentalist Homero Aridjis has remarked that there is no word in Spanish (or Nahuatl, Yucatec Maya, Zapotec, or other indigenous languages) approximating the term *wilderness*. Empty land, useless land, or unpopulated land can be described, but no single term comes laden with the grandeur—and the political and cultural baggage—of an untrammeled, self-willed land. But this does not mean actual wilderness fails to exist in Mexico or in countries further south. This conflation—the absence of a concept versus the absence of a concrete reality—is where debates over wilderness and conservation have misrepresented the natural and cultural history of the larger American hemisphere.

Critiques of wilderness have become rote in the past twenty years, and too often have employed sloppy thinking and dubious scholarship. Consider the history of Mexican national parks just described in reference to the rise of "new conservation," or the set of ideas laid out most emphatically (and hubristically) by Peter Kareiva, Robert Lalasz, and Michele Marvier in 2011 with their call for conservation to move beyond parks and protected areas and into programs for rural development and human well-being.[2] They argue that "the modern protection of supposed wilderness often involves resettling large numbers of people" and that "ecologists and conservationists have grossly overstated the fragility of nature." Such claims play into a classic trope, one that places indigenous and non-Western peoples at the supposed mercy of Northern scientists and overlooks their agency to build and create rather than to merely react. Not only is there little new about proposals to merge managed and natural landscapes—a move Mexicans (and likely others) pioneered in the 1930s—but there is little to show that this will result in improved livelihoods or more vibrant ecosystems.

Has conservation alone solved problems of poverty, inequality, and uneven development? No, and that is not what it set out to do. But to assert that conservation has caused these problems, or even has been complicit in them, is to ignore conceptions of conservation and wilderness that do not translate into a U.S.-centered narrative of nature protection.

An academic context for challenging conservation

For most people, parks, wilderness areas, and other conservation lands are wildly popular. But this is less true in academic circles due in part to a fruitful mode of inquiry that filtered through the humanities and social sciences in the 1990s. This has been called the "cultural turn," and it provided fresh perspectives on the ways in which individuals and societies constitute markers of identity. Aspects that influence and transform lived experiences which were once seen as given, or biological, such as race or gender, came to be seen as largely, if not exclusively, constructed in social terms. This new view helped break down long-held beliefs about social privileges and categories of difference and it gave cause to question many stable ideas, including those surrounding nature. Yet, the cultural-turn perspective has had a harder time making sense of how the ecological crises facing humanity (of climate change, habitat loss, species extinction among others) have been socially constructed. Instead, several tropes emerged from it to critique the standard practices of environmental protection—things as classic as wilderness and as nouveau as carbon trading—as imagined categories invented as tools of the capitalist majority to wrest power away from the weak. Parks and the international conservation institutions that support them, according to more critics than a nonspecialist might expect, "expose themselves to accusations of imperialistic interference and neo-colonialism, of meddling in other people's affairs and countries."[3] As a result, important debates about phenomena like nature conservation have remained mired in circuitous finger-pointing and simplistic critiques of power have lost their utility even as a thought exercise. The cultural perspective—deconstructing the world as something entirely socially made by relations of power and resistance—is not enough to understand the dire material circumstances of the real ecological situation we have created for ourselves.

With this in mind, when is the last time you read something from a social scientist that painted parks or nature conservation in a positive light? Writings such as Roderick Nash's link between wilderness and American-ness have given way to a more critical (in its wholly negative sense) reading of what conservation contributes to being human. Instead, wilderness has become troubled, conservationists perpetrate unspeakable acts that create refugees, and nature protection is a capitalist tool usurping sovereignty. Certainly, there exist rigorous studies with ample evidence set in specific contexts that address peculiarities and point to such conclusions.[4] At the same time, the examples of popular, local, and socially designed parks have had less press. So has the role of governance of all kinds in supporting conservation. As a result, cumulatively, sweeping generalizations about conservation paint a disturbing, fragmented picture that distorts conservation's dynamism and multifaceted past.

In the past few years popular books and articles have given new wind to these arguments, in part playing on a false timeline. Kareiva, Lalasz and Marvier's claim that "conservation became a global enterprise in the 1970s and 1980s" repeats a truncated chronology that overlooks the contributions of countries such as Mexico or Argentina, where park creation began as early as 1903 and boomed in the 1930s. Far from new, examples of conservation from Latin America—including parks made by Mexican revolutionaries, Argentine geographers, Chilean botanists, Peruvian taxidermists, Brazilian ethnographers, and more—show how nature and society have long been intertwined. The history of conservation in Latin America is hardly a simple struggle between indigenous peoples and elite scientists—a wide range of actors with more complex identities and objectives have contributed to conservation's footprint.

Popular works also display an overinflated idea of conservation organizations and their influence. Mac Chapin asserts that nongovernmental conservation organizations act as "gatekeepers" and have been "*entrusted* with the enormous responsibility of defending the planet's natural ecosystems against encroachment."[5] Such claims credit too much power to conservation organizations that would not work without governments, which in fact legally steward protected areas. Journalist Mark Dowie has recently lamented the loss of people in protected areas worldwide, claiming: "If we really want people to live in harmony with nature, history is showing us that the dumbest thing we can do is kick them [native peoples] out of it."[6] But history in many cases shows that people were not kicked out; national parks were designed with them in mind. Yet, the ways parks and peoples merged did not stop the rapaciousness of development around them. The lack of historical introspection, context, or nuance in denunciations like Dowie's and Chapin's beg a reevaluation of the broader conservation landscape.

Additional arguments, such as those by Emma Marris, claim that conservation should be fundamentally changed because nature is full of hybridity.[7] Such assessments focus on lands in the most heavily peopled parts of the planet. In other words, if you want to look at the Hawaiian Islands as a case of "gardening" then you are considering examples that serve your argument—one based on ideas about island biogeography that have addressed hybridity and extinction since at least 1968.[8] It's not surprising that critics pointing to the flaws of conservation neglect regions such as Amazonia and Patagonia—South America itself is often set aside to make these arguments because it shoots holes in them. We need more and better human stories about the diverse roots of conservation and the challenges parks have presented, or thwarted, and we need these at scales beyond islands or archipelagos.

The argument that conservationists from afar sometimes prevailed over local interests might have held true in the 1890s or the 1960s. But neither science nor conservation is made up of stagnant ideas. Ecology has come a long way as has conservation in practice. Furthermore, those who hold up local conservation as a panacea have rarely worked on the ground and most likely hold naive views about the concordance of ideas and objectives at the local level. Assumptions about community solidarity, intrinsic interests, and rural harmony overlook decades of social science scholarship demonstrating that local interests are rarely hermetic or powerless. Certainly, power dynamics shape the reception of international organizations in remote wild areas—but the specifics matter and sloppy generalizations detract from that complexity. Declaring conservation "over" is premature because it fails to recognize how it has been defined and redefined, how it has changed over time and across cultures, and how contributions from not just science but shifting cultural priorities and government funding expand and contract the cycles of park creation.

Parks may not be the endgame for ensuring the natural world can function—but they are among the best things we have. Parks have not satiated, and in all likelihood never will end, the thirst for gold, hunger for oil, or the culturally constructed fascination with mahogany. But they do put a crick in the wheel of these extractive phenomena. Removing the crick (the parks) will not mean more land for indigenous people—it will inevitably mean less land for nature and less respect for a humane future. Ending parks is not a far-fetched vision; in fact, the prime minister of Australia recently called for a moratorium on park creation.

Perhaps before such an about-face, conservationists should more carefully consider the history of parks and protected areas in places around the world that have supposedly been assaulted by evictions and expulsions. We can then see more readily what results when human-centered development is privileged, or called "conservation," and we can assess whether or not these are the landscapes diverse societies ought to aim for in the future. With little effort, this journey into the past quickly reveals a more complex and diverse narrative than "new conservationists" recognize. We can clearly see that many parks throughout Latin America, such as those in Mexico, were sources of national pride, creations of sovereign political entities, and experiments in blending local, national, and international interests. To call these products of U.S. (or more broadly Western) imperialism or omnipotent global conservation organizations is to far overstate the reach of either and to ignore the agency, resilience, and creativity of the very populations the "new conservationists" claim to represent. Rather than assume outsiders call all the shots, we should recognize that domestic conservation supporters have as long and as deep a history as conservation's supposed "refugees."

In their current form, even read together, the texts of the "new conservationists" all fail to provide a satisfactory new paradigm. Erasing parks without replacing them *with* something that acknowledges self-willed land is hardly a strategy for avoiding crises of climate, extinction, and resource depletion. It is not enough to point out that nature is complicated. It is not enough to break down without building up. If you wield a hatchet, you must also carry a seed.

Conservation has been too frequently subject to false dichotomies and too often seen in stark contrasts rather than subtle gradations.[9] It is intellectually easier to draw a dividing line between nature conservation and social justice than to embrace complexity and learn from the places in the past where they have informed each other, albeit imperfectly. Easier, but incorrect. Postcolonial, developing, and sovereign countries around the world created conservation areas on their own terms, and for myriad reasons. We owe it to the future not to let these thousands of experiments over the past century go without consideration simply because inequality and social unrest persist. A need for wild land conservation remains crucial and perspectives on how to value self-willed nature have been constructed in diverse societies for more than one hundred years. It's worth considering why and how this has happened.

Examples from below

The region of Latin America, conventionally defined as the 25 countries stretching from Mexico to Chile inclusive of most Caribbean islands, is a region of vast cultural and natural diversity. From the cacti of the Chihuahuan Desert to the fjords of Patagonia, this part of the world is linked by some linguistic continuity (mainly Spanish and Portuguese although dozens of indigenous languages remain vibrant and widespread) and demarcated by geographic contiguity. The first region of the world to be dominated by European colonialism, Latin American nations also constituted the first wave of self-governing nation-states after the United States. Historians have long debated the relative lack of political and economic independence afforded to these emerging countries over the course of the nineteenth century as British capital and U.S. entrepreneurs stepped in to fill roles left vacant by the exit of the Spanish and Portuguese. Many native-born Mexicans, Peruvians, and others decided to collaborate in these enterprises, but the relative autonomy of the individual nations and the mixed-race populations within them remains a complex story. However, this timeline means that most countries had been politically—if not economically—independent for nearly one hundred years when national parks first appeared on the landscape.

Many people mistakenly assume that conservation in Latin America began with Costa Rican parks in the 1970s or with Brazil's "save-the-rainforest" crusaders in the 1980s. They would be surprised to learn that South America's first national park was conceived by a scientist, Francisco Moreno, in 1903. He gave his own property to the government under the agreement that it would be turned into the "National Park of the South," which is today Nahuel Huapi Park in San Carlos de Bariloche, Argentina. In addition to Argentina, Brazil, Mexico, and Venezuela (and possibly others) all established and expanded parks in the 1930s. By the 1960s and 1970s, most Latin American countries had started or greatly expanded their conservation programs for varied reasons under different forms of governance— from left-wing dictatorships as in Peru, center-left democracies as in Chile, or right-wing military dictatorships as in Brazil. Yet we know little about how and why this expansion of conservation programs occurred.

A major reason global generalizations about conservation are inaccurate is because the knowledge most lacking is in the region where it has had the most enduring success—South America. Here, even a glance at the historical record reveals more use and conservation for much longer—Spanish and Portuguese expeditions, scientific journeys by no less than former U.S. presidents, rubber barons, and human rights workers. Importantly, the arguments of Peruvian, Brazilian, Argentine, and other naturalists have documented the areas for the past two hundred years. Lest we forget, these are the regions that wooed the young Alexander von Humboldt and Charles Darwin. Any cursory look would show continual recognition by these scientists that these habitats have had people in them—in different scales, shapes, and usage patterns. But the scale of habitation—at least since the sixteenth century—has been less dense than elsewhere and that scale matters for the integrity of natural systems over time.

While the histories of use and conservation vacillate wildly throughout the continent, more recent proactive events have made a difference for landscapes, animals, and humans.[10] Take, for instance, the work begun in the 1960s to protect the llama's smaller wild cousin, the vicuña, in Peru. Peruvian bureaucrats and scientists Marc Dourojeanni and Antonio Brack Egg laid the foundation for a reserve system that saved the animal from poachers, reversing a century-long decline.[11] Or, consider the warnings of Chilean writer and diplomat, Rafael Elizalde, who in 1958 published *La sobrevivencia en Chile,* a five-hundred page treatise full of such specific and dire warnings about the degradation of natural systems that the author committed suicide before completing the second edition in 1970.[12] There were also conservationists born elsewhere that made Latin American countries their chosen home, for example Maria Buchinger, a scientist of German birth with an Austrian doctorate in zoology, who became the grandmother of conservation in Latin America in the 1960s.[13] In addition to publishing scientific articles and advocating local control and design of conservation areas, she spent most of her life in Argentina, eventually becoming a citizen. The lines between nationality and nature are more complicated than at first glance. Domestic conservation policies went far beyond puppet strings pulled by international conservation organizations. Denying national autonomy and individual agency, of not just politicians but able and eager bureaucrats and technicians, to develop park systems reinforces and perpetuates a perceived power differential between the West and the rest that deserves to be ruptured.

Scientists—from north and south—played transformational roles in the protection of wilderness areas in Latin America. This has been a point of controversy, especially between ecologists and anthropologists. Take, for example, Manu National Park in Peru. Created in 1973 and nearly double the size of Yellowstone, it is the epitome of self-willed land: a tropical landscape extending from the Andes to the Amazon and of such a scale and low human population density that it lacks peers. Manu protects more bird species than exist in all of North America and a single hectare might contain more plant species than the entire United States. The full suite of animals essential for ecosystem functioning—from top predators such as the jaguar to frugivores, including thirteen species of monkey—makes this forest whole. Neither the waves of colonialism that gnawed through the landscape nor the violent "rubber boom" completely transformed the region. Today the park contains a small research station, Cocha Cashu Biological Station, which has hosted approximately 700 researchers over the past forty years. No towns exist inside, but four different indigenous groups inhabit the park, the largest being around 500 Matsigenka peoples. Nearly 30 communities totaling about 75,000 people live outside the park (distributed across an area about the size of Costa Rica). These residents mainly reside in Puerto Maldonado and include Quechua-speaking highlanders, descendants of rubber prospectors, and immigrants from other parts of Peru.

Although the research station was founded in a Peruvian-German partnership, until recently, biologist John Terborgh of Duke University in the United States directed Cocha Cashu, under permission of the Peruvian government. In the 1990s, Terborgh described changes to the park he had seen in the previous twenty years, and he suggested incentives or a careful land swap for people to voluntarily relocate in order to get better access to medicine, education, and modern amenities. The most recent census shows the population inside Manu is increasing at a rate of 4.7 percent each year: What now seems a tiny population will, in a few generations, become quite large. Some have suggested people living inside can offer security against other incursions—especially by gold and mahogany prospectors—but this rate of population growth hints at a very brief window where such an arrangement might work.[14]

Terborgh's suggestions made him a prime target for those who argue conservation should accommodate humans first and that sovereignty to determine land use rests with people deemed local. Does John Terborgh's perspective on Manu, a place he's worked in for the past forty years, matter less than a fifteen-year-old miner recently arrived from Cusco, or a lawyer from Lima who has never visited the park? Why is birthright, citizenship, or ethnic identity the trump card for conservation work? These are complicated moral questions without clear answers that should make us suspicious of sharp binaries and preconceived ideas. Ironically, these critics have not focused on Hunt Oil, which is drilling in the park, or the illegal gold prospectors who ravage territories just outside;[15] instead, they identified a scientist as a scapegoat for pointing out that increased human populations will lower the animal populations and in turn transform the forest. At what point does the independence and autonomy of native peoples to grow their populations and have access to modern amenities infringe on the sovereignty of recent immigrants, of the Peruvian state, of the international scientific community, or of the jaguars and monkeys?

One remarkable facet of this story is that the park has come this far *with people in it*. They haven't been ignored or denied but have been included in every study and policy on the park since its inception.[16] In fact, nearly all Latin American parks have included attention to indigenous peoples, including parks such as Brazil's Xingu that were formed from the start as national and indigenous parks in the 1950s. These early park formulations had their drawbacks—paternalistic state policies, limited scope, and lack of integrating residents into management structures among others—but their existence reveals more complex domestic conceptions of conservation than the critics allow. While much has been made of past conservation mistakes, more can be done to acknowledge the ways conservationists have recognized indigenous peoples' rights to a presence in the park. Conservationists rarely deny that people are there or that they have claims on rights to be there, but they can question the future—something a more accurate rendering of the past would allow them to do with greater rigor.

Scholarship should acknowledge the ways conservationists have recognized the rights of indigenous peoples to live in parks, particularly in light of all we know about the follies of conservation in the past. The critique of wilderness that argues international interests have run roughshod over local livelihoods is a too-little-too-late argument that ignores entire generations of people who have made conservation their life's work—individuals ranging from Moreno, the Argentine scientist who gave his land to create a park, to Celestino Kalinowski, a Peruvian taxidermist and local resident who gave up his trade to advocate for the creation of Manu, to Yolanda Kakabadse, the Ecuadorian environmentalist who has served as president of the IUCN and WWF. Hyperbolic, sweeping proclamations about the success or failure of a hundred years of conservation overlook how conservation has been defined and redefined, how it has changed over time and across cultures, and how contributions—not just from science but also shifting cultural priorities and government funding—expand and contract the fates of various wild places.

Conclusions

If those who care about natural landscapes want both natural and cultural diversity—which in tandem will likely ensure Earth and all its inhabitants a more secure future—then we need to reflect on what conditions in the past have created events worthy of replication in the future of conservation.

The Mexican parks matter. Their existence demonstrates that environmental protection and social policy have been partners in the past and can be in the future. But to call these parks a conservation success is to overlook the sprawling, smog-filled morass that suffocates both the parks and the people for whom they were intended.[17] There is no feasible way to return these parks to intact ecosystems, and there are few possibilities to ensure that native species, such as the critically endangered axolotl salamander (*Ambystoma mexicanum*), can thrive in parks full of people and pollution. These social parks are hollow approximations of the regional flora and fauna encountered by Alexander von Humboldt in 1807 or even the self-willed land that remains, albeit at risk, in other parts of Mexico including remote canyons of Chihuahua, tropical forests of Chiapas, and deserts of Baja California.

Several lessons drawn from Latin America might offer ways forward. We should support solid and fair governance based on information gathering. Though imperfect, independent nation-states—not large international conservation organizations—remain the largest stewards of natural areas making national governments the most important factor facilitating conservation. Weaker states allow chaos to thrive and individual (often profit-driven) choices to overrule public values. Conservation remains an alliance between government institutions and diverse publics that should be strengthened and supported rather than dismissed as misguided or imperfect. Training and learning from national, local, and native scientists in wild areas foster such collaborations. There remains a great need for basic science and scientific-capacity building among local communities and regional scientific institutions. Who is training this next generation? Cocha Cashu is the alma mater of most Peruvian conservationists, and

John Terborgh has trained more Peruvians in tropical field biology than has any Peruvian institution.[18] There is no silver bullet to protect wilderness or promote conservation; an assortment of strategies worked out in different contexts over time makes more sense. And scale matters. Costa Rica protects 25 percent of its territory—but all that land is smaller than a large soybean field in Brazil. Larger size and preservation of contiguity promote viability of wildness.

Why does this matter? What are the policy implications? Cries that conservation is taking over the world subtly call for the end of conservation work and ask about its relevance. If this is heeded, and is filtered into policy recommendations, we risk the real threat that humanity cannot redo our relationship with wild nature in the short term. The problem with conservation losing its credibility is that we don't have a model to replace it that speaks for the nonhuman silence. The world will be impoverished if parks are not sustained, expanded, and functionally connected into networks of conserved lands that support biodiversity and natural processes.

Nature does not read the literature on social justice; it does not care if some conservation areas expose unequal power relations among humans of the last century and beyond. Nature only knows that whoever shoots the jaguars changes the fate of the forest, whoever logs the trees evicts the birds, and whoever builds the roads etches a cascade of effects into the landscape. Humanity does and should care, yet this caring undergirds our responsibility to see injustice in its fullest perspective. Do the poor bear the brunt of uneven development, of land scarcity, and of instable tenancy and property transactions? Yes. Are they poor because of conservation? Hardly. Conservationists, by blaming each other, take our eyes off the larger forces—an insatiably hungry energy regime that has no regard for nature or culture, transnational resource trading without accountability, economic systems that disregard ecosystems, and fickle but ravenous consumer desires. These forces conspire not just against the poor but also against wild places.

Parks are an old technology that retains relevance in a world of new technologies because the absence of them would leave us all impoverished. The Amazonian and Patagonian regions of South America today protect some of the largest connecting expanses of intact ecosystems on the planet. These are not unpeopled landscapes, they are not exclusive enclaves, but they are spaces that hold unique and magical reserves in the public sphere as a compromise with the future. And people in these countries recognized their worth decades ago. It is time social science literature does the same.

The Fight for Wilderness Preservation in the Pacific Northwest

BROCK EVANS

THE TIME HAS COME to speak a word for the American wilderness: still a vibrant part of American national life, history, and outlook; still a vast and growing, permanent and protected, legacy out there on the land itself. Strong protections, enshrined in the Wilderness Act of 1964 and in related legislation, have in turn guaranteed the survival of significant portions of the continent's native biota.

Reflecting here on that fact, and on the emotional and political power of the wilderness idea in the minds and hearts of the American people to this day, brings into focus the rapid rise and development of the wilderness and park movements in the Pacific Northwest in one seminal generation (1963–1984). That generation's great achievement was to secure the permanent protection of millions of acres that were otherwise destined for commercial exploitation. I believe that the reason wilderness became the primary chosen designation of nature and landscape protection holds lessons for environmentalists today.

I say this because there has been of late some commentary in scientific journals and in other public forums, advocating the following:

► There is no such thing as "real wilderness" any longer. Everything which once might have *seemed* to be such (as described in the Wilderness Act of 1964) has long been permanently changed, by the powerful impact of humans and their dramatic rise toward physical domination over the entire planet and its life-forms.

▶ Those who have devoted so much of their lives and passion to add more areas to the Wilderness System are dreamers, wasting their time pursuing a chimera that doesn't exist.

▶ Controversial advocacy for strong protection of what is called the "natural world" should be abandoned. Proponents of such advocacy should instead join forces with the "realists" among us, who treat all nonhuman species and "natural-appearing" landscapes of the planet for what they really are: a *human garden*, which needs to be managed as such.

These opinions all seem so silly—so out of touch with what was actually happening to the wild forests and rivers, mountains, and meadows of the Pacific Northwest forty and fifty years ago. That was when tens of thousands of determined, ordinary citizens rose up to protect millions of acres of public lands, *as new* Wilderness Areas and National Parks.

Understanding why we did so is perhaps the best answer to today's "wilderness critics." The answer is simple: *It was a matter of life or death*, permanent loss or permanent rescue. We stood and fought, because whether or not a beautiful forest or river was protected was, in those desperate times, a matter of survival for that place.

Consider the political situation at the time in four of the northwestern United States (Washington, Oregon, Idaho, and Montana—the area of my "territory" when I was Sierra Club's Northwest Representative, between 1967 and 1973). There were *no* environmental laws whatsoever. No National Environmental Policy Act. No Endangered Species Act. Not even effective Clear Air or Clean Water laws—much less the National Forest Management Act, with its host of associated rules and regulations, which now purport to guide activities of the U.S. Forest Service or the Bureau of Land Management. Of these, there were just none.

Our only hope for any protections whatsoever was to persuade Congress to create a new Wilderness, National Park, or similar designation in the contested lands. But in those times, especially the 1960s, our numbers were few, and the political and cultural zeitgeist was totally at odds with any such folderol as "nature protection." Timber was king wherever the big trees were, and dam sites were queen wherever there were rivers to be plugged up. The entire Pacific Northwest political establishment, from chambers of commerce to (most of) organized labor to nearly all politicians, stood firmly in this resource-minded camp.

Those of us who loved these wild mountains, forests, and rivers had already learned the hard way that there was to be no redress, no significant protection of *anything* on public lands that had loggable trees, or dammable rivers, or mineable ores. We had asked, met with, appealed, and petitioned the relevant agencies many times. We were always turned down, whether by words or by half-measures.

And so the chain saws, bulldozers, and drills snarled on, tearing away every day at a vast and beautiful wild heritage. That heritage was then relatively unknown, except to those of us who had actually been there and seen what was happening. Indeed, the most disconcerting, common experience in those days was to return to some favorite trail—seeking the wild and beautiful forest which we had hiked the previous summer—only to discover that the trail and its surrounding ancient forest had vanished. It was now just another great muddy jackstraw of mangled slash, eroding logging roads, and silted-up streams.

That was the experience of our growing ranks, those of us who had moved to the Northwest in search of its beautiful and unspoiled landscapes; it was also the experience of the many locals, who were appalled at the destruction of a heritage which they had treasured since childhood.

We went to war, there being no other choice. It was a matter of life and death for all the places we valued and loved. We usually called the places we fought to save "wilderness": It was the political nomenclature of the times and the language that politicians understood. Few had ever heard of more recent concepts, such as "biodiversity," "connectivity," or even "ecosystems"; certainly not politicians or the general public! Maybe a few academics knew, but most of us activists were ordinary citizens, with few scientists (Dr. Gordon Orians being an outstanding exception) in our ranks.

So we fought for the wilderness out of love. We knew and loved these places. We fought for them to be safe, in order to no longer have to endure the feelings of loss, ache, and emptiness that we had experienced all too often—as when a last-ditch appeal was denied and the forest was logged or the river damned. We fought for the joy of knowing that the places we cherished, once safe from agency "management" (the euphemism in those times for logging), would be there forever, and would be there for our children and grandchildren too.

Let us take a quick look at what was actually protected during those battles in the Northwest and consider the strategies followed, as well as the language—the political language—we had to use, the parlance of *those* times. For we knew that if we were to get to first base with decision makers, we needed a compelling narrative—one emphasizing that national parks and wilderness areas were *good* things for the economy, for the nation, and for future generations.

The narrative we chose had to resonate with those all important decision makers. Early on we realized that an idiom of "science" could not be the central message. As we had already discovered in the angry flames of many public hearings and debates, the real task was to persuade politicians, the media, and as much of the public as we could. Not only were the concepts of biodiversity, interconnectivity, and ecosystems unknown (or nonexistent) a few decades ago, but—even had we learned of them and had them available—they would have carried no political sway.

So what *was* the convincing narrative of those times? Odd as it may sound today, we emphasized how beautiful the forests (especially those at low elevation) were, how rare and becoming rarer, and how population growth and recreation were overwhelming everything: Thus we needed to protect such places, now and forever.

The struggle in most parts of the Northwest was almost always over the *forest*: We knew that there lay the greatest danger. In one of our first efforts to publicize this fact, I prepared a "Lowland Forest Trails Resolution," passed by Seattle Mountaineers, in 1966. This was considered very radical at the time, because it extended the ambit of our concerns way beyond just protecting certain areas with specific boundaries, into safeguarding the whole ancient forest that remained.

That resolution and our nascent attack on clear-cutting that commenced in 1968–1969 in Northwest Montana were the first times that we had even considered taking on the dominant political paradigm (in which logging was a key part of so-called multiple-use management). These were the first times that we activists dared to think that we could take on an overwhelmingly powerful industry on *its home ground* and maybe even win!

Lowland forests was the term we had at the time; same with *clear-cutting*, which proved to be an instantly understandable narrative, crystallizing our concerns in one easy-to-grasp concept. *Ancient forests*—a term conceived later by our Ancient Forest Alliance (1988–1994)—was another example of creative vocabulary. Industry tried to call them "old growth," using a vaguely pejorative word, but "ancient" prevailed in that debate. Today, we have another language with new and more science-based terms like *large landscapes, connectivity,* and *biodiversity.* These are compelling and useful concepts, even gaining some traction with land-management agencies, all for the better.

But looking back, I am amazed at how many large landscapes in the Pacific Northwest we actually protected as "Parks" or "Wilderness" (and related designations), even if we didn't think of them as having "landscape-scale protection." These places harbor much biodiversity and connectivity as well, now securely in place as giant building pads for future efforts.

What about the assertion, however, noised about in some quarters, to the effect of, "Well, even if you did protect some landscapes and habitats, they are insufficient—mostly what can be labeled 'rocks and ice,' of little biological value"? To better understand, we need to remember some basic political "facts of life" from those distant times. These facts governed and dictated everything we did or attempted, given our small numbers and the dearth of public understanding of basic biological principles.

Consider the following:

1) We who were there then, and who had to take on the wilderness/ park battles, always wanted to protect the places in greatest danger—the forests and the rivers.

2) Every political tactic we chose in an effort to secure better nature protection was almost always determined by what the other side (industry and agencies) was doing. Thus, in the beginning, our strategies were mainly defensive or preemptive: We tried to get there *first*, before the chain saws came. Even the North Cascades National Park campaign (1957–1968) took a defensive tack in that sense—to protect a vast landscape from an agency (the U.S. Forest Service) whose stated policy (and guiding ethos) was to log its wilderness forests. The Hells Canyon National Recreation Area (straddling northeastern Oregon and western Idaho) was another such campaign.

3) Because there were no environmental laws, there were no policies to enforce in any court, as is possible today. We had to make them as we went along.

4) It wasn't so-called rock and ice that we fought so hard to save. We *always* wanted to protect what was most jeopardized, mainly the

forests. Thus, it again was the politics—where the U.S. Forest Service was and what they had proposed to do—that always determined where we had to begin. We had to start there, because that was the only rationale that the public understood. Start *there*, a real "somewhere," which those whose political support we needed in order to get things protected could understand, in the context of those times. And that "somewhere" almost always included *both* high-elevation terrain and low.

In the campaigns of the 1960s and early 1970s, we had to start where the U.S. Forest Service already had reserves. When the Wilderness Act was passed, it mandated a review only of *existing* Primitive Areas (Section 3 (b)). That meant that another 50 to 60 million acres of wildlands—which we termed *de facto* wilderness—could be exploited at will. So in the early 1970s we mounted a new campaign, using the newly available environmental laws to protect those places too.

At the time at which we conceived of this campaign, *de facto wilderness* was considered a new, daring (and unlikely "political") concept: For example, the first two—the proposed Scapegoat Wilderness in Montana and the proposed Alpine Lakes Wilderness in Washington—were immediately denounced by commercial interests and opposed by the U.S. Forest Service, then, and in nearly every campaign since.

Strategically, while we could not avoid them, we could use the defensive campaigns to achieve much larger, proactive goals (for example, protection of forests and lowlands that are today correctly understood to be biodiversity-rich places). That is exactly what we sought to protect then as well, even though the language we used was the language of the times, the one we had to deploy in order to win.

For example, the Hells Canyon National Recreation Area campaign began over a last-ditch, seemingly hopeless effort to defeat dams in the spectacular deep gorges of the Middle Snake River. But because we realized that much more, beyond the canyon itself, was valuable, large, wild, and beautiful, our early discussions, which began about 1967, circled around how to protect those wildlands beyond the great free-flowing river itself. How could protection be extended even beyond the vision of the not-yet-passed Wild & Scenic Rivers Act? One possible solution that I proposed at the time was the creation of a national park, for which these lands qualified in every respect, but this proved politically impossible, and ultimately in 1975 a 652,000-acre National Recreation Area resulted, which mandated new wilderness protections and banned the proposed two dams forever.

The North Cascades strategy aimed, first and foremost, to secure a national park, knowing that such a political "statement" in the middle of several national forests would not only afford better protection but also slow down our most powerful and effective opponent, the U.S. Forest Service.

What was the final result of our sustained mission to save what could be saved of the wildest and best lands and waters before it might all be lost? A state-by-state partial review shows a significant record of achievement, in terms of protecting both large landscapes and biodiversity:

Washington. This is where the campaigns began. The Olympic National Park, established in 1938 with additions in the 1980s, has protected over 1 million contiguous acres of Pacific Northwest life-forms and landscapes. In the North Cascades, the campaigns of those years succeeded in protecting about 2.5 million acres, almost all in one contiguous unit. Other large protected and near-contiguous areas are in the Alpine Lakes, covering 400,000 acres, and Mt. Rainier National Park and nearby wildernesses, protecting some 500,000 acres.

Oregon. It was already politically impossible by the 1970s to save many very large landscapes in the Cascades or Coast Range: The topography was much easier to log, the politics very tough, and the cut-at-any-cost ethos even more dominant than in Washington. Even just to protect the remaining uncut forests of the 25,000-acre French Pete Valley in the Central Cascades was a 21-year struggle (1957–1978). The long drawn-out campaign to save it ennobled all those unsung grassroots leaders who did so, and it opened up more opportunities to rescue other (and smaller) places, but much was already lost by the 1960s. The timber industry still dominates Oregon forest politics, and most environmentalists consider its current "Forest Practices Act" to be a giveaway.

We attempted a countermeasure, the proposed Oregon Volcanic Cascades National Park (first introducing the bill in 1969); but it just didn't, couldn't, gain support of the Oregon congressional delegation. Nevertheless, its statement of a grand vision, of a protected area encompassing 900,000 acres, roused many people and educated a new generation of Oregonians to the fact that much could still be saved, in smaller bites.

Idaho. The Hells Canyon issue warrants a bit more discussion because of its tremendous effect upon the morale of Idaho conservationists of the times, proving that they could actually win some things. Idaho, always conservative, was nowhere near as far right-wing then as it is now; it was so moderate that conservation-minded Democrats like Senator Frank Church could flourish.

The drowning-out of those last great gorges of the Snake River was considered a political done deal as late as 1967; only a chance legal statement (an *obiter dictum* judicial opinion by Supreme Court Justice William O. Douglas), gave our fledgling small groups a toehold from which to wage what became one of our most stunning large-landscape victories, protecting a vast biodiversity-array of plants, animals, and their habitats. After our legal intervention, and come-from-way-behind political struggle, Congress created the Hells Canyon National Recreation Area, mandating wildland and wildlife protections.

The stories of the other great conservation/wilderness protection efforts in Idaho from the mid-1960s to 1980 are tales for another time. But the result of all of them was spectacular with regard to protecting and *connecting* large landscapes.

Montana. The Glacier National Park established in 1911, along with the Bob Marshall Wilderness in 1939, and the Scapegoat Wilderness designated in 1972 form a mostly-connected, vast complex of over 3 million acres of Northern Rockies wildlands. This region also boasts an Absaroka-Beartooth Wilderness/Spanish Peaks/Hyalite complex just north of Yellowstone National Park, consisting of about 2.5 million acres, and the Upper Missouri National Wild and Scenic River, which encompasses about 150 miles of riverine High Plains habitat.

So what about all that "rock and ice"?

I have always been puzzled by this one, wondering if those who utter the dismissive phrase have ever actually hiked through the places we saved back then against such odds. Yes, there were large areas of rocky terrain (and some glaciers) in most of the areas we fought over. But that's because they were contiguous to the forested valleys and uplands that we sought to protect. Faced with the urgent political imperative to persuade decision makers, we had to start where the U.S. Forest Service did, which was always up in the high country.

But sometimes this critique seems to go way over the top. In the case of the Alpine Lakes Wilderness in Washington state, often cited as being *just* rocks and ice (by those who seem to have never hiked in it), the main struggle was over the U.S. Forest Service's proposed road up Jack Creek to log the largest remaining native forest tract in our proposed wilderness area. We won, protecting a 393,000-acre unified and diverse area, not the Forest Service's proposed 180,000 acres, which were *real* rock and ice (and split into two different rocky parts).

The same holds for the North Cascades story. To those who maintain it was not much, a hike up any of about 25 whole valleys full of ancient low-elevation forests (places like the Agnes, Buck, Downey, and Sulfur Creeks, or the valleys of the Suiattle and Whitechuck Rivers in the Glacier Peak Wilderness) might change minds.

In Oregon, in addition to those French Pete mid- and low-elevation forests, I recommend the Minam River Valley of the Eagle Cap Wilderness—60,000 acres of some of the finest mixed-conifer eastside giants I have ever seen—all protected through a campaign waged by locals against a determined timber industry in 1972. Many more stories to these can be added.

It is true much was logged, or otherwise lost, often before we had a chance to arrive on the scene. But much, given the heavy odds, was saved by that embattled generation. So the way I answer the question, "Was it enough?" is with two observations and two questions:

First, the wilderness areas and national parks discussed above, and so many other unnamed but now safe places, were very "wild" to us, far more so than anything outside them. Perhaps some human from the Pleistocene had wandered through there and built a campfire, or there have been airplane contrails in the sky, or invasive species had crept in, or there's been some other human influence. So what?

Those campaigns led from the 1960s through the 1980s—and ongoing to this day—to rescue and save wilderness were not academic exercises about this or that fine point. Using the legal and political tools of the time, they were and still are *love battles,* to save what can be saved from destructions far worse.

If successful, such campaigns would ensure no more logging or logging roads, no more slashing away on steep slopes and fouling the once-productive fish habitats below; no longer the grating and sad snarlings of the chain saw in the ancient forests or the roar of motorbikes along their trails. These, and so many other achievements—including the spiritual refreshment to the soul just to enter the peace of such places—these were why we fought for wilderness. The fine print debating whether or not they were totally "pristine" nature seemed to us ridiculous arguments, designed solely to promote even greater destructions.

We then knew only one thing for certain: Had we waited, the places we fought to save, and did save, would otherwise most surely be *gone*—roaded, logged, mined out, or dammed.

My second observation is that I too wish I lived in a world where nearly everyone agreed with our values and proposals; but since we do not live in such a world, we have to struggle for everything we are able to protect of the natural world.

And my two questions: What if those of us who cared had not roused ourselves, had not stood and fought, for what we loved? What if there had been no environmental movement at all in the Pacific Northwest, then what?

Of Tigers and Humans: The Question of Democratic Deliberation and Biodiversity Conservation

HELEN KOPNINA

DEMOCRATIC LEGITIMACY is not necessarily related to the success of con- servation policies. Examples include the creation of East African parks by undemocratic colonial governments, as well as evidence of success of environmentally benign authoritarian regimes in Gabon or the Domini- can Republic,[1] in promoting environmental policies and regulation. Pa- leontologist and conservation activist Richard Leakey became celebrated for his successful fight to preserve wildlife in Africa. In order to address the poaching of elephants, Leakey created well-armed anti-poaching units that were authorized to shoot poachers on sight. While successful in pro- tecting elephants, this approach earned Leakey a critique of his human rights credentials.

Recently *The Guardian* reported that the Indian Maharashtra state "has declared war on animal poaching," permitting forest rangers to fire at hunters in order to curb tiger killings. According to the Maharashtra forest minister, guards should not be "booked for human rights violations when they have taken action against poachers."[2] The state has promised to send more rangers into the forests and offer secret payments to informers who give tips about poachers and animal smugglers:

Where forests were once guarded by a thin force of men with sticks, an infusion of new recruits are armed with new powers, plenty of guns, and a paid network of informants in villages where the forest is a source of livelihood. Underlying it all is the implicit question: does conserving tigers justify curbing the rights of humans?[3]

Can top-down policies be both effective and ethically justifiable in conservation? The question of democratic legitimacy and environmental ethics in the context of conservation deserves our attention here. Political theorists have argued that there is nothing about democracy as a form of government (especially within a neoliberal, global economic regime) that guarantees successful conservation. In fact, in the context of conservation, *democracy* is always a term of participatory deliberation reserved strictly for humans. The issue of justice for nonhumans all too often is entirely bypassed. The case of Russian tiger conservation is briefly touched on as a catalyst for my own position that including eco-advocates in deliberative democracy is necessary to ensure that the interests of nonhumans are represented. I argue that democratic government can indeed become effective in conservation, if eco-advocates' representation of nonhumans becomes an essential component of environmental justice.

Tiger conservation

While 2010 was the Chinese Year of the Tiger, as well as the International Year of Biodiversity, there was little good news about wild tigers. In historic times, tigers roamed across most of Asia, but today their distribution is restricted, fragmented, and confined to protected areas. Approximately 97 percent of tigers have been extinguished in just over a century, and only about 3,200 tigers are left in the wild.[4] Poaching tigers and overhunting their prey, demand for tiger "parts," and the loss or fragmentations of habitat are the main culprits of the tiger's accelerated demise.[5] Climate change also threatens one of the Bengal tiger's largest habitats, the Sundarbans mangrove forest in Bangladesh—but, beyond "climate adaptation policies" targeting human populations, there is little political will to address the issue of rising water levels threatening to destroy unique tiger habitats.[6]

Project Tiger, launched in 1972 in India with the political support of Prime Minister Indira Gandhi, offered considerable promise for the plight of tigers.[7] Success was overshadowed, however, by the accusations of "non-democratic" approaches that the Gandhi government used to achieve its conservation aims, such as forced human resettlements or measures taken in an effort to control human population.[8] More recently, weak enforcement coupled with corruption of local officials and rangers have led to tiger extirpations in two Indian tiger reserves, Sariska in 2004 and Panna in 2010.

In the Russian Far East, annual monitoring detected a dramatic decline in tiger numbers, also associated with both a decline in enforcement and increased poaching.[9] Siberian tigers, also known as Amur tigers, are classed as endangered by the World Conservation Union, with only about 450 individuals left in the wild.[10]

Vladimir Putin, president of Russia, has turned out to be an unexpected potential ally. The Tiger Summit was hosted in St. Petersburg in November of 2010 and hailed as the most significant meeting ever held to discuss the fate of a single nonhuman species.[11] The Russian state currently is also working to reintroduce the Persian leopard to southern Russia where the species became extinct in 1970. Putin vouched to restore their population in order to compensate for the negative environmental impact of the Olympic Games in Sochi.[12]

Even so, the democratic legitimacy of Putin is widely questioned. Since protests erupted after the allegedly rigged parliamentary elections in December of 2011, Putin has allowed demonstrators to protest, while "reserving the right to ignore their demands."[13] Western media did not hesitate to comment on Putin's "predatory" annexation of Crimea, a previously autonomous republic of Ukraine, in March of 2014. Yet might the idiosyncratic antics of a controversial head of state make a difference for tiger protection?

Efficacy of conservation

Some political scientists have argued that liberal democracies may be ill-suited for the task of enforcing environmental regulation, because these regimes are part of the problem.[14] Liberal democratic regimes are often influenced by corporate elites and their short-sighted and profit-driven motives and are thus incapable of effectively addressing the urgent challenges of conservation.[15]

Still others contend that undemocratic environmentalism is doomed to failure.[16] A number of authors have warned that conservation will fail without addressing human rights to livelihoods and "access to landscapes," and they warn that the cost of maintaining conservation areas created without local support will be prohibitively high.[17] When local communities are allowed to participate in conservation, it leads to a new sense of environmental responsibility.[18] Nora Haenn notes that conservation success increases when local communities gain more by protecting the wildlife—for example through ecotourism—than by destroying habitat and killing wildlife for short-term gain.[19]

But despite the participation of local communities in lucrative ecotourist activities in certain cases, poaching and destruction of habitat overall have not abated. Thus, local participation does not always guarantee the protection of nonhumans. An example of this occurred in 2013, when approximately 900 dolphins were slaughtered by local people of the Solomon Islands in the course of a dispute with conservation group Earth Island Institute. The islanders claimed that the conservation group failed to remunerate them, as agreed, for ending the traditional hunt. The Earth Island Institute maintained that community leaders appropriated the money paid for abstaining from hunting.[20] Moreover, there are many examples of indigenous communities gaining the right to their land and then selling the natural resources to commercial companies or starting commercial exploitation themselves, as in the case of Tarawera Land Company owned by the Maori of New Zealand. Lastly, as populations swell, communities expand their urban and agricultural settlement and treat wild animals as intruders. As William Catton notes, modern people have become not only hyper-numerous but also hyper-voracious.[21] The very scale of human presence can thus override any gains by local participation in conservation efforts.

Environmental justice

Debates abound as to exactly what type of political system is best suited for environmental protection, and they are often closely intertwined with notions of environmental justice for people.[22] As I have elsewhere discussed in greater detail, the environmental justice typology is four-fold.[23] First, environmental justice seeks to redress inequitable distribution of environmental benefits to vulnerable groups.[24] Second, environmental justice flags the unequal exposure to environmental risks of disempowered people (in both developed and developing countries).[25] Third, environmental justice focuses on intergenerational justice issues concerning the state of the planet bequeathed to future generations. Finally, nonhuman environmental justice—also known as ecological justice—advocates justice between species.[26]

Critics of top-down approaches to conservation have marred conservation as a neocolonial fortress.[27] Some anthropologists argue that environmentalism resonates with the particular cultural values of white, upper-middle-class Westerners.[28] Relatedly, Dan Brockington argues that wildlife conservation in Africa has more to do with Western views of the environment than with what is appropriate for African people and their domestic herds and traditional livelihoods.[29] Organizations like Survival International, or platforms such as Just Conservation, tend to focus exclusively on social justice, defending what they see as the right of local communities to profit either from traditional practices like hunting and fishing or from the commercial exploitation of "their" lands.

But critical scholars have countered that nonhuman rights to "their" lands are rarely considered, and thus the ideal of biospheric egalitarianism is de facto excluded from moral deliberations. Ironically, defenders of indigenous rights who equate the conservation enterprise with neocolonial Western, environmental nongovernmental organizations (NGOs) often downplay the ecocentric values and native environmentalism of certain traditional societies; for example, Aboriginal Australian and Maori cultures once valorized respect for, and collaboration with, the nonhumans.[30] Instead, critics of conservation—privileging anthropocentric conceptions of environmental justice—mirror and reinforce Western-centered moral myopia in relation to nonhumans, ignoring or belittling the significance of the plight of all those driven to extinction by economic development. As Veronica Strang has noted,

There remains a thorny question as to whether anyone, advantaged or disadvantaged, has the right to prioritize their own interests to the extent that those of the nonhuman are deemed expendable. Discourses on justice for people often imply that the most disadvantaged groups should have special rights to redress long-term imbalances. However, if the result is only a short-term gain at the long-term expense of the nonhuman, this is in itself not a sustainable process for maintaining either social or environmental equity.[31]

Conservation critics tend to pass over in silence the fact that many indigenous and traditional peoples are becoming as "modern" as Westerners and adopting attitudes of nature exploitation for the sake of development. Another irony is that those who promote the rights of local communities simultaneously support both their "right" to profit from conservation and their "right" to hold onto their traditional practices and way of life. Considering that the right to profit is part and parcel of a neoliberal market economy, while a traditional way of life implies preindustrial values, promoting both objectives is oxymoronic.

Around the world, traditional ways of life are giving way to modernization and development. The majority of traits that once enabled traditional societies to live in greater harmony with the environment are slowly diminishing.[32] Some local communities view animals and plants as something not worth protecting.[33] The right to modern mobility is disproportionately privileged over the collateral damages to wilderness areas and roadkill.[34] Aboriginal communities in Australia, for example, have the "right" to technologically upgrade their traditional practices—to shoot rather than spear wallabies—to the point that the once plentiful population of wallabies in Cape York has dwindled to critical levels.[35] Obviously, such rights, often extended and defended in the name of "social justice," are not meant to support nonhumans or to include any moral consideration for their lives.

In the absence of a universal ethics, the question of whether conservation measures are justified depends on one's point of view. It also depends on how conservationists, activists, policy makers, and others answer the question: What is more important, democratic decision making or biodiversity protection?

There is an ongoing debate about whether nonhuman species should be regarded as having intrinsic value or as possessing only instrumental value.[36] According to the shallow ecological perspective,[37] the value of nature hinges solely on the satisfaction of human wants, whether in material or aesthetic terms.[38] From this view, for example, tigers have enormous value to people, whether providing a resource for Chinese traditional medicine or for offering aesthetic enjoyment in zoos. Tigers can also become a great human asset insofar as they attract tourism and generate income for local communities. By this logic, human-created ecosystems in which tigers roam in zoo-like enclosures can be a resource celebrated by all on a gardened planet managed by the rightful rulers of the Anthropocene.[39]

The instrumental view of nature leaves many species and ecological processes by the wayside. It is silent with respect to the fate of functionally "useless" species, the precipitous decline of populations and constriction of habitats, the inhumane confinement and slaughter of billions of animals for consumption, or the entitled use of animals in experimentation of dubious value. Instrumental value, in other words, obscures the big picture of grave damage done to nonhumans.[40] What's more, humanity can be sufficiently supported by monocultures and is unlikely to suffer profound negative side effects from extensive biodiversity loss; this implicitly makes the existence of much of the planet's remaining biodiversity "redundant."

While tigers can generate income through tourism, income can also be generated by the building of a dam or a car factory in the former place of tiger habitat. When it comes to the exercise of democracy within the present-day economic system there is a disproportionate imbalance of power in favor of the economy.[41] Indeed, "environmental considerations continue to be subordinated to economic ones."[42]

Democracy and ethics

Proponents of deliberative democracy argue that authoritarianism is not the answer for effective conservation.[43] Yet once the disprivileging of, and discrimination against, other species is fully grasped, the point of departure and measure of success should be the efficacy of conservation policies. Without more comprehensive representation of ecocentric advocates, there exist no guarantees that nonhuman species will be considered in decision-making processes; on the contrary, their interests are likely to continue being neglected or given low priority.[44] Different forms of ecologically enlightened regimes were suggested by authors who offered arguments that nonhuman agency, creativity, and autonomy ought to be recognized and respected within democratic deliberation.[45]

Who are the human advocates who speak for nature?[46] In the case of tigers, the only ethical representation will be through advocates who weigh the survival of tigers as more important than any cultural or economic considerations.

Human rights advocates presume *their* arbitration to be a universal good. Impartial reasoning, however, provides no cogent grounds for thinking that humans are superior to other living beings, or that human interests should invariably come first. We may wonder how the dominant

Western zeitgeist has succeeded in propagating the illusion that the moral prerogative lies exclusively with our species. How would human rights advocates react to the statements that the poor should be left to their own devices since the rich are more "fit" to survive in this world, or that it is "natural" for women to be subservient to men?

Such proclamations deserve the label of social Darwinism at best, or a prison sentence. Racist, fascist, proslavery, or eugenics claims that challenge consensual morality are simply unacceptable in polite academic society; discrimination against certain human groups is morally wrong. By contrast, arbitration on behalf of tigers and other nonhuman species is marginalized as the "minority perspective" of eco-warriors and animal rights activists,[47] who are labeled (and perceived) as radical and undemocratic. And the suggestion, for example, that we should end our population growth and reduce our global numbers for the sake of other species and their habitats is branded as misanthropic in the current understanding of the democratic model. But this so-called democracy is pretty much a one-species-only democracy, in which, to rephrase George Orwell, one type of animal—the human—is much more "equal" than all the others.

In this context, the answer to the question of whether the top-down conservation policies can be both effective and ethically justifiable is "yes"— especially in the case of endangered animals who, without strict protection, will continue to be ruthlessly poached and driven toward the precipice of extinction. Ecologically enlightened political leadership might be needed to make "unpopular," in the short term, decisions by sacrificing some aspects of democracy on the altar of abating biodiversity loss. If the deep ecological perspective were to be taken seriously, the voice of the "minority" of advocates would actually be recognized as the voice of the *majority* of biospheric citizens, and the discrimination against nonhuman species would come to be seen as a case of grave environmental injustice.

Conclusion

For conservation success local participation is desirable but it might not be enough. In the case of tigers, for example, we might hope for local communities to support their protection without economic incentives or political pressure; but when a rich supplier of tiger parts offers the local guards more money to shoot tigers than a conservation NGO offers to protect them, the more lucrative bribe could win. Other means, including so-called fortress conservation, might be necessary to save tigers. Or a nondemocratic government, headed by an individual who happens to like tigers, might make a big difference, at least in the short term.

Yet there is no guarantee that ecological elites will be able to implement conservation policies without popular support. Thus, while top-down policies can be effective in conservation, their long-term sustainability remains a large concern. There should be a better way.[48]

I support the democratic representation of nonhumans through human eco-advocates in all global political assemblies in order to determine what works best for wildlife and wild habitats, as well as for humans. To achieve this, we need a new mind-set, one that centers on empathy, compassion, and being proactive in defending ecological justice for all planetary citizens. In other words, we need compassionate conservation,[49] supported by collaborative justice between humans and other beings,[50] based on the robust inclusion of political representation of nonhumans through eco-advocates.

This representation needs to be all-encompassing, to include humans as well as nonhumans who, unable to speak for themselves, deserve an equal voice in a democratic dialogue for the future. We need to reach beyond the ancient Greek root of the word *democracy*—from "demos," meaning people—to a forward-thinking definition that extends representation to all species, so that our Earth's modern-day democracy regards equally its entire biospheric citizenry.

Protected Areas Are Necessary for Conservation

ANTHONY R. E. SINCLAIR

THE WORLD'S FEW REMAINING protected ecosystems are becoming progressively threatened from human exploitation. They are also under threat from a new polemic, namely that protected areas have failed to adequately safeguard native ecologies and biota and are unlikely to do any better in the future. In contrast, it is argued that ecosystems in human-dominated landscapes are stable and have been for a long time; it is there that we must concentrate future conservation efforts even at the expense of protected areas.[1] A recent debate in conservation biology urges society to move away from the protected area paradigm and to focus on altered landscapes outside parks, which are being taken over and modified by humans. While we recognize that new approaches to conservation are needed in a world of burgeoning human numbers, this does not mean that protected areas have no crucial function. The debate surrounding protected areas begs three important questions: First, do protected areas play a role in conservation that is not achieved in human ecosystems? Second, and if so, why are protected areas not achieving their goals and how can this be rectified? And third, how can human-dominated ecosystems contribute to conservation objectives; in particular, can protected areas and human-dominated areas support each other?

Do protected areas play a role in conservation that is not achieved in human ecosystems? Protected areas[2] (all areas where human activities are restricted and biota are conserved) are the basis for the traditional approach to conservation. This strategy has the advantage of solving the thorny problem of how to prevent an increase in the number of people already living in an area by having none present in the first place. Protected area conservation is essential for the preservation of large carnivores, rare species that cannot tolerate humans, and gene banks for resilience and evolution; for providing a refuge from overexploitation; and to act as an ecological baseline to detect unwanted changes from human activities elsewhere. Protected areas are also needed to protect unique ecosystems, such as the Serengeti. With this much at stake, we cannot do without them.

The original, historical policy of conservation has been to secure areas such as national parks and reserves in order to maintain a suite of biota that was disappearing in the face of human exploitation. Yellowstone National Park in the United States was an early example, a response to the combination of illegal settlement, vandalism, and wildlife slaughter which led the U.S. Army to take charge of the park in 1886.[3] Kruger National Park, South Africa, was the first such protected area in Africa (proclaimed by the Transvaal Republic in 1898 as the Sabi Game Reserve), a reaction to encroaching agriculture and extermination of wildlife from grazing lands.[4] Since then a large number of protected areas have been set up around the world specifically to provide protection for native life,[5] and clearly larger ones do provide protection.[6] A selected set of protected areas has been designated as World Heritage Sites since 1972.

Long-term research in the Serengeti National Park, spanning some fifty years, has documented the conservation value of protected areas.[7] Research within this protected area has increased the number of known species of several groups including microbes, nematodes, insects, rodents, and birds. Synthesis of the half century of data on the wildebeest migration by Grant Hopcraft and colleagues establishes demographic changes, the spatial extent of the population, and the impacts on the Serengeti ecosystem.[8] They confirm the important lesson that the Serengeti without the wildebeest migration would have completely different dynamics and, reciprocally, that wildebeest would not be so abundant but for the unique features of the protected Serengeti; the two are firmly interconnected.

Unique features of the Serengeti ecosystem include the impact of fire, which drives changes in tree populations, determines the movements of migrant ungulates, and changes grass structure for insects and birds. Spatial mosaics provide the variability that determines the migration patterns.[9] Comparison of biodiversity inside and outside the protected area reveals a consistent pattern where restricted range species of butterfly, rodents, and birds inside the park are lost outside—only the globally occurring or Africa-wide species (that is, the generalist species) are found there.[10] Even microbe species assemblages show changes with the different grazing regimes inside and outside the park because inside grazing is seasonal, while outside it is more persistent through the year.[11] Top carnivore species are lost outside the park, particularly in agricultural areas and, to a lesser extent, in pastoralist areas.[12] Loss of top predators, such as raptors, outside the park leads to increases in rodent densities and possibly disease transmission in human ecosystems.[13]

Not only are large mammals safer inside the park, they are *aware* they are safer: This has now been documented, for example, for elephants. Our long-term records of elephant births have shown a high birth rate in the early days of the park when protection was high (1960s–1970s). The 1980s was a period of severe elephant poaching with some 80 percent of the population being killed. During this period females did not give birth. This low birth rate indicated higher stress levels inhibiting conception— stress levels resulting from human killing. This stress factor has now been confirmed by Heidi G. Tingvold and coauthors:[14] Elephants have higher stress hormones not only when they leave the park but even when they approach the boundaries of the park prior to leaving. With the increased protection since the 1990s the birth rate has risen again to prior levels.

In summary, as a protected area the Serengeti National Park functions as a refuge for rare endemic species, migratory populations, top carnivores, and mega-herbivores. It provides a safe area where stress imposed by human interference is reduced. None of these kinds of species can survive in human-dominated ecosystems, a conclusion which confirms the function that large protected areas provide around the world.

Why are protected areas not achieving their goals of sustaining biodiversity for the long term, and how can this be rectified? First, there are simply not enough natural areas protected around the world to include all species. A considerable proportion of the world's biota, some 50 percent, falls outside of protected areas.[15] Unless new areas are set aside to protect more of this biodiversity, we must turn to community-based conservation (discussed shortly). And, in a world of ongoing human demographic and economic growth, it is increasingly unlikely that much more new area will be reserved.

Secondly, far from new areas being set aside, established protected areas are experiencing attrition of territory through an insidious excising of land for human exploitation. This stems from the legal insecurity of the boundaries. Despite legal demarcation, many protected areas suffer changes of boundaries set by governments as demands for land increase. Boundaries are realigned to suit political whims and over time the area diminishes; we have seen this realignment of boundaries and reduction of protected area in the Mara Reserve and Maswa Reserve of the Serengeti ecosystem, and it is common practice around the world. If protected areas are to serve their function then the only solution is to replace lost area with other area of similar biological value, a policy that is so far unrecognized and unpracticed.[16]

Thirdly, biota are being lost even within protected areas.[17] Individually, protected areas are often not large enough to protect populations that can continue to survive if all members of that species are eliminated outside the boundaries. The result is that species are being lost from the protected area over time; there is evidence that this loss is already occurring in African protected areas.[18] In a twenty- to thirty-year analysis covering 60 tropical forest reserves around the globe, William F. Laurance and his fellow researchers found that about half of the reserves experienced biodiversity losses over a wide array of animal groups.[19] Habitat modification, exploitation, and hunting were the main disturbances—meaning that the reserves are actually inadequately protected.

Fourthly, no protected area is a self-sustaining system in isolation, not even the largest areas.[20] The above-mentioned analysis of forest reserves showed that environmental changes occurring *outside* were as important as those occurring inside in determining the course of ecological change. All protected areas rely on processes that emanate from outside, whether these be water flows from rivers, recolonization of plant communities, or dispersal of animals. So to maintain a protected area indefinitely it is equally imperative to maintain the greater ecosystem within which it is embedded.

Fifthly—and perhaps most important of all—protected area conservation rests on delimiting an area with a legal boundary which is then fixed in perpetuity. Current ecological research around the world, including our work in Serengeti, shows that ecosystems are changing as climate changes; and they have been changing for millions of years. We know this has been the case for the last 4 million years in Serengeti and such change will continue into the future.[21] So static boundaries will not accommodate the changes in distribution of plants and animals as climate changes their environment; indeed it is likely that fifty years from now none of the current areas will be protecting what they were intended to protect—the communities, if able to, will have changed their location. The only way we can deal with this shift is to have either very large areas or a patchwork of interconnected small areas that can capture a moving ecosystem. Perhaps the British system of Sites of Special Scientific Interest (SSSIs)[22] that cover the country might be a model for such an approach, but only if the "patches" are large enough. Unless conservation takes up this challenge, protected areas will fail in the long run.

What are the problems for conservation in human-dominated systems?
Conservation in human-dominated systems, known as community-based conservation (CBC), attempts to maintain sustainable biological communities in the presence of human exploitation, largely in agriculture- and forestry-dominated systems.[23] The problems with protected area conservation discussed above provide the rationale for giving renewed attention to conservation efforts in human ecosystems. Much of community-based conservation still focuses on preserving the biota rather than the needs of the people,[24] but unless the aspirations of humans are given top priority there will be no conservation.[25]

Because significant amounts of natural resources, including biological species, lie in areas used by humans there has been a push toward trying to conserve species through sustainable use of or at least limited impact on areas by way of community-based conservation. It is an essential approach because human-modified landscapes now cover over 90 percent of the terrestrial surface of the planet. In developing countries community-based conservation has focused on exploiting natural areas to provide income for local peoples, in the hope that they come to value the areas and the native species that lie within them.

On the surface this idea sounds convincing, but in practice it has yet to overcome several intractable problems. Around the world, implementation of CBC has led to problems and its rationale has not always yielded successful policies.[26] For example, CBC programs in Africa often benefit local authorities or elites but not individuals in the community.[27] By definition all CBC areas have people living in them, and these people expect to receive their share of natural resource benefits or profits—for example, they might receive the income from selling a portion of wildlife harvest in an African game reserve. While this sort of plan may have been reasonable when first devised—with the killing having been correctly calculated for the numbers of wild animals that live in the area and the income shared out fairly—in the long-term such arrangements tend to fail for any number of reasons.

Projects of this sort are advertised as great successes for community-based conservation, but in reality they are often short-sighted.[28] First, the number of people increases in the region, leading to a demand to increase the harvest; but the wildlife in a set area does not tend to increase, its numbers remain steady and thus so must the harvest if it is to be sustainable. (An increase in harvest will eventually cause the extinction of the wildlife, as has occurred in areas where control disintegrated with political and social upheavals.[29] A steady harvest means that each person now receives a declining income. Secondly, each person is not content to receive even a steady income for their whole lives, let alone a declining income—people expect an increasing income so that the demand for increasing harvest is exacerbated. Thirdly, the area set aside for CBC declines over time due to expanding populations, increase in urban development, and loss of soil so that the wildlife population from which a harvest is taken decreases. For these reasons community-based conservation areas often become unsustainable in the long term.[30]

Fourth, CBC favors only those species that are either useful to or tolerant of humans, and the latter are often those least in need of protection. Other species that are detrimental to humans, such as large carnivores, are often excluded and even persecuted. In addition, CBC relies on species providing some value—usually economic value and often through commercial exploitation—so as to advance human welfare. Yet, even with so-called useful species, where economic value has been assessed it rarely exceeds 10 percent of the potential agricultural value, and so there is a strong incentive to replace the few useful wild species with domestic ones.[31] Thus, CBC does not conserve the full complement of biota, which is what is needed for a sustainable environment. As mentioned earlier there is ample evidence to show that this distorted community of species results in a collapse of the system and society has been forced to subsidize it by having to provide artificial food for birds and mammals, eradicate pests, and control predators.[32]

The "new conservation" platform argues that a world already at 7 billion and heading toward 10 billion people will simply overrun protected areas by the year 2100 in the scramble for new resources, and we may as well recognize that eventuality; to some extent this is already under way.[33] These billions of people, largely in the developing world, emulating present-day western societies, will demand and achieve energy-expensive lifestyles. Thus, if we are to save the world's natural heritage we must embrace technology and "garden" our environments.[34] Humans, it is argued, do not live in natural ecosystems but in ecosystems modified by agriculture, forestry, urbanization, and industry, and these areas have been resilient to human population growth and climate change over the past centuries.[35] This view contrasts with what these proponents claim was a prevailing concept of nature as fragile, ready to collapse with any disturbance. Thus, it is argued, conservation in the twenty-first century must embrace human-made systems. If it is to be relevant, conservation must move away from protected areas as the old model, and use technology to conserve the biota. This is the argument of the new "gardeners" of the world.[36]

However, there is overwhelming evidence that human-dominated ecosystems are unstable and unsustainable. As mentioned above, certain types of species and processes simply cannot exist in human-dominated systems. Additionally, neither ecologies nor species can recover from persistent overexploitation.[37] For example, there is a continuing loss of biodiversity and ecosystem processes in agriculture in Europe.[38] Progressive salinization of soils in Australia is causing ongoing loss of agricultural production.[39] There are not enough insects left in India to pollinate the fields.[40] In short, although one can point to a few examples where biota have returned to human-modified landscapes, there is a far greater array of cases showing that the historical impacts of humans have been impoverishing and unsustainable and will continue to be so into the future.

Conclusion: How can human-dominated ecosystems contribute to conservation objectives? Thus, we must conclude that neither community-based conservation nor protected area conservation is, by itself, sufficient and that both approaches are required to form a coordinated policy for sustainable conservation of the natural world. In addition, both call for new and daring policies to make them viable.

There are two direct ways CBC can contribute to conservation, as mentioned above. First, protected areas rely on ecosystem processes that emanate from outside so we must maintain the greater ecosystem within which they are embedded. This is in the interests of human society because protected areas provide reciprocal services for agriculture. For example, pollination rates in agriculture are higher closer to patches of native, wild vegetation.[41] Secondly, ecosystems are changing their boundaries as the environment changes so that the biota will shift their location. The present static boundaries of protected areas will no longer be providing protection—the biota will be trying to move into human-dominated landscapes in the next fifty years. Unless we keep such landscapes habitable for the majority of species, among the results will be increasing extinctions, loss of "ecosystem services," and a decline in human welfare.

So, community-based conservation is essential for long-term ecological sustainability. There is an urgent need to find ways of counteracting the destabilizing trends discussed above while maintaining the full complement of species. We must find innovative ways of both providing benefits to peoples, without losing biodiversity through extinctions, and reducing the impacts on human livelihoods.[42] In the end the costs of conservation must be met by those who benefit the most, mainly those in the developed nations who desire the aesthetic aspects of nature. These nations must devise adequate benefit programs for local communities[43]—and by "adequate" I mean that people should be better off from the CBC compensation than if they had adopted other forms of resource use with no conservation. Additionally, instead of considering human population growth a given, we must invest in and emphasize humane policies that stabilize and lower human numbers.

The assertions made by the new "gardeners" of human ecosystems that they are sustainable and resilient need to be tested by comparison with areas that have less human impact. These are de facto the protected areas; they are the controls for human impacts. This is one fundamental reason why protected areas must not be lost; they are the best way of judging whether community-based conservation is sustainable and human ecosystems are truly robust. What protected areas are not—and in the modern context not intended to be—are "pristine, prehuman landscapes" as suggested by Peter Kareiva and others.[44] While some historically may have thought that way,[45] it is not the prevailing concept of protected areas today.[46]

TWO

REWILDING EARTH, REWILDING OURSELVES

I Walk in the World to Love It

EILEEN CRIST

"THE WORLD TODAY is nothing if it is not sprawl," writes nature poet Mary Oliver.[1] It was not until the nineteenth century that a minority of people glimpsed this eventuality, and it was only at the end of the twentieth and dawn of the twenty-first that the sprawl's scope became fully transparent.

Today, knowledge of humanity's impact on the planet's systems—biodiversity, atmosphere, climate, freshwater, wetlands, forests, oceans, soil—is available to anyone interested enough to seek it. Two far-reaching consequences follow from our systems-level impact: Earth's biological impoverishment, via the loss, degradation, and homogenization of its Holocene-rich diversity of life; and the transfiguration of the planet into what author Bill McKibben recently dubbed *Eaarth*. "The world hasn't ended," McKibben notes, "but the world as we know it has—even if we don't quite know it yet. We imagine… the disturbances we see around us are the old random and freakish kind. They are not. It's a different place. A different planet."[2]

Despite the looming consequences, there are reasons to sustain hope. "The enormity of what we are doing," as David Brower enjoined, is beginning "to pervade our thinking."[3] Many people are grieving but also taking action. Despite the downsides of the electronic revolution—extractive industries, e-waste pollution, and endless media distractions—in an interconnected world knowledge and information can spread. Human solidarity with the biosphere, and toward a life of human integrity within it, may yet be born because our connection with Earth is primal; in the words of

E. O. Wilson, "despite all our fantasies and pretensions, we always have been and will remain a biological species tied to this particular world."[4]

Another reason for remaining hopeful is the foresight, and equally the afterthought, of an always-ambivalent human establishment to exempt certain lands and (to a lesser extent) waters from the sprawl. Nature conservation "constitutes hope for an implacable counterforce to the momentum of totalizing imperial power";[5] as such, it has rarely been an uncontested or voluntary gesture. Its origins reach back to pioneer thinkers of nineteenth-century North America, who advocated and inspired a movement for protecting areas of the natural world so as to arrest the planet's resource-hungry engulfment. Such pioneers understood that "nothing dollarable is safe" (John Muir). They also envisioned the ideal of every human habitat bordering the wilderness (Henry Thoreau): for the sake of diversity and balance, for the sake of beauty and quietude, for the sake of justice for nonhumans and respect for their homes.

The movement for free zones against human exploitation (as stingy and disputed as that movement tends to be) has spread around the world. Despite the fact that only about 13 percent of the land and 2 percent of the ocean are protected,[6] in recent years the globalization of nature protection and especially of parks and wilderness preservation has been indicted as impositions of American ideals. As David Quammen summarizes this argument: "protecting landscape and biological diversity by creating national parks is [censured as] another elitist form of cultural imperialism."[7] This political critique of parks and wilderness reserves is off track for at least three reasons. For starters, it belittles the ability of all people, regardless of cultural background, to discern the obvious: that without formally agreed upon, legally binding, and enforced restraint to accessing certain parts of the natural world, the sprawl would not end until it had ended everything except itself.

Another reason that the condemnation of strict nature protection as a Western burden is amiss is that different cultures elaborate different aspects of collective and historical experience, and such diverse elaborations—if resonant with inclinations that are universal to the human spirit—become the common heritage, the *real* commonwealth, of humanity.[8] (Thus, for example, millions of Westerners who do yogic practices today would not think of themselves as duped by a Hindu lifestyle and metaphysics.) It is true that the value of conservation (in its modern guise) was first nurtured on the North American continent. This occurred because a few people (partial to the European-rooted Romantic movement, the first Western

intellectual platform to oppose human domination and hubris) stood witness to the breakneck pace and horrendous violence with which an entire
continent—its people, plants, animals, forests, rivers, and rich ecologies—
was desecrated. Of course, ever since the Neolithic period human beings
have been overtaking large swaths of the natural world, but never before with
such speed, arrogance ("Manifest Destiny"), deadly germs, high-impact
technologies, and large-scale cruelty (witness the decimation of indigenous
people, passenger pigeons, bison, salmon, wolves, among so many other
natives) that occurred in North America, especially after industrialization
and population growth took off.[9] This continent-wide ecological blitzkrieg
was a (world) historic wake-up call—for a minority, it is important to remember, and not for American culture as a whole.

The third reason that the critique of modern conservation as cultural
imperialism goes astray is that closer inspection of its "American" roots reveals that the sensibility of cherishing and protecting nature was hardly a
strict Euro-American nineteenth-century innovation. Reading Thoreau's
Walden, one cannot but be struck by the repeated allusions to Eastern
philosophy and contemplative practice—both of which exalt a cosmic
view of nature's primacy and power over the human realm. And Thoreau
is *the* intellectual architect of the ideal of wilderness preservation as imperative for defending nature's autonomy against human subjugation and
instrumentalism. Indeed, it is not widely known that Thoreau first introduced the idea of a "park"—of nature free from relentless human use—
as a preserved expanse to grace the environs of every human settlement.
Muir may have been the great activist-writer, the sermonizer for parks.
But the case against civilized man's blindness to the magnificence of the
more-than-human world, and to that world's inspirational potential and
inherent right to thrive, was unequivocally made by the still-unsurpassed
blade of Henry's pen. In making that case Thoreau drew from a repository
of knowledge well beyond the Western canon. Indeed, citizens of India
might relish that the man who so influenced Mahatma Gandhi's activism
had first been inspired by Gandhi's own spiritual heritage. For example,
Thoreau had this to say about one of India's (and the world's) most holy
texts: "In the morning I bathe my intellect in the stupendous and cosmog-
onal philosophy of the Bhagvat Geeta [sic]." A few sentences later he adds:
"The pure Walden water is mingled with the sacred water of the Ganges."[10]

While the ideal and practice of safeguarding portions of self-willed
nature from the sprawl is now a shared heritage—"truly a significant con-

tribution to world civilization," in the words of environmental philosopher Thomas Birch,[11]—it must be admitted that in major ways the sprawl is already everywhere. Changing the planet's atmosphere and climate as well as the global unleashing of biocidal chemicals attest to the sprawl's life-menacing victory. What's more, the sprawl has seized Earth's best soil. The most fecund lands, the temperate grasslands, once rich in life-forms, ecological processes, and migrations ("moving ecosystems") are mostly plowed under. "Agriculture gets what it wants," as author Richard Manning nails it.[12] Indeed, along with the soil, agriculture has demanded much of the freshwater. Because protected areas are rarely large (or interconnected) enough to shelter entire river catchments, the loss of freshwater biodiversity has been enormous. (It has also been largely undocumented and blithely ignored.) According to biologist David Dudgeon and colleagues, "fresh waters are experiencing declines in biodiversity far greater than those in most affected terrestrial ecosystems."[13]

As insufficient, nonpristine, and ecologically and politically precarious as protected areas are, they still stand as safe havens where civilization's invading tide, though far from halted, is kept at bay. While in today's world even parks and wilderness reserves are losing species, the hemorrhaging is far slower than what is occurring outside protected areas. In a recent review of the status of biodiversity, conservation biologist Stuart Pimm and his coauthors write that "the rate at which mammals, birds, and amphibians have slid toward extinction over the past four decades would have been 20% higher were it not for conservation efforts." "Protected areas," they urge, "are essential for reducing extinctions."[14]

Strictly protected areas—or biodiversity reserves, as I refer to them interchangeably—are sanctuaries safeguarding more than meets the eye. As noted, they protect species (as well as subspecies, varieties, and populations), especially those who are endemic, sensitive, or averse to people's presence, wide-ranging and incompatible with human settlements and roads, or under dire threat of targeted slaying.[15] Additionally, biodiversity reserves allow ecological dynamics to unfold without chain saws, drills, plows, pesticides, trawlers, and guns to disarray them; such ecological dynamics include, for example, the movements of large herds of mammals who need vast, unbroken spaces for their mobile or migratory life cycles.[16] Protected areas are sanctuaries for animals, trees, fungi, and ecological communities, giving them a chance to ripen into old age: both for the sake of their own lives and for ecological effects uniquely shaped by larger-sized organisms, such as ancient trees.[17] For wild animals, sheltered places avail them a chance to enjoy lives free from being shot, poisoned, snared, run over, hooked, netted, or caused to starve.[18] Networked biodiversity reserves[19] also serve as necessary refuges for the massive movement of life that will occur (and has begun) in response to rapid climate change; recent studies reveal that organisms are already availing themselves of protected areas disproportionately in their climate-change-induced peregrinations.[20] Importantly, protected areas are havens for biodiversity's long-term potential, safeguarding the genetic variability required to keep viable the evolutionary promise of as many of Earth's life-forms as possible.

Protected areas are sacred for people who want to preserve indigenous or create neo-indigenous wild lifeways—choices which, while likely to be eschewed by many, remain the rightful heritage for those who now and in the future would embrace them. Biodiversity reserves also counteract what has been called "the extinction of experience" in the wake of the downhill spiral of generational ecological amnesia: This refers to the narrowing range of potent experiences of the natural world, accompanied by a cumulative collective ignorance of how rich life on Earth is when left free of human chiseling and hammering.[21] "With each ensuing generation," biologist John Waldman explains, "environmental degradation generally increases, but each generation takes that degraded condition as the new normal." Conservation is thus vital for counteracting "the insidious ebbing of the ecological and social relevancy of declining and disappearing species."[22] Beyond protecting natural areas, actively restoring the wild can relieve what author George Monbiot calls "ecological boredom" in a humanized world.[23] Last but far from least, protected areas are sanctuaries of human dignity, for they affirm that we are not so depraved as to lay instrumental claim to every object, being, and place on the planet. The thought alone of humans causing a mass extinction makes most people's conscience sting. In such conscious or subterranean desire to preserve life lies real hope, and protected areas are crucial for saving global biodiversity and averting a human-driven mass-extinction event.[24]

Indeed, land and marine protected areas are so indispensable for the existential and experiential horizons of all life—nonhuman and human—that everything possible must be done to enlarge, restore, and interconnect them. This mandate necessitates the restriction of human access, for were people allowed to explore or live within strictly protected areas, the "impact on the fauna and flora... would be fatal to a large fraction of the species."[25] Barring people from sources of livelihood or income within biodiversity reserves (prohibiting settlements, agriculture, hunting, mining, and other high-impact activities) needs to be offset by coupling conservation efforts with the provision of benefits for local people.[26] Conservation practitioners agree that this is not only the right thing to do but mandatory, for without people's support "any conservation gains will be ephemeral," as Paul Ehrlich and Robert Pringle note."[27]

The long-term ecological and human possibilities ensured by wilderness preservation do not resonate with everyone immediately—though over time, new circumstances, changing values, and emerging economic opportunities can move (and in many cases have moved) societies toward deeper appreciation of protected areas.[28] To enlist the allegiance of local communities with conservation practice, tangible benefits of protecting wild nature must be both emphasized and generated (for all, not just local elites[29]). Not only are the benefits economic (such as income created through ecotourism), they are also social, educational, and health-related.[30] For example, people often come to feel pride in their national parks, especially when these are well maintained, globally prominent, and protective of rare or widely valued species. Transboundary parks, also known as "peace parks," can encourage good relations between neighboring countries, thus contributing to social and political stability.[31] Additionally, conservation practice expands humanity's knowledge horizons through fostering a dialogue between indigenous/traditional and modern scientific ways of knowing. Thus conservation programs that actively engage local people are crucial both for the long term success of conservation plans and for the growth and flow of biological knowledge.[32] According to conservation scientists Clive Hambler and Susan Canney, conservation efforts that involve public participation and citizen science "enhance learning and engagement, and reduce feelings of powerlessness and hopelessness."[33]

For these reasons, conservationists agree that the goodwill and participation of people living near biodiversity reserves need to be procured. Protected areas must be designed with the intention of supporting local communities and, more broadly, of enhancing the quality of human life everywhere.[34] Over the last few decades it has become clear that not only should human costs of conservation be avoided or compensated for, but public enthusiasm for protecting wild nature needs to be cultivated.

PROTECTED AREAS TODAY—especially reserves that tend to enjoy the highest levels of protection—may be regarded as an analogue to Tiananmen Square's "Tank Man": They represent bold and always-precarious action against nature's final takeover by modern civilization. In a time of growing human numbers, escalating energy use, consumer accumulation of ever-more things, global trade, and technological somnambulism,[35] nature conservation constitutes "an essential holding action."[36] Lisi Krall recently described conservation practice as *resistance* against the occupation of the natural world, defending its remaining free enclaves, wild stands, and nonhuman nations from the avalanche.[37] Appearances notwithstanding, I argue that the avalanche being resisted is not a human avalanche, *per se*, but more accurately the avalanche of history, driven by the mindset and ammunition of the civilized conqueror.

Since the end of the last century into the present, those who campaign for biodiversity reserves safeguarded from all but our lightest-footprint activities (like walking or bird watching) have had to contend with the smear of "misanthropy" (literally meaning "hating man").[38] Specifically, wilderness defenders who maintain that civilized people[39] need not, and indeed *should not*, be permitted full access to the biosphere have been critiqued as promoting two false, misanthropic views: one, that there exists a gaping dichotomy between humans and the rest of nature; and two, that humans defile or taint the natural world, which would remain pristine in their absence. A notable dimension of these allegations against wilderness advocacy is that those who level them regularly fail to foreground civilized humanity's unrestrained expansionism over the planet, including mining sea beds, decapitating mountains, despoiling marine life, pervasive killing of wild animals, and appropriating the lion's share of topsoil and freshwater (to mention some outstanding examples). Defending the world against such egregious occupation can only be an act of love, and to malign the defenders as misanthropes is a charge as damaging as it is incoherent.[40]

Those who love the natural world—and want to protect its freedom, diversity, abundance, and inexhaustible beauty and mystery, as well as our covenant with all this which preceded and once surrounded our very existence—also, on pains of irresolvable contradiction, love human *being*. For as the natural world is foundationally good and beautiful, so does human nature contain the ingredients for an identity that is good and beautiful within the natural world. This perspective rings "romantic," because that is exactly what it happens to be: It is heir to the worldview of Romanti-

cism, informed additionally by ecological knowledge of nature's integrated flows and often tempered (as in Thoreau's case) by timeless spiritual
intuition of nature's unity. The Romantic worldview embraces the more
encompassing truth of a positive understanding of the natural world—as
emerging through reciprocal relations, the creation of abundance, the
building of diversity, and the breathtaking forging of *umwelts*—over the
limited truth of a killjoy understanding of the natural world—captured in
such catchphrases as "nature red in tooth and claw," "the selfish gene," or
"a dog-eat-dog world."

The positive view of nature implies that it is highly unlikely that there
is something inherent in human nature that makes it intractably adver-
sarial to the more-than-human world. Of course our species—being generalist, brainy, and technologically dexterous—has the built-in capacity to
be the proverbial "bull in the china shop" (as prehistoric human-driven
extinctions testify). But the gravest trouble lurks in how civilization has
usurped the already bigger-than-life human animal, trapping him (us)
into a calamitous identity that is conquering, instrumental, killing, incon-
siderate, and controlling—in a word, supremacist. The human supremacist is conditioned to be myopically self-serving, co(s)mically conceited
(in learned or lay fashion), and, delusions of grandeur notwithstanding,
existentially constricted—he disparages dwelling from a sacred sense of
wonder within the biosphere as secondary or superfluous by comparison
to the compulsion to live in take/compete/survive mode most of the time.

Nature's adversary is not human *being* in some essential sense, but the
supremacist identity fashioned by the dark side of civilization. As dominant
as this overlord identity has become, it is dangerously misleading to conflate
it with human nature: To make that conflation is to distort and underestimate the human, "to confuse our 'self' with the narrow ego."[41] While our nature certainly seems susceptible to the supremacist persona, this identity has
been socioculturally instilled, and historically hardened, from the inception
of civilization onward. It was coeval with the spread of agriculture and domestication, the erection of walled city-states, the emergence of resource-
driven wars, the construction of social hierarchy, the never-ending (to this
very hour) deforestation, and the annihilation of indigenous (as well as less
powerful) peoples and their ways. Perhaps most importantly, alongside the
spread and variegated forms of entrenching the above, the overlord identity
has been fashioned through a raft of philosophical, theological, political,
and pseudoscientific ideologies—leached into commonsense—that have

repeatedly (re)declared the human to be both superior to all life-forms and rightful user of the natural world. In brief, civilization (not wilderness protection) has long cultivated the human sense of being separate and supreme, and underwritten the still-reigning normative violence against the nonhuman world. It is this human identity that nature must be protected from, not some fixed essence of the human.

Thus advocacy for protecting, restoring, and interconnecting large swaths of nature, and exempting such places from all but our lightest presence, is not motivated by the alleged view that there exists a gaping dichotomy between humans and rest of the natural world. *That* dichotomy has been inflicted by the civilized human,[42] who, having categorically disavowed his animal-being, has not sought to be integral with Earth's life community but mostly to dominate and convert nature. Indeed, a human-nonhuman apartheid regime conjured by historical humanity has legitimated our self-consigned prerogative to occupy, use, displace, and eradicate the natural world at will. The mainstay of the wilderness idea, and of the activism to preserve the wild, has been conscientious opposition to this rampage and to the human-nonhuman constructed hierarchy that underpins it. Protecting wild nature is thus *precisely* intended to shield the natural world from the invented, exploitation-facilitating human-nature split— and not to assert the existence of an essential separateness between people and the nonhuman world. Even so, since the 1990s, wilderness defense has been mindlessly disparaged as "self-evidently" propagating an artificial divide between people and the natural world, while the wilderness concept has been dismissed as a white-male-American social construct.[43]

Rather than zooming in on the fact that occupying nature does not signal our unity with it, such critiques of wilderness silently press the interpretation that civilized humanity's sprawl shows our inseparability from the natural world: thus are people befuddled into *confounding* swallowing-up-nature with being-at-one-with-nature. Simultaneously, those who defend the natural world from human assimilation are censured as believing in a human-nature dichotomy. This bogus reasoning has worked only to discourage deeper thinking about our relationship with the biosphere. For it requires virtually no thought to say, "Humans and nature are not separate, therefore no wonder everything looks the way it does." But it requires critical reflection to discern that the millennia-old stance of human entitlement, with its proliferated conceptions of "the Human Difference" and its amoral instrumentalism, has all but utterly divorced humans from nature—*therefore no wonder everything looks the way it does.*

Slavery, racism, and discrimination against women and other groups, while persisting in the world, are today socially spurned; but not that long ago they were the norm, institutionalized by economic and political arrangements and upheld as self-evidently valid by mainstream opinion. Despite evidence for humanity's moral evolution regarding members of our *own* species, human ownership of land and seas along with the virulent exploitation and/or displacement of nonhumans continue to rule, congealed into realities by economic, political, and ideational institutions, and endorsed by mainstream opinion as the way things self-evidently are, need, and ought to be.[44]

Yet the arc of the moral universe bends toward justice. The time for justice for the nonhuman world—for the simple recognition of the goodness of letting places, processes, and beings abide in their own natures free from excessive interference—is surely coming, though it may take another generation or longer. Some environmental observers, however, argue that this hoped-for extension of moral consideration to nonhumans and their homes is naive, failing "to recognize the depth of our own species narcissism."[45] There are good reasons to disagree with such ripostes to the possibility of universal justice: Our own species narcissism does not have all that much "depth." Real depth inheres in what ancient spiritual and indigenous traditions have directly recognized and Charles Darwin articulated with evidence-based precision: the knowledge that we are all family on this Earth plane. While human attitudes toward nonhumans and the natural world might always remain complicated, dissimilar, and even discordant, with time, humanity is apt to converge on a broad and lucid biocentric view: that all beings are better off wild, free, cared for (in the case of the domesticated), released from inflictions of unnecessary suffering and exploitation, living in accordance with their natures and life cycles, their habitats respected and unmolested, and their unknown evolutionary destinies valued and left unobstructed.

So here we can circle back to deepen the inquiry into the mandate of protecting "big chunks of linked wilderness," as Brower colloquially put it.[46] The goal is not to maintain remnant "museum" pieces of the natural world to serve as vacation destinations, future resource reserves, science laboratories, roomy zoos, or ecological-service providers; in other words, the point is not to incarcerate portions of wild nature for various human purposes in perpetuity. In his celebrated paper, "The Incarceration of Wildness: Wilderness Areas as Prisons," Birch laid to rest such conservation rationales as alter exhibits of civilization's vise-grip on the natural world. Were such rationales for parks and wilderness to prevail in the future, protected areas would indeed turn out to be glorified Disney Worlds—assigned proper uses in a world dominated and managed by modern humans. Protected areas for "epoch Anthropocene" would serve various consumer diversions, such as sighting exotic animals, trophy hunting, safari adventures, outdoor recreation, or stress release. This warped vision for conservation is consistent with a humanized world order, in which "wilderness and wildness are placed on the supermarket shelf of values along with everything else, and everything is enclosed *inside* the supermarket."[47] A supermarket (overt or covert) rationale for long-term nature protection must be brought to light and discredited.

From a biocentric standpoint, protected areas are the best shelters of Earth's biological wealth and evolutionary potential until the time when such areas will *no longer be needed*. The practice of conservation constitutes "part of a larger strategy that aims to make all land [and seas] into, or back into, sacred space, and thereby to move humanity into a conscious reinhabitation of wildness."[48] The entire Earth will then become what Brower envisioned as Earth Park, except that the word "park" will be as unnecessary as human-nature *de jure* boundaries. But protected areas are indispensable until that day when human beings share a sensibility that cringes at the mere thought of ivory, rhino horn, tiger bone, dried-up sea horses in "medicinal" ziplock bags, shahtoosh, snow leopard fur, all fur, trophy hunting, bushmeat, exotic pets, bear bile "farming," "performing" cetaceans and other animals, shark fin soup, tortoise/turtle shell knick-knacks, wetlands for cane sugar, rainforests for palm oil or meat, prairies for corn and wheat fields, intact ecosystems for diamonds, gold, or oil, mountains for coal, sagebrush landscapes for natural gas, boreal forest for tar sands, and life-filled oceans for seafood. For the time being, though, nonhumans and their habitats must be shielded, sometimes with militant vigilance and force if they are to survive.[49]

Parks, wilderness, and other nature preserves are biodiversity arks, protected for Earth's future restoration into wholeness when humanity will desire to be interwoven within Nature's expanse rather than establishing an imperial, parasitic civilization upon it. A key task for working toward that time is to "set aside the largest fraction of Earth's surface possible as inviolate nature reserves. One-half would be nice."[50]

WHILE NETWORKS OF BIODIVERSITY RESERVES are needed more than ever in a time of extinctions and rapid climate change, they have been called into question by vociferous voices. Strictly protected areas like parks and wilderness have been denounced as "fortress conservation" that can displace people while also undermining their means to rise out of poverty.[51] In response to such sweeping denunciations, recent research has revealed that systematic data about the impact protected areas have had on local communities worldwide (and under what conditions that impact has been beneficial or detrimental) is "seriously lacking."[52] What's more, the overwhelming majority of the world's rural and urban poor do not live near wilderness areas.[53] But the shrill rhetoric of the fortress critique, along with the intimidating high moral ground of human rights it professes, have driven conservationists into the defensive and induced an observable shift (in discourse and practice) toward "people-centered" conservation approaches.[54]

While there is a broad agreement about the need to couple conservation efforts with active community involvement (as previously discussed), a vocal camp known as social (or new) conservationists[55] are contending that conservation objectives should primarily serve human interests— interests that are openly or implicitly equated with conventional definitions of economic development and prosperity. On this view, conservation practice motivated by wild nature's inherent value, and by the desire to save species and ecosystems, is shunted aside. As one observer naively phrases the supremacist assumptions underlying this perspective, "conservation is about people in relation to place; it is not only about the inventory of *objects* in nature."[56]

The literature challenging traditional conservation strategies as locking people out, and as locking away sources of human livelihood, rarely tackles either the broader distribution of poverty or its root social causes; rather, strictly protected areas are scapegoated, and wild nature, once again, is targeted to take the fall for the purported betterment of people, while domination and exploitation of nature remain unchallenged. The prevailing mindset of humanity's entitlement to avail itself of the natural world without limitation is easily, if tacitly, invoked by arguments that demand that wilderness (the last safe zone for species, processes, ecologies, non-human individuals, climatic disruption, and indigenous ways) offer up its "natural resources"—in the name of justice.[57] The cause of justice, however, would be better served by opposing a dominant economic and ideological order which is constitutionally founded on the ceaseless exploitation of all nature (people included) in the pursuit of "prosperity"; a dominant order which, in the course of generating prosperity, spawns ecological impoverishment as well as both real and perceived human poverty.

As long as the reigning idea and reality of prosperity remain unchallenged, all calls for ending poverty willy-nilly echo the mainstream answer to poverty alleviation—namely, the obligation to raise all people into the consumer ranks.[58] But what counts as consumer prosperity is built on defining the living world as "natural resources," turning countless living beings (and their homes) into consumable dead objects, converting entire biomes for crops, livestock grazing, seafood, wood products, and freshwater use, and ramping up mining operations worldwide in the service of infrastructure expansion, insatiable energy consumption, and nonstop industrial and consumer product output. As environmental commentators Michael Shellenberg and Ted Nordhaus correctly, albeit approvingly, state: "The degradation of nonhuman environments has made us rich. We have become adept at transferring the wealth and diversity of nonhuman environments into human ones."[59] To remain untouchable, this prosperity-augmenting regime must perpetuate the moral invisibility of the more-than-human world, and it must obstruct from view the brutal practices, ecological ruins, as well as human indignities that prosperity's coveted goods—from meat to cell phones, from palm oil to apparel, from sushi to automobiles, from roads to electricity generation—are beholden to.[60]

Rather than dissecting the devastating consequences of global consumer society for the biosphere—and the demographic reality (current and projected) that immensely amplifies the ruination—social or new conservationists claim that protecting wild nature from human use is iniquitous. This perspective has gained traction not because it has any intrinsic merit but because it fits with—indeed perfectly echoes—a more general present-day trend: the mission to drive civilization's parasitic tentacles more deeply into the natural world as the fundamental strategy for solving humanity's self-inflicted challenges. Wherever we turn we find diverse expressions of this single strategy: whether it is the pitch for genetically modified crops to "feed the world"; the call for desalinization projects to solve freshwater shortages; the increase of aquaculture operations (fish factories) to generate "protein" for people; the manipulation of atmospheric composition to rectify climate disruption; the expansion and diversification of biofuel production to gas up the growing global car fleet; *or* the pressure to surrender remaining wilderness areas for people's economic advancement. Unifying these superficially dissimilar projects is the human imperial mission to continue manipulating, invading, and unlocking the bounty of nature as *the* means to tackle humanity's current and coming tribulations.

The civilization-as-usual mindset of always turning to use and take from nature blocks from view the more virtuous (and incidentally more effective) alternative of addressing our problems by choosing to change *who we are* and *how we live*: abandoning a conception of prosperity that is premised on colonizing the biosphere; prioritizing the humane, drastic reduction of our global numbers; embracing ecological models of food production; and envisioning bioregional ways of reinhabiting Earth as shared home, not resource satellite. Instead of entrenching the domination of nature to secure civilization's future—and today extending the reaches of exploitation into genes and cells, biosphere-scale engineering and manipulation, and the final takeover of wild places—the biocentric standpoint advocates reinventing ourselves as members of the biosphere, to borrow Aldo Leopold's classic phrasing.

Biocentrism rewrites civilization. Returning to the Stone Age is not required for making beautiful human inhabitation a reality. What is required is the will to live in reciprocity with the more-than-human world, not at its expense: the will to create a new humanity that respects nature's freedom and desires to dwell within wild Earth's unbroken, diverse, and life-abundant loveliness. "I walk in the world to love it," writes Mary Oliver. Her words speak for the human spirit rising.

Rewilding Europe

CHRISTOF SCHENCK

ONCE UPON A TIME *there was a sweet young girl. Everyone who knew her liked her, but none more so than her grandmother, who had given her a little cap made of red velvet. Because it suited her so well, the little girl wore it all the time and soon came to be known as Little Red Riding Hood. One day her mother said to her: "Come Little Red Riding Hood. Here is a piece of cake and a bottle of wine. Take them to your grandmother. Behave yourself on the way, and do not leave the path." But upon entering the woods, Little Red Riding Hood came across a wolf, and as the tale tells us, "She did not know what a wicked animal he was."*[1]

The rest of the story is well-known: The wolf told the girl to collect some flowers, then he ran to the grandmother's house and ate the grandmother, and soon after he ate the girl as well. Finally a huntsman arrived, cut open the belly of the wolf, rescued grandmother and Little Red Riding Hood (who amazingly were still alive!), and filled the belly of the wolf with stones, which finally killed the horrible creature. This fable of the wild woods and the bestial wolf has haunted the minds of children for more than three hundred years. Moreover, it reveals a deeply embedded human perception regarding the environment and world at large: Only the village is safe; any deviation from our well-trodden path will thrust us into peril and darkness. Mischief and bane are domiciled in the wilderness.

In the fifteenth century the term *wilderness—Wildnis*—appeared for the first time in the German literature.[2] Germany was settled by an estimated 10 million people, little more than one-tenth of its present population. Over 80 percent lived in small villages, hamlets, or single homesteads—small pockets of civilization in a vast wilderness. Everything had to be defended. Livestock had to be protected against the teeth and claws of a wide range of hungry predators. Large bears and wolves routinely killed valuable cows, sheep, and goats. Smaller martens and weasels readily snuck through loopholes into the henhouses. Painstakingly cultivated plantations needed constant attention in the fight against overgrowth by natural wild plants. Carnivores were called "Raubtiere," looting animals, while plants were separated into two groups—those that were economically useful and those that were pests. *Wilderness* was a synonym for remoteness, the deserted areas, the badlands, and the term was equated with waste, infertility, ugliness, desolation, uselessness.[3] It was the absence of culture, the absence of humanity. Wilderness was to be avoided. It was bad.

From wilderness to plantation

Not surprisingly, the centuries that followed saw the European landscape change dramatically: The wild woods were cut down or turned into production forests with foreign tree species; rivers were regulated; wetlands were drained. Large predators were shot and poisoned to extinction. Wilderness remained, if at all, as tiny islands in a sea of cultivated land, roads, and growing cities.

For another three hundred years, well into the eighteenth century, human population density remained low, agriculture was based on small family farms, and species diversity was still relatively high. The extensively cultivated land offered compensatory habitats for birds, insects, reptiles, and amphibians. A number of additional species emigrated from the Eastern Steppes or northern tundra, attracted by open land and the absence of natural forests. Nevertheless, ecosystems were progressively changed, natural dynamics were repressed, and large herbivores and carnivores were wiped out or restricted to small areas.

And yet, Europe had reached only the halfway point between what once had been wilderness and what would become today's industrialized landscape. In the end, small fields have been transformed into large factory farms, where the soil is treated with fertilizers and pesticides for increased profits. The contamination of water, soil, and air has reached alarming rates. Germany is now inhabited by 81.8 million people.[4] Its road network comprises over 400,000 miles,[5] and every day more than 80 hectares (198 acres) are paved for additional settlements.[6]

Green power and conserved cultivation

European industrialization and the resulting loss of countless species and wild as well as cultural lands have, however, also given rise to a strong conservation movement. A handful of big and hundreds of small conservation organizations, foundations, and societies are presently active thanks to millions of committed members and donors. The Green Party in Germany has become a political heavyweight. German conservation laws are strict, and Europe is the only place on Earth where 27 states have developed a common network for the protection of fauna, flora, and habitat.[7] Today, even the presence of rare hamsters, newts, or bats can have significant impacts on plans for new construction.

Since most wild lands, as old growth forests, marshes, or meandering streams with dynamic floodplains, were destroyed long ago, the taste of the average European tends toward cultivated lands and eye-catching species. This predilection created a European conservation specialty—the protection of cultivated lands. While most places across the globe focus their conservation efforts on protecting existing areas of natural habitat, European efforts lean toward the conservation of gardens, orchards, heath, meadows, white storks, marsh orchids, and the like. Yet millions of dollars, ironically, are invested to oppose wild growth and control nature, in an effort to keep it in a man-made, managed state that was economically meaningful decades or, in some cases, centuries ago. Hundreds of European scientific studies are published regarding the mowing and grazing of meadows, sustainable forest management, and artificial river restoration. Millions of bird boxes have been hung in trees as hardly any old-growth forest was left to provide natural nesting holes. Landscapes and species composition are designed not along the lines of evolution and natural processes but with an eye toward accommodating the whims, needs, and desires of humans.

The European conservation approach has nevertheless contributed significant achievements. It has raised awareness regarding human impact on nature, and many endangered species have survived due to a variety of protection programs, species reintroduction, and efforts to facilitate natural recovery, as well as strategies that have improved water and air quality. The return or recovery of the peregrine falcon, bearded vulture, common crane, beaver, wildcat, and lynx are examples of the success stories of modern European conservation efforts.

Biodiversity as justification for conserved cultivation

The term *biodiversity* was introduced in the late 1980s and became prominent in the 1990s. According to the 1992 Convention on Biodiversity, "biological diversity means the variability among living organisms from all sources . . . and the ecological complexes of which they are part: this includes diversity within species, between species and of ecosystems."[8] As the protection of biodiversity became an increasingly global preoccupation and was incorporated into the Millennium Development Goals,[9] the concept was also integrated into the European conservation approach. But this integration has involved a reinterpretation of the definition of biodiversity that focuses on *species* diversity only: In European biodiversity conservation, the formula is simple: The greater the number of species in a designated, often small area, the better. So a mountain pasture with flowers and insects would be valued more highly than the beech forest, which would naturally regenerate as soon as farmers or conservationists left. Thus, "biodiversity" became a new justification for active conservation management that included grazing, mowing, burning, and clearing.

This approach has a number of fundamental conceptual errors, the first being that biodiversity encompasses much more than simply the number of species in restricted areas. It implies a global scale and the overall number of species. Our planet's biodiversity cannot be increased by artificially augmenting the number of species within select areas. Cultivated land or conservation areas with artificially higher numbers of species based on intensive management in reality do not increase biodiversity at the global scale. Management and cultivation favor certain species and replace natural species compositions. There is no global net gain as a result. In fact, human activity has never contributed to the increase of global biodiversity; to the contrary, it has led to a dramatic decline.

A second problem related to the notion of artificial, man-made species compositions is that species interact with and adapt to their environments. Sumatran tigers (*Panthera tigris sumatrae*) kept in zoos for centuries, for example, will still continue to look like Sumatran tigers, but eventually they will behave differently and will become different genetically. The same will be true for the chess flower (*Fritillaria meleagris*) of Atlantic-Mediterranean origin, which was introduced into Central Europe and is now highly protected there. Change the environment and you will change the species—this principle has been known and accepted by the scientific community since Darwin's time. Human-directed conservation is changing species in the long run. This means that even in conservation areas, set aside for nature protection, humans take a lead in evolutionary processes, with limited understanding of the results.

Third, biodiversity refers to ecosystems formed through natural, not artificial, processes and interactions. So when a blooming man-made meadow, obviously rich in plant and insect species, is compared to a dark beech forest with little plant and animal diversity, the comparison is false. The right type of forest for comparison is missing; in other words, the wild woods are gone. Absent are the large tracts of ancient forests—forests where the trees are not cut but allowed to grow for hundreds of years before they enter a slow phase of decomposition, which might last another hundred years. There are no large, diverse, and dynamic forest ecosystems that have been impacted by storms, snow, fire, and other natural factors to form a natural species composition. The comparison of a man-made meadow with a man-managed forest composed of younger trees, less open space, less dead wood and, consequently, far fewer species gives us little information pertinent to biodiversity. What counts for biodiversity is the natural diversity of genes, species, and ecosystems. And all three levels are not static. They emerged from natural processes, and only by allowing the processes to continue will we be able to keep the biodiversity we inherited.

The return toward wilderness

At the outset of the new millennium, a new and groundbreaking approach in conservation thought started to develop in Europe: the return toward wilderness. Some European conservation experts started to recognize that something was missing in their fundamental approach to conservation, and they began to take the biodiversity concept more seriously. They have realized that the third component of biodiversity, diversity of ecosystems, must include inherently natural processes.

A big stimulus came from inside the national parks. There, adminis-trations started to operate in closer accord with international categories for protected areas as established by the International Union for Con-servation of Nature (IUCN), the largest global environmental organiza-tion—having nearly 11,000 voluntary scientists and experts. In defining category II (national parks), the IUCN states: "Category II protected areas are large natural or near natural areas set aside to protect large-scale eco-logical processes." Under "distinguishing features" it is mentioned: "The composition, structure and function of biodiversity should be to a great degree in a 'natural' state or have the potential to be restored to such a state." Then the 75 percent rule is added and described in the process for applying categories: "The primary objective should apply to at least three quarters of the protected area." This means that for each national park, 75 percent of its area remains hands-off to all landscapers, hunters, foresters, geo-ecologists, and land planners.[10]

Bottom-up

Established in 1970, Bavarian Forest National Park, Germany's first, pio-neered this new wilderness approach. Between the 1980s and the mid-1990s, heavy storms felled large numbers of common spruce, which were planted in the first half of the twentieth century and had displaced a dif-ferent type of natural mixed forest. The park administration and Dr. Hans Eisenmann, Bavarian State Minister for Agriculture and Forestry, decided for the first time in August 1983 to leave the dead trees in the forest. The large amount of dead wood together with a favorable climate and general increase of temperature caused by climate change led to a calamity of the bark beetle. Millions of four-millimeter-small, inconspicuous insects ulti-mately killed thousands of trees, transforming several hundreds of hectares of forest. The little beetle divided the Bavarian public into two factions—the haters and the lovers of wilderness. An acrimonious dispute took place for several years, until it became more and more clear that a new and healthier forest with even more species had sprung up in the devastated areas.[11] The goal was set and 14 additional German national parks were evaluated from that point on based upon their commitment to wilderness and the non-intervention management of at least 75 percent of their area.

The reunification of Germany in 1990, and the end of the Cold War in Europe, served as another trigger for the push for wilderness conservation. In the federal state of Brandenburg, for example, visionary conservationists found a unique opportunity to buy ex-military training areas, formerly used by the Red Army, and turned them into new wilderness areas. The preconditions were favorable for this, as military use took place only on limited areas and parts of the forests hadn't been managed for over a hundred years—allowing for forest conditions otherwise difficult to find in Central Europe. Hunting was banned, forest fires were allowed to burn unchecked, and natural dynamic processes soon started to change the appearance of the terrain. It soon became wilderness that was shaped and managed only by "the will of the land" itself.[12]

New wilderness-related NGOs emerged, such as Wild Europe, Re-Wilding Europe, the European Wilderness Society, and the Foundation for Natural Landscapes Brandenburg. Networks of landowners, for example the recently established National Nature Legacy Network in Germany, dedicated their activity toward wilderness and natural processes protection. Wilderness was promoted through campaigns like Wild Wonders of Europe, and traditional conservation organizations such as the Frankfurt Zoological Society reshaped their conservation program in Europe exclusively to support the protection of biodiversity and wilderness.

Top-down

Alongside these bottom-up processes, we also have seen the new wilderness approach begin to develop in a top-down manner. Forced by the Convention on Biodiversity, in 2007 the German government launched the National Strategy for Biodiversity with the approval of the Federal Cabinet. The change of paradigm is tucked away on page 40 in a few phrases: "By the year 2020, Mother Nature is again able to develop according to her own laws throughout at least two percent of Germany's national territory, for example in post-mining landscapes, in former military exercise zones, on watercourses, along coastlines, in peatlands and in the high altitude mountains."[13] Though hidden and concise, the statement constitutes a huge step toward a precedent-setting commitment to wilderness regeneration from one of the biggest global economies, within a densely populated country that has suppressed wilderness for centuries.

Two percent seems little, but the challenge is not an easy one, as 2 percent of the German territory equals 714,000 hectares (1.76 million acres). The Federal Agency for Conservation estimates the current wilderness area to be between 0.5 and 0.7 percent, which means that more than 400,000 hectares (roughly 1 million acres) of wilderness have to be added over the next seven years. Based on the average (small) size of German national parks, four national parks will have to be added per year,[14] and there is still strong local resistance to the establishment of new parks. In most cases, however, this opposition quickly turns to support when the parks, after a few years, begin to invite tourism and stimulate the local economy.

The EC (European Commission) Presidency Conference on Wilderness and Large Natural Habitat Areas, held in Prague in May of 2009, with 250 participants from 36 countries, raised the profile of wilderness and wild areas in Europe and recommended an agenda for the protection and restoration of such areas.[15] As Ladislav Miko, the then Minister of the Environment of the Czech Republic, said, "Europe should be proud and treasure the wilderness it still has, but it needs to do more," recognizing the fact that wilderness and wild areas, while a crucial facet of Europe's natural heritage, remarkably cover less than 1 percent of Europe's surface. Pavan Sukhdev, an economist and study leader of the Economics of Ecosystems and Biodiversity (TEEB) report noted, "We are prisoners of a system which favors manmade capital over national capital and human capital and favors private goods over public goods… that is the problem." And he adds: "Wild areas are the insurance for our future, and investing in them remains critical."[16] In February of 2009, the European Parliament passed, by an overwhelming 538 votes, a resolution calling for improved protection and funding for Europe's last wilderness areas.[17]

Why wild?

The reasons for wilderness protection were delivered along with the "Message from Prague": Wilderness and wild areas are important because of their indirect and direct economic, health, social, research, and cultural values. They have intrinsic value, are essential laboratories for research into biodiversity and natural processes, and provide gene banks for the future. They can also contribute to mitigation and adaptation to climate change, and they provide a wide range of ecosystem services. At a human level, they afford an enormous scope for spiritual inspiration and physical recreation and renewal.[18] Wilderness goes back to the fundamentals of sustainability. Sustainable development, according to the Brundtland Commission, is "development that meets the needs of the present without compromising the ability of future generations to meet their own needs."[19] Our maximum legacy in that sense is to leave as much wilderness as possible untouched. It is the most altruistic approach. It represents a commitment to speak for plants and animals without voice and vote, as well as a promise to preserve our world for the as yet voiceless, future generations of humans.

Today, wilderness is on the rise in Europe. The decreasing European population (Europe is the only continent where this is occurring), might open additional opportunities. More than a hundred wolves again roam German forests. Their population is steadily growing, and some even live close to big cities like Berlin. Today's Little Red Riding Hood could have the chance to meet a wolf again, were she to come to life more than two centuries after she appeared in the Brothers Grimm fairy tale collection. In some rare areas, she might even leave her well-trodden footpath and perhaps experience, instead of a humanized landscape, true wilderness.

And she might witness even more than that expressed in the words of the Brothers Grimm: "Little Red Riding Hood opened her eyes and saw the sunlight breaking through the trees and how the ground was covered with beautiful flowers."[20]

The British Thermopylae and the Return of the Lynx

GEORGE MONBIOT

Y GODODDIN **IS ONE OF THE FEW** surviving accounts by the Britons of what the Anglo-Saxons did to them. It tells the story of what may have been the last stand in England of the Gododdin—the tribes of the *Hen Ogledd*, or Old North—in AD 598. A force of 300 warriors—the British version of the defenders of Thermopylae—took on a far greater army of Angles at a town named in Brittonic as Catraeth: probably Catterick in Yorkshire. Like the Spartan 300, they fought for three days, during which all but four were killed.

The Anglo-Saxon conquest appears to have crushed the preceding cultures much more decisively than the later suppression of the Anglo-Saxons by the Normans. One indication is the remarkable paucity of Brittonic words in English. Even if you accept the most generous derivations, there appear to be no more than a couple of dozen, of which only four are used in daily conversation: *dad, gob, beak,* and *basket.* (If you thought "gob" was recent slang, you couldn't have been more wrong.) It was an obliteration, almost as complete as that of the Native American cultures in the United States.

The account was written by one of the four survivors, the poet Aneirin. He tells how the last warriors of the Gododdin gathered in Din Eidyn, the town we now call Edinburgh. (Several Scottish cities, including Glasgow,

Aberdeen, and Dundee, have Welsh—or, more precisely, Cumbric—names). They feasted there for a year before marching south, toward certain death in Catraeth.

In the middle of Aneirin's gory saga is something incongruous: a sad and beautiful lullaby called *Pais Dinogad* ("Dinogad's Shift"), in which a mother tells her son of his dead father's mastery of hunting.[1] It names the animals he killed. Most were easy for scholars to identify: pine marten, roe deer, boar, grouse, fox. But one animal was for many years a mystery: *llewyn*. It looks like a cognate of the modern Welsh for lion: *llew*. But what did it mean? Nothing seemed to fit, until 2006, when a bone was found in the Kinsey Cave on Giggleswick Scar,[2] 30 miles as the raven flies from Catterick or Catraeth.

Until this discovery, the lynx—a large spotted cat with tasseled ears—was presumed to have died out in Britain at least six thousand years ago, before the first sod was turned by the first farmer. But this find (and three others in Yorkshire and Scotland) drags its extinction date forward by around five thousand years. It was likely to have been familiar to Aneirin and his people.

This is not quite the last glimpse of the animal in British culture. A ninth-century stone cross from the isle of Eigg shows, alongside the deer, boar, and aurochs pursued by a mounted hunter, a speckled cat with tasseled ears.[3] Were it not for the fact that the animal's backside has succumbed to the dilapidations of time, we could have made a certain judgment, as the lynx's stubby tail is unmistakable. But even without the caudal clincher it's hard to see what else the creature could have been. The lynx might have clung on in forest remnants—perhaps in the Grampians—for another few hundred years. It was survived by the wolf, whose last certain record in Britain was the beast killed in Sutherland in 1621.[4] The lynx is now becoming the totemic animal of a movement that is transforming British environmentalism: rewilding.

Rewilding means the mass restoration of damaged ecosystems. It involves letting trees return to places that have been denuded, allowing parts of the seabed to recover from trawling and dredging, permitting rivers to flow freely again. Above all it means bringing back missing species.

One of the most arresting findings of modern ecology is that ecosystems without large predators behave in radically different ways from those that retain them. Some of them drive dynamic processes—trophic cascades—that resonate through the whole food chain, creating niches for hundreds of species that might otherwise struggle to survive. The killers turn out to be bringers of life.

Such findings present a radical challenge to British conservation, which has often selected arbitrary assemblages of plants and animals and sought, at great effort and expense, to prevent them from changing. It has tried to preserve the living world as if it were a jar of pickles, letting nothing in and nothing out, keeping nature in a state of arrested development. But ecosystems are not just collections of species; they are also the dynamic and ever-shifting relationships between them. And this dynamism often depends on large predators.

It is not just for scientific reasons that many of us now wish to bring back missing species; it is also an attempt to rekindle some of the wonder and enchantment that, in this buttoned-down land, often seems to be missing. Where farming is retreating from barren land, and where people are beginning to question why vast tracts of the uplands should be denuded by deer-stalking and grouse-shooting industries that serve only a tiny elite, there are new opportunities for change.

At sea, the potential is even greater: by protecting large areas from commercial fishing, we could once more see what Oliver Goldsmith described in 1776—vast shoals of fish being harried by fin and sperm whales, within sight of the English shore.[5] (This policy would also greatly boost catches in the surrounding seas: The fishing industry's insistence on scouring every inch of seabed, leaving no breeding reserves, could not be more damaging to its own interests.[6])

Rewilding is a rare example of positive environmentalism, in which campaigners articulate what they are *for* rather than only what they are *against*. You cannot sustain a movement only by responding to the moves of your opponents. One of the reasons why the enthusiasm for rewilding is spreading so quickly here is that it helps to create a more inspiring vision than the usual green promise: "Follow us and the world will be slightly less crap than it would otherwise have been."

Lynx present no threat to humans: There is no known instance of one preying on people. They are specialist predators of roe deer, a species which has exploded in Britain in recent decades, holding back—through their intensive browsing—attempts to reestablish forests. They will also winkle out sika deer: an exotic species which is almost impossible for humans to control as it hides in impenetrable plantations of young trees.[7] The attempt to reintroduce this predator marries well with the aim of bringing trees back to parts of our bare and barren uplands.

The lynx requires deep cover, which means that it presents little risk to sheep and other farm animals, which—as a condition of farm subsidies—are supposed to be kept out of the woods. But the real reason for choosing this species first is that lynx are magnificent. To know that Dinogad's father's quarry, the *llewyn* in Aneirin's saga, inhabits the woods through which you walk feels like the shadow that fleets between systole and diastole.

David Hetherington, Britain's leading expert on lynx, estimates that the Scottish Highlands could currently support around four hundred, which is likely to be a genetically viable population.[8] On a recent trip to the Cairngorms, I heard several conservationists suggest that lynx could be reintroduced there within twenty years. If trees return to the bare hills elsewhere in Britain, the big cats could soon follow.

There is nothing radical about these proposals—from the perspective of anywhere else in Europe. Lynx have now been reintroduced to the Jura mountains, the Alps, the Vosges in eastern France, the Harz mountains in Germany, and several other places, and they have reestablished themselves in many more. The European population has tripled since 1970, to around 10,000.[9] Like wolves, bears, beavers, boar, bison, moose, and many other species, lynx have been able to spread as farming has left the hills (where yields are very low) and people discover that it is more lucrative to protect charismatic wildlife than to kill it, as tourists will pay well for the chance to see it. Large-scale rewilding is happening almost everywhere—except Britain.

Here, attitudes are just beginning to change. Conservationists are starting to accept that the old, preservation-jar model is failing, even on its own terms. People are beginning to ask why magnificent wildlife is allowed to return everywhere else in Europe, but not here. Already projects like Trees for Life in the Highlands or the transformation of the Knepp Estate in Sussex provide a hint of what might be coming.[10] The organization I am helping to set up will seek to catalyze the rewilding of land and sea across Britain. Our aim is to reintroduce that rarest of species to British ecosystems: hope.

Letting It Be on a Continental Scale: Some Thoughts on Rewilding

JOHN DAVIS

LIKE A DULL TWO-BIT AXE, indolence cuts roughly both ways. As Americans and other modern peoples have become more and more dependent on machines—and thus lazier—some formerly cultivated areas of the overdeveloped continents have been abandoned. People have moved away from lands considered marginal for agriculture, forestry, and other extractive uses toward more fertile lands, with increasingly intensified production through modern technologies. This has harmed wild nature by increasing energy consumption and the concomitant extraction of fossil fuels, but it has also permitted large areas of the planet to grow back into native vegetation. An outstanding example is the eastern United States, where European settlers cleared most of the original forest to make way for agriculture and which is now again more than half-forested, though not yet with trees of presettlement stature and grandeur.

Unbuild it, and they will come

With returning forests come once-extirpated creatures. In some places, then, residents now face a choice of whether to let nature be—let rewilding proceed on a large scale and with it all the benefits of returning bears, wolves, otters, big cats, beavers, trout, raptors, and the like—or decry the abandonment of once-productive land and force it back into growing things for people.

In this debate, which unfortunately pits good groups against each other, such as agrarian proponents against defenders of wilderness, I stand with the wild bunch, but my hope is that the rival camps can find common ground. I believe we should miss no opportunity to give land back to wild nature, let wildlife reclaim ancient homes, honor the livelihoods of wild species whose practices—sustainable foraging, gathering, and hunting—stretch back thousands of years, since long before the rise of agriculture, and served to maintain the beneficial balance of vegetation and browsers.

Why, utilitarians may ask, let neglected farmlands regrow into forest? Why let wild nature reclaim formerly humanized landscapes?

The answer should be obvious: Because we've taken far too much. Humans have fragmented, altered, and devitalized most ecosystems on Earth, and the results include a burgeoning extinction crisis, with tens of thousands of species doomed to premature demise. Wild animals need big, wild, connected lands and waters to thrive. Many of us humans need these natural areas, too, for mental and physical well-being. Movement is as essential to animals' lives as are sun, water, food, and family; yet we modern humans have deprived our fellow denizens of most of their living and traveling spaces. Across much of the world, wildlife habitats are so diminished and fragmented by roads, dams, cities, agro-industrial fields, and other human developments that only by protecting and restoring broad corridors of natural habitat—wildways—can we stanch the loss of biological diversity. Whenever and wherever we can do this through the simple action, or inaction, of benign neglect, as with the eastern forest recovery—with relatively little active restoration needed—we should oblige gratefully.

Isolated habitats, such as those found in many countries' scatterings of small refuges and parks, do have value and the potential to meet the needs of relatively sedentary species; but small habitat remnants generally will not long afford secure homes for sensitive and wide-ranging animals like bears, otters, wolves, big cats, migratory ungulates, raptors, songbirds, butterflies, trout, salmon, whales, and seals. As human-caused climate chaos worsens, many plant species, too, will be susceptible to effects of habitat fragmentation, and some will go extinct if not given grounds and waters to move northward and upward. The solutions to isolation are *large interconnected wildlife reserves*; and the needs they meet may be summarized in five broad categories: food, sex, cover, genes, and change.

Food. Predators need to roam widely to find ample prey. Herbivores, pollinators, and frugivores need to move along with the leafing, flowering, and fruiting of plants. Many animals move seasonally to track dietary preferences. Black bears in North America, for example, wake from hibernation early in spring before much food is easily available. They may depend then on intact wetlands with succulent vegetation. In summer, bears may hunt smaller animals and scavenge carcasses of prey taken by other carnivores, and they may fish, rob bees of honey and larvae, and dig for insects (particularly ants) until berries ripen in late summer. In autumn, bears feast on acorns and beechnuts. In late autumn, bears may head up to high, dense spruce/fir forests, dining along the way on mountain-ash berries, before finding dens beneath the soon-to-be snow-covered thickets.

Sex. We all want it. Some of us must travel far to find it. Attractive mates may not be available nearby; and of course, for most animals, it is crucial to choose a mate not closely related, lest inbreeding depression occur. Commonly in carnivore species, young males light out for the territory, wandering far and wide to find a home range and mate of their own. In isolated habitats, such wild wanderers may be shot or run over before they find safe ground; and after some generations of this, the carnivore species is likely to go locally or even regionally extinct. Some of the most poignant stories in North America today involve young cougars, lynx, red wolves, gray wolves, black bears and grizzly bears, wolverines, and other wide-ranging species bravely striking out on their own. Two such recent stories offer examples of this: One tells of a young male wolverine who somehow made it safely from the wilds of the Greater Yellowstone Ecosystem south through southern Wyoming's Red Desert and into the High Rockies of Colorado, where he was still—as of my exploratory traverse of this region in summer of 2013—looking for a mate. Another story is of a young male gray wolf, named "Journey" by his fans, who has ventured through Oregon and into northern California over the last couple of years and been confirmed as the first wolf in California in many decades, but had to return to Oregon to find a mate.

Cover. Wild animals need shelter just as much as domestic animals, like us, do. Intact old forests provide snags, hollow logs, rock caverns, dense vegetation, and other structure that afford animals thermal shelter and places to hide from predators and raise young. Good cover is most generously provided in unbroken natural areas. In a typical year, moose, for instance, may seek cool and lush wetlands during summer, but in autumn after the rut, they may head up into the boreal zone, where evergreen browse is ample. Brook trout, for another example, need cool, well-oxygenated pools during the heat of summer, but they later may need to travel upstream or downstream in winter to livelier waters that won't freeze.

Genes. Again, populations need to mix genetically if they are to produce healthy individuals for the long term. Just as it would be unhealthy for a small community of people to be isolated from other communities, it is unhealthy for individuals to be limited to potential mates with whom they are related. Deleterious recessive genes then express themselves; populations slowly decline through inbreeding depression. Wolves are more genetically tolerant of intrafamilial pairings than are most animals, yet even among these gregarious canids, population health depends on some young pack members dispersing to either join other packs or start new ones.

Change. Even before humans started domesticating and polluting the planet, storms, earthquakes, volcanoes, and other natural disturbances stochastically altered environmental conditions. Change is the norm in nature, in the form of weather, succession, erosion, and other climatic, biological, and geological forces. Animals and plants may respond to changes by shifting their ranges, in part to track their optimal or preferred climate envelopes. The double whammy of industrial civilization on the natural world is that we have pushed rates of change way past those to which wild species are adapted—especially in the form of global heating—and we've fragmented landscapes so that species can no longer easily move to stick with their required environmental conditions. Even without climate chaos, humankind would be exterminating wildlife species by the thousands per year, through habitat destruction, overkill, and introduction of invasive species (which then sometimes outcompete natives). With anthropogenic climate change, extinction rates will reach catastrophic levels in the coming decades. If people do not begin reconnecting wildlife habitats, rewilding landscapes, and greatly reducing our emissions of carbon and other pollutants, we will exterminate millions of species in the space of a few generations; some projections have nearly one-third of wildlife species going extinct in the next century.

Wildlife corridors (also known as linkages or habitat connections or wildways) may be as narrow as a riparian buffer along a stream or wider than a mountain range. The safest rule about wildlife corridors is: The wider and wilder, the better. In many regions, we can make the greatest gains for wildlife (and for human-powered recreation) in the near term by protecting waterways and the lands alongside them, making the buffer of natural vegetation as wide as possible, and protecting mountain ranges, which tend to be more intact than lowlands by virtue of their ruggedness. At the same time, we should install safe wildlife crossings on major roads (again to the benefit of wildlife and people, as collisions with animals are reduced), and seek conservation easements or public acquisitions on private lands between existing public reserves.

More of the world could be rewilded within our lifetimes than you might imagine. Again, in the eastern United States, forests have returned to many places cleared for agriculture a century or more ago; and with the returning forests have come once-extirpated or once-diminished species like white-tailed deer, moose, river otter, beaver, black bear, and bobcat. In the North American East now, a top ecological priority is to help cougars, red wolves and gray wolves, bison, and elk recolonize the recovering forests and forgotten grasslands (the latter, little-known ecosystems so beautifully described by Reed Noss in his *Forgotten Grasslands of the South*).[1]

The most successfully rewilded part of the American East is, arguably, New York's Adirondack Park, where state-owned Forest Preserve lands have been protected for over a century (after wide-scale deforestation for lumber and tanneries) by the Forever Wild clause of the New York State Constitution. Farseeing conservationists and businesspeople in the late 1800s—alarmed by massive logging and subsequent fires that were damaging watersheds critical to New York's great cities—drew a protective "Blue Line" around northern New York's Adirondack Mountains and adjacent valleys. These leaders, including lawyer Louis Marshall, father of Wilderness Society cofounder Bob Marshall, declared that lands therein purchased by the state would be *forever kept as wild forest*, with no logging or commercial development allowed. Through the twentieth century, the New York State Department of Environmental Conservation purchased wildlands that went on the market; and late last century, the state established the Adirondack Park Agency to determine zoning for and partially protect the private lands (to this day, still more than half the Park) within the 6-million-acre park.

While the Adirondack Park is not a perfect conservation model (exurban and shoreline development have fragmented much more of the private land than should have been permitted), it does prove that rewilding can succeed. By most measures, the land in this exemplary public/private park is more wild today than it was a hundred years ago; and it may be the most promising landscape east of the Mississippi for recovery of the full suite of species that were here at the time of European colonization, including cougar, lynx, and wolves. The waters of the Adirondack Park, and many other half-rewilded parts of the East, however, have not fared so well, having been afforded less protection, and stocked with popular but nonnative game species. Full rewilding of the Adirondacks would mean not only healthy numbers of apex terrestrial predators but also of aquatic predators. The biggest freshwater body in the area, Lake Champlain (sixth largest in the United States after the five Great Lakes), and its tributaries in the Adirondacks and Vermont's Green Mountains, have lost most or all of their American eel, land-locked Atlantic salmon, lake sturgeon, lake trout, brook trout, and harbor seal (yes, a freshwater population persisted into the 1800s, dating back to when Lake Champlain was a sea, closely connected to the Atlantic Ocean).

Rewilding waters, sometimes more difficult than rewilding lands, may necessitate active restoration efforts. To extend the Lake Champlain example, if we wish for this lovely lake to flourish biologically again, we must remove dams on its outlet, the Richelieu River in Quebec, and on its major tributaries in Vermont and New York. We must try to fish out the many introduced species (like alewives, carp, foreign trout, and so on). We must greatly reduce phosphorus pollution (runoff from urban areas and farms, chiefly). Full restoration would probably be nearly impossible in Lake Champlain and in many other water bodies that have been commerce routes, for nonnative freshwater species and subspecies of mussels, like zebra mussels and quagga mussels, now number in the billions on lake substrates. Still, conscientious and appropriately scaled human societies could restore much of the biota of Earth's natural water bodies, provided we could: muster the political will and wisdom to remove dams, modify culverts and bridges to allow animal movement, reduce pollution, and stop introducing alien species.

Along with Appalachian and Adirondack lands, other successful rewilding stories abound in many areas where conservationists are active. The reintroduction of gray wolves to Yellowstone National Park, in Wyoming and Montana, is among the most dramatic rewilding successes. Wolves have brought some relief to riparian vegetation heavily depleted by elk browsing, especially after periods of elk population surge. Riparian forests are recovering, and with them beaver, trout, frogs, songbirds, dragonflies, and a rich array of species that do best near streams. Wolves aid grizzly bears, who are better able to scavenge carcasses left by their pack-animal neighbors than to hunt sizeable prey like elk, mule deer, or bison—with the wolves doing the heavy lifting while the grizzlies clean up after. Wolves have also reduced mesopredators like coyotes, reducing predation on the montane fox (a red fox isolated since the last Ice Age in high mountains of the West) and pronghorn fawns, thus increasing both fox population and chances of pronghorn survival. Owing to wolves, the incidence in elk of the exotic disease brucellosis has been reduced, because wolves force elk to scatter widely, thus reducing herd concentrations that otherwise might facilitate transmission of the disease from animal to animal.

Species recovery efforts constitute the beginning of rewilding, as seen with those undertaken for the bald eagle, osprey, peregrine falcon, whooping crane, alligator, black-footed ferret, and red wolf in the United States; the capercaillie, griffon vulture, wisent (European bison), and ibex in Europe; wombats and flightless birds in Australia; and many other species worldwide. Rare plants have also been successfully restored in some areas. An ambitious effort is under way in the United States to breed blight-resistant chestnut trees to eventually restore the monarch of North America's eastern deciduous forest, the American chestnut. A similarly ambitious recovery effort is under way in Europe to select for extant aurochs genes in domestic cattle, their descendants, and bring back the largest herbivore to have survived the Pleistocene overkill of the megafauna. (Elephants, rhinos, hippos, and many other huge herbivores were exterminated from Europe thousands of years ago, but aurochs persisted into the 1600s.)

Rewilding as a theme has widespread appeal as an antidote to the diminishment of wild nature wrought by humans in recent centuries. We've spent the last few hundred years wrecking nature. Let's spend the next few hundred restoring it, passively *and* actively. Read books like Dave Foreman's *Rewilding North America*, Jim Estes and John Terborgh's *Trophic Cascades*, John Terborgh and Michael Soulé's *Continental Conservation*, Reed Noss and Allen Cooperrider's *Saving Nature's Legacy*, Cristina Eisenberg's *The Carnivore Way*, Will Stoltzenberg's *Where the Wild Things Were*, Caroline Fraser's *Rewilding the World*, David Quammen's *Song of the Dodo*, E. O. Wilson's *The Diversity of Life*, and George Monbiot's *Feral*, and you learn not only why rewilding is ecologically necessary but also why it is socially and spiritually inspiring. Listen to Dave Foreman get a crowd howling for wolves, or to Harvey Locke make the true pitch for *giving Nature half*, or to Michael Soulé summon allies for a Great American Corridor along the

Rockies, or to Cristina Eisenberg poetically describe the Carnivore Way, or to George Monbiot's TED talk on Rewilding and Wonder, and you feel an exciting sense that we really can help big wild animals return!

Guided by these visionary works, especially Dave Foreman's foundational book, *Rewilding North America*,[2] and by Wildlands Network and Rewilding Institute colleagues, I undertook continental, muscle-powered treks in 2011 and 2013, first from the Florida Keys north through the Southeast Coastal Plain and Appalachians to Quebec's Gaspe Peninsula, then from Sonora, Mexico, north through the Sierra Madre and Rocky Mountains to British Columbia, Canada. In walking, pedaling, and paddling my way through the most intact parts of these continental corridors, I came to the guardedly optimistic conclusions that Eastern and Western Wildways are still possible, but they will require unprecedented levels of collaboration and cooperation among conservationists, outdoor recreationists, landowners, and everyone who cares about securing North America's great natural heritage.

In simplest terms, I concluded that in the American East, cougar recovery is the top rewilding priority; and that in the American West, gray wolf recovery is the top rewilding priority; and that all over the country, making the human-built environment more permeable to wildlife movement and more durable in the face of climate chaos is a societal imperative. By restoring, protecting, and linking enough habitat to sustain wide-ranging carnivores, we could actually rewild enough land to enable most other native species to thrive as well. Some biologists speak of the wolf, wolverine, and cougar as "umbrella species," because their habitat needs are so great that if we meet them, we cover the needs of most other species, as well.

In most areas, then, critical steps in rewilding are: protecting sufficiently large and connected habitats to allow apex predators to either return on their own or be successfully reintroduced, putting safe wildlife crossings on major roads, and dismantling dams. Lands and waters are not truly rewilded until they have their native hunters—and especially, their apex predators—back in ecologically effective populations.

In the eastern United States, enough land has regrown its natural forest cover after past clearing that an Eastern Wildway—a continental conservation corridor spanning the Southeast Coastal Plain, the Appalachian Mountains, the Adirondack Mountains, and nearby valleys—is at least a theoretical possibility within a few cougar generations. Part of what conservationists must do now to prevent any backsliding is: Dissuade officials and landowners from clearing regenerated forest or grasslands. The agri-business and energy sectors pursue these regenerating lands with an eye toward planting monocultures of corn, wheat, soy, or fast-growing trees. Left unchecked, these economic forces could denude the eastern Unit-ed States all over again and start a new Dust Bowl in the Great Plains of midwestern North America, where some areas, until recently depopulat-ing, are facing new onslaughts from energy extraction and agribusiness. Rewilding advocates need to show how much richer the East is with the recovery of forests and the return of extirpated species—like the beaver, moose, bobcat, fisher, and river otter—and how much richer still it can be with return of others—the cougar, red wolf and gray wolf, brook trout, American chestnut, American elm, butternut, wildflowers, and more.

Beside the moral and ecological imperatives for rewilding, the au-thors mentioned above share strategic reasons for embracing rewilding and for spreading its values far and wide: which reasons might best be summarized with such words as *wonder, joy,* and *beauty*. Sometimes the best way to fight bad things is to promote good things. As conservation-ists, we spend most of our time averting threats. Too seldom do we pro-mote positive, active, vibrant solutions; even less often do we engage in life-affirming work on the ground. Rewilding—ecological restoration on landscape and continental scales—affords us the opportunity to use our hands and heads to make the world wilder, lovelier, happier. It is an excit-ing vision that will inspire and draw in new advocates for the wild.

Many new advocates for the wild today are at home on a continent that some of us in the Western Hemisphere have assumed was developed beyond hope—often having written it off as the "Old World"—but which is now being showered with a reinvigorating outpouring of rewilding talk and work. Look at the website of Rewilding Europe, and you can catch a glimpse of the excitement and opportunity.[3] Networks of conservationists are exploring rewilding opportunities on marginal farmlands in France, Scotland, Western Iberia, the Carpathians, and elsewhere in Europe.

Neither Africa nor South America has ever been so badly overde-veloped as have much of Europe and the eastern United States; but even lightly developed regions of the Southern Hemisphere, degraded in many places by agricultural practices, will benefit from rewilding work.

Although much rewilding is done through government action, ex-emplary leadership by the Conservation Land Trust and Conservacion Patagonica (founded by Douglas and Kristine Tompkins) demonstrates the important role that private philanthropy can play in rewilding. Together, these wildlands philanthropists have secured more than 2 million acres, in the Alerce forest, Patagonian steppe, the Iberá wetlands, and other imperiled ecosystems. They have protected and restored such charismatic species as the huemul (south Andean deer), guanaco, puma, Geoffroy's cat, giant anteater, and marsh deer, and are working to reintroduce jaguars to the Iberá marshlands region from which the great cats had been extirpated.

Laurie Marker's Cheetah Conservation Project in Namibia is another conservation success story, pointing to additional rewilding opportunities. Cheetahs are among the African species most sensitive to persecution and habitat fragmentation; so a landscape made safe for them will be safe for most other native wildlife living there.

In North America, rewilding opportunities are especially promising in the northern Appalachian and Adirondack Mountains of the northeastern United States and southeastern Canada; on the Southeast Coastal Plain of both the Gulf of Mexico and the Atlantic; and throughout the Great Plains, particularly in eastern Montana. Additionally, without much help from us, large carnivores are rewilding parts of the Rocky Mountain Front, the Cascades, and the northern Midwest.

Give these wide-ranging predators—jaguar, puma, ocelot, gray wolf, red wolf, coyote, wolverine, otters, grizzly and black bears, eagles, trout, salmon—protection and room to roam, and they'll recolonize former habitats quickly. Indeed, the wide and rapid dispersals of these carnivores almost seem like an osmotic force at times, with individuals of the species (usually young males looking for mates and new territory) making heroic journeys of hundreds of miles. One young male cougar, for instance, dispersed from the Dakotas in 2011 and somehow got past numerous roads and towns and made it to the relatively safe, wild forests of the Adirondacks. He probably found ample food and cover there, but he found no mate, alas, so resumed his wandering, only to be hit and killed by a car in Connecticut. This theme is all too familiar, as our furred and feathered friends try to rewild old homelands but are all too often done in by cars or guns before they find new territories or mates.

WE HOMINIDS, meddlesome though we are, have the power, whether through benign neglect or as a consequence of thoughtful rewilding, to stop the extinction crisis, but doing so will require enacting conservation and engaging in cooperation on a scale we have seldom, if ever, practiced before.

We will need to protect much—probably *at least half*—of Earth's areas of terrestrial and aquatic habitats in large reserves interconnected by wildlife corridors and buffered by compatible-use zones such as agroecological farming. In North and South America, we should establish continental conservation corridors (which would be mixes of public reserves and private lands where owners are offered generous financial incentives for rewilding efforts) through the Southeast Coastal Plain, Appalachian and Adirondack Mountains, Great Plains, Rocky Mountains, the Andes, Patagonia, Pacific Coast Ranges, and Boreal Forest.

We will also need to actively restore forests and grasslands and sharply reduce our carbon emissions, to return CO_2 levels in the atmosphere to about 350 parts per million. (These conservation and restoration programs, by the way, could provide good jobs for millions of people.) In Europe, marginal lands should be allowed and helped to regrow native vegetation, and native animals—like the aurochs, wisent, ibex, wolf, lynx—should be assisted in returning. In Europe and Asia, too, the great Boreal Forest should be left intact. In Africa, we still have the opportunity to keep alive the great megafauna and their wild habitats, and this should be recognized as a global ecological and social priority.

We can and must make conservation and restoration work wildly fun, to inspire the young folks who will inherit a badly overused and fragmented world. (And elders, too, who are living longer and need meaningful work in their retirement years.) The youth of today too often rely on video games and other electronic, virtual experiences for excitement, in part because, for some, the Big Outside is now too far away and too degraded, and because, for others, with or without wilderness right outside their door, the adults they grow up shadowing turn on the Internet more often than they tune in to the "Outernet." In bringing back biodiversity and wilderness, let's bring back our ancestral traditions of plugging into Nature and tuning into the wild. Let's bring back the bison, aurochs, wolf, cougar, and lynx, the bats, eagles, songbirds, butterflies, frogs, rattlesnakes, trout, salmon, and whales with their migrating, leaping, flying, fighting, rattling, dancing, mating, singing splendor. Let wild nature *be* on a large enough scale, and we'll all live richer, more joyful lives.

Yellowstone to Yukon: Global Conservation Innovations Through the Years

HARVEY LOCKE AND KARSTEN HEUER

FOR THE LAST ONE HUNDRED AND FIFTY YEARS the Yellowstone to Yukon region of western North America has been at the forefront of conservation. For this reason it remains home to many free-flowing rivers, wild animals, beautiful national parks, and wilderness solitude. It also is home for many humans. If every region in the world were to have benefited from the same conservation actions as this rugged mountainous region there would be no global extinction crisis. Today the Yellowstone to Yukon Conservation Initiative (Y2Y) seeks to build on that legacy and carry it forward as an example of a sane relationship between humans and the rest of life. The shared vision of those leading this initiative, citizens of both Canada and the United States, is to create an interconnected system of wild lands and waters stretching from Yellowstone to Yukon, harmonizing the needs of people with those of nature. It has become a symbol of hope around the world.

Pioneering conservation

Sometime around 1850, people of European descent began to notice a new phenomenon. Through our sudden technological power and population growth we were beginning to transform the world in new and unrecognizable ways. Whereas earlier we had farms, forests, clear skies, and wild rivers, increasingly these yielded over to mines, dams, and soot-filled skies—a result of coal-burning in factories and cities. This led to the rise of the Romantic movement, one of whose basic perspectives was that the natural world is beautiful and should be appreciated in its primeval sublimity. Around the same time, Charles Darwin and Alfred Russel Wallace came to understand evolution and the essential role of natural processes in shaping nature.

Population pressures and technological advances led to the great western migration of Europeans within North America. They moved westward mostly to exploit and occupy a land that had been inhabited by people of the wilderness and fur-traders. It was called progress. But then something new happened. First, artist George Catlin expressed the original idea of a national park after a trip to the Great Plains across the wild Missouri River in 1832: After seeing the destructive path of European settlers moving inexorably westward, he asked, "Why could not the Indian, the buffalo, and their wild homeland be protected in a magnificent park? . . . A nation's Park, containing man and beast, in all the wild freshness of their nature's beauty."[1] Then an expedition sponsored by the U.S. government encountered the Yellowstone Plateau and its astonishing natural features. They developed a new view of the meaning of progress. Progress in the face of such awe-inspiring natural beauty consisted in leaving it intact for both the people of the present and for future generations to appreciate, free of industrialization. Yellowstone National Park was created by the U.S. Congress in 1872, in time to preserve all of the area's native species, including wild bison. This was a conscious act of self-restraint for the greater good. And that national park idea immediately spread around the English-speaking world.[2]

The next large national park created after Yellowstone was Rocky Mountains Park (what is now known as Banff National Park) in the Canadian Rockies. It started out small in 1887 but grew quickly. It was the third national park created in the world. It was followed soon after by Yoho and Glacier National Parks. Before the end of the nineteenth century, national parks had also been created in Australia, New Zealand, South Africa, and in other parts of the United States. In the twentieth century the idea spread around the world and now many countries have national parks. Thus the national park idea, born and raised in the Yellowstone to Yukon region, became an international phenomenon.

The Rocky Mountains of the Yellowstone to Yukon region, like the Serengeti-Mara grasslands of East Africa and the Galápagos Islands of Ecuador, enjoy a special status in the global imagination. They begin in Wyoming, where the Green River rises between the two long mountainous limbs of the Wyoming and Wind River Ranges. They extend in a northwesterly direction through Montana and Idaho, into Alberta and British Columbia, and then into the Yukon and Northwest Territories of Canada. They were shaped by the glaciers of the Wisconsin Ice Age, and to this day their climate remains cool. The remnant glaciers and deep winter snowpack makes them the source of the West's great rivers: the Colorado, the Missouri, the Columbia, the Fraser, the Saskatchewan, the Peace, the Liard, the Mackenzie, and the Yukon. Aboriginal people from adjacent prairies and forests moved in and around the mountains for hunting and spiritual pursuits, sometimes living year-round in the grassy valley bottoms. While the area supports abundant and diverse wildlife, it contains very little arable land. Instead it has deep forests. These too have led to other forms of innovative conservation.

As the Euro-American and Canadian pioneers swept westward—homesteading, clearing forests and ploughing the prairie, mining the hills and streams—the appreciation of nature reasserted itself. In 1891 the first national forest was created in the United States, to keep the land in public hands and to be managed for conservation. It was the Shoshone National Forest, established as part of the Yellowstone Timberland Reserve, adjacent to Yellowstone National Park. While what exactly "conservation" should mean on national forest lands has been debated over the last hundred years, there is no question that they are of great value to biodiversity in the United States.

With the tide of humanity came the near extinction of large mammals and birds. In the last half of the nineteenth century North Americans slaughtered the wildlife for their hides, for food, or for fun. Just in the nick of time, wildlife laws of general application were passed to prevent the disappearance of so-called game species, such as elk and pronghorn antelope. Writers began to take up as their cause the defense of all species, including animals like wolves and grizzly bears that were previously thought of as "vermin." Ernest Thompson Seton and his contemporaries coined the term *wildlife,* to replace the more utilitarian categories of "game" and "vermin." They wrote widely read books about what life is like from an animal's perspective. Acknowledging that nonhuman species by nature do not recognize national borders as they move around in search of food and mates, Canada and the United States began cooperating. They entered into treaties to protect from indiscriminate slaughter both migratory birds across the continent and marine mammals on the west coast. Civic organizations like the American Bison Society were created to protect that nearly extinct species. The honorary chairs were each country's head of state, Earl Grey, then Governor General of Canada, and Theodore Roosevelt, then president of the United States.

Once again the Yellowstone to Yukon region was at the forefront of conservation. A small but genetically vital plains bison herd was protected when Yellowstone Park was created in 1872. The National Bison Range was created by the U.S. federal government as a refuge for the conservation of bison in Montana's Flathead Valley beginning in 1908. North of the border, the government of Canada began conserving remnant wild plains bison in Banff National Park in the 1890s.

Elk range once extended from the Appalachian Mountains to the Pacific, with the elk's last stronghold being the greater Yellowstone region. When settlement and ranching took up much of the great Jackson Hole, Wyoming, elk herd's winter range, there was great die-off. American society responded by creating the National Elk Refuge in 1910. Through actions like these, ungulate populations began to rebound and later, in the second decade of the 1900s, elk from Yellowstone were reintroduced to Banff National Park.

Transboundary cooperation for conservation was pioneered in the Yellowstone to Yukon region. Alberta Waterton Lakes National Park was initially created as a forest reserve in 1895, and then it was upgraded to national park status. It lay adjacent to Glacier National Park in Montana, which was created in 1910. Rotary clubs in Alberta and Montana promoted the idea of joining the two as Waterton-Glacier International Peace Park. By act of Congress in the United States and Parliament in Canada the world's first peace park was created in 1932. The idea has since spread around the world.

But the old bias against so-called vermin continued. Even in national parks wolves were persecuted and extirpated. Pelicans were killed for eating game-bird eggs. In the lower 48, grizzly bears saw their range almost entirely confined to two national parks: Yellowstone and Glacier. Bison, though saved from extinction, were seen as competition for cattle and not allowed to run free. The landscape was denied the bison's keystone function. Bison were classified as domestic animals, which meant they had to be kept under control. They have been fenced in, even in national parks like Banff and Waterton, and they are often shot if they leave Yellowstone.

Aboriginal people have always been present in the Yellowstone to Yukon region. They too have been innovators in nature conservation. The Pablo-Allard buffalo herd that came to flourish on the unbroken grasslands of the Kootenai-Salish Reservation in Montana's Flathead Valley was key to the recovery of plains bison. Unfortunately the herd had to be sold when the Flathead Allotment Act of 1904 allowed homesteaders to buy land and break the grass there. The government of Canada bought most of the herd and shipped it to national parks in Alberta. The remnant of the herd was protected by the U.S. government in the nearby National Bison Range.

The Northern Arapaho and Shoshone Bannock people on the Wind River Indian Reservation in Wyoming worked to protect (in 1934) 188,000 acres in the Wind River Range as the first tribal area devoted to wilderness conservation on their reserve lands. Similarly, the Kootenai and Salish people created the Mission Mountains Tribal Wilderness on their reserve in 1982 to prevent logging and to protect honored species such as grizzly bears. On their lands in Idaho, the Nez Perce people were leaders in the reintroduction of wolves to the western United States. But like their wild, nonhuman relatives the bison and the bear, Aboriginal people were often victims of intolerance from the white majority.

Conservation near people

These myriad conservation actions in the southern Yellowstone to Yukon region did not occur in remote places. They took place near rail lines and where people lived in significant numbers in the landscape. They were conscious efforts to preserve wild nature. However, much of the Yellowstone to Yukon region was roadless and lay protected by its remote character even in the absence of conservation efforts.

This began to change with World War II. Great dams were built on the Columbia River system to provide electricity for an aluminum smelter and on the Bow River to provide electricity for munitions plants and to light the city of Calgary. During World War II, American soldiers carved the Alaska Highway into the remote landscape of British Columbia, an arc along and across the wild Northern Rockies of British Columbia and across the Yukon, designed to provide land access in the event of a Japanese invasion of Alaska.

Oil was found and developed on the Mackenzie River and a road built across the Mackenzie Mountains to supply the Alaska Highway with oil.

When the war was over, returning soldiers and peacetime prosperity fueled a housing boom and roads pushed into forests to give access to loggers. More dams were built. Suddenly the wilderness landscape became almost as scarce in the southern half of the region as it was elsewhere in the United States and southern Canada. In response, the wilderness movement hit its stride. In 1964 the U.S. Congress passed the Wilderness Act, a remarkable statute that could put a wilderness conservation overlay on any federal land. This law was used to legally protect several areas in the Yellowstone to Yukon region including the two biggest wilderness areas in the lower 48 states: the Selway-Bitteroot Wilderness in Central Idaho and Western Montana (nearly 1.24 million acres) and the Bob Marshall Wilderness south of Glacier National Park, Montana (950,000 acres). The province of Alberta also legally designated three small wilderness areas adjacent to Banff National Park and the Bob Marshall-sized Willmore Wilderness Park adjacent to Jasper National Park's northern boundary. In British Columbia the remote heart of the Purcell Mountain Range was protected in the Purcell Wilderness Conservancy. But the northern part of the Yellowstone to Yukon region remained essentially wild and unprotected with the exception of Nahanni National Park Reserve, which, in 1975, conserved a spectacular river corridor from hydroelectric development but protected very little wildlife habitat.

Over the years more provincial parks were added adjacent to Banff and Jasper and more formally designated wilderness areas were added adjacent to the Bob Marshall Wilderness area, Yellowstone National Park, and Selway-Bitteroot in Central Idaho and Western Montana. As a result, the southern half of the Yellowstone to Yukon region contains the world's largest complex of protected areas. These huge green islands stand out on maps of the world, draw tourists from every continent, and have been studied by park professionals around the globe.

In 1972 the Yellowstone to Yukon region set another first for conservation. When Canada and the United States joined in the World Heritage Convention, Nahanni and Yellowstone National Parks were two of the first five natural sites in the world recognized for their outstanding value to humanity. Since then the Banff-Jasper-Kootenay-Yoho park complex and Waterton-Glacier International Peace Park have also been recognized as World Heritage sites.

Conservation biology shifts the scale

The first century of conservation action anchored by parks and wilderness protection in the Yellowstone to Yukon region was a remarkable success for nature. However, the emerging science of island biogeography began to demonstrate that these protected areas, while highly effective, in isolation from each other would not be sufficient to hold onto nature indefinitely. Islands tend to lose species over time. This is because even the biggest parks protect only a portion of a viable population of wide-ranging animals like grizzly bears or wolverines. A new discipline called conservation biology emerged and developed theories about how to maintain viable populations of species over time. Radio-collar technology attached to animals by researchers began to reveal the vast international movements of individual lynx and wolves. Golden eagles and swans were found to migrate up and down the Y2Y corridor, breeding in the Northwest Territories and Yukon and wintering in the greater Yellowstone area.

Thus, as profoundly important as the parks and wilderness areas were to the well-being of nature, we learned that they would not be sufficient unless they were linked together across the landscape. This in turn required that conservation attention be paid to overcoming barriers to secure wildlife movement in relation to such obstacles as highways, towns, and rural housing subdivisions. In 1992, a North American organization called the Wildlands Project was formed to promote such thinking. In 1993, it hosted, along with the Canadian Parks and Wilderness Society, a meeting of Canadian and American scientists and conservation activists in the Canadian Rockies. They agreed that the Yellowstone to Yukon region was really one gigantic ecosystem that should be managed in a cooperative way and that society should be engaged to achieve an interconnected landscape. The Yellowstone to Yukon Conservation Initiative was born.

The Yellowstone to Yukon Conservation Initiative

The goal of the Yellowstone to Yukon Conservation Initiative is an interconnected system of wild lands and waters stretching from Yellowstone to Yukon, harmonizing the needs of people with those of nature. In the largely undeveloped and unprotected north that has meant adding new parks and wilderness areas, in other words creating the Yellowstones and Banffs of the twenty-first century. In the fragmented but still largely intact area from Jasper south to Missoula, Montana, working toward that goal has meant ensuring that public lands are stitched together across roads and private lands in a way that also meets people's needs. In the more fragmented south, centered on the Greater Yellowstone region, that has meant restoring missing species like wolves and reconnecting grizzly bear populations between there and the vast wilderness areas of Central Idaho and from there up into Canada through the Cabinet-Yaak region of western Montana and from Idaho across to the Bob Marshall Wilderness.

The Yellowstone to Yukon idea is based on two key innovations: one, the conscious creation of a community of people thinking at the continental scale about how the whole biome hangs together; and two, an organization that serves to catalyse action through the cooperation of a wide variety of players instead of trying to do everything itself, acting only where there is an unaddressed need. This nonhierarchical and collaborative approach to social change was new. It has required a lot of thinking and it had a few false starts. Even so, this vision-driven approach to shared conservation goals realized by multiple actors has made remarkable progress in twenty years.

In the wild north, the Muskwa-Kechika Management Area in northern British Columbia was created in two steps through a land use planning process in the late 1990s. Proposed by conservationists, supported by the Kaska Dena people, and agreed to by a broad cross-section of society including the oil and gas industry, it resulted in 2 million hectares (4.94 million acres) of wilderness parks and 5 million hectares (12.36 million acres) of special management zones that allow resource extraction subject to the long-term goal of wildlife and wilderness preservation. In the first decade of the twenty-first century, at the urging of the Dehcho First Nations and conservationists who engaged people from across Canada, the park protecting the vast and spectacular South Nahanni watershed has been expanded sixfold to cover 3 million hectares (7.41 million acres), making it one of the world's largest national parks. In 2012, with the support of the Sahtu Dene First Nation, the 489,500-hectare (1.2-million-acre) Nááts'ihch'oh National Park was created upstream and adjacent to Nahanni. While both the national parks in the Nahanni watershed and the Muskwa-Kechika Management Area have some imperfections that need attention, they represent giant conservation advances by any global standard. In the Yukon, prolonged efforts by First Nations and conservationists to protect a vast area of the beautiful Peel River watershed have met stiff resistance from extraction interests, but the struggle continues. Near Mile Zero of the Alaska Highway in Northern British Columbia, at the Peace River Break, which divides the wild north from the more fragmented middle region of Yellowstone to Yukon, the Site C hydroelectric dam proposal is being fought vigorously for it would be a grievous impact to connectivity of the region as a whole.

In the middle region, Banff National Park has developed the world's most extensive system of highway crossing structures for the full range of wildlife species. A monitoring system shows that over 200,000 individual species movements have occurred through the structures over and under the road to which animals are guided by a continuous fence. It is not perfect but has reduced roadkill by over 90 percent and allowed safe passage to many species including grizzly bears, wolves, lynx, wolverine, elk deer, moose, and bighorn sheep.[3] It has been emulated on Highway 93 for use by many of the same species on the Kootenai-Salish Reservation in Montana and near Pinedale, Wyoming, with a special focus on use by pronghorn antelope. Work continues to see a similar system built near Jackson Hole, Wyoming, and along Highway 3 in the Rockies of southern Canada just north of the border.

Serious efforts are under way to expand Waterton-Glacier International Peace Park into the Flathead Valley of British Columbia and to connect it up to Banff with a wildlife management area. Recent revelations that open-pit coal mining in the Elk River Valley have created a toxic load of selenium and heavy metals downstream near the U.S. border have made this work all the more urgent. On the U.S. side of the border, efforts are under way to add wilderness areas in various parts of the Flathead watershed, and road removals on the Flathead National Forest have improved conditions there. Recent legislation in British Columbia has banned oil and gas mining in the transboundary Flathead River watershed and, at the time of writing, bills in the House and Senate in the United States would do the same on Flathead National Forest, and the government of Canada has recently promised to ban coal mining on its lands in the watershed.

Private lands conservation has also moved ahead rapidly, always with willing sellers. In the United States, The Nature Conservancy's various transactions, by which it has acquired extensive valley bottom lands for connectivity from Plum Creek, have taken a giant step toward linking the Bob Marshall and Selway-Bitterroot Wilderness Areas. The Trust for Public Land's work on a private land conservation easement deal with Stimson

Lumber Company along with private lands conservation efforts by Vital Ground and Y2Y in the Yaak area of Montana have largely restored a corridor for grizzly bear movement.[4] Important parcels for connectivity have been secured on Canada's Highway 3 by Y2Y working with the Nature Conservancy of Canada (NCC) and with the Nature Trust of British Columbia. At Duck Lake, Yellowstone to Yukon Conservation Initiative and NCC have secured almost an entire corridor across private lands between the Selkirk and Purcell Mountain Ranges that is known to be used by grizzly bears, wolves, and mountain caribou. In aggregate, these strategic private land projects represent perhaps the largest coordinated acquisitions for connectivity in the world.

In the more fragmented south some important gains have been realized. The U.S. Fish and Wildlife Service, the National Park Service, and the Nez Perce tribe have achieved the restoration of a wolf population across the landscape. Wild swans steadily have been reintroduced. Old logging roads are being removed from National Forests. Significant parts of Yellowstone's northern winter range that lies outside of the park have been secured. Wild bison now range freely in Jackson Hole. The Path of the Pronghorn, by which that species migrates out of Grand Teton National Park to its winter range, has been the focus of solid conservation actions. Connectivity for grizzly bears and wolverines across the High Divide between Greater Yellowstone and the Selway-Bitteroot has been the subject of much study and is now ripe for concentrated action. Restoring this linkage is especially important in a warming world.

Yet all is far from perfect. Oil and gas drilling in the Upper Green River Basin has done great harm to that winter range in recent years. Important habitat continues to be lost to housing subdivisions. Road-building continues in some wild landscapes. And climate change has the potential to have an especially heavy impact in the most southerly reach of Yellowstone to Yukon.

Climate change is already affecting the entire region. Study after study suggests that securing large core areas with varied elevation and aspect connected across the landscape is the most effective way to help nature adapt to a warming world. The north-south orientation of the Yellowstone to Yukon landscape and the high topographic variation of the region combined with efforts to secure connectivity at the landscape scale give us some hope that the region's species may be able to adapt to this human-caused impact. Studies show that we need to protect at least half of a given region in an interconnected way in order to hold onto all its native species and processes. In the southern region of Y2Y close to half is protected so there is lot to work with. And in the wild north this underscores the urgency to make very large protected areas in places such as the Peel River watershed and upper Yukon River.

Inspiring hope for conservation around the world

The vast scale of the Yellowstone to Yukon Conservation Initiative, the iconic nature of the region, and the tangible conservation success we have been able to achieve have attracted global interest. In many ways Y2Y has become the global icon of large landscape conservation.[5] The Yellowstone to Yukon Conservation Initiative has been asked to work with people on many continents to help adapt large landscape conservation ideas to their circumstances. There is thus hope for another first: that large landscape conservation anchored on large parks and wilderness areas that work for nature and people can become the new norm, instead of a unique case; for all the world is beautiful and deserving of conservation at the scale of Yellowstone to Yukon.[6]

Yellowstone as Model for the World

GEORGE WUERTHNER

THE IDEA OF SETTING ASIDE LANDS from most commercial development and settlement started almost as an afterthought in 1872 when the United States did something extraordinary. In an age of unbridled westward expansion in the post–Civil War, and at a time when Manifest Destiny was a widely held expression of American conviction in the morality and value of expansionism, the United States Congress withdrew the Upper Yellowstone River region from commercial and private development establishing Yellowstone National Park. Nothing like that had ever been done anywhere before on such a grand scale.

Historically, hunting preserves held by royalty and sacred realms where people were forbidden to go had existed, but the idea of setting aside a large parcel of the landscape for permanent protection as a wildlands reserve—and of making that landscape available to the public, not just the private preserve of the wealthy or elite—was something new.

Yellowstone became the nation's and the world's first national park. The act of March 1, 1872, set the area apart as a "pleasuring ground for the benefit and enjoyment of the people," and at the same time required "the preservation, from injury or spoliation of all timber, mineral deposits, natural curiosities or wonders within said park and their retention in their natural condition."[1]

The creation of Yellowstone National Park set a new standard for land management where preservation, rather than exploitation, of nature became the guiding philosophy. It is an idea that has been emulated by more than a hundred countries around the world.[2] Indeed, its creation story and ongoing history is a reflection of the issues that conservationists have faced in the formation and management of nearly all national parks.

In a sense, the history of Yellowstone is the history of every park everywhere. It is not difficult to see the profound effect that the creation of Yellowstone National Park had on the world's thinking about wildlands, and conservation strategy. Yellowstone has been at the forefront of conservation efforts since its very inception.

It is the first place where an endangered animal was saved (bison). One of the first places where another species was restored (wolf). It was the first place in the United States and perhaps the world that ended predator control. It was one of the first places where naturally occurring wildfires were restored. It was the first place where ranger-led interpretative talks and walks were implemented. It was one of the first places to implement catch-and-release fishing. It was the first place where the concept of a "greater ecosystem" came into popular support. And it is now the anchor for an even more ambitious plan to link a series of protected parklands from the Yukon to Yellowstone. Yellowstone has remained a philosophical model of how to preserve natural processes by minimizing resource exploitation and internalizing self-restraint.[3]

Critique of the Yellowstone model

Some critics deplore the fact that the so-called Yellowstone model is widely adopted around the globe, suggesting that it is yet another form of "imperialism" or "colonialism."[4] Such an argument falls flat, however, when one considers that human culture has always borrowed and adopted good ideas from many places. The Greeks invented participatory democracy that has been widely adopted around the globe, and no one decries the widespread adoption of democracy as a valid and desirable form of political discourse just because the Greeks were the first to initiate the concept. Good ideas are always emulated and transferred from culture to culture.

One can find fault with democracy, but as is often pointed out, it is better than any other form of political enterprise. Similarly, while one can poke jabs at the Yellowstone model, the reason it is widely adopted is because it works better than any other form of conservation.

It works so well that the park was declared an International Biosphere Reserve in 1976 and a World Heritage Site in 1978.[5]

Locals almost always oppose parks

The park's creation was a radical idea at a time when the majority of the public domain within the United States was open to hunting, trapping, homesteading, mining, logging, farming, ranching, and other exploitation.

Indeed, there was much local opposition to removing any land from potential exploitation and settlement. Upon learning of the creation of Yellowstone National Park, the *Helena Gazette* in Montana opined: "We regard the passage of the act as a great blow to the prosperity of the towns of Bozeman and Virginia City."[6]

Local opposition to new conservation designation is nothing new or unique. By definition, creation of a park or other reserve means restrictions on human activities that previously were permitted or tolerated. However, that should never be a reason to avoid advocacy for new parks and wildlands. Subsequent generations nearly always are thankful that earlier citizens have set aside lands for protection.

In the years following its establishment, Yellowstone's naysayers introduced a number of bills into Congress to reduce the park size or completely dismantle it. When these attempts to dissolve Yellowstone National Park failed, park opponents tried other mechanisms to eliminate the park, including an attempt to split off the northern part of the park so a railroad could be built. To justify removing this area from the park, Montana's delegate characterized the Lamar Valley as "wholly unattractive country," hence not worthy of park protection. Today the Lamar Valley is one of the most popular attractions due to the easily observed wildlife found there. Others proposed damming the Yellowstone River just below Yellowstone Lake for hydroelectric power. This too was prevented, but only by the intervention of dreaded "outsiders" from the eastern United States.

To appreciate how contrary to ongoing government policy the establishment of Yellowstone National Park was, keep in mind that in the post–Civil War era it was the general policy of the United States government to encourage western development and American occupation. The 1864 Homestead Act encouraged settlement of the frontier by giving free land to anyone who would farm and develop vacant government territory. At the same time the U.S. government, through its railroad land grants legislation, bestowed more than 185 million acres of land upon railroads as an incentive to build transcontinental tracks across the country. Add to these laws other prodevelopment legislation, like the Mining Law of 1872 that encouraged mining claims and the 1878 Timber and Stone Act designed to assist lumber companies through the sale of western forestlands, and it is easy to understand how contrary it was to national policy in that era to create a national park off-limits to privatization and development.

Human-free zones?

Some critics of nature reserves suggest that park advocates consciously created the idea of human-free wilderness to facilitate the removal of indigenous peoples. A number of interpretations of Yellowstone's early history suggest that the settlement of Native Americans on reservations was advocated by park advocates as a ploy to create the illusion that parks were vacant lands with no human historical use.[7]

That is a strawman designed to sully the idea of parks, not to mention that, in most instances, it is simply not true. The tribal people who lived near or traveled through what is now Yellowstone National Park were resettled on reservations *before* the park was created as part of national Indian policy to set the stage for America's rapid western expansion, not park creation.

As early as 1851 with the signing of the Fort Laramie Treaty, various tribes inhabiting the lands surrounding Yellowstone were being assigned to reservations. For instance, the Crow tribe was given a reservation centered on the Upper Yellowstone near what is now Livingston, Montana, downstream from present-day Yellowstone National Park. In 1855, other tribes of the region like the Flathead Indians agreed to a reservation north of present-day Missoula, Montana. In the same year, the Blackfeet Indians signed a treaty and agreed to reside on a reservation east of present-day Glacier National Park.

By 1868, four years before anyone had voiced support for setting aside Yellowstone as a park or other reserve, the tribes most immediately associated with the Yellowstone country were settled on reservations. The eastern Shoshone Indians and northern Arapahos settled on the Wind River Reservation in Wyoming, and the Crow Reservation was shrunk and shifted eastward to the lower Yellowstone in Montana. The "Sheepeater" Indians, an isolated band of the Shoshone tribe who inhabited the mountains surrounding Yellowstone, joined their brethren on the Wind River Reservation by 1871.[8]

Though the designation of reservations was supposed to eliminate conflict between Indians and whites, not all relationships went smoothly. Often there was bloody resistance to these policies. Some have suggested that 300 Shoshone Indians were slaughtered by a U.S. Army to clear the way for Yellowstone National Park creation. However, the only major conflict with the Shoshone tribe anywhere close to Yellowstone occurred in 1863 near Bear Lake on the Utah-Idaho border. The Shoshone were killed in retaliation for the theft of some cattle and in response to several earlier conflicts where white settlers had been killed (never mind the Indians were starving due to appropriation of their territory).[9]

As with many other conflicts around the West, this event had nothing to do with park creation. Bear River is several hundred miles from Yellowstone, and the massacre occurred nearly a decade before anyone even suggested there should be a park.

Events like the Bear River Massacre convinced many of the remaining tribes that settlement on reservations was preferable to war with the far superior U.S. Army forces.

There were additional skirmishes between whites and Native Americans that took place in the Yellowstone region for years afterward, but none of these battles were designed to create the illusion of human-free wilderness as some suggest. General George Custer and his men were killed in 1876 by Sioux warriors on the Little Big Horn River, a tributary of the Yellowstone not more than a few hundred miles from what is now Yellowstone National Park. The following year, in 1877, a band of Nez Perce Indians led by Chief Joseph passed through Yellowstone in a failed attempt to evade the U.S. Army while fleeing Idaho en route to Canada. But the Nez Perce were not "driven" from the park to make it a human-free wilderness; rather, the Nez Perce were merely traveling through the park to evade the military units that were in hot pursuit.

Similar reserves for tribal people in the more remote parts of the Amazon Basin and in parts of Africa, Australia, and Asia continue to this day, and few in fact are established to depopulate the land for park creation. Rather as with the American West, these reserves are designed to assimilate tribal people into the larger culture, and to free up land for resource exploitation.

Like the Yellowstone experience, the settlement of indigenous peoples on reserved lands or the movement to villages or towns to take advantage of schools and jobs has resulted in a de facto depopulating of some areas. But this population shift typically has little to do with the forced removal of people explicitly for park creation. We see the same demographic shift occurring in many parts of the world, such as the Great Plains where population decline has been occurring for decades as residents migrate from rural areas toward jobs and big city lights beyond their primary region.

Far more people have been removed from their homes for reasons related to resource development than for nature reserves. We regularly remove people of all backgrounds to make way for mines, oil fields, logging, highways, transmission lines, or hydroelectric dams. The Three Gorges Dam in China, for instance, displaced more than a million people living in 13 cities, 140 towns, and 1,350 villages.[10]

The human influence

Others suggest that the Yellowstone model excludes the influence of indigenous peoples from the land, suggesting that humans are part of nature too. Certainly human presence can be shown to have affected wildlife and plant communities. Humans-as-predators no doubt had an influence upon big game numbers, just as other top predators do today, such as wolves, lions, hyenas, and cougar (puma). And in some plant communities, regular burning set by human ignition favored certain plants over others and changed the structure of plant associations.

But many who champion the human influence apply this universally and fail to understand that human manipulation and impact was generally local and had distinct geographical limits. For instance, in Yellowstone National Park, most of the landscape is high-elevation forest of lodgepole pine and subalpine fir. These forests do not burn and cannot burn in most years because they are more or less fireproof due to climatic conditions. It takes extensive drought combined with low humidity and high winds to burn these forests. Fire ecologists often joke about these being "asbestos" forests due to their general inflammability.[11] As a consequence, though Native Americans may have regularly camped, traveled, and hunted on the Yellowstone Plateau, it is doubtful that they significantly altered the fire regime due to the inherent resistance to fire found in these forests.[12]

Similarly, in the days before the advent of the horse, hunting large game animals was difficult. Except for special circumstances like bison jumps (driving animals over cliffs) as they crossed the Great Plains, spearing caribou as they swam Arctic rivers, catching salmon as they darted over falls on rivers, and other methods, mass killing of large game and fish was impossible. Furthermore, if you must carry a bison carcass back to camp on your back or with the help of dogs, you are not going to hunt far from your home location. Therefore, there were huge areas where little or no hunting occurred, providing refuge from human predation. And because of the ecological demands of humans for wood, water, and other resources, many areas of the landscape were simply unusable for large human groupings.

Groups did hunt Yellowstone; in particular, the Sheepeater Indians used dogs to corral and trap bighorn sheep on cliffs where they could then shoot them with arrows, but again the locations where such methods worked are geographically limited. The influence of humans as predators and their effect upon game populations was not uniform in either time or space.

But this fails to recognize two truisms.

Given the limited technology and low population density of their time, indigenous peoples' ecological footprint was relatively modest in comparison to the footprint of today's industrial culture. Though native people were perfectly capable of wiping out species on small islands and in other unusual circumstances, in general their influence of the landscape and wildlife was minor.

That, however, is not true today. Even the most isolated indigenous peoples now rely on technological innovations to some degree, which increases their ecological footprint well beyond historic conditions. The acquisition by indigenous peoples of rifles, trucks, motorboats or snowmobiles, chain saws, axes, and even something as simple as a metal knife, not to mention modern medicine that has increased survival rates, increases greatly the potential human footprint, posing threats to native plants and wildlife.

As we humans have occupied more of the world, and as we've come to commandeer even more of the globe's resources, it has become clear there is both an ethical and scientific justification for creating, supporting, and enlarging parks and protected areas. Just as speed limits are necessary to avoid chaos and harm when people adopted modern transportation methods, parks and reserves are needed to curtail the unbridled human species as it colonizes and appropriates much of the global Net Primary Productivity.

Yellowstone's real value—wildlife preserve

The original legislation establishing Yellowstone National Park's borders was rather arbitrary with the U.S. Congress imposing a square boundary upon the Yellowstone Plateau designed to encompass most of the major geothermal features in the park. The primary purpose of the Yellowstone legislation was to protect "natural wonders" like Old Faithful, the biggest regularly erupting geyser in Yellowstone, and other geological features. In this regard the park has lived up to its original goals—conservatively, Yellowstone contains about 10,000 thermal features including more than half of the world's geysers.

Yet within a short decade after the park's establishment in 1872, it became clear that perhaps the greater value of Yellowstone was as a sanctuary for wildlife and natural processes. When Yellowstone was created by congressional action, most of the surrounding land was part of Montana and Wyoming territories—the states did not yet exist. In fact, other than a few trapper brigades in the 1820s and 1830s, as well a number of prospectors bent on discovering the next El Dorado in the 1860s, much of the Yellowstone country remained largely a mystery to non-Indians.

Because the high elevation discouraged settlement and its geology did not favor gold or other mineralization, there was little interest in the region. One civilian expedition known as the Cook-Folsom expedition explored Yellowstone in the summer of 1869. But the scenic wonders were so beyond the imagined or known realities to date that when one of the expedition members attempted to publish an article on their experiences, the manuscript was rejected by a national magazine because they claimed they did not publish fiction.

Two additional exploratory expeditions, the Washburn in 1870 and Hayden in 1871, documented the major geological features of what would soon be Yellowstone National Park. Members of the Hayden expedition, in particular, had political connections in Washington, D.C., and other influential eastern cities, and they brought national attention to the region's special features. Their lobbying efforts convinced Congress to set aside the area as a national preserve.

Establishment of the park was just in the nick of time. Rapid changes were closing in on the Yellowstone country. Gold was discovered: in Emigrant Gulch, a tributary of the Yellowstone River, just 30 miles north of the future park boundaries, in 1864; in Bear Creek near Gardiner, in 1867; and at the headwaters of Soda Butte Creek, near present-day Cooke City, Montana, in 1870. Indeed these last two gold discoveries defined the north and northeast boundaries of the park.

As these and other developments started closing in on what would become Yellowstone National Park, it became clear that Yellowstone's value was at least as significant for wildlife as it was to protect the geological wonders that inspired the park's creation. Like many new national parks in developing countries today, Yellowstone was more a park on paper than in reality. When Congress first set aside the park, there were no funds to sustain a staff or operate any facilities. Yellowstone was the "wild West" where anything goes, and did. Market hunting for the park's wildlife was not only legal but popular.

In 1875, Captain William Ludlow with the U.S. Army led another military expedition to the park and reported widespread slaughter of wildlife, particularly of elk. Philetus Norris, the first superintendent of the park, traveling through Yellowstone that same summer, wrote that he witnessed more than 3,000 elk slain in the park.[13] Another visitor, General William Strong, in the same year also reported that nearly 4,000 elk had been killed in or near Yellowstone for their hides (worth $6 to $8 a piece).[14] Just as poachers today kill elephants for their tusks or snow leopards for their hides, local people in the late 1800s readily exploited wildlife for money. And, as in many poorer countries today, there were no rangers to patrol the new park.

Because of this ongoing slaughter of wildlife, voices were raised to make Yellowstone a wildlife preserve—and just in time. By the year 1900, elk were nearly extirpated from most of the West and persisted only in a few places like Yellowstone National Park. Again, this is not unlike the situation today in other parts of the world, where national parks remain critical as the last stand for many wildlife species. Indeed, Yellowstone became the source for transplants that established many of the elk herds in the American West.

Like so many other firsts associated with Yellowstone, the park was the first place in the world where large charismatic megafauna, the American bison, was saved from extinction. Bison, which some estimate numbered in the tens of millions, were slaughtered for their hides, first by Native Americans armed with rifles and horses, then later by market hunters, until one of the last remaining wild herds resided in Yellowstone. Attempting to preserve this vestige of wild bison against poachers became one of the prime goals of the newly established park, just as parks in other parts of the globe today protect some of the last Russian tigers, snow leopards, black rhinos, and other endangered megafauna.

At a time when bison were threatened with potential extinction, even elk were overhunted both inside and outside of the park.

Although no one even knew anything about genetics when Yellowstone bison were saved from extinction, today protection of the "wild" genome is recognized as yet one more value of Yellowstone's establishment. Unlike most other domesticated bison herds around the West, Yellowstone's bison are one of only a handful of bison herds with the original wild genome (most bison have some cattle genes in their genetic code).

Yet within a decade of the park's designation, it was apparent that Yellowstone's boundaries were insufficient to protect the wildlife that was increasingly under duress outside of the park. Slaughter for hides and market trade decimated bison herds. Destroying the bison herds was seen as desirable public policy as a way to reduce resistance from Plains Indians by eliminating their food supply. By 1874, just two years after Yellowstone's establishment, a bill was introduced into Congress to stop the slaughter of bison, but President Grant pocket vetoed the bill agreeing with his military strategists who argued that extirpation of the bison would reduce the resistance of the plains tribes.

After a visit to Yellowstone in 1882, General Phil Sheridan, appalled by the market hunting that was decimating Yellowstone's wildlife, recommended that Congress expand the park 40 miles to the east and 10 miles further to the south to protect the migration routes of elk that summered in the park's high country. Sheridan's recommendation languished for nearly a decade due to local opposition, but in 1891, President Benjamin Harrison proclaimed a 6-million-acre area east of the park as the Yellowstone Forest Reserve, what was to become the first national forest, followed six years later with the Teton Forest Reserve to the south of the park.[15]

But like most national parks, Yellowstone was a political creation, not based on sound conservation science, and at least at first, inadequately staffed and funded. The first superintendent, Nathaniel Landford, did not even have a salary and had no staff. Eventually, in 1886, administration for the park was transferred to the War Department, and the U.S. Army was brought in to patrol the park, protect the wildlife from poachers, and build a rudimentary infrastructure of roads and ranger stations. It was not until 1916 that a professional core of park administration was created when Congress created the National Park Service to manage and oversee the nation's growing collection of national park units. Just as Yellowstone faced during its early years, many national parks established today face similar conflicts with poachers, and sometimes they respond with armed rangers to protect wildlife.

Spare the vandalism of improvement

For decades private interests worked to open the park to business interests, always arguing that the public experience would be improved with greater development. However, by 1886 park supporters in Congress had won the political debate that parks require "retention in their natural condition" as originally envisioned by the 1872 legislation. The idea that Yellowstone should be managed to maintain natural conditions was yet another philosophical transition that has defined national parks everywhere. A congressional committee reported to Congress expressed this position by concluding: "The park should so far as possible be spared the vandalism of improvement. Its great and only charms are in the display of wonderful sources of nature, the ever varying beauty of the rugged landscape, and the sublimity of the scenery. Art can not embellish these."[16]

Yellowstone initially suffered the same fate as many newer national parks do today. At first it was largely a protected area only in name—a problem repeated throughout the world where "paper parks" exist on maps but have little actual protection on the ground.

Market hunters freely accessed the park, killing elk, bighorn, and bison. Tourists came and dismantled or damaged thermal features. Hucksters set up camps claiming ownership of the land. Despite a goal of protecting park wildlife, bias against predators still dominated the early park administration's agenda, and wolves, mountain lions, and coyotes were killed regularly. At the same time, natural ecological processes like wildfires were suppressed and unsavory practices like feeding bears for public display were condoned.

But attitudes and ideas about management changed over time. By the 1930s the biologist Adolph Murie was questioning national park predator policies, calling for the protection of coyotes, bears, and cougars rather than killing them.[17] Viewing predators as equally important to park natural landscapes as elk, bison, or bighorns soon was emulated in other national parks. Today, around the world, most park areas at least tolerate predators and some parks are established to specifically protect predators like snow leopards, tigers, wolves, and jaguars. But this change in attitude about predators had its origins in Yellowstone.

By the 1950s and 1960s, due to killing of large predators like wolves, elk numbers in Yellowstone had grown to the point where some suggested elk were having a negative impact on woody vegetation like aspen and willows (much as some suggest elephants are doing in African parks). In response, the National Park Service initiated an elk culling program, using rangers to kill thousands of elk. The spectacle of elk being slaughtered in a presumed sanctuary created a public outcry and backlash.

The National Park Service then commissioned an outside review committee to oversee and advise the Park Service on not only its elk management but its overall mission and policies. The committee was chaired by the eminent ecologist, A. Starker Leopold, son of the late conservationist and ecologist Aldo Leopold. The Leopold Report, as it came to be known, recommended among other things that the goal of national parks should be restoring natural processes to the greatest degree possible.[18]

Among the more notable lines in the report was the affirmation that: "As a primary goal, we would recommend that the biotic associations within each park be maintained, or where necessary recreated, as nearly as possible in the condition that prevailed when the area was first visited by the white man. A national park should represent a vignette of primitive America."

The Leopold Report noted that such a benchmark is both difficult and elusive; in many parks some species are extinct, there is natural variation in species composition due to climatic change, or invasion by nonnative species has altered the natural regime. It was the pursuit of this ideal that was important even if it could not be fully realized. The committee concluded: "Yet, if the goal cannot be fully achieved it can be approached. A reasonable illusion of primitive America could be recreated, using the utmost in skill, judgment, and ecologic sensitivity. This in our opinion should be the objective of every national park and monument."

The Leopold Report had a profound effect upon Yellowstone's management as well as national parks around the globe. Wildfires, which previously had been suppressed in Yellowstone as well as other national parks, were now welcomed as a natural ecological process. In Grand Canyon National Park, where natural flood regimes on the Colorado River were destroyed by upstream dams, restoration of periodic high water floods to emulate the natural water flows were reestablished. In Olympic National Park, several dams on the Elwha River are in the process of being removed to restore salmon runs and natural hydrological processes. In Everglades National Park, natural water flows are being restored by removal of dikes and canals and restitution of upstream wetlands. And recognizing the importance of top predators for ecosystem health, instead of rangers shooting elk to reduce populations, wolves were reintroduced to Yellowstone and Grand Teton National Parks to achieve the same goals, but through selection by native predators.

Yellowstone is also one of the first freshwater wildlands reserves established, setting the stage for the later creation of global marine reserves. Commercial fishing in the park was banned early on (originally guests were treated to trout caught in park waters). Over time, even sport fishing was limited, with catch-and-release fishing implemented for most park waters. And slot size limits were put into place, effectively protecting the largest fish.[19]

Just as with marine reserves now being designated in oceanic waters, the banning of commercial fishing and placing limits on sport fishing had a profound effect upon the park's fisheries. Spawning runs of trout increased dramatically and were utilized by many other park species from grizzly bears to bald eagles. Otters, loons, white pelicans, minks, and even wolves have enjoyed the bountiful fish populations that serve as an important part of the food chain. (Unfortunately, the introduction of nonnative lake trout into Yellowstone Lake has led to a profound decline in native cutthroat trout, which lake trout prey upon.)

Greater ecosystem

Given that parks cannot often by themselves sustain biodiversity, Yellowstone acts as the centerpiece of the Greater Yellowstone Ecosystem (GYE), a 28-million-acre landscape consisting of Yellowstone National Park, adjacent Grand Teton National Park, plus other surrounding federal lands including national forest wilderness, national wildlife refuges, and Bureau of Land Management lands. The recognition of the Greater Yellowstone Ecosystem has led to greater coordination of land management agencies to achieve protection of the whole landscape.[20]

Together these public lands form the vital heart of the much more ambitious Yellowstone to Yukon initiative that seeks to link up protected lands along the spine of the Rockies from the Alaskan border to the GYE in Wyoming.[21]

Yellowstone continues to stand at the forefront of global conservation. As the world's first park, it continues to inspire people around the world. A country's true wealth is not what it can develop and consume, but the degree to which it can preserve its natural heritage. In that regard Yellowstone is the gold standard by which the world's conservation efforts are measured.

Rewilding Our Hearts: Making a Personal Commitment to Animals and Their Homes

MARC BEKOFF

IT IS COMMON KNOWLEDGE that we are losing species and habitats at an unprecedented rate in a geological epoch some are calling the Anthropocene, "the age of humanity." We are deep into a time when humans are devastating numerous species and their homes and behaving in heartless and selfish ways. The age of humanity is anything but humane.

Simply put, we humans are the major cause of such massive and egregious ecocide because—as big-brained, big-footed, overproducing, overconsuming, arrogant, and selfish mammals—we freely move all over the place recklessly, wantonly, and mindlessly trumping the interests of countless nonhuman animals (animals). There are too many of us. No one truly knows how many of the changes we have wrought are irreversible. But if we don't change our ways, we will certainly only continue along our self-destructive path. Ecocide is suicide.

Every second of every day we decide who lives and who dies; we are *that* powerful. Of course, we also do many wonderful things for our magnificent planet and its fascinating inhabitants, but right now, rather than patting ourselves on the back for all the good things we do, we need to take action to right the many wrongs before it is too late for other animals and ourselves. We need to keep the wild *wild*. Protected areas and wilderness are the foundation for conservation; in order to make sure we preserve whatever wilderness remains, we need to respect not only the land on which we and other animals live but also the animals themselves. Our interests should not and must not always trump theirs.

I see at least two ways to begin digging out of the environmental and moral muck in which we have become mired. The first centers on paying careful attention to the international and interdisciplinary field called "compassionate conservation,"[1] and the second is choosing to go through a personally transformative process that I call "rewilding our hearts."[2] Rewilding our hearts calls for a social revolution based on a personal commitment to change how we interact with other animals, with other humans, and with the land on which they live. It mandates a global paradigm shift on a deeply personal level.

Compassionate conservation: *The lives of* individual *animals matter*

I have been studying nonhuman animals all my life. As a child, I sensed that other animals had emotions and awareness, and much of my career as a scientist has been devoted to discovering *if this was true* (it is), and then *how* and *in what ways*. Among researchers and scientists today, there is no longer much debate over the fact that many animals are emotional, intelligent, and sentient beings. This paradigm shift has been extremely gratifying to witness, and I'm proud to have played a role in it.

The goals of compassionate conservation are clearly stated in the mission statement for the Centre for Compassionate Conservation at the University of Technology, Sydney (Australia),[3] and in *Rewilding Our Hearts: Building Pathways of Compassion and Coexistence,* my most recent book.[4] The mission statement for the Centre for Compassionate Conservation promotes the protection of captive and wild animals as *individuals* within conservation practice and policy. Finding ways to both compassionately and practically share space (coexistence), via trade-offs among different values, is vital if we are to reduce harm to animals.

A simple and morally acceptable approach is to utilize the universal ethic of compassion (and empathy) to alleviate suffering in humans and other animals as well as to resolve issues of land sharing. A compassionate and practical ethic for conservation that focuses on individual well-being, in combination with other values, provides a novel framework of transparency and robust decision making for conservation that will benefit all stakeholders.

Compassionate conservation stipulates that we need a conservation ethic that prioritizes the protection of other animals as individuals: not just as members of populations of species but as beings valued in their own right. This is important because of what we now know about their consciousness and sentience. Compassionate conservation requires that we must protect animals as individuals—they are not merely "objects" or "metrics" to be traded off for the good of populations, species, or biodiversity.

A paradigm shift in our approach to other animals is vital because of what we have come to understand about their cognitive and emotional capacities and their ability to suffer and experience joy (sentience).[5] With a guiding principle of "first do no harm,"[6] compassionate conservation offers a bold, virtuous, inclusive, and forward-looking framework that provides a meeting place for different perspectives and agendas to address issues of human-animal conflict when sharing space. Peaceful coexistence with other animals and their homes is needed in an increasingly human-dominated world if we are to preserve and conserve nature as best we can.

Surely, adhering to the principles of compassionate conservation will go a long way toward reducing the ecocide in which we are now engaged and for which we all are responsible.

Rewilding our hearts and minding animals

In *Rewilding Our Hearts,* I lay out the details for a much-needed social movement and paradigm shift that can help extricate us from our destructive ways and help us to maintain our hopes and dreams for a more peaceful world for all beings in very trying times. We live in a world in which "unwilding" is the norm rather than the exception. If we did not *un*wild we wouldn't have to *re*wild.

The concept of rewilding is grounded in the premise that caring is okay. In fact, it is more than okay; it is essential. It is all right to imagine the perspective of nonhuman animals in order to take their well-being into account. People who care about animals and nature are often made to feel they must apologize for their views. They are disparaged for "romanticizing" animals or being sentimental, and they can be portrayed as "the radicals" or "the bad guys" who are trying to impede "human progress." This book takes a hard look at that progress, and it proposes that by fighting better for and caring better for animals, we will also be fighting better for and caring better for humanity. When I was in Sydney, Australia, in February of 2013, I had a stimulating talk with environmental scientist and writer Haydn Washington. After I mentioned that I was sick and tired of people who cared about animals having to apologize for their compassion and empathy, he said something that really moved me: "People should not have to apologize for their sense of wonder." Amen.

Rewilding our hearts is about becoming re-enchanted with nature. It is about nurturing our sense of wonder. Rewilding is about being kind, compassionate, and empathic and harnessing our inborn goodness and optimism. In the most basic sense, *rewilding* means "to make wilder" or "to make wild once again." This means many things, but primarily it means opening our hearts and minds to others. It means thinking of others and allowing their needs and perspectives to influence our own.

We are the re-generation. Over the past few years I have come to see that we are always "*re*-ing" one thing or another. Rewilding in the real world requires us to try to *re*store and *re*create ecosystems by, for example, reintroducing or repatriating animals into areas where they once lived. But since we really cannot recreate or restore ecosystems "to what they were," it has been suggested that we *re*build rather than *re*wind as we move into the future. Rebuilding surely is part of the process of rewilding.

We also talk about the need to rekindle, rebalance, refine, reconnect, reenvision, reintegrate, reimmerse, reeducate, rehabilitate, rethink, and reshape our relationships with other nature. Many of these efforts are reactions to environmental and ecological problems we can no longer ignore, but being strictly reactive—the "putting out the fire" mentality—does not work. As we rewild our hearts, there is an urgent need to be proactive. Instead of looking to the past as a guide, we have to envision the positive future we want and actively work toward it.

A long time ago I developed the notion of "minding animals."[7] I still like this phrase and use it in two main ways. First, "minding animals" refers to caring for nonhuman animals, respecting them for who they are, appreciating their own worldviews, and wondering what and how they are feeling and why. We mind animals when we try as hard as we can to imagine their point of view. But the phrase also acknowledges and honors the well-established fact that many animals have very active and thoughtful minds. We may never know everything that nonhuman animals think and feel, but we do know that they see and react to the world with awareness and emotion.

In the same way, we can also "mind Earth." We must care for her and appreciate, respect, protect, and love her. To do this, we must imagine the Earth's perspective, which is to say, the collective perspective and well-being of all her inhabitants. In the end, we are "all one." All beings and all landscapes connect and interact in reciprocal ways. This is a social and ecological truth. What happens in my hometown of Boulder, Colorado, influences and is influenced by what happens outside of Chengdu, China, where I go to work in the Animals Asia moon bear rescue center.[8] Minding animals and minding Earth in this way increases our wisdom. It helps us not by accumulating more objective "facts" but by guiding us to make wiser choices about our actions in the world. Wisdom recognizes that our actions always impact others—even others whom we don't currently realize or see, that we always make choices in how to live, and that there are better and worse decisions having vastly different impacts. As Pat Shipman says, it is imperative that we make decisions today with global impacts in mind.[9]

When I mind animals in this way, I practice what I consider "deep ethology." That is, as the "see-*er*," I try to become the "seen." When I watch coyotes, I become coyote. When I watch penguins, I become penguin. I will also try to become tree and even rock. I name my animal friends and try to step into their worlds to discover what it might be like to be a given individual—how they sense their surroundings, how they move about, and how they behave in myriad situations. This isn't just a flight of fancy. These intuitions can sometimes be the fodder for further scientific research and lead to verifiable information, to knowledge. As a scientist, I know that it's never enough to simply imagine another animal's perspective. But as a person, I know that it's never enough to accept unclarity or uncertainty about how animals' minds work as a reason to not care for them, or as an excuse for inaction or willful harm directed toward them. This distinction is important.

In *Rewilding Our Hearts,* a more interdisciplinary work than my previous books, I consider a more global and holistic perspective; I go beyond my specific areas of expertise in ethology and compassionate conservation to consider biology, psychology, sociology, philosophy, and anthropology. All of these, in fact, inform studies of animal behavior, animal minds, and conservation biology, but they are not always acknowledged. As an activist arguing for social change, I believe, ultimately, that what we need is not more information about animals but rather a social movement and revolution in how we interact with animals and nature, a movement based on peace, compassion, empathy, and social justice. My vision of this movement is not that it represents a single idea or a specific program (there is no "membership" to acquire); instead, I posit that we are all already members, as living, breathing human beings who move in circles of coexistence.

Rewilding Our Hearts describes a positive and inspirational social movement about what we can and must do, as individuals within a global community, working in harmony for common goals, to deal with the rampant and wanton destruction of our planet and its innumerable and awe-inspiring residents and their homes. We really do need wild(er) minds and wild(er) hearts to make the changes that must be made right now, so that we can work toward having a wild(er) planet. The Earth is tired and broken and is not infinitely resilient. Like a fatigued person teetering on the brink of burning out, our wondrous and magnificent planet needs all the help it can get. I see wild as beautiful, but—as Terry Tempest Williams writes so eloquently—today we must often attempt to find "beauty in a broken world."[10]

The word "rewilding" became an essential part of the discussion among conservationists in the late 1990s when two well-known conservation biologists, Michael Soulé and Reed Noss, wrote their now-classic essay: "Rewilding and Biodiversity: Complementary Goals for Continental Conservation."[11]

Dave Foreman, a true visionary and the director of the Rewilding Institute in Albuquerque, New Mexico,[12] sees rewilding as a conservation strategy based on three premises: "(1) healthy ecosystems need large carnivores, (2) large carnivores need big, wild roadless areas, and (3) most roadless areas are small and thus need to be linked."[13] Conservation biologists and others who write about rewilding or work on rewilding projects see it as a large-scale, even continental, process involving projects of different sizes that both include and go beyond carnivores, such as the ambitious, courageous, and forward-looking Yellowstone to Yukon Conservation Initiative. Of course, rewilding includes a lot more than carnivores, as it must.

The core words associated with large-scale rewilding projects are *connection* and *connectivity*, the establishment of links among geographical areas so that animals can roam as freely as possible with few if any disruptions to their movements. For this to happen ecosystems must be connected so that their integrity and wholeness are maintained or reestablished.

Regardless of scale—ranging from huge areas encompassing a variety of habitats that either need to be reconnected or need to be protected to personal interactions with animals and habitats—the need to rewild and reconnect centers on the fact that there has been extensive isolation and fragmentation "out there" in nature, between ourselves and (M)other nature, but also *within* ourselves. Many, perhaps most, human animals, are isolated and fragmented internally concerning their relationships with nonhuman animals, so much so that we're alienated from them. We do not connect with other animals, including other humans, because we cannot or do not empathize with them. The same goes for our lack of connection with various landscapes. We don't understand they are alive, vibrant, dynamic, magical, and magnificent. Alienation often results in different forms of domination and destruction, but domination is not what it means "to be human." Power does not mean license to do whatever we want to do just because we can.

Rewilding projects often involve building wildlife bridges and underpasses so that animals can freely move about. These corridors, as they're called, can also be more personalized. I see rewilding our heart as a dynamic process that not only will foster the development of corridors of coexistence and compassion for wild animals but also will facilitate the formation of corridors within our bodies that connect our heart and brain. In turn, these connections, or reconnections, will result in positive feelings that will facilitate heartfelt actions to make the lives of animals better. These are the sorts of processes that will help the field of compassionate conservation flourish. When I think about what can be done to help others, a warm feeling engulfs me and I am sure it is part of that feeling of being rewilded. To want to help others in need is natural, so that glow is to be expected.

Rewilding is an attitude. It is also a guide for action. As a social movement, it needs to be *proactive, positive, persistent, patient, peaceful, practical, powerful,* and *passionate*—which I call "the eight Ps of rewilding."

To summarize, "rewilding" is a mind-set. It reflects the desire to (re)connect intimately with all animals and landscapes in ways that dissolve borders. Rewilding means appreciating, respecting, and accepting other beings and landscapes for who or what they are, not for who or what we want them to be. It means rejoicing in the personal connections we establish and which we need so badly. Indeed, I see the process of rewilding as, most of all, a personal journey and transformative exploration that centers on bringing other animals and their homes, all ecosystems, back into our heart. It is inarguable that if we are going to make the world a better place now and for future generations, personal rewilding is central to the process. Laws and public policy will not do it, and neither will more science. Instead, each of us must undergo a major personal paradigm shift in how we view and live in the world and how we behave. Researchers agree. For example, Andrew Ford and Richard Cowling stress that "conservation is primarily not about biology but about people and the choices they make."[14] California State University psychologist P. Wesley Schultz notes, "Conservation can *only* be achieved by changing behavior."[15]

Compassion begets compassion, and there's actually a synergistic relationship, not a trade-off, when we show compassion for animals and their homes. There are indeed many reasons for hope. There's also compelling evidence that we and other animals are born to be good and that we're natural-born optimists. Therein lie the many reasons for having hope that in the future we will harness our basic goodness and optimism and all work together as a united community. We can look to the animals for inspiration. So, we need to tap into our empathic, compassionate, and moral inclinations to make the world a better place for all beings. We need to add a healthy dose of social justice to our world right now. We can all make more humane, gentler choices to expand our compassion footprint.

When all is said and done, and more is usually said than done, we need a heartfelt revolution in how we think, what we do with what we know, and how we act. We can no longer act as *Homo denialius*, as if nothing is really happening.[16] Rewilding can be a very good guide. The revolution has to come from deep within us and must begin at home, in our heart and wherever we live. I want to make the process of rewilding a more personal journey and exploration that centers on bringing other animals and their homes, ecosystems of many different types, back into our heart.

For rewilding to become a transformative social movement, people from all walks of life, and with often vastly different interests, will need to work with one another. This will happen only if rewilding itself is regarded as a flexible concept that can be adapted to fit a wide range of different contexts and needs, and if the movement itself is undertaken from a spirit of humility, grace, kindness, compassion, and empathy. This is my vision of rewilding. To succeed, we must be hopeful and pragmatic, idealistic and realistic, persistent and flexible, and kind to, and critical of, one another. We need to rewild our hearts and build landscapes of hope and heart. We must live with hope, not in fear. We need to recognize and be proud of the fact that we are also animals and therein lies hope for a much better future. The resilience of other animals and nature as a whole is being tested and strained to its limits, and at some point the rubber band will likely break; what a tragedy that will be for all beings.

The time is right, the time is now, for an inspirational, revolutionary, and personal social movement that can save us from doom and keep us positive while we pursue our hopes and dreams. Our planet is tired and dying and not as resilient as some declare it to be.

I really like the phrase "Leap and the net will appear," an idea put forth by American naturalist John Burroughs. We need to have faith that what we do will have positive effects. In many ways we intuitively know what we need to do, but we can be afraid to commit to something when we are unsure of what the results will be. Instead, we keep our hopes and dreams alive by taking the step into action, doing something, anything, based on what our heads and hearts are telling us. We need to step out of our comfort zones and think outside the box and work with others. We need a new mind-set of cooperating with others who also care about animals and Earth. Hard work pays off. A report issued in May of 2012 by the Center for Biological Diversity showed that about 90 percent of endangered species are recovering on time. The report notes that we still have a long way to go before we can know how well many species are doing, but there are success stories across the United States. These include the Aleutian cackling goose, California least tern, American crocodile, black-footed ferret, whooping crane, gray wolves in the northern Rocky Mountains, and the shortnose sturgeon.

So, what do we need to do? We must rewild now. We need to take the leap. It will feel good to rewild because compassion and empathy are very contagious. *Ecocide is suicide.* When "they" (other animals) lose, we all lose. We suffer the indignities to which we subject other animals. We can feel their pains and suffering if we allow ourselves to do so.

We live in a magnificent yet wounded world. Despite all of the rampant destruction and abuse, it remains a magnificent world filled with awe and wonder. If you are not in awe, you're not paying attention. So let's get on with it. Open your heart to nature and rewild as you go through your daily routines and rituals. The beginning is now. We can always do more as we rewild. Rewilding is a work in progress from which we must not get deflected. How lucky we are that we are able to partake in this process, gratefully and generously blurring borders between "them" and "us" and their homes and ours.

Let's make personal rewilding all the rage. We are all intimately interconnected, we are all one, and we all can and must work together as a united community to reconnect with nature and to rewild our hearts.

The Humbling Power of Wilderness

SPENCER R. PHILLIPS

The central epiphany of every religious tradition always occurs in the wilderness.

—ROBERT F. KENNEDY JR., *HUMANKIND*[1]

LET'S STIPULATE THAT RELIGIOUS EPIPHANY requires an understanding of one's relationship to the divine . . . to the creator . . . to God. I would further submit that this understanding is fundamentally a matter of humility. Humility is the recognition that we are not masters of the universe—not even of our own little corners of it—and that we need something more than ourselves if we are to make sense of our lives. What Kennedy's observation suggests is that this understanding—this *humility*—is best attained in wilderness.

I am not going to argue that other human experiences cannot have this effect. Try giving birth, for example. Or, if you are not properly equipped, watch your wife do it. Listen to a symphony. Or head to a museum or gallery and see what Georgia O'Keeffe or Ansel Adams saw when they looked at the wild.

But I will suggest that experiencing wilderness is the most effective way to get the proper perspective on life. As John Muir wrote, "the clearest way into the universe is through a forest wilderness."[2] That must mean that all those other ways we try to find our way into the universe—via even the highest art that humans have wrought or our dearest relationships with other people—are not so clear.

Even so, spiritual renewal or religious significance often gets short shrift in our consideration of the value of wilderness to people. For example, one conservation organization's website lists "nine surprising reasons for kids to get outside this summer."[3] A litany of intermediate goals and instrumental values that parents might wish for their children so they can be more productive and less bothersome little human beings, it includes items like: less stress, increased attentiveness, better sleep, building crucial life skills, enhanced learning and creativity, reduced violence and crime, more defenders of wild lands.

Not that there's anything wrong with lower stress, not being a criminal, and defending wild lands. But speaking as a parent, I find something conspicuously missing from this list: learning humility, appreciating one's place in the universe, and the spiritual transformation these produce. I am also speaking as one who has had to learn this lesson myself—the hard way—and, of course, in wilderness.

The Sacandaga ice-water enema

The Siamese Ponds Wilderness is part of New York's Adirondack Park and could well be called the immediate inspiration for the Wilderness Act of 1964. It borders the land where the Zahniser family has its camp, which is where Howard Zahniser drafted much of the Act.[4]

I was there in May of 1996, squeezing in a short solo backpacking trip before leading a newly designed economics workshop later in the week. I had a plan for the trip, and my plan included fording the East Branch of the Sacandaga River to complete a brilliantly laid out loop.

My plan, however, was not the wilderness's plan. The wilderness didn't care about my brilliance. It was just doing its wilderness thing, which on that day happened to be regulating the water flow unleashed by a storm the night before and from still-melting snow farther upstream. The river itself seemed narrow enough, maybe 20 meters, but it was high, raging, and very cold.

I should have turned back and picked another route. But I had *my* plan, and it called for fording. I put my clothes and boots in my pack (so they'd be dry on the other side). There was a cable stretched over the river to ease fording in milder conditions, so I clipped my pack to the cable, tied a rope to the carabiner, and, not wanting to lose the connection to my pack, tied the other end of the line around my waist and waded in. "I got this," I thought.

By the time I was in up to my knees, I knew I'd have to move fast to avoid hypothermia. I moved a bit farther from the bank, into deeper water. Before I could give another thought to the cold, the current knocked me over. As luck would have it, I literally reached the end of my rope in a rapid downstream. With my middle tethered to the cable upstream, the river doubled me over, and the hydraulics slammed my bottom down to the river's bottom. Repeatedly.

All I could do at the end of my rope, with my brilliant plan having gone suddenly and horribly awry, was say or think "Jesus, help!" or maybe it was more like "Jesus! . . . [glub, glub, glub] . . . Help!" Either way, and after another bounce or two, my *feet* finally found the river's bottom, and my hands found the rope behind my back. I hauled myself upstream a bit and pendulumed back to the bank I'd had no business leaving in the first place.

My attitude went from "I got this" to "I get it."

I needed to learn humility—to set aside my will, my intention, my self—and be subject to the reality of the wilderness. The lesson included, of course: *Never practice "live bait" swift-water rescue alone.* More broadly, I learned that my plans, however brilliant, are not all that important, and I might pursue them at my peril. In the words of Solomon: "There is a way which seems right to a man, but its end is the way of death."[5]

The physical lesson about allowing nature to take its course and to rule over and curtail my hiking plans had a metaphorical connection to my life at the time. You see, even though it was taking a toll on my family, I was set on my way in a particular direction with my work. I thought that my progress in that direction should take precedence over all other concerns.

I had my plan laid out and I was going to follow it, no matter the hours, the travel, or the distraction from my closest relationships. I was going to follow my path, come hell or—so I thought until the Sacandaga had its say—high water.

As I lay in my sleeping bag that night following the river's lesson, I watched the stars through the canopy of centuries-old hemlocks and reflected on how close I had come to becoming a really bad newspaper headline, something like: "Naked Environmentalist Wins Darwin Award." And it sank in that maybe my way wasn't quite the right one. I saw that I needed to set my plans and priorities—all of them—aside and (humbly) take a different path.

I'm certainly not the first to have learned humility in the wilderness. Consider Moses, the son of Hebrew slaves raised in the Egyptian palace. Moses knows who he is, and he thinks he knows how to help his enslaved brethren. After killing an Egyptian whom he'd witnessed hitting a slave, Moses flees Egypt and spends the next forty years lying low. He marries, has children, and becomes a humble shepherd. Then one day, leading the flock "to the far side of the wilderness," he sees the burning bush and hears God's call to return to Egypt to lead Israel out of bondage and, not incidentally, into the wilderness.

Moses has some doubts. He says he's not much for public speaking, for example. And he wants to know what he's supposed to say if the Israelites demand some proof that he is operating on good authority. God's answer is tell them that "I am" sent you. In other words, Moses, you have no authority, only the command of the one who sent you. This is not about you.

It takes all of those forty years, the transition from prince to shepherd, and (I submit) the separation from civilization that wilderness provides, before Moses can get to a place, spiritually, from which he can actually lead. Moreover, he is able to lead only by humbly following someone else. Moses eventually does lead Israel out of Egypt and into the wilderness, but perhaps ironically, it takes *another* forty years before the people are ready to enter the Promised Land.

Contrary to popular belief, the Israelites don't wander about in the desert for forty years because Zipporah's husband (Moses) refuses to stop and ask for directions. Rather, their wilderness trek is in part punishment for doubting their ability, under God's care, to succeed right off. It's also a means of preparing the people to eventually be successful. The people have to get over their grumbling and learn, in the wilderness, that God is all they need.

In the book of Deuteronomy—his swan song delivered just before the rest of the nation crosses into the Promised Land—Moses tells the people:

God, your God, is leading the way; he's fighting for you. You saw with your own eyes what he did for you in Egypt; you saw what he did in the wilderness, how God, your God, carried you as a father carries his child, carried you the whole way until you arrived here.[6]

It is a reminder first of all that they had not come so far, nor would they be going any farther, either alone or under their own power. Later, when Moses says, "Remember how the Lord your God led you all the way in the wilderness these forty years, to humble and test you,"[7] it is a reminder that the thing they would need most going forward would be humility.

A goat, a prophet, and a carpenter walk into a wilderness . . .

During their time in the wilderness, the people of Israel also receive the law, including what to do on Yom Kippur, the annual Day of Atonement. On that day, the sins of the entire nation, a whole year's worth, are to be laid on the head of the (scape) goat who then will carry the sin away into the wilderness.[8]

This ritual of confession and sacrifice comes after, and is in addition to, the prayers and sacrifices made to cover over various individual sins as people went about their lives throughout the preceding year. All that effort—the prayers said, the incense and grain burned, the oil and blood poured out—evidently, was not sufficient: The nation still needs the wilderness to take away its transgression. The people cannot do it for themselves: They have to humbly let the scapegoat and his walk into the wilderness do it for them. (How fitting it is that the National Wilderness Preservation System includes the Scapegoat Wilderness.)

Jumping forward a couple thousand years and into the New Testament, we find John the Baptist "crying out in the wilderness, 'prepare the way of the Lord.'"[9] He does in fact do his preaching "in the wilderness of Judea, saying, 'Repent, for the kingdom of heaven is at hand.'"[10]

What strikes me as significant is that John does not call the people to the temple, nor to the palace, and certainly not to the marketplace, to get in touch with their spiritual need. Instead, his call to repentance comes from the wilderness, a place where social status does not count, the cares of daily life do not distract, and the comforts of home do not dull people to what God might have to say.

Jesus himself walks into the wilderness so that John can baptize him. This is itself an act of humility, as even John protests that he is unworthy to baptize his cousin (and his Lord).

Afterwards, Jesus walks farther into the wilderness to be tested in preparation for his earthly ministry. The Message, a modern, more idiomatic translation of the Bible, tells the story this way:

Jesus prepared for the Test by fasting forty days and forty nights. That left him, of course, in a state of extreme hunger, which the Devil took advantage of in the first test: "Since you are God's Son, speak the word that will turn these stones into loaves of bread."

Jesus answered by quoting Deuteronomy: "It takes more than bread to stay alive. It takes a steady stream of words from God's mouth."

For the second test the Devil took him to the Holy City. He sat him on top of the Temple and said, "Since you are God's Son, jump." The Devil goaded him by quoting Psalm 91: "He has placed you in the care of angels. They will catch you so that you won't so much as stub your toe on a stone."

Jesus countered with another citation from Deuteronomy: "Don't you dare test the Lord your God."

For the third test, the Devil took him to the peak of a huge mountain. He gestured expansively, pointing out all the earth's kingdoms, how glorious they all were. Then he said, "They're yours—lock, stock, and barrel. Just go down on your knees and worship me, and they're yours."

Jesus' refusal was curt: "Beat it, Satan!" He backed his rebuke with a third quotation from Deuteronomy: "Worship the Lord your God, and only him. Serve him with absolute single-heartedness."

The Test was over. The Devil left.[11]

Fittingly, Jesus quotes Deuteronomy, Moses's post-wilderness-odyssey debrief, to counter the tempter's appeal to what he assumes would be Jesus's pride. Jesus and Moses draw the same lessons from their experience of wilderness. In Jesus's case, it is that he, *even he*, has to relinquish control and be humble—that is, he is not to use his power in service of his own interests, whether in food, position, or power. As he later puts it in Gethsemane, "Not my will but yours."[12]

The Bible is rife with this idea that humility is spiritually essential. To give one example, again in the *Message* translation, "You're blessed when you're at the end of your rope. With less of you there is more of God and his rule."[13] The same verse in *New Living Translation* reads "God blesses those who are humble, for they will inherit the whole earth."

This need for humility is not only fundamental to spiritual survival, it's also a need that wilderness is uniquely able to fill. When it's just you and the wilderness, it's awfully hard to *honestly* say "I got this." Because the minute you do say that, you find yourself at the end of a rope, maybe drowning in a frigid river, or tumbling off a rock. At a minimum you will simply be missing the most important thing you might have come to the wilderness for, even if you don't know yet know why you are there.

Two paths diverge in the future of wilderness

With the Wilderness Act now fifty years old, and human impacts on even the remotest wilderness becoming ever more obvious, some urge that we reconsider the efficacy and the wisdom of letting wilderness do its own thing. People of this view worry about the loss of iconic species and landforms (climate change driving the Joshua trees from Joshua Tree National

Park and the glaciers from Glacier, for example), and contend that people should actively intervene to maintain natural, or at least historically familiar, conditions in wilderness areas.

I, on the other hand, worry much more that such intervention is the opposite of humility, and it would therefore hinder our spiritual transformation while diminishing the ability of the wilderness to teach humility to our future selves.

In the first version of the future, we think we know better than nature what nature needs, at least if we define what nature "needs" as that which produces what we want from it. In that future, we favor "naturalness" over "freedom" and set about manipulating ecological processes in order to mimic the production of a certain familiar set of natural outcomes on the right side of some particular set of administrative boundaries. You know, this many glaciers here, that many elk there, some particular mix of vegetation, and the same palette of sunsets and wildflowers for the delight of recreationists adorned in their own glorious hues.

This is essentially the view Christopher Solomon takes in his much-discussed *New York Times* column: Echoing a group of scientists, resource managers, and—to be fair—wilderness lovers, he urges a transition of our role as the guardians of wilderness to one of being gardeners of wilderness.[14]

It is perhaps tellingly *un*-humble that the *Times'* headline pronounces that the fifty-year-old Wilderness Act "is facing a midlife crisis"—as if the completely human and artificial concept of a mid-(human) life crisis can or should be applied to what one hopes is a timeless legal institution or, worse, to the "bits of eternity"[15] that the institution protects. If the Act's turning fifty means it's time to "rethink the wild,"[16] should we be prepared next year to rethink the right to vote when the equally venerable Voting Rights Act hits the half-century mark?[17]

Moreover, the idea that we can do better than nature alone at delivering natural outcomes is a fundamentally proud one. Solomon's and the gardeners' faith in human intent or capability must confront the reality that the reason nature no longer gives us precisely what we want is that we have already so royally screwed up its ability to do so. Having failed to steward the original fruitfulness of the Earth, who could honestly believe that humans will outdo nature at the much harder task of restoring Earth's fruitfulness?

In a better future, we humbly let the wilderness be wild and favor its freedom over its naturalness. This is the view embodied in Bob Marshall's assertion:

There is just one hope of repulsing the tyrannical ambition of civilization to conquer every niche on the whole earth. That hope is the organization of spirited people who will fight for the freedom of the wilderness.[18]

If we are humble, we can choose to refrain from intervention in wilderness—even in the face of climate change and the myriad other effects of our use, benign and otherwise, of the rest of the planet. We can also let the ecological, aesthetic, social, and economic chips fall where they may. And if we do, we will still have the enduring resource of wilderness that the Act was established to secure. Even an "unnatural"—but still untrammeled—wilderness will teach a cautionary tale about the inescapable limits of our own brilliant plans.

Most importantly, we will have learned humility and put ourselves in a position from which our lives can then be lifted up, or "exalted," as in the verse above. Wilderness will continue to teach humility, and the humble will be blessed.

We've got to know our limitations

In summary, if we insist on trusting in ourselves and following what seems right to us . . . if we believe that we can "help nature adapt"[19] and that "we got this," we are doomed.

Beyond what Moses, Isaiah, Jesus, and the others had to say, this wisdom is echoed by a more modern sage: Clint Eastwood. In the final scene of *Magnum Force,* Eastwood's Dirty Harry character sends his (proud) nemesis to a fiery doom and snarls, "Man's got to know his limitations."

Wilderness is most powerful as a place, an idea, and an institution that teaches us our limitations: our limitations as individuals, our limitations as a civilization, and our limitations as a species. To ignore this lesson is to insist that we know better. And the drive to become gardeners rather than guardians of wilderness is really just a new expression of "the tyrannical ambition of civilization to conquer every niche on the whole earth."

Taking fuels reduction, invasives removal, fixed climbing anchors, and the like into the wilderness[20] might be a gentler or more enlightened means of conquest than converting wild areas to vacation resorts, timber plantations, gas fields and wind farms, but the freedom of the wilderness will be just as lost.

Lost with it will be the chance to learn humility and to find, as John Muir wrote, "our way into the Universe." My wilderness prayer is that by not insisting on our way, we will instead find it.

THREE

PROTECTED AREAS: THE FOUNDATION FOR CONSERVATION

Conservation in the African Anthropocene

TIM CARO

ACROSS MOST OF AFRICA, the idea that multiple-use areas can be an effective conservation strategy for large and medium-sized mammals has little merit. Human populations are increasing very rapidly, faster than on any other continent, along with concomitant conversion of wild habitats to agricultural landscapes. Currently, there is a new "scramble for Africa" as governments and foreigners extract resources and many new development and infrastructure projects are being planned or implemented. Several forms of biodiversity have no place in these human-modified landscapes. The aim of this chapter is to demonstrate this for larger mammals and to suggest that we must adhere to and increase our commitment to fully protected areas; they are the best conservation tool at our disposal.[1] I do this using data from a fully protected area in which I have worked for twenty years. My goal here is to counter the idea held by the "new conservationists" that we should direct future efforts toward working landscapes where animals and plants are managed for the benefits of people.[2] Their view of the future of conservation as being "gardening of wildlife" for human benefit contrasts strongly with my original view of conservation in the Anthropocene.[3]

I work in Katavi National Park (KNP), which encompasses 4,471 square kilometers, in the Great Lakes area of East Africa north of Lake Rukwa in western Tanzania.[4] The area is part of the central Zambezi miombo woodlands ecoregion,[5] but, unusually for miombo, it is characterized by *Terminalia* and *Combretum* tree genera.[6] The park was established in 1974 to protect a great diversity and abundance of large mammals that collect along rivers and forage on floodplains during the dry season and was then doubled in size in 1998.[7] Like other national parks in Tanzania, the park is administered and patrolled by Tanzania National Parks authorities; no settlements or exploitation are allowed within national park boundaries.[8] The other major protected area in the Katavi-Rukwa ecosystem is the adjacent 4,323-square-kilometer Rukwa Game Reserve (RGR) that lies to the east and south of the KNP. It is administered by the Wildlife Division but is patrolled less frequently; tourist hunting occurs there.[9] When I first arrived in Rukwa Region in 1995, KNP was smaller, and to the east was Mlele Game Controlled Area, where resident and tourist hunting, tree cutting, and grazing were allowed. To the northeast of KNP lies the Msaginia Forest Reserve where selected hardwood extraction is allowed but settlements are forbidden. To the south of KNP and RGR, within the Division of Mpimbwe,[10] lies Usevya Open Area. There Sukuma, Pimbwe, Fipa, and Rungwa people live in and around 22 villages where they graze cattle and practice agriculture (principally sorghum, maize, millet, cassava, peanut, and rice cultivation.)[11] It is illegal to hunt animals in Tanzania without a license, but—in practice—illegal subsistence hunting is widespread in Mpimbwe, with incursions principally made into KNP and RGR because large mammals have disappeared from village land.[12]

When I first arrived in Katavi I set out to estimate densities of large and medium-sized mammals in areas under four different sorts of land use: KNP, the multiple-use Game Controlled Area and Forest Reserve, and the agricultural landscape of the Open Area. For fourteen months I drove along 20 transects, once per month, throughout all management areas, and I found overwhelming evidence for KNP containing far greater abundances of mammals ranging in size from elephants to small carnivores.[13] The Game Controlled Area mammal abundances were lower than KNP but were still reasonably high, whereas those in the Forest Reserve and Open Area were very low indeed.[14] The chief factors responsible for lowered mammal abundances outside Katavi National Park were illegal hunting rather than differences in habitat.[15] These early data showed that state-owned conservation areas permitting human activities cannot be relied upon for conserving large and middle-sized species in this taxonomic group in western Tanzania.

Exactly the same pattern occurs across Tanzania as a whole. These data were instead obtained from aerial census data collected by the Serengeti Ecological Monitoring Programme, Tanzania Wildlife Conservation Monitoring Programme, and Conservation Information Monitoring Unit based on repeated systematic reconnaissance flights across the country.[16] Large mammal biomass is significantly higher in protected areas with no hunting than in protected areas where hunting by foreign tourists is sanctioned. Lumping national parks and game reserves together (areas that do not allow any form of human activity except, respectively, photographic tourism or tourist hunting), there were significantly higher densities of the largest mammals than in combined adjacent game controlled areas and open areas, both of which allow many more human activities. Although these are not randomized controlled tests, so confounding factors may be involved, the data suggest human presence results in larger, often edible, mammals going missing from human-dominated landscapes.

When we extended our studies to non-charismatic fauna and flora in and around Katavi National Park, however, we found that species richness of small mammals, frogs, butterflies, birds, and trees did not decline along a four-step gradient of increasing human activity. Rather, different management areas hosted distinct communities of each taxonomic group.[17] This highlights the import of developing landscape-scale conservation strategies for those taxa not yet heavily exploited by people in areas that are still subject to a relatively light human footprint, a position long advocated by the landscape ecologists as well as the new "gardeners of wildlife."

So what about the criticism that protected areas have failed to protect biota in Africa in the long term? Meta-analyses show that populations are declining in many protected areas across the tropics,[18] particularly populations of mammals on the African continent, albeit at different rates in different regions.[19] That may be so, but a key question is whether they are declining at faster rates than are populations outside protected areas. We examined this too for Tanzania. We found that while large and medium-sized mammal populations are declining,[20] they are declining far more rapidly in game controlled areas and open areas than in national parks and game reserves.[21] More species fared well (either increasing or remaining stable) in areas that limited human activities than in areas that permitted them. Furthermore, significantly more species declined in areas that had poor protection and heavy human activity than increased in those areas. In short, fully protected areas are in increasing trouble but not as much trouble as areas where people extract resources and live. A subsequent study in the Masai-Mara ecosystem in Kenya showed that persistent large herbivore declines have occurred over a thirty-two-year period due to an expanding human population in ranches and with livestock influences spreading into the nominally protected area.[22] Nonetheless, there are some long-term successes with Community-Based Natural Resource Management areas especially in Namibia and Botswana.[23]

In essence the "new gardeners" have simply repackaged the old debate that compares the "fences and fines" approach with the "use it or lose it" approach to conservation. Then, as now, what we really require are proper experiments that compare ecological outcomes of different methods of wildlife management over the long term, or correlational studies that try to eliminate as many confounding variables as possible.[24] Good studies may eventually persuade us that we need a multitude of approaches to conserving natural resources, dependent on which natural resources and on context,[25] but, as it stands now, strictly protected areas are our best conservation strategy for larger mammals.

If we bypass the idea of multiple-use areas in Africa that support communities of small non-edible taxa but often fail large mammals, then how can we bolster the strictly protected area network? First, we need to protect additional species and habitats as many are not protected at all.[26] Wildlife in Tanzania is fortunate as the nation is still creating national parks, including Saadani, Kitulo, and Saa-Nane Island National Parks in the last twenty years. Second, we need to enlarge strictly protected areas,[27] as it is generally agreed that larger protected areas are the best conservation tools. Tanzania has been good at this too: recently expanding Katavi and Ruaha National Parks. Another option is transboundary conservation areas; again Tanzania has been effective by creating Mkomazi National Park adjacent to Tsavo National Park in Kenya. Third, buffer zones are required for as many strictly protected areas as possible in order to insulate them from the negative impacts of anthropogenic activities occurring immediately outside and to increase the effective size of the protected area.[28] Many adjacent game reserves perform this service for national parks in Tanzania but the old model of game controlled areas buffering strictly protected areas no longer works: Game controlled areas have been eroded over the last thirty years by hunting, logging, and grazing—all those activities espoused by the gardening model. Wildlife management areas in which economic returns from resource extraction go to local Tanzanians may hold some promise as buffer areas, but they have yet to be evaluated.[29]

Fourth, corridors between protected areas are now seen as vital because they can enable species to disperse between protected areas, maintain genetic variability within populations, rescue populations from local extinction, facilitate species' range shifts due to global climate change, and provide more area for species requiring large home ranges.[30] For instance, decreased connectivity between protected areas has led to reduced gene flow between elephant (*Loxodonta africana*) populations in Tanzania.[31] In that country, several wildlife corridors have now been identified and some research has started.[32] Corridors may simply be historical migratory routes, or else the shortest distance between two protected areas; alternatively they may be uncultivated lands between protected areas, without or with information on animal movements.[33] In Tanzania, there are at least 31 wildlife corridors still in existence at the time of writing, five in extreme danger of being cut, 18 in critical condition, and eight in moderate condition.

Addressing many of the direct and indirect threats to strictly protected areas will not be solved by abandoning them; it will instead depend on the effectiveness of management. For example, stopping illegal extraction requires law enforcement and negotiating with local communities; tackling invasive species requires prevention and removal techniques; and managing fire may require suppression or prescribed burning. Good management is the way to bolster strictly protected areas. Thomas Struhsaker advocated effective law enforcement, secure long-term funding, permanent collaboration with an overseas organization, scientific presence and monitoring, a flexible management plan, and local and national educational support.[34] Clearly, good management varies according to context, but these general rules apply to most protected areas in Africa.

In finishing, it should be noted that from a biological perspective there is nothing special about large mammals in Africa. Some may act as keystone species, such as elephants, but the majority does not. For an ornithologist or lepidopterist, larger mammals are just members of another taxonomic group. However, for the vast majority of people, both Africans and foreigners, lions (*Panthera leo*), leopards (*Panthera pardus*), elephants, buffalo (*Syncerus caffer*), and rhinoceros (*Diceros bicornis* and *Ceratotherium simum*) species—the "Big 5"—are special,[35] and they attract disproportionate visitors to areas where they are protected.[36] Guests bring money to developing African countries and so these species and others, such as giraffe (*Giraffa camelopardalis*), zebra (*Equus burchelli*, *E. grevyii*, and *E. zebra*) and wild dogs (*Lycaon pictus*), indirectly help national and local economies. These African flagship species simply do not fare well in human-dominated ecosystems. So if the so-called Anthropocene proponents want to manage wildlife for the benefits of people, they will need—counter-intuitively—to embrace strict protectionism more closely.

The author would like to thank Monique Borgerhoff Mulder for comments.

The Silent Killer: Habitat Loss and the Role of African Protected Areas to Conserve Biodiversity

KATHLEEN H. FITZGERALD

> *The survival of our wildlife is a matter of grave concern to all of us in Africa. These wild creatures amid the wild places they inhabit are not only important as a source of wonder and inspiration, but are an integral part of our natural resources and our future livelihood and well-being. In accepting the trusteeship of our wildlife we solemnly declare that we will do everything in our power to make sure that our children's grandchildren will be able to enjoy this rich and precious inheritance.*
>
> —FIRST PRESIDENT OF TANZANIA, JULIUS K. NYERERE, 1961[1]

SITTING ON THE BANKS of the Olifants River in Kruger National Park, we watch as over 60 elephants gather in the river. They are cooling themselves, drinking water and spraying themselves with moist river sand. The herd comprises all ages—an awesome assortment of sizes. The matriarch, an enormous female, starts walking downstream and all the elephants slowly follow. The terrain is steep, rocky, and variable, but the elephants navigate their way in single file. Along the bank is an area of sand that slopes toward the river. When the matriarch approaches the top of the bank, she looks down, leans onto her back knees, and slides down. Imagine a three-ton animal sand-sledding. It is incredible to watch; the scene makes it hard not to imagine hearing an anthropomorphic "Yee-haw" coming out of their mouths. We sit in awe watching as each elephant in turn follows the matriarch's action and does the same.

When one of the baby elephants follows suit, rather than sledding easily down like the others, she is forced into somersaults by the river bank's steepness and she rolls down, spiraling like a tire going down a hill, and lands at the bottom on her back with her legs flailing up in the air. One of the other elephants trumpets, and immediately six elephants run to help her. They protectively surround the baby and nudge her over and up onto her feet, whereupon she wobbles off, flanked by her protectors, the collective herd giving an amazing glimpse into the complex familial systems of elephants.

THE AFRICAN ELEPHANT (*Loxodonta africana*) is just one of Africa's iconic species threatened by a severe poaching crisis gripping the continent. Driven by an insatiable demand for ivory in Asia, more than 25,000 elephants were poached in 2011, as estimated by the Convention on International Trade in Endangered Species of Wild Fauna and Flora (CITES). Other evidence suggests the year-to-year figures are much higher. Enormous time, energy, and resources are necessarily being invested in Africa's wildlife in an attempt to stop the poaching, trafficking, and demand. Even if we stop the current onslaught of poaching,[2] however, viable populations of in situ wildlife in Africa will not survive given present rates of habitat loss. Habitat loss is African wildlife's silent killer, and it needs urgent attention.

The survival of Africa's wildlife is dependent on large, wild protected lands and requires a deliberate choice by African governments to protect habitat for these species. The range of the African elephant, a conservation dependent species, for example, has declined significantly over the past two decades. Only 31 percent of the elephant range lies in protected areas, which cover approximately 9 percent of the continent, putting the future of this magnificent species at risk.[3]

A similar situation exists for Africa's four great apes, which are concentrated in forest landscapes in West and Central Africa. The chimpanzee, the most populous of all great apes, has four subspecies: Central, Eastern, Western, and Nigeria-Cameroon chimpanzee, and all subspecies are in decline and listed as endangered with only 22 percent of their suitable habitat secured in protected areas.[4]

Drivers of habitat loss

What are the main factors leading to accelerated habitat loss across the continent?

The simple answer is growth. This includes economic, population, development, resource extraction, agricultural, and international growth—all of which is directly and indirectly resulting in habitat loss.

In the past decade, Africa's growth rates have been approaching those of Asia. In 2011, seven African countries were among the world's ten fastest-growing economies, with each having an annual growth rate of 8 percent or more.[5] The African Development Bank projects that by the year 2030 Africa's population will grow to 1.6 billion—up from 1 billion today—representing 19 percent of the world's population. With more people and an expanding economy come new and increasing demands on land and natural resources, resulting in habitat conversion and fragmentation if not managed properly.

Economic and population growth brings with it large-scale infrastructure, and vice versa. Roads, oil pipelines, and railways are increasingly a part of Africa's new landscape. Today it is possible to travel on good highways throughout southern Africa. The Chinese are developing a new East African railway line that will connect Kenya, Rwanda, Uganda, Burundi, and South Sudan.

One factor driving Africa's economic growth stems from the removal of Africa's natural wealth through mining, drilling, and other forms of extraction, and it too is increasing in scope and scale across the continent. Be it a coal mine in Zimbabwe or a transmission line across northern Kenya into Ethiopia, these developments have an impact on habitat. Infrastructure development and resource extraction also threaten a large number of Africa's parks and reserves including: Tanzania's Selous Game Reserve (uranium mining), Zambia's Lower Zambezi National Park (coal mining), Zimbabwe's Mana Pools National Park (sand mining), Uganda's Murchison Falls National Park (oil extraction), Kenya's Nairobi, Amboseli, and Tsavo National Parks (highway development), and Namibia's Namib-Naukluft National Park (uranium mining).

Africa's forests and woodlands are also subject to accelerated extraction. Comprising 17 percent of the world's forest cover, Africa hosts the second-largest tropical forest in the world, the Congo Basin forest, 250 million hectares (618 million acres).[6] In addition to harboring extraordinary biodiversity—including four of the world's five great apes—the Congo Basin and other forest systems across Africa provide regional and global ecological services as carbon sinks and water catchments. However, deforestation rates in Africa are four times the world average.[7] Over the past twenty years, 200,000 square kilometers of ape habitat has been lost as a result of forest depletion due to increased logging, small-scale mining, palm oil plantations, and other extractive industries.[8] This habitat loss combined with the bush meat trade has resulted in all African ape subspecies becoming endangered or critically endangered. With developing economies, increased access to forests through infrastructure development, and the lack of a firm regulatory framework, deforestation will continue to accelerate, eroding not only key habitat for primates and other wildlife but destroying a critical carbon sink and vital ecosystem services in the process.

Rapid growth is also taking place in the agricultural sector. Small-, mid-, and large-scale farms are expanding across the continent. With increased global attention on food security from international and national governments and donors, subsidies and support for agricultural expansion have increased across the continent. This expansion is taking place without proper planning, leading to dramatic declines in water resources and habitat. For example, inside Southern Ethiopia's Gambella National Park, which hosts the great white-eared kob migration, the second-largest mammal migration in Africa, thousands of hectares were allocated to foreign companies for agricultural development. Likewise, the Zambezi River in Zambia is lined with agricultural development, prohibiting elephant movement along traditional corridors that extend from Botswana and Zimbabwe into Zambia. Both the expansion of agriculture and increasing food security are understandable priorities for many African countries, but achieving these must be carried out with proper planning, water management, and other methods that support the surrounding environment.

International growth is also fueling change in Africa. Foreign governments and multinational corporations are buying up large tracts of land in Africa due to a high global demand for food, biofuel, and minerals. Between 2000 and 2010, 134 million hectares (331 million acres) were purchased in Africa.[9] The targeted lands are highly productive for agriculture. These acquisitions result in large-scale development and land conversion, displacement of wildlife and people, and ecological degradation on a colossal scale. The demand for land is expected to rise with the global population nearing 9 billion, consumption patterns shifting toward more resource-intensive foods, and bio-based resources replacing fossil fuels used in transport and plastics. The world needs more land to produce more, and Africa is widely viewed as the continent with the most land to spare.

Despite Africa's growth, most Africans remain poor. While Africa's urban areas are rapidly expanding and its middle and upper classes growing, a majority of Africans are rural and directly dependent upon natural resources for their daily survival. Biodiversity and ecosystem services underpin every aspect of human life, including food security, livelihoods, health, ethnic diversity, and cultural enrichment. A quarter of the total wealth of low-income countries comes from "natural capital," compared to only 2 percent in wealthier nations.[10]

What does all of this mean for the long-term survival of wildlife and wild lands in Africa? Africa hosts a significant percentage of the globe's biodiversity and is rich with endemic species. For example, one-quarter of the world's mammals and more than a fifth of the globe's birds occur in Africa.[11] Africa's diversity and density of wildlife is recognized globally and remains unparalleled on any other continent. From the massive elephant herds of southern Africa to the world-renowned wildebeest migration in eastern Africa to the awe-inspiring mountain gorillas in Central Africa, without a doubt the continent holds some of the world's most unique, rare, and precious wildlife.

Africa is at a crossroads with development increasing and habitat and wildlife decreasing. However, with proper spatial planning and strategic conservation investment, Africa can host dynamic and productive economies while simultaneously supporting an expansive Pan-African network of protected areas, connected and complemented by community and private conservation areas. African governments have an opportunity to demonstrate to the world that conservation and economic development can coexist and that a continent does not need to sacrifice its natural heritage to develop.

While there is global recognition of the need to protect Africa's natural heritage, the prioritization of wildlife and wild lands conservation must be led and championed by Africans.

Value of protected areas and large landscape conservation in Africa

Protected areas have served historically as the main conservation tool in Africa, and they remain the fundamental building blocks of biodiversity conservation. They have protected a diversity of ecosystems, and they continue to provide key habitat and safe havens for wildlife and to support vital ecosystem services upon which wildlife and people depend.[12]

Protected areas are important to national, regional, and local economies. For example, Kenya's wildlife-based tourism accounts for 70 percent of the country's tourism revenue, is the third-largest contributor to national gross domestic product (GDP), and is a leading earner of foreign exchange, generating approximately US$745 million in 2007, up from US$247 million in 2002.[13] South Africa's tourism economy is the most robust and diverse on the continent and is strongly underpinned by nature-based tourism. Over 60 percent of visitors to the country visit at least one protected area during their stay. South Africa's world-renowned parks, such as Kruger National Park, play a significant role in attracting international tourists. Tourist arrivals to South Africa grew by 10.2 percent in 2012 compared to the global tourism visitation growth of 3.8 percent for the same period.[14]

Wildlife-based revenue goes far beyond fees paid for lodging and park entry. A suite of expenditures are made by tourists—such as domestic flights, vehicle transport, hotels in major cities, shopping, tipping, and dining. Other economic benefits derived from protected areas include spin-off businesses and employment. Much of this income is not calculated when considering the economic value of protected areas.

Protected areas are key components in climate change mitigation strategies. While Africa contributes little to climate change through CO_2 emissions, Africa's people, wildlife, and economies are particularly vulnerable to the effects of climate change given limitations in their ability to adapt to the projected changes. Climate change is recognized as a driver of species and habitat loss, and its impacts are projected to escalate in the future.[15] Climate change adaptation initiatives could cost African countries more than 5–10 percent of their GDP.[16] An expansive protected area network can help to effectively mitigate the ecological, social, and economic risks and costs related to climate change.

There are more than 1,100 national parks and reserves in Sub-Saharan Africa. Since 1970, total protected-area coverage in Africa has increased nearly twofold and now encompasses 3.06 million square kilometers of terrestrial and marine habitats. Protected areas currently cover 15.9 percent and 10.1 percent of total land surface in the East/Southern African and West/Central African regions, respectively.[17] Despite the number of protected areas, wildlife continues to decline at an alarming rate across the continent for the following reasons:

- ▸ *Too Small, Too Isolated.* Protected areas are too small and too isolated to support viable populations of certain species, ecosystem dynamics, natural processes, biodiversity, genetic exchange, and wildlife movement.
- ▸ *Encroachment and Degradation.* Some protected areas are surrounded by incompatible land use, resulting in encroachment on and degradation of the protected area and species loss as they move outside protected area boundaries.
- ▸ *Poorly Managed.* Many protected areas are poorly managed due to limited capacity and resources and do not effectively protect biodiversity or ecosystem services.

Overall, evidence from a broad range of African protected areas indicates that the main cause of wildlife declines is that many protected areas, due to size and shape, do not encompass the full range of functional resource gradients, migratory corridors, and seasonal habitats required to maintain a diverse array of productive wildlife populations.[18] As a result, wildlife are dependent upon both protected areas and adjacent lands, resulting in a source-and-sink situation in many landscapes where the lands adjacent to protected areas are not managed in a conservation-friendly way.

The source-sink dynamic is aptly displayed in Amboseli National Park in southern Kenya. The Amboseli ecosystem stretches from the park to the Chyulu Hills and Tsavo West National Parks in Kenya to Mt. Kilimanjaro National Park in Tanzania. Amboseli National Park (392 square kilometers) forms the core of the ecosystem, while six surrounding group ranches—a form of communal ownership—surround the park. While Amboseli is world-renowned for its elephants, the park is too small to support viable populations of elephants, predators, and certain ungulates. Wildlife is dependent on the unprotected areas outside the park, which is held by Maasai pastoralists. Many of the group ranches have subdivided the land into plots ranging in size from 10 to 60 acres. Fencing, cultivation, development, and other forms of habitat fragmentation, along with increased hostility toward wildlife due to predation on livestock and competition over resources, have a dire impact on wildlife and have resulted in a "sink" area.[19]

While protected areas often represent the core of a larger ecosystem, they must be ecologically connected to the lands, forests, and water sources that surround them. The benefits of conserving and restoring ecosystems and large landscapes make ecological and economic sense. For example, a 2012 United Nations Environment Programme report on the contribution of montane forests and related ecosystem services to Kenya's economy reported that the cumulative negative effect on the economy of deforestation through the reduction of water-regulating services was an estimated US$40 million annually, more than 2.8 times the cash revenue generated by deforestation.

Solutions

African governments and partners can reverse the trends of habitat loss and protect viable populations of Africa's wildlife and natural heritage by:

▶ increasing the number and size of protected areas;
▶ improving protected areas management;
▶ engaging communities in conservation in a meaningful way; and
▶ increasing awareness and prioritization of the ecological and economic value of conservation.

Reference to protected areas refers to the International Union for Conservation of Nature (IUCN) definition, which includes six distinct categories ranging from strictly protected nature reserves and parks to protected areas with sustainable use of natural resources.[20]

There is an ongoing academic debate between those pushing for strictly protected areas and those pushing for community-based natural resource management. The debate revolves around which approach is more effective for biodiversity conservation.[21] For those of us who live in Africa and work in the field with protected area authorities, private landowners, and communities across the continent, the answer to this debate is quite simple: We need both. If biodiversity is going to survive in the long term there must be a robust, well-managed network of large protected areas that is complemented by good private land and community-based natural resource management and conservation areas outside protected areas.

Increasing protected areas

Expand and increase parks and government reserves. Protected areas networks need to be expanded, linked to and complemented by other conservation areas that are well established and managed, and legally binding. As Africa continues to grow, there will be more pressure on land and natural resources. National parks provide the most secure means of protecting wildlife and habitat, since they are relatively legally secure and, in most African countries, any degazetting of an established park requires an act of parliament.

Across the continent private land is for sale from willing owners. These lands are being purchased by land speculators (both foreign and the emerging African elite), developers, and agricultural companies. Strategic lands should be purchased for protected areas expansion. These lands can be transferred to governments for management as national parks or retained privately for conservation. Many African governments have requested this kind of support. Some governments, such as South Africa's, have protected area expansion strategies, while others—despite having been approached by willing sellers—lack the necessary funding or the ability to perform the transaction.

In many African countries land is owned by the central government; therefore, the establishment of a protected area must be done through legal governmental processes. For example, in the Democratic Republic of Congo (DRC), the African Wildlife Foundation (AWF) worked with local communities and the government to establish two faunal reserves— the 3,625-square-kilometer Lomako-Yokokala Faunal Reserve, and the 1,100-square-kilometer Iyondji Community Bonobo Reserve, which were gazetted in 2006 and 2013, respectively. Part of the Congo Basin forest, these reserves protect tropical forest habitat for the endangered bonobo and other primates, forest elephants, the elusive Congo peacock, and other species. Similar to AWF's work in DRC and other countries, there is an opportunity to work with communities and governments across the continent to create new protected areas through existing legal frameworks.

Expand and increase community and private conservancies. Across the continent, the number of "conservancies"—whereby communities and/or private landowners decide to set aside their land for conservation purposes—has increased. In Namibia, for example, approximately 16 percent of the country is in community conservancies.[22] In Kenya, there are over

150 conservancies—private and community-owned. The establishment of conservancies, if set up properly, can help expand land under conservation and, importantly, directly benefit communities and landowners. As an approach that incentivizes conservation it should be supported across the continent.

Conservancy legislation differs country by country, and conservancies vary in size, structure, and land tenure. Despite the diversity among them, conservancies throughout Africa share somewhat universal benefits. Conservancies:

- ▶ complement state-owned protected areas by providing additional wildlife habitat;
- ▶ diversify the tourism economy by offering a different type of tourism product than state-owned protected areas, such as walking safaris and cultural interaction;
- ▶ diversify land management, providing a range of habitat types to support a broader diversity of wildlife and ecosystems; and
- ▶ directly engage and empower communities and private landowners in taking part in and benefiting from conservation, thereby incentivizing protection of wildlife and habitat, increasing the number of people benefiting from conservation, and decreasing animosity toward wildlife.[23]

The African Wildlife Foundation assessed conservancies in Namibia, Botswana, Zimbabwe, South Africa, Tanzania, and Kenya and found the following consistent factors that lead to the long-term success of conservancies:

- ▶ Well-defined property, land, and wildlife user rights.
- ▶ A vibrant national tourism economy and a diversity of tourism opportunities in the conservancy.
- ▶ Meaningful engagement of landowners and adjacent neighbors to ensure local support.
- ▶ Parties obtaining ownership/equity in conservancies bring resources, money, land, expertise, and assume a level of risk—handouts do not work.
- ▶ Strong legal structure, with bylaws and constitutions to ensure good governance, transparency, adherence to conservation parameters, code of conduct, membership obligations, and revenue sharing.

- ▶ Adopted and updated scientifically based habitat and wildlife management plans.
- ▶ Professional management, a solid business plan, and a formal institutional structure.

The motivation to establish a conservancy varies. For some, it is the best land use, whereas for others it is to preserve special cultural sites and traditions. In northern Kenya for example, communities have established conservancies as a form of security against Somali terrorists and cattle raiders. Bottom line, conservancy benefits must be determined by the communities and landowners, and designed in a way that meets their needs.

In Zimbabwe for example, private conservancies were established as landowners realized managing wildlife in arid zones was more profitable than managing livestock. In 2003, private wildlife conservancies comprised 1.9 percent of Zimbabwe's total land base and 10.9 percent of the conservation land in Zimbabwe,[24] playing a key role in the country's wildlife conservation. Today, as a result of unplanned resettlement and irregular land allocations due to Zimbabwe's land reform process and other associated legislation, there are less than approximately four viable private wildlife conservancies in the country. The 320,000-hectare (790,737-acre) Save Valley Conservancy is one of these last remaining conservancies in Zimbabwe. Located in the Lowveld (the lowlands) of southwestern Zimbabwe, the Save Valley Conservancy hosts significant populations of endangered rhino, elephant, lion, and wild dog and is at risk because of unplanned settlement and lack of clarity around wildlife user rights and land tenure.

Zimbabwe, like other countries in Africa, has an incredible opportunity to increase conservation land and engage communities in conservation by incorporating community land into existing conservancies to expand the conservation area and to support new landowners in the establishment of conservancies. Providing the technical and financial support to expand and launch new conservancies is critical.

There is substantial economic and ecological complementarity between parks and conservancies,[25] which further demonstrates the need for both kinds of protected areas. For example, AWF helped establish community-owned conservancies outside Amboseli National Park. The park serves as a critical source of wildlife, without which the conservancies would not be ecologically viable on their own. Likewise, the park would not survive without the community conservancies as they protect a key wildlife corridor, dispersal area, and protective buffer to the park. The revenue that the conservancy members are generating has made them conservation supporters.

The term "national park" is well understood around the globe and draws tourists. While conservancies are becoming more recognized, tourists are still more inclined to visit landscapes with parks. Conservancies enjoy many of the same visitors as parks do by offering different experiences that cannot be undertaken in state-run protected areas, such as walking safaris, cultural experiences, horse-back riding, and night game-drives. Many tourists now spend time in parks and conservancies, bringing revenue to both protected area authorities and conservancy owners, as well as increasing revenue to the country since tourists stay longer to enjoy the diversity of activities offered.

Improve protected area management

For Africa to maintain its wildlife, protected areas—state, provincial, private, and community-owned and community-run—must be well managed. Africa's protected areas range from well-supported and highly functioning, such as Kruger National Park in South Africa and Volcanoes National Park in Rwanda, to less well functioning, such as Bouba Ndjida National Park in Cameroon and Comoe National Park in Ivory Coast. Protected area management in Africa is faced with a diversity of challenges: restricted funding, limited capacity, and lack of political prioritization. Park management is generally more successful in countries having autonomous protected area authorities, robust tourism economies, and tourism and ecosystem services that are valued as important parts of the economy, such as in South Africa, Namibia, Kenya, and Botswana. Autonomous protected area authorities have the ability to manage protected areas with limited political interference, collect and spend revenue, and make management decisions without the requirement of going through a central government.

Another key aspect of successful protected area management is where revenue is shared between parks. For example, in Tanzania significant revenue comes from Kilimanjaro and Serengeti National Parks. This revenue in turn subsidizes less frequently visited, yet ecologically significant parks, such as Ruaha and Kitulo National Parks in southern Tanzania. Despite revenue from tourism driving sound operations of protected areas, most countries still receive some level of additional financial support from central government for protected area management.

In less developed countries, such as Ethiopia, Burkina Faso, Democratic Republic of Congo, and Cameroon, the challenges of park management are significant. In Ethiopia for example, the country's wildlife authority is not autonomous. All revenue generated from parks goes to the central government and the wildlife authority receives an annual budget that is generally below its required operational budget. In DRC, Africa's largest country—host to globally significant forests and endangered species, such as the mountain gorilla and the bonobo—the annual operating budget of the protected area authority is far from adequate to support the country's network of protected areas. In West Africa, Parc W (the "W" National Park) is a tri-national park, 11,283 square kilometers comprising parts of Burkina Faso, Niger, and Benin. The park is one of the last major expanses of intact Sudanese-Sahelian savannah in West Africa, provides large tracts of habitat for species that require extensive areas for seasonal migrations, and is on the frontline against the advance of the Sahara Desert. Given the park's low visitor numbers, park authorities lack the necessary income to manage the park. As a result, the park is used extensively as a grazing zone by migrant pastoralists.

Protected area authorities are seeking management partners to help support and transform struggling parks and sustain key areas of biodiversity. Providing sustained support to wildlife authorities, and doing so in a way that builds up the capacity of the protected area authority and sustainability of parks, is vital for the long-term sustainability of Africa's protected areas.

Similarly, private conservancies and community conservation areas must be well managed. Support should be provided to ensure that these areas are managed optimally and are economically viable, to ensure their long-term sustainability.

Some protected areas will be able to support the majority of operations through tourism; some, however, although having significant ecological value, are located in countries that for one reason or another do not attract tourists, and so they struggle to become self-sustaining. These include protected areas in countries with high levels of conflict or which are perceived as politically unstable, such as South Sudan, Central African Republic, DRC, and Chad. These countries host globally significant wildlife. If not supported, their governments are likely to allocate protected areas for different types of land use as pressure on habitat increases. Biodiversity offsets and credits, as well as carbon credits, offer potential market solutions to sustaining parks, but for now support for these areas is driven by philanthropy as the markets are not fully established.

While certain countries are supporting conservation successfully through tourism, it is important that this not be the only source of revenue. For example, because of the impact of terrorism activities in Kenya, tourism over the past two years has declined. With fewer people visiting Kenya's protected areas, there is less revenue. As a result, wildlife rangers and scouts have been laid off, thereby increasing the vulnerability of wildlife and habitat and hampering conservation management. In addition, staff members who have lost their jobs may seek alternative income through poaching. Economic diversification is thus fundamental in supporting Africa's conservation areas.

Engage communities in conservation
Conservation must matter to the local landowners and communities living with wildlife. If they do not benefit from conservation, it will not work—it is that simple. There are numerous examples across Africa whereby people from surrounding communities invade conservation areas, kill wildlife, or bring down fences because they are not benefiting from conservation. Living with wildlife can be challenging and it places an additional burden on already stressed lives. Communities lose livestock due to predation, and crops due to elephant raids. There are, however, many ways to enlist communities in long-term conservation and to incentivize and motivate them to protect wildlife. As discussed previously, one of the best ways of doing so, wherever feasible, is by supporting community conservancies.

There is debate in conservation circles about the success of community conservation. The challenge is not how we replace community-driven approaches with other models, but how we design and implement community-based nature protection programs to maximize their ecological and economic benefits and to stand the test of time. Most community-based projects are focused around incentivizing communities to protect a particular area or wildlife in return for incentives that range from money to social benefits or employment. However, many community-based projects are flawed because of poor structure, lack of good governance, unsustainability, and top-down approach. In addition, Africa is riddled with small community projects that generate revenue that is too little, unreliable, or both for the community's benefit; thus, they fail to have a meaningful impact on people's lives and to support a conservation outcome.

For community-based programs to work, the following factors must be met:

- ▶ Community engagement must be voluntary.
- ▶ Communities must be engaged from the beginning of the project and their participation should be institutionalized so they play meaningful roles in governance and management.
- ▶ There must be clear conservation targets, such as the protection of specific lands or the conservation of certain species.
- ▶ Conservation benefits must be tied to conservation responsibility in a *quid pro quo* scenario making communities responsible for conservation outcomes.
- ▶ Conservation benefits must be at a scale that deters nonconservation behavior. If a community can make more money from farming as opposed to keeping wildlife, they will do so.
- ▶ Community benefits should be reliable. If a community is uncertain as to if and when benefits will be derived, they may resort to nonconservation activities.
- ▶ Handouts do not work, and communities need to both assume a reasonable level of risk and bring something to the project, such as land, wildlife, money, or skills.
- ▶ Project structures must be transparent and set up to ensure equitable distribution of benefits and avoid elite capture.

Many community-based projects are set up on the assumption that communities will automatically engage in positive conservation behavior if provided with certain benefits. This kind of wishful thinking does not work. For example, one may speculate that if a high-yield crop is introduced into an agricultural intensification program, the farmer will grow more food in a smaller area and will not expand the farm into the local forest—the conservation target. However, if this has not been codified through an agreement or a land use plan, the farmer will most certainly expand the farm area to grow more crops for market.

The African Wildlife Foundation utilizes a suite of conservation covenants in its programs to protect a particular natural asset, such as a forest, conservation area, or wildlife. In exchange for meeting these covenants, certain economic or societal benefits are derived—such as revenue from a business, help with access to a market, support for business development, educational support, or a combination of these. These conservation-derived benefits must be at a scale to have a meaningful impact on the communities. If, however, these covenants are not met, benefits are withheld. It is a *quid pro quo* arrangement that is secured through a legal agreement with the community. Communities are part of the process from the beginning and have the full freedom to choose not to be part of a program.

AWF's conservation enterprise program has succeeded in establishing community tourism programs that incentivize conservation and improve people's lives, because the community benefits are substantial, reliable, and institutionalized with community equity. AWF has successfully helped communities that own land, customary and legal tenure, to establish conservation lodges in Botswana, Zambia, Rwanda, Uganda, Tanzania, and Kenya. With AWF's model, the community owns the fixed assets and the lodges while agreeing to set aside land for conservation, subscribe to a set of conservation covenants, and partner with a private sector operator who manages the facility on their behalf. The revenue goes back to the community and is tied to conservation performance, making nature conservation an incentive for communities. The engagement of the private sector in these models is important to ensure the long-term economic sustainability of the operation.

AWF also requires that a percentage of the individuals employed at the lodge be from the local community, thus generating more revenue to and increasing the skill base of the community. I met a young Maasai man five years ago at one of the AWF-supported lodges in southern Kenya. He initially had been hired as a busboy, earning money for his extended family. Place settings, tablecloths, and napkins were foreign to him, but he learned quickly. He had a special knack for birding, which was recognized by the lodge management. They provided him with guide and natural history training, and today he is one of their lead guides. He has a driver's license, is certified as a guide, and is currently enjoying a sought-after job in Kenya. He is a local champion for wildlife and his family appreciates the direct benefits they enjoy from wildlife.

This model can also be applied to communities who, although they do not own land, can—through loan and grant arrangements—acquire equity in existing lodges in conservation areas, thus incentivizing conservation of that resource. AWF conducted interviews with communities around Zimbabwe's largest and arguably one of its most important parks, Hwange National Park. All communities complained that they were not benefiting from the park. This dynamic is not unique to Zimbabwe. Imagine if these communities had equity in some of the lodges in the park—their attitude would be radically different. Meaningful community equity is the direction community-based natural resource programs must go.

Governments can play a central role in incentivizing conservation for communities and private landowners. Many African countries, for example, provide economic and legislative benefits for agricultural land use. If governments provided similar incentives for wildlife and conservation land management, it would result in more land being managed for conservation purposes.

Make conservation a priority

Expanding protected areas is and will continue to be difficult in Africa until conservation of wildlife and wildlands becomes a priority. Conservation in Africa competes for attention and resources with other key issues such as poverty, infrastructure, health, and employment. However, conservationists are demonstrating that healthy ecosystems are vital to poverty alleviation, sustainable agriculture, and livelihood enhancement and that thriving ecosystems make countries stronger and more resilient in the face of climate change.

In order for senior government officials to prioritize conservation their constituents must support and advocate for conservation. Even as I write this essay, pastoralists in northern Kenya's Laikipia region have taken to the streets and are protesting *against* wildlife. Laikipia is one region in Kenya with an increasing wildlife population, which has resulted in an increase in human-wildlife conflict. After a number of people there were killed by elephants, the local communities gave the district government one week to deal with "their elephants." (Reference to "their elephants" rather than "our elephants" demonstrates how few members of the population view their country's wildlife as their own.) If the local community felt that they were benefiting from conservation—through wildlife-based tourism, for example—and if these benefits outweighed the losses resulting from human-wildlife conflict, the situation undoubtedly would be different.

For conservation to become a priority there must be greater awareness of the overall value brought to countries and communities by protected areas and wildlife. There is an increasing appreciation for the role protected areas play in safeguarding ecosystem services. Ecosystem services support every aspect of human life and a majority of Africans are directly dependent on these services for their daily survival. As African governments work to address poverty and food security, the protection of ecosystem services through protected areas should be a key strategy.

African governments are also starting to recognize the important economic value of ecosystem services. Historically, the economic value of protected landscapes was determined by calculating park entry fees or lodge revenue, both of which are mere portions of the benefits derived from conservation. An assessment done on Ethiopia's protected areas took into consideration the "indirect benefits" of nature preservation such as watershed management, flooding reduction, natural water treatment, ground water recharge, soil erosion reduction, air filtration, and carbon sequestration. The economic value of protected areas was valued at approximately US$432 million annually.[26] This is in a country with little wildlife-based tourism. Figures like these, which underscore the economic value of healthy ecosystems, can help change the discussion with policy makers as they make decisions about land and habitat.

Conclusion

Walking through an East African savannah woodland, I quietly follow my guide. It is early morning. The sun is rising and the mourning doves greet us with their common call. I am relishing the sounds of the savannah, the stillness, and the birdsong. My guide is passionate about this landscape. He knows its natural history, inhabitants, and rhythms. He explains that as a senior guide he supports his children in good schools, and provides them with clothing, a nice home, and ample food. Wildlife conservation changed his life.

We are walking in a community conservancy. My entry fee goes toward the community, and the luxury lodge where I stayed the night before is owned by the community. This landscape was once degraded; however, now this conservancy is flourishing with wildlife—cheetah, lion, elephant, hyena, aardwolf, and more. Before the creation of the conservancy, this community fought wildlife—the people were not benefiting and wildlife was perceived as a nuisance. They now support wildlife and conservation. As we move deliberately between the whistling acacia, we see a group of ten elegant Maasai giraffe browsing. They watch us, determine that we are not a threat, and continue eating. We sit together on a fallen tree branch and watch the giraffes in silence, letting the morning unfold.

This conservancy demonstrates what is possible.

Africa is endowed with vast and varied wild nature. Its wildlife is unparalleled and its landscape diversity exceptional. The alarming trends of habitat and wildlife loss can be reversed. Across Africa, governments, nongovernmental organizations, communities, landowners, and the private sector are joining together to create sustainable and viable protected areas. These creative partnerships are crucial now more than ever. For Africa's wildlife and wild lands to survive, more well-managed protected areas and community and private conservation areas are needed, and communities must be meaningfully engaged in conservation. The value of conservation must be recognized at all levels. Africa has a unique opportunity to develop in a way that preserves its natural heritage for generations to come. Africa has a chance to show the world that economic development does not need to come at the expense of its precious wildlife and natural environment.

Another Inconvenient Truth: The Failure of Enforcement Systems to Save Charismatic Species

ELIZABETH L. BENNETT

IN SPITE OF SIGNIFICANT recent advances in understanding how to conserve species we are failing to conserve some of the most beloved and charismatic, with severe population losses, shrinking ranges and extinctions of subspecies. The primary reason is hunting for illegal trade of highly valuable body parts, increasingly operated by sophisticated organized criminal syndicates supplying wealthy East Asian markets. Current enforcement systems were not established to tackle such crime, and weak governance, low capacity and inadequate resources facilitate the trade. To save these species this trade must be treated as serious crime, with allocation of sufficient resources, highly trained personnel, and appropriate technologies to allow it to be tackled effectively. Success in tackling this trade will necessitate commitment from governments and nongovernmental organizations and the support of civil society.

In the first decade of the twenty-first century we have learned much about how to conserve species more effectively. We have become more skillful in strategic planning,[1] and in applying this to range-wide priority setting and species-focused action planning.[2] We are becoming more sophisticated in understanding how to identify and engage appropriate stakeholders in developing and implementing conservation programs,[3] in balancing the needs of conservation with those of local communities,[4] and in developing incentives to conserve species.[5]

We are failing, however, to conserve some of the most charismatic and beloved species. The Sumatran rhinoceros (*Dicerorhinus sumatrensis*) is almost certainly now extinct in Thailand, and probably in Peninsular Malaysia.[6] In spite of increases in both black (*Diceros bicornis*) and white rhinoceroses (*Ceratotherium simum*) overall, two subspecies of African rhino have almost certainly gone extinct in the past decade as a result of illegal hunting: the western black rhinoceros (*D. bicornis longipes*) and, in the past three years, the northern white rhinoceros (*C. simum cottoni*).[7] Even formerly seemingly secure populations are now at risk: South Africa lost almost 230 rhinoceroses to poaching between January and October of 2010, one every thirty hours.[8] The saiga antelope (*Saiga tatarica*) has suffered a catastrophic decline, with a loss of greater than 95 percent of its total population in the fifteen years prior to 2005.[9] Less than 3,500 tigers (*Panthera tigris*) now occur in the wild, occupying less than 7 percent of their historical range,[10] and, of these, fewer than 1,000 tigers are likely to be breeding females.[11] With the tiger, we are witnessing the tragic winking out of one of the planet's most beloved animals across its range, one population at a time, with recent extinctions in Nakai-Nam Theun in Lao PDR where tigers were seen frequently fifteen years ago,[12] and Sariska, Panna, and possibly Sanjay in India within the last three years.[13]

The primary reason for all of these declines is hunting for illegal trade in highly valuable body parts. Such trade is increasingly controlled by organized criminal syndicates with sophisticated smuggling methods and modes of operation, frequently operating through countries with high levels of corruption.[14] The trade is large-scale and commercialized: elaborate and costly hidden compartments in shipping containers or below wholesale shipments of sawn timber, fish, or scrap products, in which are concealed massive quantities of wildlife products from ivory to bear paws and frozen pangolins.[15] The traders are also light on their feet, frequently changing routes and modes of operation as enforcement commences in any one place and continually working through the routes and means of least resistance.[16] The legislation and methods of addressing illegal wildlife trade in many countries were not developed to tackle this type of organized crime. Trade through e-commerce from websites whose location is difficult to detect and who operate beyond the current realms of wildlife legislation and enforcement is a further challenge.

What is responsible for this increase in organized wildlife crime? The single greatest factor is the increasing demand for wildlife products from the wealthy countries of East Asia and the high prices these products command.[17] Many of the criminal networks radiating out across Asia and Africa ultimately link to the markets of East Asia. Within Africa this often involves nationals from China, Thailand, Vietnam, and other Asian countries operating within the continent.[18] The trade is facilitated by weak governance and lack of capacity in many of the countries where the animals are hunted and in transit, compounded by the close link between government officials and big business, both legitimate (blue-fin tuna traders, for example), illegitimate (such as pangolin traders), and the legally shady area between the two (tiger farms, for instance). Weak governance also extends beyond governments: Ivory being transported by air from Africa to Asia in shipments greatly exceeding individual travel allowances shows that certain airlines are either lax or corrupt.[19]

The scale of the trade is immense. Between January 2006 and September 2009, a minimum of 470 African rhinos were poached; snaring of rhinos for bushmeat has largely been replaced by targeted shooting, using assault weapons and high-powered rifles, to obtain the horns.[20] Given its nature, obtaining exact trade figures for other species is impossible, but data from seizures give some indication of the level of operations: the 24 tons of pangolins seized by Vietnamese authorities in March 2008[21] in two linked shipments from Indonesia destined for China; the 332 tiger bones and two tiger skulls, 531 saiga horns, and 283 Asiatic black-bear paws seized by the Russian authorities in 2007 near the border with China;[22] the 239 African elephant tusks weighing an estimated 2 tons seized at Bangkok International Airport en route from Nairobi to Lao PDR in February 2010;[23] the 6.2 tons of ivory from Tanzania via Malaysia seized by the Vietnamese authorities in March 2009;[24] and the total of 361.4 tons of ivory seized globally between 1989 and 2009.[25] The proportion of trade represented by these confiscations is unknown, but it is likely to be the tip of the iceberg: of the 1,521 African rhino horns allegedly destined for East Asia between January 2006 and September 2009, only 43 were seized by authorities and a further 129 recovered in the field.[26]

We have taken our eye off the ball. Enforcement is critical: old-fashioned in concept but needing increasingly advanced methods to challenge the ever-more sophisticated methods of smuggling. Where enforcement is thorough, and with sufficient resources and personnel, it works, both at sites[27] and along trade chains.[28] Success stories involve long-term programs based on good science and local knowledge, sufficient capacity supported by appropriate legal mechanisms to establish and enforce regulations, and monitoring programs to facilitate adaptive management.[29] Successes also involve multiple partners in clear, multi-agency relationships to provide different skill sets and, critically, to provide accountability and transparency, leading to good management even in countries with high levels of corruption.[30]

But such programs are lamentably rare, and resources applied to combating such crime generally grossly inadequate. In most countries wildlife and protected area authorities are given low priority and thus are severely understaffed, undertrained, and underresourced. Wildlife laws are often anachronistic, from a past when this type of wildlife crime was rare or nonexistent. More often than not systems are weak for protected area enforcement and even weaker for enforcement along trade chains and in markets, where the responsibility for enforcement is legally ambiguous and often lies with transportation or urban authorities whose interest and training in wildlife crime is negligible. The same lack of resources applies internationally. The ASEAN (Association of Southeast Asian Nations) Wildlife Enforcement Network is often held up as a good example of an international initiative to combat wildlife crime,[31] but its home base of Thailand remains one of the three countries most heavily implicated globally in the illicit trade in ivory.[32] CITES (the Convention on International Trade in Endangered Species of Wild Fauna and Flora) and Interpol each have only a single person in charge of enforcement of wildlife crimes.

Tackling the issue by focusing on demand reduction is a challenge, given deeply ingrained cultural beliefs in the efficacy of certain wildlife medicines, leading to tacit support for the trade across many sectors of Asian society. Any change is likely to be on a generational timescale, but we do not have that luxury of time for many of the species currently targeted by trade. In the short term the only practical way to reduce demand is through enforcement, both acting as a deterrent and also demonstrating that this is not a socially acceptable norm. Meanwhile, in-depth research into what will cause widespread behavior change is urgently needed.

To save some of the highly charismatic species before it is too late we have to start taking wildlife enforcement seriously. We must dedicate the intellectual, funding, and personnel resources needed to supersede those of the criminal organizations involved. This requires greatly increased numbers of highly trained and well-equipped staff at all points along the trade chain: most especially in core sites where the species are being hunted but also along key transportation routes and in end markets. It involves use of a wide array of technologies, whatever is most appropriate for the task in hand: sniffer dogs and X-ray machines for vehicles and shipping containers, user-friendly DNA testing kits and Smartphone apps to aid in species identification, and state-of-the-art software to detect Internet crime. Success necessitates a total change in the way that wildlife crime is treated by governments and wider society. Law enforcement agencies including customs and police must regard this as serious crime and its enforcement as part of their job. Encouragingly, in Asia the United Nations Office on Drugs and Crime has recently listed wildlife crime as one of their core foci and, in November 2010, the potentially powerful International Consortium on Combating Wildlife Crime (ICCWC) was signed into effect.[33]

To be effective in tackling wildlife crime, national governments, drawing on the expertise of ICCWC members and others as needed, should start dedicating the scale of resources to illegal wildlife trade that they do to other serious crimes, including the provision of highly trained enforcement personnel. Members of the judiciaries in countries along the trade chain should be well informed, giving sentences appropriate to the value and scale of the crime. Critically important, enforcement agencies in developed countries should greatly step up their technical support to the less developed countries that are so often the sources of the traded wildlife, as well as curb demand at home, and multilateral, bilateral and private funding agencies should dedicate the level of resources needed to support such operations. Nongovernmental organizations with in-depth, on-the-ground knowledge and technical skills can facilitate much of this through their local, national and international networks and knowledge bases. All of this requires the support of civil society and their appreciation of the full implications of illegal wildlife trade. Unless we start taking wildlife crime seriously and allocating the commitment and resources appropriate to tackling sophisticated, well-funded, globally linked criminal operations, populations of some of the most beloved but economically prized charismatic species on the planet will continue to wink out across their range and, appallingly soon, altogether.

The author is grateful for comments from John Robinson, Arlyne Johnson, and two anonymous reviewers.

America Needs More National Parks

MICHAEL J. KELLETT

From the very beginning, every single park has had opposition.
At the end, everybody goes, "Wow, what were we thinking?"
—KEN BURNS, FILMMAKER, *THE NATIONAL PARKS: AMERICA'S BEST IDEA*

THE PEOPLE OF AMERICA invented the national park with the congressional establishment of Yellowstone in 1872. Since then, our National Park System has grown to more than 400 units, including such legendary places as Yosemite, Grand Canyon, Great Smoky Mountains, Independence Hall, Mount Rushmore, and the Statue of Liberty. Each year, almost 300 million people from across America and around the globe visit our national parks. The success of our park system has inspired more than a hundred other countries, from Afghanistan to Zimbabwe, to create hundreds of their own national parks.

Despite our magnificent national park legacy, less than 7 percent of America's lands are preserved in the National Park System or in the National Wilderness Preservation System outside of national parks—and most of the acreage is in Alaska. Several hundred million acres of undeveloped federal, state, and private lands and thousands of square miles of marine, estuarine, and Great Lakes waters have inadequate protection. Most of these areas are threatened by increasing development.

Many places of great natural and cultural significance could qualify for addition to the National Park System. National park designation is unmatched in providing permanent preservation, world-class education and recreation, diverse economic benefits, and broad public recognition and support that ensures long-term ecological integrity. Urgent action is needed to expand the boundaries of threatened existing parks and to add high-priority new areas to the park system, before they are seriously damaged or lost.

Priorities for National Park System expansion

Expansion of Existing Parks

Development activities on adjacent national forest, Bureau of Land Management (BLM), state, and private lands are increasingly endangering existing National Park System units. This is because many national parks are not large enough to encompass complete ecosystems or historic landscapes, safeguard wide-ranging predators, and connect vital habitats. The expansion of incomplete national parks often represents the best way to ensure their long-term protection.[1]

Potential park expansions include: Biscayne (FL) and Delaware Water Gap (NJ, PA) to prevent encroaching urban development; Dinosaur (CO) and Theodore Roosevelt (ND) to terminate fracking for oil and gas; Crater Lake (OR) and North Cascades (WA) to stop logging and road building; Canyonlands (UT) and Glen Canyon (UT) to prohibit drilling, mining, and off-road motorized abuse; Glacier (MT) and Yellowstone (ID, MT, WY) to halt the killing of wolves, grizzly bears, and bison; and Mammoth Cave (TN) and Oregon Caves (OR) to avert exploitation of integral watersheds.

Threatened Ecosystems

At least 50 percent or more of the Earth may need to be protected to sustain native biological diversity.[2] However, less than 6 percent of the coterminous United States is now safeguarded in nature reserves.[3] One study has estimated that three-quarters of America's terrestrial ecoregions are endangered, critical, or vulnerable,[4] while another study has rated 126 of the continent's ecosystems as critically endangered, endangered, or threatened.[5] The creation of new national parks could greatly expand the protection of ecosystems across America.

New ecosystem-based national parks could include: biodiversity hot spots, such as Ancient Forest (CA, OR) and Kauai (HI); immense, untamed landscapes, such as Red Desert (WY) and Tongass (AK); rare native grasslands, such as Kissimmee Prairie (FL) and Sheyenne (ND); vulnerable coasts, such as Cape Fear (NC) and Lake Michigan (MI); expansive wildlands in regions with inadequate protected areas, such as Maine Woods (ME) and Mobile-Tensaw Delta (AL); iconic landscapes such as Hells Canyon (ID, OR) and Mount St. Helens (WA); and exceptional paleontological and geological areas, such as Tule Springs (NV) and Valles Caldera (NM).

Natural River Systems

More than 75,000 large dams have drowned 600,000 miles of America's rivers under reservoirs—some 17 percent of total river miles.[6] Three-quarters of our freshwater ecoregions have been identified as being in endangered, critical, or vulnerable condition.[7] The National Park Service has identified 3,400 river segments totaling 63,000 miles, which have "outstandingly remarkable values" of national significance.[8] Only about 200 of these river segments, totaling 12,500 river miles—just 4/10 of 1 percent of the nation's total river miles—are included in the National Wild and Scenic Rivers System.[9] National Park System expansion could safeguard many of these imperiled rivers.

Potential national parks could protect segments of great American rivers such as the Colorado, Columbia, Connecticut, Mississippi, Missouri, Ohio, Rio Grande, and Snake, as well as outstanding river segments listed on the Nationwide Rivers Inventory (NRI), such as the Allagash (ME), Big Darby (OH), Big Fork (MN), Clinch (TN, VA), Gila (AZ, NM), Green (CO, UT, WY), John Day (OR), and Suwannee (FL).

Wild Marine and Coastal Areas

Poorly represented in reserves are America's marine, estuarine, and Great Lakes waters, and most are open to harmful industrial activities.[10] The National Park Service has long experience with parks encompassing significant waters, such as Biscayne, Channel Islands, and Isle Royale. An expanded National Park System could considerably increase protection for America's territorial waters.

Potential water-oriented national parks include existing national marine sanctuaries (NMSs) and national estuarine research reserves (NERRs), administered by the National Oceanographic and Atmospheric Administration (NOAA), and other significant waters, such as Big Bend Seagrass Beds (FL), Bristol Bay (AK), Delaware Bay (DE, NJ), East End, St. Croix (USVI), Frenchman's Bay-Gulf of Maine (ME), and Western Lake Superior (MI, WI).

Endangered Wildlife

Over 1,500 American plant and wildlife species are listed under the federal Endangered Species Act (ESA), and countless others are in jeopardy, mainly due to habitat destruction and industrial development. One of the primary reasons for creating national parks, including Denali, Everglades, and Glacier, has been to safeguard native wildlife and habitats. The expansion of the National Park System could help to save many additional at-risk species.

New national parks for imperiled wildlife could include: Georges Bank (MA) for blue, fin, North Atlantic right, and sei whales; Giant Sequoia (CA) for California condor, California spotted owl, Little Kern golden trout, and Valley elderberry longhorn beetle; Gila-Apache (AZ, NM) for jaguar, Mexican wolf, Mexican spotted owl, and Gila trout; High Allegheny (WV) for West Virginia northern flying squirrel, Eastern small-footed, Indiana, and Virginia big-eared bats, and Cheat Mountain salamander; Northeast Ecological Corridor (PR) for West Indian manatee, Puerto Rican plain pigeon, Puerto Rican boa, and leatherback turtle; and Thunder Basin (WY) for black-footed ferret, black-tailed prairie dog, greater sage-grouse, and blowout penstemon.

Carbon Preserves

If kept intact, forests, prairies, and wetlands absorb and store massive amounts of carbon, helping to offset greenhouse gas emissions that fuel climate change. [11] However, on most lands outside national parks and wilderness areas, massive amounts of carbon are being released by industrial activities such as logging, livestock grazing, drilling and mining, intensive agriculture, and commercial development. National parks protecting carbon-rich ecosystems from these activities could make a major contribution toward mitigating climate change.

Examples of potential carbon-preserve national parks include old-growth forests such as the Chugach (AK), Nez Perce-Clearwater (ID), Okanogan-Wenatchee (WA), Shasta-Trinity (CA), Willamette (OR), and BLM Medford District (OR), as well as high-density, second-growth forests, such as the Allegheny (PA), Chequamegon-Nicolet (WI), Green Mountain (VT), Mississippi (MS), Quabbin (MA), and Ottawa (MI).

Restoration Parks

With little of America remaining in pristine condition, the restoration of degraded lands and waters is increasingly important. The international Convention on Biological Diversity (CBD) calls for the restoration of at least 15 percent of degraded ecosystems by 2020.[12] The National Park

Service has a century of experience with restorative national parks, such as Big Bend, Redwood, and Shenandoah. This experience could be applied to many other damaged lands and waters across America.

New national parks could restore rivers such as Detroit River (MI) and Rio Salado (AZ), wetlands such as Grand Kankakee Marsh (IL, IN) and Sharp Park (CA), forests such as Great Trinity (TX) and Tuskegee (AL), and coastal ecosystems, such as Ormond Beach (CA) and Western Lake Erie (MI, OH).

Cultural Treasures

Despite its rich resources, the National Park System does not embody the full breadth of American cultural diversity. For instance, while the system includes many battlefields and presidential homes, it has few sites representing immigration. Dozens of cultural treasures merit further consideration as new national parks.

Potential new cultural national parks could represent early industry at Blackstone River Valley (MA, RI), Native American heritage at Cedar Mesa (UT), colonial history at Castle Nugent (USVI), conservation and social justice movements at Walden Woods (MA), and a World War II program with global impact at Manhattan Project (NM, TN, WA). Expansion of existing parks could broaden public understanding of workers' rights at Cesar Chavez (AZ, CA), the fight to end slavery at Fort Monroe (VA), Native American culture at Ocmulgee (GA), crucial Civil War battles at Petersburg (VA), and Spanish colonial history at San Antonio Missions (TX).

Parks for the People

Large metropolitan areas are home to two-thirds of Americans, but few of them are within 50 miles of a major National Park System unit. More than 90 percent of total national park acreage is west of the Great Plains, while only a small percentage is in the East, South, and Midwest. Millions of people in underrepresented cities and regions would benefit from new national parks that connect them with nature, explore our history, and promote public health.

New national park candidates in or near large cities include Bankhead-Talladega (Birmingham), Big Darby (Columbus), El Yunque (San Juan, PR), Great Salt Lake (Salt Lake City), Midewin Prairie (Chicago), Mount Hood (Portland, OR), Piney Woods (Houston), and Santa Ana Mountains (Los Angeles). Potential new parks in underrepresented regions include Berkshire (MA), Pawcatuck Borderlands (CT, RI), and White Mountains (ME, NH) in the Northeast; Land Between the Lakes (KY, TN), Lowcountry (SC), and Ouachita (AR, OK) in the Southeast; and Driftless Rivers (IA, WI), Ozark Highlands (MO), and Ohio Valley (IL, IN, OH) in the Midwest.

The benefits of national parks

Strength of Nature Preservation Mandate

The National Park System is the gold standard for American protected areas. The unique mandate of the 1916 National Park Service "Organic Act" requires our parks to be managed "to conserve the scenery and the natural and historic objects and the wild life therein and to provide for the enjoyment of the same in such manner and by such means as will leave them unimpaired for the enjoyment of future generations."[13] The agency's "Management Policies" specify that, "when there is a conflict between conserving resources and values and providing for enjoyment of them, conservation is to be predominant."[14] Combined with the additional overlay of designation under the 1964 Wilderness Act, national parks have the most robust safeguards of any lands and waters in America.

Some people mistakenly believe that our national parks are being "loved to death." On the contrary, more than 52 percent—43.9 million acres—of parklands are designated as roadless, undeveloped wilderness areas, by far the largest amount of any public land system. Over 80 percent of the park system is encompassed by designated or recommended wilderness, including 92 percent of Yellowstone, 89 percent of Yosemite, and 85 percent of Zion National Parks.

Conversely, some people have the inaccurate impression that national park designation inordinately restricts public use. In fact, national parks welcome far more visitors than any other land or marine management system. Each year, millions of people readily access famed tourist destinations, such as Old Faithful, Yosemite Valley, and Zion Canyon, by public transportation or road. Others leave their vehicles to explore vast expanses of pristine backcountry that are open to the public.

Strength of Historic Preservation Mandate

Unlike other land and water agencies, Congress has made historic preservation a central part of the National Park Service mission. Two-thirds of park units were designated to protect historical, architectural, or archaeological resources. Many cultural parks have global importance, such as the Statue of Liberty, Philadelphia's Independence Hall, and Mesa Verde

National Park's thousand-year-old cliff dwellings, which are UNESCO World Heritage Sites. Because of the National Park Service's unparalleled expertise, Congress has charged the agency with maintaining the National Register of Historic Places, which has more than 89,000 listings.

Quality of Education and Recreation Programs

A quarter-billion people flock to America's national parks each year to enjoy extraordinary educational and recreational opportunities. Most take advantage of the National Park Service's superlative visitor centers, maps, and guided tours. Families on affordable vacations enjoy secluded picnic areas and hospitable campgrounds. Children encounter living classrooms with towering trees, amazing wildlife, and famed historic sites. Wilderness lovers find adventure and renewal in expansive wilderness. In our increasingly diverse and urbanized society, the natural and historic connections provided by our national parks are more important than ever before.

Resources Dedicated to Preservation, Education, and Recreation

Contrary to a common misconception, the American people can well afford our national parks. The National Park Service budget is about $2.6 billion a year, or a mere 1/15 of 1 percent of the total federal budget. The average American household pays only $2.56 in taxes annually for the operation of our park system—a little more than the price of a cup of coffee at Starbucks.[15] The public views our parks as a tremendous bargain; 90 percent of respondents in a 2012 bipartisan opinion survey said they support maintaining or increasing the National Park Service budget.[16]

We can also afford to expand our National Park System. Most potential parks are already administered by other federal agencies, which have operating budgets that can be transferred with the land. If needed, additional funds could be reallocated from questionable programs, such as annual subsidies of $16 billion to the fossil fuel industry and $20 billion for the problem-plagued F-35 fighter jet. Parks authorized to encompass private lands can be acquired through the federal Land and Water Conservation Fund, landowner donations, and private contributions.

Diversity of Economic Benefits

The National Park Service's emblematic arrowhead logo, one of the world's most valuable brands, signifies national park designation, which confers global prestige and recognition, drawing millions of park visitors who spend billions of dollars in and around parks. National parks also attract professionals, entrepreneurs, and other new residents, who move to gateway communities for a healthy, outdoor lifestyle.[17] In 2012, every taxpayer dollar invested in our National Park System generated an estimated $10 in economic activity, which nationally returned $26.75 billion in annual revenue and supported 243,000 American jobs.[18] The 2013 federal government shutdown, which closed the parks for 16 days, cost local communities almost 8 million visitors and $414 million in revenues.[19]

Depth and Breadth of Public Support

Despite public skepticism toward government in recent years, Americans continue to enthusiastically support our national parks. A 2014 public opinion poll found that 84 percent of Western voters approve of the job the National Park Service is doing—more than any other federal land agency.[20] The appeal and affordability of national parks attracts large numbers of visitors, even during difficult economic times.[21]

Why national park creation has stalled

Although the new national park movement is flourishing in other countries, it has stalled in the United States. Between 1961 and 1981, more than 150 National Park System units were established, including 14 premier national parks (for example, Redwood)—a rate of 7.5 parks per year.[22] Encompassing 53 million acres, these additions more than doubled the size of the park system. Since 1981, a total of 82 National Park System units have been designated—a rate of only 2.3 parks per year. Equal to just 11 percent of the acreage of the previous two decades, 6 million acres of parks have been added. No premier national park has been created that did not involve existing parkland.

There are two major reasons for the decline. First, in the 1980s, the then U.S. president Ronald Reagan and his congressional allies ushered in an era of hostility toward conservation. They opposed expansion of the National Park System while encouraging the development-oriented U.S. Forest Service and BLM to maximize resource extraction. Second, conservationists responded by going on the defensive. Most of them abandoned new national park advocacy, focusing instead on holding back harmful public land development projects and designating alternative types of protected areas that seemed less controversial. Both of these trends continue today.

By taking national parks off the table, conservationists surrendered their most powerful preservation tool. During the last three decades, this has resulted in protected areas that are usually not as large, not as strictly safeguarded, nor as popular as comparable national parks would have been. Most of America's lands and waters remain vulnerable, requiring endless defensive battles by conservationists. This is not a solid foundation for addressing the conservation challenges of the twenty-first century.

The limitations of national park alternatives

Strength of Nature Preservation Mandate

National Forest Special Management Areas. The National Forest System, encompassing 193 million acres, is dominated by "multiple-use" activities, such as logging, livestock grazing, drilling, and mining. In an effort to protect high-priority lands, conservationists have increasingly relied on designating special management areas (SMA). These SMAs include presidentially proclaimed national monuments (NMs) and congressionally established wilderness areas (discussed below), national recreation areas (NRAs), national scenic areas (NSAs), national wild and scenic rivers, national trail system units, and inventoried roadless areas (IRAs) under the Roadless Area Conservation Rule.

Although an improvement over standard management, these SMAs fall far short of National Park System protection standards. They remain under the "multiple-use" mandate, allowing a variety of destructive industrial activities. These activities include clear-cut logging in Giant Sequoia NM (CA), wolf hunting in Hells Canyon NRA (ID), feed crop cultivation in Land Between the Lakes NRA (KY, TN), hardrock mining adjoining Mount St. Helens NM (WA), off-road motorized recreation in Oregon Dunes NRA (OR), and oil and gas drilling in Spruce-Knob-Seneca Rocks NRA (WV).

National Landscape Conservation System. The 248 million acres of Bureau of Land Management lands also have a "multiple-use" mandate. As with the national forests, BLM management favors industrial development over conservation. The National Landscape Conservation System (NLCS), created by Congress in 2009, was meant to shift the BLM "corporate culture" toward preservation. The NLCS includes national monuments, wilderness areas, national conservation areas (NCAs), national wild and scenic rivers, national trail system units, wilderness study areas, and assorted other units.

Unfortunately, the NLCS provides significantly weaker protection than the National Park System. The NLCS authorizing legislation leaves lands under "multiple-use" management instead of providing additional statutory protection. This allows numerous harmful activities, such as oil and gas drilling in Canyons of the Ancients NM (CO), off-road motorized recreation in Grand Canyon-Parashant NM (AZ), intensive livestock grazing in Missouri River Breaks NM (MT), target shooting in Sonoran Desert NCA (AZ), and hardrock mining in White Mountains NRA (AK).

National Wilderness Preservation System. Designation under the Wilderness Act offers the strongest safeguards available for lands under national forest, BLM, and national wildlife refuge management. However, these wilderness areas are inferior to National Park System wilderness areas.

- ▶ *Weaker protection.* National forest, BLM, and national wildlife refuge wilderness areas allow a number of damaging "nonconforming uses," due to politically negotiated compromises incorporated into the Wilderness Act.[23] These uses may include livestock grazing, hunting and trapping of predators, artificial habitat manipulation, game fish stocking, and motorized access to support certain activities. These uses are rarely, if ever, allowed in National Park System wilderness areas, because of the added safeguards of the Organic Act.
- ▶ *Less land protected.* National forest and BLM lands are heavily fragmented by industrial activities and national wildlife refuges are often small, previously damaged areas. This, along with agency resistance, has suppressed the size and number of wilderness areas. The average BLM wilderness area is a mere 5 percent as large as the average National Park System wilderness.[24] This figure increases to only 11 percent for national forest wilderness and less than 40 percent for National Wildlife Refuge wilderness. Just 19 percent of national forest, 14 percent of NWR, and 4 percent of BLM lands are designated as wilderness, versus 52 percent of the National Park System.
- ▶ *Only roadless areas protected.* The Wilderness Act can preserve roadless wildlands, but it cannot restore roaded and seriously degraded landscapes. As a result, national forest and BLM wilderness areas are usually isolated tracts surrounded by roaded lands open to industrial "multiple-use" activities. In contrast, national parks can preserve roadless lands as wilderness, restore previously degraded lands, and reconnect them all as a single protected unit, such as Shenandoah and Everglades National Parks.

National Wildlife Refuge System. The wildlife-oriented mandate of the 150-million-acre National Wildlife Refuge System has been important in protecting native biodiversity. However, many refuges are undermining this goal through intensive habitat manipulation—often to maximize game populations—and other harmful activities. Examples include livestock grazing at Charles M. Russell NWR (MT), genetically modified feed crops at Crab Orchard NWR (IL), commercial farming at Klamath Refuges (OR, CA), for-profit trapping at Kenai NWR (AK), forest clear-cutting at Moosehorn NWR (ME), artificial water impoundments at Shiawassee NWR (MI), and oil and gas extraction on more than one-quarter of national wildlife refuges. With rare exceptions, these destructive uses are prohibited in the National Park System.

National Marine Sanctuaries and National Estuarine Research Reserves. The NOAA-administered National Marine Sanctuary System encompasses 170,000 square miles of marine and Great Lakes waters. However, the system is constrained by inadequate statutory authority, funding, and political support. The 1.3-million-acre National Estuarine Research Reserve System, administered cooperatively by NOAA, states, and other entities, does not provide additional federal statutory protection. Accordingly, these waters are frequently open to damaging activities, such as commercial fishing and mineral extraction, which are usually banned in National Park System units.

State and Private Land Protection. National Park System designation is usually considerably more protective than state or private ownership. Some state parks provide robust safeguards and excellent programs, yet the vast majority of state lands suffer from a variety of damaging industrial uses and extremely limited budgets. Private landowners and nonprofit organizations have preserved many important places, but they cannot offer the permanency of public ownership. National Heritage Areas, designated by Congress and affiliated with the National Park Service, offer valuable assistance to conserve largely private, "lived-in" landscapes, but they do not provide federal ownership and protection.

Strength of Historic Preservation Mandate
National forest, Bureau of Land Management, and national wildlife refuge lands contain a remarkable array of cultural sites and artifacts. Unfortu-

nately, these agencies do not have the mandate, funding, or staff needed to adequately preserve them. The Forest Service has completed cultural surveys on only 20 percent of its lands, while just 6 percent of BLM lands have been surveyed. Irreplaceable historic sites and artifacts are being harmed by commodity extraction, intensive recreation, and vandalism.

Quality of Education and Recreation Programs

Other federal land and water management agencies are not able to provide education and recreation programs comparable to those of the National Park Service. With inadequate budgets for these programs, these agencies have minimal visitor centers, informational materials, and staffing. The Forest Service and BLM are increasingly focused on recreation that maximizes revenues, such as ski resorts and off-road motorized "play areas," on boosting user fees, and on closing or privatizing unprofitable facilities. National Wildlife Refuge visitor programs are dominated by hunting and fishing, with scant resources for other activities. Marine sanctuaries and estuarine reserves offer some commendable education programs, but they are hobbled by insufficient funding.

Resources Dedicated to Preservation, Education, and Recreation

The National Park Service budget dedicates $27.00 per acre of land per year—85 percent of its budget—to park preservation, education, and recreation. In contrast:

- ▶ The Forest Service allocates approximately $7.50 per acre annually—only 6 percent of its budget—to wilderness and other special management areas, although they comprise 22 percent of national forest lands.[25] Most of the agency budget goes to subsidized logging, road systems, and fire suppression.[26]
- ▶ The Bureau of Land Management devotes about $2.50 per acre each year—just 6 percent of its budget—to the National Landscape Conservation System, even though it encompasses 27 percent of BLM lands.[27] Three-quarters of the BLM budget is dedicated to subsidizing commodity extraction, such as livestock grazing.[28]
- ▶ The U.S. Fish and Wildlife Service allots a little over $5 per acre yearly—less than 40 percent of its budget—to the National Wildlife Refuge System.[29] Three-quarters of this is used for wildlife management, including intensive habitat manipulation, and refuge maintenance.

Diversity of Economic Benefits

Inadequate education and recreation programs and damage caused by industrial development undermine the public appeal of national forests, BLM lands, national wildlife refuges, and NOAA sanctuaries and reserves. As a result, these areas generally receive significantly fewer visitors than national parks, and nearby communities tend to attract fewer new businesses and residents. Local people are more economically dependent on boom-and-bust resource extraction. This helps to explain why these communities tend to have lower job, income, and population growth rates than those near National Park System units.[30]

Depth and Breadth of Public Support

Most Americans can name one or more national parks, but few can name even one wilderness area, national forest or BLM special management area, national wildlife refuge, marine sanctuary, or estuarine reserve. Campaigns for these little-known public lands have difficulty gaining public support beyond the state level. This gives local special interests inordinate political influence to reduce the number, size, and level of protection of proposed special management areas. In contrast, campaigns for new national parks can draw on a nationwide constituency to override special interests and gain the strongest possible protection.

Needed: a campaign for new national parks

Considering today's political climate, it would be easy to assume that expanding our National Park System is an impossible dream. On the contrary, most successful national park campaigns of the past overcame challenges at least as great as those we face today.[31] Yellowstone was established during the height of Manifest Destiny's push to "conquer" the West. Isle Royale, Everglades, Big Bend, and Olympic were authorized in the depths of the Great Depression. Grand Canyon, Grand Teton, Kenai Fjords, North Cascades, and Voyageurs all required years of pressure by citizen advocates to prevail over stubborn opposition.

Grassroots groups and activists are rediscovering the potential of the National Park System and proposing new parks in their regions. Thus far, they have been largely working on their own, held back by insufficient resources, entrenched opponents, and limited assistance from mainstream organizations and political leaders. If these individual efforts were united, organized, and adequately funded, they could serve as the foundation of a powerful, nationwide campaign to expand our National Park System.

Such a campaign could provide an inspiring, positive agenda to reinvigorate a tired and reactive conservation movement. It could rally tens of millions of national park supporters from across the country and convince Congress and the president to take positive action. It could help the long-beleaguered National Park Service to reclaim its role as the leading voice for the preservation of our nation's natural and cultural heritage.

In 2016, Americans will celebrate the 100th anniversary of the National Park Service. There could be no better time for a bold campaign to expand the National Park System for the next century. Why not 100 new parks to mark the centennial? The last time the American conservation movement united behind such a sweeping vision, Congress passed the landmark 1980 Alaska National Interest Lands Act and doubled the size of our National Park System. We did it then and we can do it again. Future generations will thank us for having the foresight to save our unprotected natural and historic treasures as their priceless national park legacy.

A New Era of Protected Areas for the Great Plains

CURTIS H. FREESE

TEMPERATE GRASSLANDS, including the Great Plains of North America, are one of the least protected biomes on Earth.[1] Keystone species and large-scale ecological processes that shaped the Great Plains' biodiversity are now missing or much diminished.[2] Fortunately, native prairie persists over significant portions of the Great Plains[3] and the potential exists to fully restore the region's native biota with a network of small and large protected areas. Despite ongoing threats to the region's biodiversity, changing public attitudes and economic and demographic trends may present opportunities for the creation of new protected areas in the Great Plains—with the term *protected areas* here meaning any land devoted primarily to biodiversity conservation—that are sufficiently large to harbor the full suite of native species and ecological processes.

Great Plains biogeography, history, and conservation needs

The Great Plains encompasses the region of mixed- and short-grass prairies bordered on the west by the Rocky Mountain Front and on the east by the tall-grass prairie, which begins around the 97th or 98th meridian west, and extends from southern Alberta, Saskatchewan, and Manitoba to south-central Texas.[4] Rapid Euro-American colonization of the Great

Plains during the last half of the 1800s largely preempted the creation of a system of Great Plains national parks and similar nature reserves. For all practical purposes, Great Plains wildlands—unfenced prairie with abundant wildlife—were gone by 1930, as the prairies had been parceled out to livestock production or converted to crops.[5]

The 1930s and 1940s brought a small surge in protected-area creation in the U.S. portion of the Great Plains as the U.S. government bought homesteaded lands from landowners struggling through the Great Depression and the Dust Bowl. A small percentage of these lands became national wildlife refuges and national parks.[6] However, protected-area coverage in the U.S. portion of the prairies has grown very little since. The biggest jump in Canada's protected areas in the Great Plains occurred over the last three decades with the creation of Grasslands National Park and Suffield National Wildlife Area. Today, roughly 1 percent of the Great Plains is in protected areas.[7]

Nearly two-thirds of the Great Plains remains in native or seminative prairie, primarily managed for livestock production.[8] Energy extraction, invasive plants, poor livestock management practices, draining of wetlands, damming of rivers and streams, and conversion of prairie to cropland, among other factors, are serious threats to the region's biodiversity.[9] The resulting erosion of Great Plains biodiversity is well documented. Many birds are exhibiting significant population declines.[10] Two keystone species, the black-tailed prairie dog and American bison, occupy small fractions of their original ranges. The gray wolf and grizzly bear are extinct in the Great Plains except for animals that occasionally enter the western margins from the Rocky Mountain Front. One keystone ecological process—fire—has been largely eliminated and another—ungulate grazing—highly altered.[11]

Existing protected areas of the Great Plains fall far short of being a cornerstone for biodiversity conservation. Apart from the small proportion of land in protected area coverage, no protected area—whether nonprofit land or national park, wildlife refuge or other public land—harbors the full suite of native species, nor is any federal protected area actively pursuing restoration of all native species and processes. Large mammals, particularly bison, elk, wolves, and grizzly bears, are the most commonly missing species. Protected area lands are commonly leased for domestic cattle grazing, usually as a habitat management tool. The fragmented and unusual configurations of many of the region's most prominent federal protected areas complicate management. The two largest—the 1.1-million-acre Charles M. Russell National Wildlife Refuge (CMR Refuge) and the 244,000-acre Badlands National Park—are elongated and irregular in shape. Three other large protected areas—Grasslands National Park (123,000 acres), Suffield National Wildlife Area (113,000 acres), and Theodore Roosevelt National Park (70,467 acres)—are all divided into two geographically separate management units. Thus, other than the CMR Refuge and Badlands National Park, no protected area in the Great Plains includes a contiguous management unit larger than about 70,000 acres. This is of particular concern in grassland ecosystems where the size of areas needed to accommodate both large-scale ecosystem processes, such as fire and ungulate grazing, and populations of large predators, may be much larger.

Conservation opportunity

Restoring and conserving large-scale ecological processes (such as fire, hydrologic regimes, natural grazing patterns, and migratory routes) and wide-ranging species (large ungulates and predators, for example) of the Great Plains will require very large and interconnected protected areas. Conserving the region's diversity of ecosystems—the Glaciated Plains of Alberta, Saskatchewan, and Montana, the Nebraska Sandhills, and the Flint Hills of Kansas and Oklahoma, to name but three of many—and the biodiversity of each will require a network of strategically placed protected areas across the Great Plains. These may range widely in size, but our vision should be for several ranging in size from 1 to 3 million acres each and others of hundreds of thousands of acres each.

Fortunately, large, mostly intact areas of high-biodiversity value remain across the Great Plains. A recent assessment identified 38 high-priority areas that range between 211,000 and 3.66 million acres in size and represent roughly 10 percent of the region. Fifteen of these areas are over 1 million acres in size,[12] large enough to support sizeable populations of umbrella species like bison and big predators. Allowing for population fluctuations and room to roam, 1 million acres could probably support 10,000–20,000 bison. If wolf densities in nearby regions of the Rocky Mountains[13] are indicative of potential wolf densities on the Great Plains (and they may not be), a reserve of 2 million acres may be necessary to support several packs totaling anywhere from one hundred to two hundred animals. Journal records from the Lewis and Clark Expedition suggest an area this size might support a similar number of grizzly bears. Recent analyses of the Expedition's observations of grizzly bears yielded a density of 8 bears per 100 square miles along their route through the plains.[14] For long-term genetic health, populations of a few hundred animals would require connectivity with other wolf or bear populations.

The biodiversity of Great Plains protected areas depends in large part on the ecological integrity of the larger landscape surrounding them, as well as on the health of distant lands important for migratory species. The soft edges provided by a buffer zone of biodiversity-friendly ranching or agro-ecological farming should generally be much better for protected area management than the hard edge of a wheat or corn monoculture. To create truly soft edges we need a paradigm shift in range management, as Samuel Fuhlendorf and colleagues have proposed, from a utilitarian focus to managing for "pattern and process" that includes the "conservation of all species and life forms, habitat structures, and processes across complex landscapes."[15] Some of the management changes can be made without reducing livestock profitability.[16] However, per the proposed paradigm shift, the metric of livestock profitability may become increasingly secondary, as society demands and is prepared to pay for a broader range of ecosystem services—outdoor recreation, wildlife, carbon sequestration, and so on—from rangelands.[17]

Major socioeconomic and demographic changes in the Great Plains portend potentially large shifts in land ownership and management.[18] Across much of the Great Plains, the number of people living on ranchlands and in small towns continues to decline as remaining ranch owners—predominantly baby boomers and older—leave the land and their children migrate to better economic opportunities. As these ranches become available on the market, they attract increasing numbers of outsiders who buy for investment and recreational purposes and for whom livestock production is often secondary.[19] The region's larger cities and those areas with attractive natural amenities and services (and those affected by the current boom in fossil fuel extraction) will continue to grow. Together with broader public demand across the continent, these places may use their growing economic and political leverage to alter prairie management to deliver noncommodity ecosystem values, in particular the restoration of wildlife and wildlands. This change coincides with both the growing ecological movement for rewilding and emerging methods of payment for ecosystem services of rangelands.[20]

Building a network of large protected areas across the Great Plains will require a diversity of strategies on public, private, and tribal lands. Extraordinary levels of public support, both political and financial, will be crucial. New and innovative partnerships and collaboration among landowners and natural resource agencies will be needed to overcome the disparate approaches to land stewardship that result from fragmented ownership and management jurisdictions. Business as usual will not get us to scale.

In the northern half of the Great Plains, public lands, particularly Crown lands in Canada and Bureau of Land Management lands and National Grasslands in the United States, cover millions of acres in high-priority areas. Strong public demand will be mandatory for transforming public lands to protected area status. Most high-priority areas, however, include extensive private lands and therefore both for-profit and nonprofit landowners are crucial if a new surge in protected area creation is to occur. As demonstrated by Grasslands National Park, government purchase of private lands for creating protected areas remains an important tool for protected area development.

Individual and corporate landowners, whether motivated by for-profit enterprise or a philanthropic undertaking, or some of both, have a potentially major role to play in protected area development if they wish to seize the opportunity. Some landowners have a strong interest in wildlife and, with the goal of improving ranch profitability, are increasingly involved in nature tourism, fee hunting, conservation easements, and other financial levers for improving wildlife habitat. Some voluntarily manage for biodiversity for its own sake without expecting a return on investment, while others manage with profit in mind. Those trying such new approaches to incorporating wildlife conservation into land management range from the traditional, multi-generation ranch family (for example, the Switzer family of the Switzer Ranch and Nature Reserve in the Sandhills of Nebraska)[21] to well-heeled owners who are relatively new to the ranching enterprise (Turner Enterprises, for example, owner of seven ranches totaling nearly 615,000 acres in the Great Plains).[22] These new landowners generally stay in commodity production (cattle or bison), but they often are more open than traditional ranchers to diversifying land stewardship to include wildlife values.[23] Part of a long-term strategy for Great Plains protected areas should be to encourage land owners who have the means to continue U.S. and Canadian traditions in wildlands philanthropy by eventually dedicating their lands to protected-area status, whether through placement in a public trust, donating the land to another organization for that purpose, or other means.

Apart from wildlife and land-use policy work, purchasing and holding conservation easements, and other efforts to conserve biodiversity on public and private lands, nonprofits play a pivotal role in the Great Plains by acquiring and managing lands of high biodiversity value and by researching and demonstrating how to restore and conserve prairie lands. The most ambitious is the American Prairie Reserve in northeast Montana whose goal is to create a 3-million-acre protected area by stitching together private lands purchased by the Reserve and public lands—largely CMR Refuge and Bureau of Land Management grazing allotments.[24] Nature Conservancy Canada and The Nature Conservancy have acquired and manage several properties of high conservation value ranging from hundreds to tens of thousands of acres in size across the Great Plains.[25] We need to greatly amplify these and other nonprofit land investments that focus on restoring and conserving priority prairie landscapes.

The sound management of millions of acres in American Indian reservations is also a key component of a protected area strategy for the Great Plains. Reservations have established bison herds with spiritual and cultural values and land health as a guiding goal; many support endangered species recovery efforts, and some have attempted to establish Tribal National Parks or Reserves. The complex checkerboard ownership of reservation lands by various private and public entities, and the fractionated ownership of American Indian trust lands, present major hurdles to creating large protected areas on American Indian reservations.[26] However, the transfer of the 133,300-acre South Unit of Badlands National Park, within the Pine Ridge Indian Reservation, to the Reservation and Oglala Sioux Tribe for management—the nation's first tribal park[27]—surely marks an historic milestone for both Great Plains tribes and protected areas.

Conclusion

A system of large protected areas is needed to restore and conserve the large-scale ecological processes and associated species that have characterized the biodiversity of the Great Plains since before Euro-American colonization. Opportunities for doing so exist both ecologically and socioeconomically. Largely intact, high-priority areas of millions of acres remain where the full range of native prairie biodiversity could be restored. The next decade or two will likely bring vast changes in land ownership and management across the Great Plains. Continuing depopulation of rural areas and growth of metropolitan areas will almost surely be accompanied by major shifts in social, cultural, and economic interests and incentives for managing both private and public prairie lands.

This period of change calls for a paradigm shift from commodity-focused management of rangelands to biodiversity-focused restoration. For this to happen, we need to recognize the extraordinary biodiversity and wildland value of many of the region's public lands. Support for expanding the size and improving the care of existing public protected areas is needed, and many public grazing lands should be converted to protected area status. We need to support entrepreneurial landowners—traditional and new, for-profit and nonprofit—who are willing to try novel and collaborative approaches to restoring biodiversity and creating privately owned nature reserves. We need to foster strong public demand and financial support, both regionally and across the continent (and even globally), for restoring and conserving the spectacular natural heritage of the Great Plains on both private and public lands. If successful, we will usher in a new era of creating great protected areas for the Great Plains.

The author would like to thank Eileen Crist, Steve Forrest, and Kyran Kunkel for many helpful comments on the essay, and Mary Elder Jacobsen for her skillful copyediting.

Human Impact on Protected Areas of the Peruvian Amazon

MARC J. DOUROJEANNI

SIXTEEN PERCENT OF THE AMAZON BIOME is part of Peru, nearly a quarter of which Peru has designated as protected areas under several categories. The oldest protected area in the Peruvian portion of the Amazon biome is the small Cutervo National Park, established in 1961, located in the north of Peru. Some of the most important protected areas of the Peruvian Amazon (including Pacaya-Samiria National Reserve and the Manu National Park) were created in the 1970s. Today there are 11 national parks and a total of 45 protected areas, both national and regional. Peru protects more than 18.1 million hectares, approximately 23.4 percent of its Amazon biome, which would seem quite a considerable area under protection, but a large portion of this area remains only partially protected, with about 55.3 percent of it allowing human presence and restricted economic uses ("direct-use"), including such categories as: national reserves, communal reserves, reserved zones, protection forests, and regional conservation areas. The fully protected areas ("indirect-use") are national parks, national sanctuaries, and historical sanctuaries, and these areas stretch across 44.7 percent of the protected land.

Most consider protected areas having people inside and permitting utilization of resources (direct-use) as not fully guaranteeing biodiversity conservation. Subsequently, the proliferation of direct-use or "soft" protected areas may sell the illusion of biodiversity conservation while, as a matter of fact, these provide no protection or only partial or insufficient protection.

The topic is not new. Several studies have already been carried out showing that fully protected areas in the humid tropics, without inhabitants or users of resources, have remained quite intact over decades despite human pressure and lack of funding.[1] Recent studies, especially in the Brazilian Amazon, demonstrate that protected areas for indirect-use are better maintained, with less deforestation, than those for direct-use.[2] However, still other studies show that there are no significant deforestation differences between the two groups of categories.[3] And, especially in Brazil, a persistent radical current of social-environmentalism advocates for the noncreation of protected areas for indirect-use and actively promotes human occupation within them.[4]

In this essay I will consider current information on deforestation and forest degradation in protected areas of different categories in the Peruvian Amazon and will compare impacts of deforestation in protected areas of the Peruvian and Brazilian Amazon.

Deforestation in protected areas

The main and most obvious expression of human intervention in tropical forests is deforestation that drastically alters the original ecosystem with elimination of practically all original species, transforming the deforested area into a simple anthropic ecosystem. Therefore, deforestation is an excellent indicator of protected area's health or capacity to conserve biodiversity and it is easier to measure than forest degradation: the greater the deforestation, the lower the protection.

Deforestation has not been officially measured in Peru since 2000, when it reached 11 percent of the Amazon.[5] Then, deforestation in protected areas of all categories had attained 116,000 hectares, which at the time equaled 0.6 percent of the deforested area in the entire Peruvian Amazon (Andean and lowland) and 0.8 percent of the protected land. As Table 1 shows, the deforestation in indirect-use protected areas covered 0.22 percent while in direct-use areas it reached 1.34 percent. Thus, the percent of deforestation has been six times larger in areas under direct-use than in those for indirect-use. This estimate does not include any areas recognized as "reserved zone," a transitory category that—according to ongoing studies—may result in protected areas or indigenous areas or, as well, be destined to forestry or agriculture.

A second source of information on deforestation in protected areas was drawn up by the Data Center for Conservation at the National Agrarian University (CDC/UNALM),[6] Lima, Peru, based on more recent information provided by the National Service of Protected Natural Areas and other institutions, or prepared by the CDC/UNALM. Most of this information had been gathered in the period between 2000 and 2009 as part of the preparation or review of management plans.

According to this second source, which includes all protected areas of the eight departments of Peru benefited by the National Program of Tropical Forests (five from the Amazon and three from the Northern Coast), indirect-use protected areas (parks and sanctuaries) have lost 0.12 percent of their territories due to deforestation, while direct-use protected areas recognized as "national reserves," "protection forests," and "communal reserves" have lost, respectively, 1.74, 1.51 and 0.9 percent.[7] If all categories of direct-use are grouped together, deforestation in these areas reached 1.46 percent or a 12 times larger deforestation than those for indirect-use.

Table 2 was prepared with part of the baseline information of CDC/UNALM and refers to the main protected areas of the five departments included in the Amazon biome.[8] These represent almost 80 percent of all land being protected in the Peruvian Amazon, excepting reserved zones. This approximation, which aims to facilitate the comparison with the Brazilian situation where protected areas are located in lowland Amazon, excludes several medium- or small-sized protected areas of the high Andean-Amazon portion.

As Table 2 shows, this data ratifies that deforestation in national protected areas is ten times larger in direct-use (1.15 percent) than in indirect-use areas (0.11 percent).

TABLE 1. DEFORESTATION MEASUREMENTS AS OF 2000 IN PROTECTED AREAS OF THE PERUVIAN AMAZON

Type	Area (in hectares)	Deforestation Area (in hectares)	Percent
Indirect-use	8,321,460	17,937	0.22
Direct-use	6,175,660	82,524	1.34

Note: Reserved Areas are not included.

Source: H. Portugués and P. Huerta, *Mapa de deforestación de la Amazonía peruana* 2000.[5]

TABLE 2. DEFORESTATION IN PROTECTED AREAS
OF THE PERUVIAN AMAZON

Category	Protected Area	Department	Area (in hectares)	Deforested area (in hectares)	Percent deforested
National Parks (indirect use)	Ichigkat Muja	Amazonas	88,477	90	0.10
	Cordillera Azul	Loreto	709,682	1,625	0.23
		San Martín	108,479	0	0
		Ucayali	73,518	0	0
	Rio Abiseo	San Martín	274,520	363	0.13
	Alto Purus	M. de Dios	1,255,391	68	0.01
		Ucayali	1,256,703	215	0.02
	Manu	M. de Dios	1,564,503	3,159	0.20
	Bahuaja Sonene	M. de Dios	297,115	939	0.32
Total indirect use			*5,619,388*	*6,459*	*0.11*
National Reserves (direct use)	Pacaya-Samiria	Loreto	2,080,000	29,059	1.40
	Alpahuayo-Mishana	Loreto	58,069	3,162	5.45
	Tambopata	M. de Dios	280,235	3,563	1.27
	Matsés	Loreto	420,635	0	0
	Pucacuro	Loreto	637,954	221	0.03
Communal Reserves (direct use)	Chayu-Nain	Amazonas	23,598	1,031	4.37
	Tuntanain	Amazonas	94,968	112	0.12
	Amarakaeri	M. de Dios	402,439	10,506	2.61
	Purus	Ucayali	194,674	358	0.18
	Sira	Ucayali	226,690	2,782	1.23
Total direct use (in national areas)			*4,419,262*	*50,794*	*1.15*
Combined total (direct use + indirect use) in national areas			**10,038,650**	**57,253**	**0.57**
Regional Conservation Areas (direct use)	Amazonas (1) Loreto (3) San Martín (1) Ucayali (1)		2,094,453	8,576	0.41
Total direct use (in national areas + regional areas)			*6,513,715*	*59,370*	*0.91*
Grand total			**12,133,103**	**65,829**	**0.54**

Source: CDC/UNALM (2011)

Deforestation affects 0.54 percent of all categories of protected areas in Table 2. This is less than what was found by H. Portugués and P. Huerta for all protected areas,[9] and less than what has been stated by the Foundation for Agrarian Development, or "Fundación para el Desarrollo Agrario" (FDA), in Peru.[10] As a matter of fact, the inclusion of other Andean-Amazonian protected areas, given their smaller size, would not significantly change the results of Table 2, but it would reveal that deforestation is higher in all categories as the pressure on them is much higher. But the same difference would remain between deforestation in areas for direct-use and indirect-use.

The most heavily deforested protected areas in the Amazon were the Alpahuayo-Mishana National Reserve and the Chayu-Nain and Amarakeiri communal reserves. In absolute figures, the largest deforestation took place in the Pacaya-Samiria National Reserve, with a loss of 29,000 hectares. This figure is doubtful, as F. Rodríguez and coauthors,[11] with information from 1994, already indicated the existence of 54,718 hectares deforested. It is probable that recent inventories included, as usual, secondary vegetation as original forest. Of all national parks in Peru, the most affected has been Bahuaja-Sonene.

Deforestation in buffer zones

The information compiled by CDC/UNALM also includes data on deforestation in buffer zones of most protected areas mentioned in Table 2.[12] These zones are defined by the management plans, and according to law the economic activities carried out in these zones must not affect the integrity of the protected neighboring area. However, the development of agriculture, forestry, mining, or oil exploitation, among other activities, is not prohibited. Not every protected area has, at present, a buffer zone.

Deforestation in buffer zones of all protected areas included in the CDC/UNALM study reached 11.9 percent.[13] In Table 3, which like Table 2 refers to those protected areas in the five departments entirely located in the Amazon, the average deforestation in buffer zones was 9.28 percent. It is interesting to note that the deforestation pressure was higher in the buffer zones of indirect-use protected areas (10.31 percent) than in direct-use (7.42 percent). Considering that deforestation inside indirect-use areas has been much lower (0.11 percent) it is shown once again that these categories are quite successful at protecting the ecosystem.

The two national parks of the San Martín department (Cordillera Azul and Abiseo) suffered the highest pressure (their buffer zones are already 40 and 10 percent deforested, respectively), although the parks themselves are relatively intact. The buffer zone of the Alpahuayo-Mishana National Reserve, very close to the city of Iquitos, is equally quite compromised, with 25 percent already deforested, although deforestation within the reserve covers only 5.5 percent.

TABLE 3. DEFORESTATION IN BUFFER ZONES OF PROTECTED AREAS IN THE PERUVIAN AMAZON

Category	Protected Area	Department	Area (in hectares)	Deforested area (in hectares)	Percent deforested
National Parks (indirect use)	Ichigkat Muja	Amazonas	138,718	1,682	1.21
	Cordillera Azul	Loreto	1,132,019	49,546	4.38
		San Martín	924,051	372,938	40.36
		Ucayali	189,410	6,723	3.55
	Rio Abiseo	San Martín	472,145	47,313	10.02
	Alto Purus	M. de Dios	845,499	1,304	0.15
		Ucayali	630,165	2,071	0.33
	Manu	M. de Dios	312,767	3,199	1.02
		Ucayali	59,385	78	0.13
Total for protected areas for indirect use			*4,704,159*	*484,854*	*10.31*
National Reserves (direct use)	Pacaya-Samiria	Loreto	1,185,164	82,443	6.96
		San Martín	34,644	32	0.09
	Alpahuayo-Mishana	Loreto	65,957	16,538	25.07
	Tambopata	M. de Dios	233,020	34,464	14.79
Communal Reserves (direct use)	Tuntanain	Amazonas	287,677	6,602	2.29
	Amarakaeri	M. de Dios	210,265	16,784	7.98
	Purus	Ucayali	201,782	6,952	3.45
	Sira	Ucayali	385,848	29,485	7.64
Total for protected areas for direct use			*2,604,357*	*193,300*	*7.42*
Grand total			**7,308,516**	**678,154**	**9.28**

Source: CDC/UNALM (2011)

Forest degradation

Only one limited study on forest degradation, based on forest harvesting, has been conducted in Peru.[14] Forest degradation has been recognized as an urgent issue in terms of biodiversity conservation,[15] in particular its implications on greenhouse gas emissions.[16] Even practices previously deemed harmless, such as rubber extraction and Brazil nut harvesting, have significant impacts that are transmitted through the food chain (for example, introduction of disease, reduced regeneration, food-supply limitations for foraging species, etc.).[17] However, forest degradation is difficult to measure.[18]

Significant degradation results in direct-use protected areas where large portions of their surface are legally open to regulated or controlled exploitation of resources, through zoning and other measures included in management plans. These areas were established with provisions that allowed for sustainable extraction of non-timber products, hunting, and fishing. But, given the complexity of managing these areas, degradation tends to be much more widespread and intense than what is actually authorized.

For instance, the management plan of the Pacaya-Samiria National Reserve[19] allows agriculture and cattle ranching on more than 123,241 hectares (5.7 percent of the area) recognized as a "special use zone." The plan also implicitly recognizes a 265,823-hectare area (12.3 percent of the area) as having already been so severely degraded as to require its being included in a "recuperation zone." Simply put, by the year 2000 more than 18 percent of the reserve territory had been degraded. Since neither the park service nor the park's director has authority with the capacity to implement management, it is presumed that degradation is actually spreading to the other 24.1 percent considered to be a "direct utilization zone" (where extraction is allowed). Otherwise only the "strict protection zone" and the "wildlife zone" (limited to tourism)—together totaling 48 percent—will likely persist without severe disturbance. This situation is not surprising given that in 1968 only some 2,000 seasonal extractors were registered in the Pacaya sector and some 30 resident families existed in the Samiria sector,[20] while by 1995 the reserve already supported more than 42,000 inhabitants in several villages. A significant and completely illegal lumber exploitation, as well as the unregulated extraction of all kinds of forest products, hunting, and fishing, persist in large portions of the area.

Comparing the case of Peru and Brazil

The first conclusion of the foregoing information is that in spite of severe management limitations and raising pressures, the Peruvian Amazon system of protected areas has suffered little damage. Deforestation is affecting 11 percent or more of its Amazon biome but has barely caused a loss of 0.54 percent of forests inside protected areas of all categories. This is consistent with findings in the Brazilian Amazon, although deforestation of protected areas in this country reaches 1.5 percent, or almost three times more than in Peru. The second conclusion is that in Peru, as in Brazil, indirect-use protected areas have been significantly more efficient in preventing deforestation than have direct-use.[21]

However, while deforestation in direct-use federal protected areas of Brazil is 2.1 times greater than in indirect-use federal protected areas, this same relation in Peru is 10 times greater. This difference is smaller but still considerable in regional or state-administered protected areas of both countries (respectively 1.2 and 8 times). Considering that the quality of management of protected areas is as limited in Peru as it is in Brazil,[22] the fact of such significantly higher degrees of deforestation in Brazilian protected areas may be explained by the following:

- ▶ The road network in Brazil, larger than in Peru, generates greater pressure on protected areas;
- ▶ while every protected area of Peru has been established specifically to conserve natural ecosystems samples, several Brazilian protected areas categories (extractive reserves, for example) were expressly established to benefit resident populations;
- ▶ many Brazilian protected areas face serious problems around land titling regularization as related to both private and indigenous claims; and
- ▶ the social-environmental movement in Brazil is more radical and active than it is in Peru and it is being supported by the federal government.

On the other hand, this analysis confirms the obvious. The experience in tropical countries has shown that if people are living inside protected areas it is problematical to apply agreed management plans, although jointly developed with the inhabitants in categories such as the national and communal reserves of Peru or the "extractive reserves," "reserves for sustainable development," or "areas for environmental protection" of Brazil. The success of such agreements depends on two almost unachievable conditions in both countries: one, population growth and pressure on natural resources within this type of protected area must be stabilized to a sustainable level, and two, the administration of these areas must have the capacity and the means to enforce the law and the standards mutually agreed upon and in consensus with the local population when drafting the management plans.

The first condition, as seen in the case of Peru's Pacaya-Samiria National Reserve, is impossible as long as no other or more attractive economic opportunities exist outside the protected area and also because the authority has no legal or practical recourse for preventing either entrance of newcomers or invasions. The best-known Brazilian case is the Chico Mendes Extractive Reserve (Acre, Brazil) established in 1990 with 700 families of rubber tappers. By 2005, its population had reached more than 2,000 families, 62 percent of which herd livestock. By 2008, the herd had 10,000 head of cattle and over 45,000 hectares[23] had been deforested for livestock use.

On the other hand, as is well known, the administration of protected areas both in Brazil and in Peru is largely inefficient. Services of both protected areas are understaffed, undertrained, and under-budgeted,[24] as compared, for example, to Spain, where "natural parks" are equivalent to several direct-use protected areas of Brazil and Peru, but which allocates comparatively enormous funds to the budgeted management of these areas. In 2010 only four small Spanish natural parks (comprising 130,000 hectares) containing older, stable, wealthier, and better-educated populations, received a basic budget of US$5.3 million.[25] In 2010 the budget of the Peruvian protected area service to administer 18 million hectares of Amazon protected areas was only US$5.2 million (most of it international donation). In 2010, the budget for the Pacaya-Samiria National Reserve (over 2 million hectares) was US$577,000,[26] or half of what the Spanish Cabo de Gata-Nijar Natural Park (38,000 hectares) received that year.[27] Nevertheless, Pacaya-Samiria is one of the costliest reserve areas in Peru with the highest number of staff (5 professionals and 64 park rangers).

The above-mentioned facts drastically contrast with new trends of social-environmentalism around the world[28] that favors protected areas for direct-use in detriment of those for indirect-use. This tendency is strong in Brazil, and it has had a strong influence in the rapid increase in the number of direct-use protected areas—recognized locally as "for sustainable development"—that correspond to IUCN/WCPA categories IV to VI. Back in 1984 as much as 92 percent of the Brazilian protected land in the Amazon was either national parks or biological reserves, but in 2009 62 percent of the protected area of the Brazilian Amazon already belonged to the direct-use group. The remaining 38 percent corresponds to indirect-use protected areas (IUCN/WCPA categories I and II), which in Brazil includes biological reserves, national parks, and ecological stations.

The rapid growth, in number and coverage, of direct-use protected areas in the Brazilian Amazon is frequently attributed to the increasing difficulty in locating areas of biological importance without inhabitants. However, it must be kept in mind that the social-environmentalism of the 1980s led to the creation of "extractive reserves," conceived to benefit rubber tapper unions in Acre.[29] The purpose of these areas, disguised as "protected areas," has been to guarantee land tenure for a social group to exploit in exclusivity specific natural resources.[30] The easy argument that nature can be conserved while simultaneously using it was obviously well received by policy makers contributing to the proliferation of this type of so-called protected areas. In 2009, 21.1 percent of all protected land in the Brazilian Amazon was defined as "extractive reserve" or "reserve for sustainable development."

In addition, Brazil imported the idea of establishing "areas for environmental protection," an adaptation of the European "natural parks," where old cultural or anthropic landscapes are preserved through complex standards which are negotiated on a one-to-one basis with the resident population and other users of the area's resources. The concept of the "natural parks" was probably applicable to the southern developed regions of Brazil, where remaining nature is intimately associated with agricultural or semi-urban landscapes, as in Europe. However, as might be expected, governments considered this protected area category as an excellent opportunity to make claims of "protecting nature" while avoiding expropriation costs and conflicts.[31] As a result, very large portions of natural areas of the Amazon were "protected" under this relaxed category instead of being conserved as national parks or stricter categories. And to complete this scenario, legislation in 2000 transformed the national forests (13.5 percent of the area that is protected) into protected areas that additionally were opened to human occupation.

The Brazilian social-environmentalism has not limited itself to promoting the establishment of direct-use protected areas. Its main banner has been a frontal attack on national parks accusing them of being "imperialist," of infringing human rights and of freezing development, in addition to being unnecessary or inefficient to conserve biodiversity.[32] These kinds of arguments have resulted in the elimination or drastic reduction of several important national parks such as Pacaas Novos in Rondonia and Araguaia[33] in Tocantins. This latter went from being established in 1959 with 2 million hectares to just 94,000 hectares.[34]

The social-environmentalism argumentation has indirectly benefited other interests such as those of agribusiness, lumber industry, and hydro energy generation. Just as an example, it is worth mentioning that in 2010, the Rondonia Assembly eliminated 12 state protected areas that covered more than 1 million hectares.[35] The Mato Grosso State, among others, has reduced several of its most important parks, including Cristalino, arguing that "sustainable development is compatible with conservation."[36] The result of these processes is that while in appearance the proportion of the protected area of the Brazilian Amazon is increasing, the proportion of the truly protected area is actually decreasing.

Conclusion

As the details of this essay on Peru suggest, strictly protected areas for the conservation of biological diversity have significant and lasting value. However, as I have reiterated many times, along with so many others,[37] the problem is not choosing between protected areas for "direct-use" and protected areas for "indirect-use." Moreover, the protected areas for direct-use were not invented by the social-environmentalism. More than twenty years before the existence of extractive reserves in Brazil, Peruvian environmentalists had already created national reserves having residential populations and use of resources.[38] Both groups of protected areas are necessary, and they must and can coexist.

However, it cannot be denied, as the data shows, that direct-use protected areas do not substitute those for indirect-use. It is also undeniable that some Brazilian categories protect very little or nothing at all. It is indispensable for a portion of the areas to remain untouched as much as possible, because it is biologically necessary,[39] and also because it is easier and more affordable to manage; in other words, it is viable in the socio-economic conditions still prevailing in tropical countries.

Protected Areas in Chilean Patagonia

CARLOS CUEVAS

WESTERN PATAGONIA IS A LAND of deep contrasts and impressive landscapes, extending 15 degrees of latitude, or roughly 1,000 miles, along the Pacific side of southernmost South America. The Antarctic continent is only 800 miles away from Cape Horn—Chilean Patagonia's southern tip. Covering 250,000 square kilometers, roughly one United Kingdom or three times the size of Austria, western Patagonia is home to less than 2 percent of Chile's current population. (In this essay the term "western Patagonia" refers to the present-day Chilean province of Palena and regions of Aysen and Magallanes.)

The dominant factor that shaped the landscape we see today is glacial action. Almost all the land was covered by ice 2–3 million years ago until just ten thousand years ago when the ice retreated, a very short time in the evolution of life on the planet. Two ice fields, the largest outside Antarctica and Greenland, are the last visible reminders of the glacial era. The most prominent sign of glaciers shaping the area, however, is the ubiquitous presence of coastal fjords, the retreating ice leaving behind not only peninsulas but some 10,000 islands as well. While the outer coast is about 1,000 miles long, the total coastline, factoring in all the islands and fjords, amounts to some 50,000 miles. Volcanic eruptions have shaped life in Patagonia—especially the resulting ash, a main component for soil origin and characteristics.

The abiotic and biotic characteristics of the ocean are conditioned by the South Pacific Gyre, flowing from west to east. Upon reaching the continent the current is divided between a segment flowing south around Cape Horn and another, the Humboldt Current, flowing north. Both cold water currents strongly influence the country's climate. The water flow and associated upwelling areas give rise to the most productive fisheries in the world. Yet the region's rich and complex marine ecosystems are poorly understood because research has focused on only a few species of commercial value; Patagonia's terrestrial ecosystems, with characteristics and dynamics found nowhere else on Earth, are better understood.

Population and land use

More than ten thousand years ago, humans arrived in western Patagonia; the Monte Verde archaeological site remains the oldest scientifically dated human habitation site in all of the Americas (14,800 years before present). The harsh climate and cold summers did not allow crops to reach maturity, so indigenous peoples were restricted to hunting, gathering, and fishing. Human numbers remained low and Patagonia still is the least inhabited part of the country. Until the early nineteenth century, five distinct native peoples populated western Patagonia. In the coast, the Chonos lived in the northern fjords, up to the Taitao peninsula; the Yamana or Yaghan lived south of Tierra del Fuego, to the southern tip of the continent, Cape Horn; between those groups, from the Taitao peninsula to the Strait of Magellan lived the Kaweshkar or Alacalufes. With little or no contact with the former, two groups of hunters lived in the grasslands east of the Andes, the Tehuelche on the mainland and the Ona or Selk'nam on the island of Tierra del Fuego. Their numbers likely never exceeded 10,000 people among all the groups.

The first European to reach Patagonia was Ferdinand Magellan, a Portuguese captain serving the Spanish crown, who entered the strait now bearing his name in 1520. Spanish colonists made an ill-fated attempt to settle the Strait of Magellan during the sixteenth century; the English corsair Thomas Cavendish rescued one survivor and bestowed the name "Port Famine" to the once-proud City of King Philip. This settlement was the first but not the last environmental blunder in Patagonia motivated by decisions made from afar and ignorant of local conditions. Few navigators reached Patagonian shores in the three centuries after discovery; the Spaniards established trade and supply lines through the Isthmus of Panama and tried to keep out competitors like the English or the Dutch who nevertheless came when Spain was at war with them in Europe. Francis Drake made the second passage of the strait, and the Dutch captains Willem Schouten and Isaac Le Maire discovered Cape Horn in 1616. More than a century later, in 1740, Admiral Lord Anson crossed through the Strait of Magellan en route to attack the Spanish forts in the Pacific. Massachusetts whalers and seal hunters came in numbers after American independence, to the point that Americans were generally known as "Bostoneses."

One distinguished visitor, Charles Darwin, spent over a year (1832) navigating Chilean Patagonia's stormy waters and carrying out research ashore as naturalist of HMS *Beagle*, charged with mapping the coast of the former Spanish colonies. Darwin noted the land's characteristics—glaciers flowing into the sea at the latitude of southern England, the mix of plant and animal species not found elsewhere, and the impact of volcanic activity. Darwin perceived very clearly that the limiting factor for agriculture and life in general was the very cold summers and not the average yearly temperatures; his observations are still valid today. In the book written when he was not yet thirty years old, he made passing negative comments about the indigenous inhabitants, based on very superficial observations. Later in life a wiser Darwin changed his views after having access to data gathered by missionaries, such as a Selk'nam language dictionary with more than 30,000 terms showing the ability of the indigenous people of Patagonia to describe, understand, and adapt successfully to the harsh environment.

The permanent presence of a nonindigenous population dates only from the middle of the nineteenth century; this stemmed from government decision and not spontaneous movement by settlers seeking land to make a living. Chilean authorities established in 1842 a small garrison later turned into a penal colony. Punta Arenas ("Sandy Point" on the Royal Navy maps drawn by the HMS *Beagle* officers) languished for decades until steamships able to negotiate the narrows of the Strait of Magellan replaced the tall ships using the Cape Horn route. At that time the port revitalized, becoming a coaling and supply station and serving as a base for seal and whale hunters operating in South American and Antarctic waters.

Around 1880 the government brought sheep from the Falkland Islands and kick-started large-scale, wool-producing farms by selling and leasing extensive tracts of grasslands deemed "vacant"—ignoring the existence of indigenous peoples who lived there and hunted local wildlife. Near the Strait of Magellan, the operation succeeded financially but ruined indigenous communities; in the present-day Aysen Region further north, the "Magellanic model" of sheep grazing floundered due to lack of suitable grasslands. Since the beginning of the twentieth century, independent settlers occupied brush- and forestlands at the fringes of the Aysen concessions, where they intentionally set fires to easily open land for cattle ranching and sheep grazing. Forest fires damaged an estimated 10 million acres in Aysen and a lesser amount in Magallanes and Palena, but the forests are slowly recovering except where soil was lost completely due to erosion.

Indigenous peoples indeed had a certain degree of impact upon nature, but these effects were limited due to the human population's sparse numbers and modest technology. The second wave of inhabitants had more impact, but still within certain limits. At the present time, the natural and cultural heritage of western Patagonia is under a new kind of threat, stemming not from resource use by locals but from large-scale energy and fish farming investments by Chilean and international corporations.

Low-grade coal was known to exist since the nineteenth century and small mines operated irregularly depending on international prices. In the last twenty years two large coal-mining operations have been developed within a 100-mile radius of Punta Arenas, with an estimated 4 billion tons underground looming large as a potential threat. Drilling for oil was successful in 1945, production peaked in the 1980s and is declining, but the environmental consequences will remain for a long time. Further north in the Aysen Region there is no coal or oil, but salmon farming (salmon is a nonnative species) has surged (Chile is the world's second-largest exporter), reaching levels of density within pens and numbers of floating fish pens per coastal mile that would be unacceptable in other countries that have issued and enforce strict regulations for salmon aquaculture. Massive escape of these nonnative species is causing the degradation of native ecosystems while fishmeal that falls to the bottom through the pens has rendered lifeless large areas of the ocean.

While industrial salmon production is the major threat to Chile's coastal ecosystems, the potential for large-scale hydropower development of Patagonia's wild rivers presents the main conservation challenge on land. Plans for a series of huge dams proposed by private corporations for key Patagonian rivers were sidetracked in 2014 when the government withdrew one of the permits issued (to HydroAysen). Years of campaigning had rallied a majority of Chileans to strongly oppose such dam construction, but proponents are determined and have the right to reapply.

Large dams have many negative effects, including the often-overlooked loss of landscape values, seismic risk, and loss of nutrient flow to the rich estuarine ecosystems. Moreover, the electricity that would be generated has no local benefit but is intended for sale to mines located 1,000–1,500 miles to the north, far from Patagonia. Dam construction, if permitted, will only increase an already quasi-monopolistic control by corporations of Chile's power generation; if halted, abundant wind and solar power near the mines (in fact the highest solar energy rate per square meter anywhere in the world) can serve local needs without power lines.

The controversy about the dams in Aysen and the social movement against the expansion of coal mining in Magallanes have started a discussion about what kind of future the local inhabitants want. Given the climatic and ecological constraints on traditional agriculture and the low population density, nature-based tourism is emerging as one of the few sustainable options, if adequately planned and managed. Tourism might be a double-edged sword, but it is one of the few possible development options given the skills and financial possibilities of the locals. Western Patagonia, endowed with some of the most spectacular and dramatic landscapes in the world, provides tourism attractions of the highest level. In addition, roughly half of the land area is already conserved, legally declared as national parks, nature monuments, or national reserves, the oldest reserve dating from 1932 and the oldest park from 1945.

Natural heritage and conservation values

Although intuition might lead us to view the Arctic and the Antarctic as symmetric, as mirror images of one another, there are significant differences between Earth's far north and far south. The northern hemisphere is dominated by land while the southern hemisphere is predominantly water. Ecologically speaking, the difference is noteworthy: winds, ocean circulation patterns, heat transfer, ocean nutrient circulation, availability of space and connectivity for species evolution and migration differ greatly when comparing hemispheres. Additionally, New Zealand and Chile, the world's southernmost landmasses (excluding Antarctica) are part of the Pacific Ring of Fire, therefore volcanic activity is very high, strongly influencing soil conditions and the evolution of life-forms.

Two hundred million years ago, all of the planet's land was part of a single large continent, Pangaea. At that time this mega-continent started to break down, first dividing into northern and southern landmasses, and later continuing to break down as Australia, South America, Africa, and Antarctica drifted apart to become separate continents. Western Patagonia has been for millions of years at the "cutting edge" of the continent's drifting process, and the Andes Mountains have risen as the continent pushes against the oceanic plate. The Pacific Gyre brings cold Antarctic water toward the continent, creating a cooling effect; combined with predominantly westerly winds and the presence of the mountains, the conditions were set for extensive glaciation in Patagonia. Due to the common origin with other southern lands, local Patagonian flora is more closely related to New Zealand and Tasmania than to tropical America.

National parks and nature conservation

The oldest national park in western Patagonia is Cape Horn National Park at the southernmost tip of South America. Created in 1945 for its wilderness values and pristine character, Cape Horn is also a historic landmark. Not only did the captains and crews sailing past this promontory make the crossing between the two largest oceans of the planet, they achieved a special status because the journey was harsh and dangerous; dozens of ships sank trying to cross, and countless mariners perished in these waters.

Most of the land in Patagonia is government-owned, but the best agricultural or grazing land has long been in private ownership. The next step taken in protecting the outstanding natural heritage was establishing Lago Grey and Laguna San Rafael national parks in 1959. Years later, an enlarged Lago Grey became Torres del Paine National Park while Laguna San Rafael was the first "mega" protected area in Chile, with a size initially exceeding 1 million hectares (2.5 million acres) and now enlarged to 1.75 million hectares (4.3 million acres).

The late 1960s saw the largest increase in the number and total area of protected wildlands in Chile. Chile's then president Eduardo Frei Montalva demonstrated decisive conservation leadership during his term (1964–1970). No other president before or after has created more protected areas, in either number or total area conserved. Separated in time by more than sixty years, and governing in different cultural contexts, President Frei and U.S. President Theodore Roosevelt shared common traits: Both could be labeled as "Innovative Conservatives." Both came from tradition-oriented backgrounds, but neither was content administering "business as usual." Each felt the govern-

ment should take action to further the public interest, and both used government powers to such effect. By the end of Frei's term roughly half of western
Patagonia was within the boundaries of a national park or national reserve.

Progress in establishing protected areas by the Chilean government
has been very irregular: sometimes fast, as was the case with president
Frei, sometimes very slow, but never losing ground, showing at least some
growth at the end of each president's term in office.

Since 1990, private landowners joined the protected areas movement,
providing a welcome complement to government efforts, especially in
places such as grasslands and other ecosystems not present or poorly represented in the older protected areas.

Categories of protected areas

Government-created protected areas covering terrestrial landscapes in Chile
include national parks, nature monuments, and national reserves (formerly
known as forest reserves). Chile's national parks follow the same management principles as in the United States—large areas with limited evidence
of human intrusion, open to visitors but managed to achieve protection of
a region's natural heritage. Nature monuments are, in a sense, small-scale
national parks managed for the protection of single elements with high conservation value, such as cave systems, marine birds' nesting sites, or salt lakes.

National reserves do not have a close equivalent in the United States,
and America's national forests do not have an equivalent in Chile. People
in the United States, Canada, and Europe are surprised by the fact that
Chile's timber supply comes from fast-growing trees grown as a crop in
abandoned agricultural land; native forests are dominated by a mixture of
broad-leaved species, have slower growth rates, and grow in places with
steeper slopes and poor access. Even if sustainability requirements are not
added to the equation, all the above-mentioned factors turn logging native forests into a financially risky proposal. On the other hand, large areas
deforested during the nineteenth century in central Chile in order to open
lands for agriculture have thin soils, making them no longer profitable for
agricultural use, and landowners either sell out to forest corporations or
independently plant forest crops on the abandoned agricultural land. As
a result, well over 90 percent of the timber consumed locally or exported
comes from privately owned, planted forests, undercutting even more the
financial prospects of timber production from native forests.

In Patagonia, as is the case in the rest of Chile, government-owned natural forests (which are fundamental for watershed protection and other ecosystem services) generally do not have commercially viable timber tracts, especially in Patagonia, where the topographic and climate conditions are extreme. Therefore, the U.S. National Forest concept (multiple-use management including timber extraction) does not apply in Chile. Thus, our national reserves fulfill a different role—they are not potential sources of timber but rather are sources of ecosystem services, protecting fragile ecosystems such as montane forests, wetlands, and alpine ecosystems. They also serve as interim protection until a precise allocation to a different category can be made.

In developing countries, many people, including influential politicians, hold development at all costs as a central tenet and perceive national parks and other strict land and ecosystem protection legal measures as hindering the desired development. National reserves may provide a lower level of legal protection, but by using such a designation some of the development boosters' resistance may be overcome. During President Frei's administration new protected areas were more or less evenly split between parks and reserves. Twenty years later a sizable amount of reserve land was upgraded to national park status and the resulting ratio was nearly two-thirds to one-third. The largest of the reserves, the 2.5-million-hectare Alacalufes National Reserve, however, was not reclassified on the grounds that, although fulfilling all the technical and scientific requisites to be a national park, it would result in the protected areas balance between parks and reserves reaching an 80:20 percent ratio, and that was not viable politically at the time.

The anti-conservation ideology, like the Spanish colonists of the sixteenth century, totally ignores the real characteristics, limitations, and also the opportunities for new ways of using a territory; but it is a powerful force and conservation advocates have to deal with it. Time and again the two views—toward landscape preservation or toward development—have clashed in Patagonia.

Present day

Western Patagonia, while comprising only one-third of Chile's continental territory, contains 80 percent of the nation's terrestrial protected areas; the figure is more impressive taking into account that approximately 20 percent of the country's land area (South American continent and adjacent islands) falls within the boundaries of national parks, nature monuments, national reserves, or private protected areas. Depending on who speaks, these figures are used for praising or criticizing conservation efforts and achievements. Critics always insist that there is too much territory "locked up" in national parks, and, even worse, now certain private owners are "locking" their resources instead of "developing" them; the critics see Patagonian biodiversity as "over-represented" in protected areas and believe that national park land should be declassified and opened to resource extraction.

Fortunately, in Chile, this anti-conservation view has never led to decreasing the area under protection, but it has hindered the establishment or enlargement of protected areas as well as government efforts in support of private conservation and especially public–private partnerships. Although the aim of the critics is not the improvement of conservation management, it is useful to take into account the implicit questions underlying their criticisms: How much is enough? What level of ecosystem representation constitutes successful biodiversity conservation?

The key answer is that protected areas fulfill many objectives at once. In Patagonia, not enough time has passed since the glaciers retreated for new species to evolve, thus we still find a lower number of species as compared to the tropics, most of them pioneers able to exploit new opportunities. Although not a hot spot for tree species, this part of the world boasts a different kind of diversity. Here—in just one-tenth of 1 percent of the planet's land area—8 percent of the Earth's nonvascular plant species live, outnumbering the vascular species in the same area.

Within Patagonia's marine environment, protected areas are still few and small, covering as of January 2014 just some 100,000 hectares (247,000 acres) representing a fraction of 1 percent of the Patagonian territorial sea and none of the Exclusive Economic Zone. After a long struggle, two additional marine conservation units doubling the present area have been declared, a great achievement given the odds, but still painfully far from the minimum required to protect western Patagonia's marine heritage. Although the same categories used on land might be used in marine environments, the government has supported only the use of the Fisheries Law categories of marine park and marine reserve, as well as the "Multiple Use Coastal Marine Area," a management and enforcement agreement coordinating the actions of a number of government agencies with different mandates such as fisheries control, tourism, and navigation.

There is also a designated nature sanctuary in the Quitralco Fjord. Marine protected areas still do not have ranger stations or patrols as land areas have, and are not regularly monitored, but the establishment of marine protected areas is just starting in Chile and conditions should improve with time. Terrestrial areas started when the country did not have managerial experience or enough scientific expertise; in fact, the science of conservation biology did not exist. Present conditions are different and progress could be fast if the political will can be generated. The Patagonian fjords will certainly be at the center of developments regarding marine protected areas in the future.

Sometimes forgotten when forests get the limelight, Patagonian moorlands represent the third-largest wetland expanse in South America after the much better known Pantanal and Amazonian wetlands. These wetlands represent a huge carbon sink, in fact much larger than all of Chile's forest biomass combined; if disturbed or degraded they could become a huge source of greenhouse gases, therefore preservation measures are crucial.

In Patagonia, geology and the geological processes at work before our eyes are unique, including two large ice fields from which the glaciers issuing forth are the closest to the Equator that flow directly into the ocean.

Besides physical elements—flora, fauna, rocks, water or ice—in western Patagonia many relationships and associations contribute to the web of life. The intricate interactions between terrestrial and marine ecosystems—with a lengthy coastline, fjords, estuaries, ocean currents, upwellings, and tidal currents—are fragile and worth protecting. The natural fragmentation of ecosystems is the rule here; studying such processes can lead to greater biological understanding and possible ways to prevent extinctions elsewhere.

Although by area Chile is just the seventh-largest country in South America, some Patagonian protected areas are among the largest in the world. Bernardo O'Higgins National Park, with 3.5 million hectares (8.6 million acres), is larger than Belgium—or four times the size of Yellowstone. Next in land area is Alacalufes National Reserve with 2.3 million hectares (5.7 million acres), followed by Laguna San Rafael National Park (1.7 million hectares), Alberto de Agostini National Park (1.41 million hectares), Guaytecas National Reserve (1.1 million hectares), and Katalalixar National Reserve at 674,500 hectares.

All these protected areas share a land boundary or are separated by only a fjord, strait, or bay. The areas stretch continuously along the fjord district, from latitude 42 to latitude 56 South, and have no roads or large, man-made structures; human presence is restricted to a few fishing villages in the vicinity (but outside park boundaries), a landing strip at Laguna San Rafael, and navigation aids for the ships passing through the fjords. The Madre de Dios islands, surrounded by Alacalufes, were left out in order to allow mining of high-quality lime deposits. The terrestrial component of western Patagonia's coastal zone is in fact a large wilderness, but, except for the small marine protected areas, fishing and aquaculture pens are allowed in the ocean. Captive fish breeding is prohibited if the adjoining land belongs to a national park; under this statute the most environmentally damaging activity is excluded from a large share of the coast.

In addition to the six large parks and reserves already mentioned, there are 25 public and a number of private protected areas in western Patagonia, some of them abutting one of six larger ones, most others not far from the core of protected land. The best known of the adjoining areas is Torres del Paine National Park, sharing a boundary with Bernardo O'Higgins National Park along the southeastern edge of the Southern Patagonian Ice Field. Mention should be made also of Hornopirén, the northernmost of the Patagonian national parks; Cabo de Hornos, the southernmost and oldest of them; and Corcovado and Yendegaia national parks, the newest ones. Magallanes (the oldest national reserve) and Laguna Parrillar National Reserve provide watershed stabilization against landslides and drinking water for Punta Arenas, the largest city in Patagonia. Among the private conservation areas the largest are Pumalín, Patagonia Park, and Karukinka, but many others add to conservation efforts.

Private conservation in western Patagonia

Until 1990 the creation and management of protected areas was done exclusively by the national government (Chile is a unitary nation, meaning that although the national government is decentralized in 15 regions, there is no self-governing subnational level of government as found in federal nations). In recent decades a number of private conservation initiatives, large and small, have been undertaken in the region. They include profit-oriented businesses that include conservation as part of their business plan, farmers who want to preserve all or part of their properties, corporations that find themselves owning ecologically valuable pieces of native forests within landholdings used for commercial tree plantations, and plain examples of wildlands philanthropy—people who buy land in order to protect nature, without seeking financial gain.

In Chile, the private protected areas gained momentum at the height of a wave of privatization of public assets. Some people secretly and not so secretly hoped that the private sector would replace the government as the main conservation provider. A quarter of a century later, the hope has not materialized; there are solid reasons in economic theory for such an outcome. The products of conservation (scenic beauty, biodiversity, clean air and water) generally don't have market prices and there is no mechanism to charge those human "free riders" that refuse to pay voluntarily; on the other hand, conservation's direct costs (land acquisition and management, labor, infrastructure, energy, etc.) have a market price and there is no way to avoid paying it. The commitment to conservation demands an investment but cannot promise a specified financial return. In some instances it is possible to charge for the use of certain goods or services and achieve a margin of profit, but these cases are the exception and not the rule.

The six largest private protected areas in Chile, each covering more than 50,000 hectares (123,000 acres), are funded by interested sponsors because the revenues do not cover acquisition and development costs, and sometimes not even the operational costs. Two protected areas are financed by wealthy Chileans, two by U.S.-based nongovernmental organizations, and the balance by American philanthropists. Of the six, three are located in western Patagonia: Pumalín Park, Patagonia Park, and the Karukinka nature preserve.

Pumalín. Pumalín Park, encompassing roughly 290,000 hectares (716,000 acres), is located in Palena Province at the northern end of western Patagonia. The project was started by Douglas and Kristine Tompkins in 1990, who, through a charitable foundation, gradually bought private tracts of land as they came onto the market. Douglas Tompkins came to Chile for the first time in the 1960s as a downhill ski racer and later kept returning to enjoy nature-oriented sports while developing two successful business ventures in the United States. He later moved to South America and decided to devote himself to protecting the wildlife and beauty of Patagonia.

A century ago, the Chilean government gave away or sold at bargain prices most of the land in the province of Palena. The owners were expected to develop the land, cut or burn the forests, and start cattle ranches. The climate and soils were, in general, unsuitable for ranching and even less for crop agriculture. The inhabitants of the island of Chiloe, located some 40 miles west of Pumalín, had explored this coast since colonial times and did not find suitable places to make a living. This stretch of coast was spared the human-set fires that ravaged the forest near settlements located north and south of Pumalín Park.

Pumalín protects an important natural heritage, including 80,000 hectares of forest containing Chilean false larch (*Fitzroya cupressoides*), a species listed in CITES Appendix I. This represents about one-fifth of the world population of the species, which is endemic to a limited area in Chile and neighboring parts of Argentina.

Pumalín was formally declared a nature sanctuary by the government in 2005, providing a layer of official recognition to this exceptional private venture, widely acknowledged as the largest privately funded and managed nature preserve on Earth. The land is managed as a public access park, open for hiking, camping, and wilderness recreation, and has been offered as a donation to the government for the creation of a new national park. As of this writing, the government has not yet accepted it for inclusion in Chile's national park system.

Patagonia Park. All over the world—in Chile, the United States, Argentina, Brazil, China—grasslands are among the least represented biomes in national parks and other types of protected areas, and for the same reason: Places suitable for grasslands typically support agriculture or livestock, and establishing protected areas means buying property, withdrawing grazing rights, and countering a perception that grazing is a benign land use with no real impact. Going against the three hurdles is no easy task for any government.

Grasslands cover roughly 12 percent of western Patagonia, but representation in the existing protected areas is very low, about one-tenth of 1 percent. Much sought after for sheep grazing, most grassland ecosystems were sold off by the government well before the creation of the first national parks. In Magallanes, the grasslands cover 3 million hectares (7.4 million acres) in one block broken only by the Strait of Magellan; in Aysen, the grassland area is much smaller, 370,000 hectares (914,000 acres) in the three valleys, where the region's three original private ranches, or *estancias,* were located.

By the beginning of this century, the Belgian owners of Estancia Valle Chacabuco, facing rising costs, declining soil fertility, and unstable commodity prices, started to look for a prospective buyer. Conservacion Patagonica, a nonprofit organization headed by Kristine McDivitt Tompkins, agreed to buy the economically troubled 78,000-hectare sheep farm in 2004. Conservacion Patagonica devised a project to create a future Patagonia National Park by combining the acquired private lands with two adjoining national reserves, Jeinimeni to the northeast and Lago Cochrane to the southwest. The new park, comprising roughly 263,000 hectares, will be a world-class protected area with the fullest array of fauna in all of Patagonia, majestic mountains, and easy visitor access from existing road networks in Chile and Argentina. The project is now concentrating efforts on eradicating introduced plant species, eliminating fences, and generally restoring the land to its former richness and diversity. Public access infrastructure is under construction, including park personnel housing, visitor center, trails, campgrounds, and other facilities. The project aims to be energy self-sufficient and all buildings will be low maintenance.

The Patagonia Park project's permanently employed workforce is already larger than the workforce employed by the former sheep farm. The park has the potential to become, within a few years, the economic driver of the Cochrane area, much as Torres del Paine National Park did for the province of Ultima Esperanza after land use there was converted from grazing to parklands.

The Chilean government has already accepted two recent land donations for new national parks, but the Patagonia Park project will likely remain for a while in the pipeline because there is still some restoration and construction work to be completed prior to the land's donation to the national park system. Meanwhile, work is progressing to create links with the local entrepreneurs who will benefit from the new service-oriented economy now emerging.

Karukinka. The private nature reserve Karukinka is a case study in land management serendipity and also a textbook example of late-twentieth-century Chilean decision makers' attitude toward a large tract of government-owned primary forest. At the end of the nineteenth century, the government of Chile sold or leased at very low prices the grass-covered northern part of the island of Tierra del Fuego. Nobody showed interest in the southern beech forests (*Nothofagus pumilio, N. betuloides,* and *N. antarctica*) in the central part of the island, so the government kept the lands that nobody wanted. It is interesting to note that in Chile, as in other parts of the world, those unwanted lands would later provide the backbone for the creation of national park systems.

Thirty years ago, in the late 1980s, decision makers were busy implementing an agenda known in Chile as neoliberal and in the United States as neoconservative, so they decided to sell half a million acres of gently rolling public domain land, half of it primary forest, at five dollars per acre to anyone interested in logging it. The military regime came to an end in 1990 and the newly elected government announced a change: The tracts that remained unsold would now go for ten dollars an acre. And with that, U.S.-based land developers investing a few million dollars got hold of the largest continuous expanse of Nothofagus forest in the world. They set up Forestal Trillium and started to plan a large-scale logging operation (which Chilean forest activists opposed vigorously), but—despite generous governmental assurances of subsidies for machinery and buildings— the projected bottom line always remained in the red and the operation never started. After the project went bankrupt, the investment bank Goldman Sachs ended up acquiring the Trillium assets while purchasing some distressed debt. The bank ultimately donated the land in 2004 to the Wildlife Conservation Society (formerly New York Zoological Society), and the property, encompassing more than 275,000 hectares (680,000 acres), became one of the largest private nature reserves in South America.

Road to the future

After the creation of Hornopirén National Park in 1988, no new parks were established in Patagonia during the next seventeen years, although the process of parks declaration continued elsewhere in Chile. In 2005, in what was likely the largest donation of private lands for a national park anywhere in the world, Corcovado National Park was established with a core area of 80,000 hectares donated by the Conservation Land Trust (a foundation established by Douglas Tompkins) and American philanthropist Peter Buckley; their gift of private land was combined with roughly 200,000 hectares of previously unprotected public land. In early 2014, Yendegaia National Park in Tierra del Fuego was similarly established, with a core area donated by a foundation established by Douglas Tompkins (the lands originally acquired with the crucial help of Peter Buckley and Ernst Beyeler) plus the addition of a large tract of public land around the gift lands.

Besides the case of Patagonia Park, other exciting potential opportunities for private–public cooperation include Alacalufes National Reserve, the unit that thirty years ago could not be upgraded just to avoid increasing the total acreage of "hard" conservation, but which is now flanked by private land bought for that very purpose. Another area ideally fit for conservation is the land around the Melimoyu volcano, where there are three tracts of public land separated by private lands that are suitable only for protection.

In practical terms, the idea of substituting government conservation action with solely private action does not work. At the same time, since private conservation stakeholders are now active in Patagonia, the best option for the future is to join forces, combining what government and private sectors can each do best. Private entities have flexibility and can seize opportunities as they arise. The state can provide law enforcement capabilities, public policy harmonization, and steadier, if limited, funding. The end result, moving into the future, is a potentially world-leading system of protected areas that sustains western Patagonia's extraordinary beauty, favors distinctive biodiversity, and anchors a regional economy that sees wild nature as an asset to be treasured.

Rewilding the Carpathians: A Present-Day Opportunity

BARBARA AND CHRISTOPH PROMBERGER

THE CARPATHIAN MOUNTAINS have a long history of being utilized by humans, and any primeval wilderness there has remained in only small, scattered pockets of the most remote mountain areas. Deforestation, over-hunting, significant development pressure, and a change in land owner-ship are the greatest conservation threats today—and, at the same time, the biggest conservation opportunity. Conservation organizations today have the unique opportunity to acquire large areas of land to secure in perpetuity. Ecological and evolutionary processes can be allowed to convert land-scapes that still possess wilderness qualities and ecological richness back into true wilderness—for the benefit of biodiversity and people alike.

If you put a group of European conservationists into a room to dis-cuss focal areas for conservation, you will soon end up talking about the Carpathian Mountains. This 1,500-kilometer-long mountain range in Southeastern Europe covers a total of 209,000 square kilometers across seven countries—of which 33,000 square kilometers constitute high-value areas for conservation according to the WWF Danube-Carpathian Pro-gramme. In short, the Carpathian Mountains are considered the "green backbone of Europe," the "green pearl," and "Europe's last wilderness." Compared to the rest of Europe, the Carpathians indeed host the largest areas of Central and Eastern Europe's remaining ancient forests, stunning biodiversity, the highest concentration of large carnivores, and the largest unfragmented forests.

Even so, the Carpathians are not untouched; they have a long history of human utilization. Even in the absence of roads, logging activities in the back part of the mountain valleys often date back more than a century, when rivers and streams were used for timber rafting; hunting and poaching had significantly diminished populations of both chamois (small, goatlike bovids native to European mountains) and red deer—with direct adverse consequences for their predators—even a century ago; brown bears were almost driven to extinction by the middle of the twentieth century due to human persecution; and traditional livestock grazing in the alpine areas had additional impacts on wild grazers and the vegetation around timberline. Millions of people have lived in numerous villages all along the Carpathians and left their footprint. In particular, forest management has severely impacted many areas, although in other areas human impact has been more moderate and the bulk of native species has survived. Intact forests, however, have remained mostly in small pockets of steep, inaccessible valleys; only a few areas with a significant surface of untouched forest have been protected over the centuries either by their geography or by decision of the ruling elites.

To make a long story short, the relative wilderness character of the Carpathian Mountains is due less to its own pristine state and more to the fact that the rest of Europe is in an even worse condition.

The current situation: threats and opportunities

In order to understand the current situation of conservation threats and opportunities in the Romanian Carpathians, one has to look into the history of land use. In broad outline, the history of the Carpathians and the human impact on their ecosystems spans three eras:

Prior to World War II: In most parts of the Carpathian Mountains, logging was uncontrolled and clear-cuts resulted wherever people had easy access. Nevertheless, it is estimated that in 1943 1.2 million hectares [2.97 million acres]—20 percent of all Romanian forests—were still ancient or quasi-ancient forests.[1] At that time, because no regulated replanting happened, regeneration was dominated by photophilic species such as birch, rowan, or Norway spruce resulting in a shift of forest composition. The establishment of state-owned forests was initiated in 1863, with the transfer of forests owned by the Bucovina monasteries to the state.[2] By 1939, forest ownership was as follows: 30 percent of the forests were state-owned; 29 percent were private; and 41 percent were communal forests.[3] Livestock grazing developed in the alpine areas during the summer months with the presence of millions of sheep (which also transferred diseases to wild ungulates) and numerous guarding dogs, which represented the appearance of an (introduced) ferocious predator in this ecosystem: Black grouse as a ground-nesting bird at the edge of the alpine zone probably disappeared from most of the Carpathians due to predation by the guarding dogs, and any deer or chamois foraying out of the forest would be terrorized by the dogs. However, it is probably less the direct predation but more the lack of access to their summer habitats that limited the large ungulates. Although hunting was controlled in some areas, local peasants often poached for food and for control of livestock damage. The cumulative effects were low chamois populations and local extirpation of red deer and brown bears.

World War II to 1989 (the communist period): By 1948, the forests were entirely state-owned due to the nationalization process. Forests had begun being managed with forestry policies, and massive investments were channelled into forest road infrastructure and organized replanting. State policies, however, also resulted in substantial change to the forest composition via replacing deciduous species with Norway spruce for their economic value. Serendipitously, the situation for wildlife improved tremendously due to the trophy-hunting spleen of Romania's dictator Nicolae Ceaușescu, who enacted anti-poaching laws; restocked bear populations; and enforced strict hunting regulations—all resulting in an abundance of wildlife throughout the 1970s and 1980s. Livestock grazing in the alpine area continued, but the negative effects (destruction of timber vegetation along the alpine treeline, for example) were reduced due to strict laws and their ardent implementation.

1990 to the present (capitalist period): The collapse of the economy in the 1990s had rather positive effects upon the mountain ecosystem. For example, timber harvest decreased from 22 million cubic meters in 1987 to 14 million cubic meters in 1996. Forest policies remained relatively unchanged until 2004, when a land restitution process was initiated and 70 percent of the forest was returned to communes (40 percent) and private individuals (30 percent). Massive clear-cuts and deforestation on a large scale have been the results of this land ownership change throughout the last decade. Hunting was "democratized" and control weakened, leading to increased poaching and widespread decline of wildlife populations. Today, healthy chamois populations tend to be restricted to national parks where hunting is prohibited. Livestock grazing in the alpine areas has continued and destruction of dwarf pine and green alder along timberline has increased due to a lack of control.

Additionally a new threat for mountain ecosystems has emerged from European Union "rural development funds," which have included funding to build logging roads in areas that have hitherto not been accessible as well as the construction of weekend and guest houses in uninhabited mountain valleys. Also, the payment of agricultural subsidies to farmers after the accession of Romania to the European Union has resulted in the increase of livestock grazing in the alpine areas.

Overall, the trend in the Romanian Carpathians goes in two directions (as it happens in many other places): on the one hand, marginal agricultural land is being abandoned and the overall forest cover increases with consequent advantages for biodiversity; on the other, economic exploitation of productive lands (agricultural and forest) is being intensified with fewer and fewer areas remaining unmanaged.

While the process of land restitution has so far been largely detrimental, it also represents an amazing opportunity for conservation. As ownership of 30 percent of Romanian forests transfers into private hands, in most cases, there is little interest in the property per se and more interest in converting it into cash. Private owners want to sell, and what happens after a sales contract is rather irrelevant to these new owners. What if conservation organizations step dynamically into the picture?

Why wildland projects?

Protecting existing wilderness and allowing natural processes in areas that still possess some wilderness qualities and good ecological function are both an immediate priority and an opportunity to halt the loss of biodiversity in Europe. Wildlands are the key repositories for a variety of species that play a central role in the functioning of the entire ecosystem. Large predators, essential to the food web, have been persecuted tremendously during the last century, leading to the extinction of these species in many parts of Europe and a consequent cascade of negative impacts on the resilience of whole ecosystems. Additionally, Romania initiated a large-scale persecution campaign in the late 1950s to exterminate wolves and raptors, using poison, trapping, and shooting. But while other countries succeeded in completely wiping out their wolf populations, Romania's inaccessible mountain areas served as refugia where the wolf numbers might one day regrow to create Europe's largest wolf population outside of Russia.

Carpathian chamois, a flagship species for the alpine areas, is currently threatened by overhunting and poaching. For the past twenty years, chamois numbers have been officially presented as virtually constant, while in reality populations are drastically declining. Since hunting quotas are calculated based on fake evaluations, and the honest presentation of low numbers would automatically lead to no or low shooting quotas, leaseholders of hunting areas have no incentive to report more realistic figures—despite the looming consequences. Protected areas are thus playing an indispensable role in safeguarding threatened species (such as the chamois) from mismanagement, and they can ultimately work as a source for reestablishing healthy populations in a network of wildlands. This is affirmed by the situation in some national parks in Romania, where wildlife populations have increased after hunting was prohibited and efficient control of poaching was put in place.

Wilderness protection in Europe has often focused on areas of no or little economic value. Over half of the Carpathians are still covered with forests, and the economic pressure on these habitats is enormous. In 1900, it was estimated that 40–50 percent of Romanian forests were still largely intact ancient forest. Logging activities, even in areas difficult to access, led to a plummeting of this number to around 20 percent in 1943 and 12 percent in 1974. Studies conducted prior to the land restitution (in 2004) revealed a total of less than 4 percent of virgin forests, parts of which might have been logged throughout the 1990s. Forest management policies have transformed vast ecosystems of high biodiversity and natural forest dynamics into mono-functional timber-producing plantations. Tree species such as the common ash, Wych elm, sycamore maple, rowan, and European yew have all suffered declines—with yew being represented by only a few individual trees scattered across the Carpathians. While of little economic interest, these species play vital roles in the forest ecosystem, due to their fruits and leaves, their association with specific symbiotic and prey species, and their contribution to the general stability and diversity of the forest. Alder trees, for example, typically grow along mountain brooks, building and improving topsoil; their leaves can account for an annual input of nitrogen into the soil of up to 70 kilograms per hectare [roughly 63 pounds per acre]. Additionally, the alder leaf beetle (*Agelastica alni*), who feeds on alder leaves, can completely defoliate a tree in late summer; since there can be thousands of beetles and larvae even on a single tree, many fall into the water and thus serve as important food for fish along these galleries. On the other hand, spruce (typically planted after logging operations) creates acid soils, provides little living space for other species, has no positive effect on the watershed, and usually creates very unstable forests with low biodiversity.

As a result of the establishment of tree plantations, the age structure of many forests has been altered to even-aged stands that are more vulnerable to natural calamities. Compared to the standards of other European countries, where trees are harvested at the age of 80–120 years, the Romanian Forest Act still stipulates rotation cycles of 120–140 years. Though this represents a slightly better situation, one must not forget that trees harvested within that age range are still young and far from having fulfilled their ecological roles. Wandering the remote and inaccessible forests of the Carpathians one can still encounter amazing trees, elms more than 400 years old for example—trees that during Empress Maria Theresa's rule (1740–1780) would have been considered "over-aged" by the standards of modern forestry. The ecological value of such old trees cannot be overemphasized. Once dead, the standing but decaying trees will be used by different woodpecker species for foraging and excavating cavities, which in turn will provide nesting space for secondary cavity-nesters, such as bats, nuthatches, small owls, and occasionally even pine martens.

While foresters consider bark beetle infestations a calamity which has to be fought by all means, including spraying pesticides into the forests, they are actually often more the result of bad forestry practices that have led to unstable forests. These insects and their host trees have coevolved over thousands of years and are an integral part of forest ecosystems helping to shape forest structure and composition. In this context we have to understand that such "catastrophes" are often just a hint of nature showing that natural processes are never static, but very dynamic. In protected areas, these natural processes can be allowed without compromising the economic benefits of landowners.

Wildlands in favorable condition, where nature is allowed to take care of itself, will ultimately be of benefit for nature and humans alike. Being highly multifunctional, such ecosystems provide a wide range of services such as water regulation, minimization of natural hazards, air and water quality, and climate regulation—and they are simply exceptionally beautiful.

Conservation strategy

Given these realities in the Romanian Carpathians and the need for wilderness areas as refugia for the entire European continent, it becomes clear that there is a great opportunity for biodiversity conservation in these mountains. Creating new national parks would be the logical way forward to safeguard the natural treasures in the Carpathians.

The traditional way to create national parks is through government action on public land, lobbied for by different sectors of the society and with administration by public bodies. This system worked in Romania in the late 1990s and early 2000s, and 14 national parks exist today with a total of almost 900,000 hectares [2.2 million acres] (although two-thirds of this area is composed of the Danube Delta National Park). Most national park administrations are being provided and financed by the National Forest Administration (known as "Romsilva"), but after the land restitution and the loss of 70 percent of its forests, it is highly unlikely that Romsilva will agree to gazette any additional national parks on the land they administrate. The Romanian government, on the other side, is the only government within the European Union that does not provide any budget for protected areas. The remaining public sector is mostly in financial straits as well, and Romanian-based nongovernmental organizations (NGOs) struggle financially, surviving on fixed-term contracts for specific conservation activities that are financed by time-limited international public funds.

The question remains: What might be done to use this window of opportunity, in which millions of hectares of valuable forest land change ownership? In fact, here we come to the good news of this essay: Romania represents at the moment a unique opportunity for international conservation organizations to secure large swaths of land for conservation in perpetuity, by purchasing them, converting them from commercial forests into national parks and eventually—through a rewilding process—back into bona fide wilderness. It could also represent an opportunity for a different type of economic development in Romania that would not harm its natural treasures: making the country attractive to a rapidly growing European nature tourism market.

What would such a strategy look like? First, a lot of land needs to be purchased, which is already virtually impossible in most other parts of Europe, where ownership structures are settled and no large properties exist. In the Carpathians, much land is for sale and, by European standards, land prices are still very low. It may be that this is the only place in Europe where opportunities for large land acquisition exist, except perhaps for the Scottish Highlands, which were cleared of their forests centuries ago and have turned to barren land since. Secondly, an organization would need to establish and overlook conservation partnerships around these properties for three reasons: one, to create economic alternatives for local people and thus get their support for the initiative; two, to help fund the ongoing administration costs, at least until the Romanian government chooses to allocate a budget for protected areas; and three, to assist the protected area initiative to accomplish its conservation goals. Lastly, a rewilding campaign would contribute to converting altered ecosystems back into their natural composition, either by letting nature take its course or by introducing missing elements—such as native species—if deemed necessary or desirable.

And last, but not least, an initiative of this size would need the assurance that these land-holdings would one day go back into the ownership of the Romanian people, once the conditions and the necessary infrastructure for administering a modern system of protected areas are fulfilled by the Romanian State. Few in Romania realize today the treasure this country has, but if these forests can now be secured, the Romanian people will one day be proud of the Carpathians as a World Natural Heritage of extraordinary beauty and biodiversity.

Protecting the Wild Nature and Biodiversity of the Altai-Sayan Ecoregion

MIKHAIL PALTSYN

THE ALTAI-SAYAN ECOREGION is one of the 200 priority areas identified by World Wide Fund for Nature for biodiversity conservation.[1] Named after the Altai and Sayan Mountains, this region covers more than 1 million square kilometers of mountains, steppes, and forests in the very center of Eurasia, overlaying the intersection of Russia, Mongolia, Kazakhstan, and China (see map). Altai-Sayan is the birthplace of two of the world's ten largest rivers— the Ob' and the Yenisey, with watersheds covering over 5.5 million square kilometers. These rivers are crucial for the quality and health of freshwater ecosystems for an area as large as Europe. Additionally, six freshwater and saline Great Lakes of Mongolia cover 100,000 square kilometers of the ecoregion.

The wide elevation range (between 200 and 4,580 meters above sea level) and climate diversity of this mountain region define its high landscape variability and uniqueness. Dark and wet conifer forests (*taiga*) in the deep river valleys graduate into alpine meadows and tundra at higher elevations; the southern mountain slopes are covered by dry steppe and forest steppe; semi-deserts and deserts occupy wide intermountain depressions; and the highest elevations are defined by cold mountain deserts, glaciers, and snow fields. High landscape diversity is the basis for the unique species diversity of the Altai-Sayan Ecoregion—including some 10,000 known species of plants, animals, and fungi, with 3,500 vascular plant and 680 vertebrate animal species.[2] The elusive snow leopard (*Panthera uncia*), impressive Altai argali (*Ovis ammon ammon*), slim Mongolian saiga (*Saiga tatarica mongolica*), and legendary Saker falcon (*Falco cherrug*) are flagship species of Altai-Sayan Mountains and icons for biodiversity conservation in this part of Central Asia.

Altai-Sayan is home to approximately 5 million people, speaking about 20 languages.[3] This region is often considered as a cradle of the great nomadic people of Central Asia, of whom several hundred thousand still lead traditional nomadic lifestyles and depend completely on their livestock. In spite of the fact that there are many links between past cultures of the Altai-Sayan Region and modern civilization, the ancient and medieval history of Southern Siberia and Central Asia is little known to the general public.[4] This area is extremely rich in stone and cave paintings, as well as ancient burial mounds, menhirs, steles, and other historic monuments. The oldest sites of human settlements in Altai-Sayan date back to 40,000 BC.[5]

The Altai-Sayan Ecoregion in the center of Eurasia, at the intersection of Russia, Mongolia, China, and Kazakhstan.

The global distinction of the Altai-Sayan Ecoregion has been underlined by nominations for UNESCO World Nature Heritage sites for two of its regions: the Golden Mountains of Altai and the Uvs Nuur Basin.[6] Conservation of the Altai-Sayan Ecoregion offers an outstanding opportunity to preserve a gigantic, all-but-pristine landscape, along with the ecological functions it fulfills and services it delivers. Conservation of the Altai-Sayan challenges conservationists and government leaders to demonstrate that there are indeed ways to protect large swaths of wild nature and prevent large-scale degradation of ecosystems.[7]

The environment of Altai-Sayan is threatened by industrial development, which, if not opposed, will likely increase during the next decades. General threats for the region's ecosystems and biodiversity include hydropower generation, mining, degradation of pastures, deforestation and forest degradation, poaching, and poorly planned tourism development; the effects of these impacts will likely be exacerbated due to climate change.[8]

A total of 52 existing and proposed dams were identified in the Altai-Sayan Ecoregion in 2012.[9] Five of them are large hydropower dams (315–6,000 megawatts located on the Yenisey and Irtysh Rivers.)[10] The building of new dams will threaten the integrity of water ecosystems in the Russian part of Altai-Sayan and negatively influence adjacent regions.

Mining is also increasingly a threat in the Altai-Sayan Ecoregion. Mining for coal and metal ores has been traditionally concentrated in Russia's Kemerovo Region, but now the Russian government has plans to develop mineral deposits in previously wild areas of the Altai and Sayan Mountains. During the last decade, coal mining has been intensively pursued in the Mongolian part of the Altai-Sayan Ecoregion, impacting the habitats of Altai argali, snow leopard, and other endangered species.[11]

Pasture degradation from overgrazing is another serious threat on the Mongolian side of the ecoregion. Livestock numbers in Mongolia doubled between 1992 and 2007—increasing from 22 million to more than 40 million.[12] The rise in goat numbers is especially damaging for the rangelands, as goats are more aggressive grazers than other livestock. Populations of wild Altai argali and Mongolia saiga have coexisted with nomadic herders and their livestock for centuries, but in our time the impact of livestock grazing on the quality of the rangelands and the range and habitat of these wild species is very high.[13]

Illegal logging is a serious problem in the Russian Federation, including the Altai-Sayan Mountains. WWF reports that 10–35 percent of all timber logged in Russia is done illegally, while in certain regions logging up to 50 percent of timber is illegal or suspicious.[14] In Mongolia the forestry sector is dominated by illegal trade, and 85–90 percent of consumed wood is produced illegally.[15] Remote sensing data recorded about 18,000 wildfires in the Russian portion of the Altai-Sayan Ecoregion, affecting 8.3 million hectares (20.3 million acres) between 2000 and 2009.[16] It is estimated that over 87 percent of these fires were caused by humans.[17]

The poaching and illegal wildlife trades are grave threats to endangered and other wildlife species in the Altai-Sayan Ecoregion. Poaching is depressing the numbers of Altai argali and snow leopard and is also the chief factor behind the dramatic declines in populations of Saker falcon, musk deer, Mongolian saiga, and Mongolian marmot in the ecoregion.[18]

Creating a protected area network is one of the most effective and comprehensive ways to address all these threats to the ecosystems and biodiversity of the Altai-Sayan Ecoregion. The first protected area in the ecoregion (Stolby Zapovednik, a strictly protected nature reserve) was established near Krasnoyarsk City, Russia, in 1925 to protect picturesque rock pillars and conifer forests on the 47,000-hectare (116,000-acre) area. Then in 1932, the large, 1-million-hectare Altaisky Zapovednik (Altaisky Nature Reserve) was established in the Altai Mountains, Russia, thus protecting virgin boreal forests, alpine meadows, and tundra of the Teletskoye Lake and Chulyshman River watershed. Since that time the total area of ecosystems under protection in Altai-Sayan has increased seventeen times! Currently, 114 protected areas exist in the ecoregion on the territory of Russia, Mongolia, Kazakhstan, and China, covering about 18 million hectares (44.5 million acres), where various biomes and habitats of endangered species are found. Protected areas occupy about 17 percent of the entire ecoregion and protect 60 percent of the glaciers, 30 percent of the mountain tundra and alpine meadows, 15 percent of the mountain forests, 8 percent of the forest steppes, 7 percent of the steppes, 21 percent of the deserts and semi-deserts, 59 percent of the lakes, and 18 percent of the riparian ecosystems in Altai-Sayan.

There are five general types of protected areas in the Altai-Sayan Ecoregion: *zapovedniks*, or "strictly protected areas"; national parks; nature parks; *zakazniks*, or "wildlife refuges"; and local protected areas. Zapovedniks— strictly protected areas—are territories that are closed to the general public and can be visited by tourists and other visitors only on special permission. Activities like development, logging, hunting, fishing, grazing, agriculture, and organized tourism are banned in the zapovedniks. No human settlements can be located inside zapovedniks (with a few exceptions). The objectives of zapovedniks are environmental education and the protection and monitoring of near-pristine ecosystems and endangered species. After the collapse of the Soviet Union, zapovedniks in Russia and Kazakhstan started to develop ecotourism programs for a limited number of tourists in their territories. Strictly protected areas in Mongolia are generally open for visitors. Zapovedniks have their own staff of inspectors, researchers, and educators and are funded by national governments. There are 18 zapovedniks in the Altai-Sayan Ecoregion with a total area of 5 million hectares (12.4 million acres)—about 30 percent of all protected areas in the ecoregion.

National parks are protected areas established for the conservation of unique landscapes, traditional lifestyles of local and indigenous people, and tourism development. National parks have several functional zones with different regimes. Some functional zones of the parks could be open for hunting, fishing, or livestock grazing. But overall development, capital construction, and logging activities that would otherwise jeopardize unique landscapes and nature monuments are restricted or banned in the national parks. These parks may have human settlements and are open for tourism. They have permanent staff, including inspectors, educators, and tourist guides. There are 18 national parks in Altai-Sayan with a total area of around 7.5 million hectares (roughly 18.5 million acres)—about 42 percent of all protected areas.

Nature parks are regional protected areas established for the conservation of biological and cultural diversity, supporting traditional lifestyles as well as tourism development. Nature parks exist only in the Russian part of the ecoregion. They have a similar regime to national parks, but they generally have much more restricted funding and permanent staff. The budgets of nature parks depend on regional governments and are often insufficient for proper management. Only one nature park in Altai-Sayan—Ergaki, located in the southern portion of Krasnoyarsky *Kray* ("region")—has adequate funding and effective staff. But generally park inspectors have no rights to stop and fine poachers. Thus, the conservation role of nature parks is extremely limited. There are eight nature parks in the Altai-Sayan Ecoregion covering an area totaling nearly 1.2 million hectares (nearly 3 million acres)—roughly 6 percent of all protected areas.

The zakazniks—wildlife refuges—are national or regional protected areas established for the conservation or restoration of ecosystems, for the protection of endangered and game species, and for their unique geological or paleontological interest. The regime of zakazniks is often strict, including the ban of development activities, hunting, fishing, and some-times logging. Zakazniks have no staff and are protected by inspectors of the zapovedniks (the strictly protected areas described earlier), regional wildlife protection agencies, or special regional administrations for pro-tected areas. The effectiveness of regional zakazniks greatly depends on available funding for their protection. For example, zakaznik protection in the Russian Altai is very low and ineffective due to the absence of funding for their protection. At the same time zakazniks of Krasnoyarsky Kray are managed by special administrators and regularly patrolled. The total area of 74 wildlife refuges in Altai-Sayan is 3.8 million hectares (9.4 million acres)—or 21 percent of all ecoregion protected areas.

Local protected areas first became established in the Mongolian part of Altai-Sayan around 2010–2011. These areas are delineated by local gov-ernments and local communities in order to develop community-based rangeland and wildlife management and to protect mountain pastures from mining. They are protected by local communities themselves. These areas are used for traditional livestock grazing and look more like "sus-tainable use areas" than bona fide protected areas.

Overall, the main role of different protected areas in Altai-Sayan is to conserve the integrity and viability of wild lands from major industrial threats such as mining, construction, and other development. At the same time protected areas play a critical role in the conservation of endangered and game species. Thus, the northernmost snow leopard and Siberian ibex populations in Krasnoyarsky Kray were saved only through strict protec-tion and anti-poaching measures of the Sayano-Shushensky Zapovednik. In the 1970s and 1980s Altaisky Zapovednik was a perfect shelter for popu-lation of Altai argali in Chikhachev Ridge, when all other argali habitats were taken over by the livestock herds of Soviet collective farms. Musk deer population density in protected areas of Altai and Sayan is usu-ally much higher than in the surrounding areas available to poachers.[19] Kuznetsky Alatau Zapovednik also successfully protects from poachers the highly sensitive forest reindeer (*Rangifer tarandus valentinae*) popula-tion in the northern part of the Altai-Sayan Ecoregion.[20]

Sometimes protected areas are successful in saving habitats but not endangered species themselves. The endangered Saker falcon, for example, was completely eliminated by poachers from the territory of Khakassky Zapovednik between 2005 and 2011.[21] The snow leopard of the regional Shavla Zakaznik—formerly the largest population of snow leopards in

Russia—was destroyed by snare poaching in the 1980s and 1990s.[22] Since 2010, however, when part of this zakaznik was included in Sailugemsky National Park and an active anti-poaching campaign was organized by WWF and other conservation groups, this area has proven promising for the restoration of snow leopards in the Altai Mountains due to its high-quality habitats and high population densities of Siberian ibex, elk, and musk deer—key prey species for snow leopards.

Transboundary protected areas located along state borders of the Altai-Sayan Ecoregion have considerable value in conservation of transboundary populations of endangered species. Two such transboundary nature reserves (one along Russia and Kazakstan, the other along Russia and Mongolia) protect key populations of snow leopard, Altai argali, Siberian ibex, Mongolian marmot, Saker falcon, and other species. Two more will be established in the ecoregion at the border of Russia and Mongolia, protecting argali and snow leopards.

Four protected areas in the Altai Mountains of Russia, along with four nature reserves on the border of Russia and Mongolia, compose the core area of two UNESCO World Heritage Sites: the Golden Mountains of Altai and the Uvs-Nuur Basin.[23] These have recognized global significance and high conservation value. Now governments and conservation organizations of Russia, Mongolia, China, and Kazakhstan are discussing extending the Altai Golden Mountains World Heritage Site to include seven protected areas in the transboundary zone of these countries. If this initiative is successful it will establish a huge international transboundary nature reserve in the very heart of the Altai Mountains.

Despite a relatively well-developed protected area network in the Altai-Sayan Ecoregion, plans are under way for establishing additional protected areas. Currently only 16 percent of key snow leopard habitats in Russia where sustainable leopard populations exist are inside of protected areas. Thus, the Conservation Strategy for Snow Leopard in Russia 2014–2024 suggests at least 300,000 hectares (741,316 acres) of new protected areas are needed to ensure proper protection of most important snow leopard distributions.[24] The 2012 WWF Altai-Sayan Ecoregion Conservation Strategy aims to include up to 35 percent of habitats of snow leopard and Altai argali and at least 20 percent of Mongolian saiga habitats in protected area networks by 2020.[25] If these plans come true the total area of wild nature under protection in the Altai-Sayan Ecoregion will increase to 20 million hectares (nearly 50 million acres)—a total area roughly equivalent to the North American Great Lakes!

The Crucial Importance of Protected Areas to Conserving Mongolia's Natural Heritage

RICHARD P. READING, GANCHIMEG WINGARD,
TUVDENDORJ SELENGE, AND SUKH AMGALANBAATAR

VAST (1.57 MILLION SQUARE KILOMETERS), sparsely populated (approximately 2.7 million people), and relatively poor (mean income per capita in 2013 = \$3,770), Mongolia faces the daunting task of protecting its natural heritage in the face of rapid natural resource extraction efforts by multinational corporations that are promising quick prosperity.[1] Further complicating the rising extractive bonanza, Mongolia continues its struggles to transition from a communist nation with a centrally controlled economy to a democracy with a free market.[2] Expanding and improving its system of protected areas arguably represents the most important component of Mongolia's conservation efforts since political and economic transformation began in 1991.[3] Mongolia has strongly embraced the importance of protected areas to help counter its accelerating rate of development, although as demands for the country's vast mineral and fossil fuel resources grow, and as the increasingly urban population of the country becomes impatient for the promised rise in "standard of living," the challenges to protected areas expansion, management, and even retention (in certain cases) increases. In this essay, we briefly describe the historical and continuing cultural importance of conservation in Mongolia, the threats to the country's protected areas system, and the vital need to maintain, expand, and better manage the nation's system of nature protection.

As of 2012, Mongolia had an impressive 99 federal protected areas covering 27.2 million hectares or over 17 percent of the country.[4] In addition, dozens of smaller *Soum* (county) and *Aimag* (province) protected areas exist covering over 10 percent more of the country. The Government of Mongolia retains ownership of all land, except for very small (half-hectare) plots that individuals may own.

Background

Nature conservation in Mongolia traces its roots back to the country's animistic and then Buddhist traditions.[5] Since Ghengis Khan established the first Mongolian nation over eight hundred years ago, protected areas, in the form of reserves to protect hunting grounds and sacred sites (such as holy mountains), have played an important role in that conservation tradition.[6] Ghengis Khan established hunting reserves during his reign and Mongolia began codifying traditions of environmental and wildlife protection in laws during the sixteenth century. While Americans are rightfully proud of establishing Yellowstone National Park as the world's first national park in 1872, Mongolia has continuously protected Bogd Khan Mountain since 1778.[7] Following its transition from communism, Mongolia, under the leadership of then Minister of Nature and Environment Dr. Zambyn Batjargal, committed itself to establishing a network of protected areas based upon principles of landscape ecology to conserve the nation's flora and fauna. In 1992, the Mongolian Parliament adopted the lofty goal of eventually protecting at least 30 percent of the country, and in 1993 the government formed a Protected Areas Bureau (PAB) to manage the growing network of parks.[8] Unlike the situation within many nations, pressure to continue expanding the protected areas system emanates from Mongolia's rural population. Generally speaking, local people and governments outside of the few larger cities exhibit the greatest support for increased nature conservation efforts and establishing more protected areas to do so.

The Mongolian Parliament, or State Great Khural, passed a new Law on Special Protected Areas in 1994. This law recognizes four types of protected areas—Strictly Protected Areas, National Conservation Parks, Nature Reserves, and Monuments, as outlined below:

Strictly Protected Areas provide the greatest level of protection in Mongolia. These protected areas are dedicated to conserving nature for nature's sake and represent Mongolia's most wild landscapes. They include Pristine, Conservation, and Limited Use Zones, the first of which excludes all people, except protected areas managers and researchers who can only observe but cannot manipulate nature. Strictly Protected Areas fall under the International Union for Conservation of Nature's (IUCN's) Category Ia, or Strict Nature Reserve.

National Conservation Parks protected areas with relatively preserved natural conditions that hold historical, cultural, scientific, educational, and ecological importance. They include Special, Travel and Tourism, and Limited Use Zones. The IUCN classifies "national parks" as Category II protected areas.

Nature Reserves serve to conserve, preserve, and restore areas with important natural features and resources. Four types of nature reserves exist: Ecological, Biological, Paleontological, and Geologic. Mongolian law does not provide provisions for zones within Nature Reserves. Nature Reserves fall within IUCN Category III and Category IV—Natural Monument or Feature and Habitat/Species Management Areas, respectively.

Monuments protect unique natural formations or important historical and cultural areas in their natural state. These, generally small protected areas, fall under IUCN Category III.

In the years that followed this law's passage, the State Great Khural passed the Law on Buffer Zones in 1997, and the Law on a National Program for Protected Areas in 1998. The former law permits the creation of zones surrounding protected areas limiting development in order to help maintain the ecological integrity of those protected areas. The latter law outlined Mongolian policy and guidelines for managing, expanding, funding, and developing the protected areas system and its administration over the next twenty years.

The number of protected areas and the extent of their coverage grew rapidly in the first few years following Mongolia's transition from communism, slowed in the late 1990s, and then again increased over the last few years (Table 1). Although some conservationists criticized Mongolia for expanding nature protection faster than the country's capacity to manage those areas, we argued elsewhere that such expansion was necessary given the growing demands for natural resources extraction.[9] Our earlier concerns proved well-founded, as approximately 45 percent of the country is today leased for natural resource extraction or exploration, primarily for coal, gold, copper, silver, uranium, fluorite, and molybdenum.[10] Thus, many ecologically important areas enjoy at least legal protection from severe degradation, and Mongolia has worked hard over the past several years to improve and expand management of its system of protected areas.

As mentioned, currently 99 federally designated protected areas exist in Mongolia, comprising 17.39 percent of the land (Table 1, Figure 1). Additionally, as of late 2007 *Soum* (county) or *Aimag* (province) governments had protected some 16 million hectares in 899 local areas—or 10.3 percent of Mongolia (Table 1).[11] These mostly smaller *Aimag* and *Soum* protected areas, a large and growing number, are now scattered throughout the nation. Combining federal and local protected areas, an impressive 27.7 percent of Mongolia now enjoys some level of conservation status. More recent expansion of the protected areas system strives to obtain better and more equitable representation of Mongolia's major natural zones. Even so, high mountains (31 percent protected), deserts (31 percent), and taiga forests (30 percent) remain better represented than steppe (9

TABLE 1. MONGOLIAN PROTECTED AREAS SYSTEM

Type of protected area	Number	Extent (1,000 km²)	Percentage of Mongolia
Federal protected areas	*99*	*272.05*	*17.39%*
Strictly Protected Areas	20	124.11	7.94%
National Conservation Parks	32	117.09	7.49%
Nature Reserves	34	29.58	1.89%
Monuments	13	1.27	0.08%
Local protected areas	*899*	*161.4*	*10.32%*
Aimag protected areas	485	114.0	7.29%
Soum protected areas	384	35.0	2.24%
Joint Aimag-Soum protected areas	30	12.4	0.79%
TOTAL	**998**	**433.45**	**27.71%**

Note: Federal protected areas data updated in 2013 and local protected areas data updated in 2009.

percent) and forest-steppe (5 percent) ecosystems.[12] Underrepresentation of temperate grasslands reflects a worldwide trend in the conservation of these vast ecosystems, which are critically endangered primarily because they are subject to widespread conversion for intensive agriculture.[13]

The Protected Areas Bureau manages Mongolia's nature conservation system. Yet staffing and funding for PAB have failed to keep pace with the rate of expansion of the system; in 2009, PAB comprised only 320 staff, including 225 rangers and 95 specialists and managers divided into 24 administrative offices.[14] This miniscule cohort of conservation professionals is stretched beyond capacity. Some technical assistance has been provided by international donor projects such as the Denver Zoological Foundation, United Nations Development Programme/Global Environment Facility (UNDP/GEF), German Technical Advisory Agency (GIZ), The Nature Conservancy, and WWF; yet only rarely, does protected area staff receive adequate training, equipment, and budget to effectively conduct their work.

Main threats to protected areas in Mongolia

Mongolia faces a number of significant environmental threats and worrisome long-term trends that require immediate attention.[15] Despite the rhetoric, Mongolia remains far from pristine. Just because Mongolia has a

FIGURE 1. MONGOLIA'S PROTECTED AREAS SYSTEM

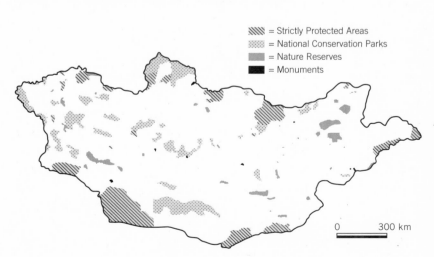

= Strictly Protected Areas
= National Conservation Parks
= Nature Reserves
= Monuments

0   300 km

low human-population density, limited development, and little industrial land transformation does not mean the country enjoys a high degree of ecologic health. Indeed, the flora and fauna of Mongolia suffer from over-harvesting and increasing habitat degradation, several regions are already devoid, or nearly devoid, of large wildlife, desertification is expanding, erosion is evident in several areas, and several species and subspecies are threatened with extinction. Arguably, the four main threats to biodiversity are the impacts of mining, poaching, expanding numbers of livestock, and lack of resources and capacity for effective conservation management.[16] Throughout most of Mongolia, protected areas provide the first line of defense—at least against the onslaughts of mining and poaching.

Mining represents by far the largest sector of the Mongolian economy. Formerly limited to just a few locations, government complicity and liberal extraction laws have encouraged rapid expansion of the mining sector. By 2010 about 45 percent of Mongolia was leased for natural resources exploitation or exploration, and international and domestic firms now mine in nearly every section of the country. Every few years mining companies and pro-development government officials call for removing crucial habitats from the protected areas system to permit mining of the valuable fossil fuel and ore deposits that those companies believe exist there. What's more, unregulated or loosely regulated activities and tens of thousands of "wildcat" or "ninja" miners (named because they often carry mining pans on their backs, thus resembling ninja turtles to many Mongolians) cause severe environmental degradation through the indiscriminate and illegal use of explosives and chemicals like cyanide. Usually, little to no restoration or reclamation occurs.

Increased poaching has dramatically impacted plant and especially animal populations throughout Mongolia.[17] Although subsistence poaching represents a significant problem in some areas, poaching to supply an international commercial market poses a far greater threat to Mongolian wildlife. As Mongolia opened its doors to international markets, poaching increased to satisfy the huge demand for animals and animal parts in Asian markets, especially for use in traditional medicines. The rapidly growing affluence of Chinese and other Asian consumers has translated into greater profits from wildlife trade, and the impacts on Mongolia's wildlife have been dramatic. Numbers of formerly more common species—such as elk (*Cervus elaphus*) and Siberian marmots (*Marmota sibirica*)—have crashed in the face of uncontrolled poaching, to the extent that both of these species are now considered critically endangered.[18] Poachers have even begun targeting species not customarily used in traditional medicine to provide "substitute" parts. For example, poachers kill argali sheep (*Ovis ammon*) for their horns, which they grind up into powder they then pass off as coming from a traditionally valued animal, such as saiga (*Saiga tatarica*).[19] Although improving, both monitoring and anti-poaching efforts remain weak and virtually nonexistent outside of protected areas. With laws only sporadically enforced, poaching has become pervasive and often brazenly open.

Overgrazing as a result of expanding livestock numbers represents another major ecological threat throughout Mongolia.[20] By law, protected areas permit grazing in at least parts of all protected areas but without providing any guidance on how managers can limit that grazing. Mongolia remains primarily a nomadic pastoralist society outside of cities and towns, and most Mongolians view nomadism as fully compatible with nature conservation and many even regard livestock as semi-wild animals.[21] These cultural perceptions become obstacles when managers of protected areas attempt to eliminate or restrict livestock grazing. Historically, Mongolian pastoralists raised livestock in herds limited primarily by the harsh climate, low human numbers, and especially social and political constraints, such as the strict, centralized market controls that existed under Communist rule and the feudal land tenure system prior to that.[22] But recent social and economic changes largely eliminated such market controls and the number of livestock has increased dramatically after the end of communism and collectivization.[23] Privatization of herds provided an incentive to rapidly increase herd sizes, while increased freedom of movement permitted pastoralists to move away from areas experiencing harsh winters, dry summers, or land degradation. As the social security and market support systems provided by communism disappeared, pastoralists have come to view large herd sizes as the best insurance against catastrophic loss of their entire herd. However, expanding herds have led to overgrazing, erosion, desertification, and eventually huge crashes in livestock numbers in the face of large-scale disasters (extended droughts and harsh winters, for example). Most pastoralists and government officials recognize the need for grazing reform, but thus far an effective solution that most pastoralists will accept remains elusive.

Finally, lack of resources and capacity hamper the ability of park staff to more effectively manage the amazing natural areas they are charged with protecting. Most conservation professionals do not have sufficient resources to enforce existing laws and regulations. Rangers report their inability to thwart illegal activities, especially poaching, due to low fines not being a deterrent (for example, the fine for illegal fishing is only about US$1–2); social hesitancy (rangers encounter destitute people who poach for subsistence or people who are ignorant of the law); and fear (poachers are well-armed and dangerous). In addition, most rangers cannot legally carry a firearm and do not have the power of arrest, so they must find a police officer—often dozens of kilometers away—to enforce the laws. Improving conservation management requires additional equipment, staff, and training, as well as drafting conservation management plans, improving existing management, and developing good outreach and local relations. Of course, doing all of this requires more money, something the Mongolian government has not been willing to provide. The government simply must both realize the immense ecological significance of protected areas and back their establishment with meaningful support. As natural resources extraction ramps up, Mongolia should dedicate a substantial proportion of the income from that industry to support nature conservation, including money earmarked toward improving protected areas management. Similarly, the PAB might ramp up even greater community support through creative, community-based programs that link conservation to local benefits. Finally, the international community must support Mongolia's conservation efforts through effective technical and financial contributions. Although some of these conservation policies and measures exist today, Mongolia needs a much greater commitment to nature protection.

Continuing importance of protected areas in Mongolia

Despite the challenges, Mongolia remains a nation with great conservation potential. Indeed, Mongolian populations of some species exceed those of all other populations throughout world combined, such as wild Bactrian camels (*Camelus ferus*), Asian wild asses (*Equus hemionus*), goitered gazelles (*Gazella subgutturosa*), Mongolian gazelles (*Procapra gutturosa*), argali, or mountain sheep (*Ovis ammon*), cinereous vultures (*Aegypius monachus*), white-naped cranes (*Grus vipio*), and more. The low human-population density and lack of modern development (only one recently completed paved road crosses the country) offer hope that improved conservation management could permit recovery of degraded ecosystems and depleted wildlife populations. The strong, deep-seated conservation ethic that pervades Mongolian culture gives further cause for hope. The power of nomadic romanticism as symbol and myth pervades Mongolian culture.[24] As such, support for conservation remains strong, especially among rural, nomadic pastoralists who view nature conservation, including the establishment of parks, as a way of helping them realize and maintain their traditional lifestyles. Yet, much work remains.

Mongolia's protected areas form the core of the county's conservation efforts. Indeed, little wildlife conservation or management occurs outside of protected areas[25] (and, as a result it is rare to see large, wild animals outside of protected areas and most animals outside of parks are extremely cagey): This must change. Protected areas function best when they exist within a conservation-friendly landscape. No federal agency exists to safeguard wildlife outside of protected areas, for example.[26] Conservation beyond protected areas in Mongolia would go a long way toward improving the conservation prospects for the nation, as well as the integrity of the protected areas.

And maintaining the conservation value of Mongolian protected areas is vital. Several protected areas, created specifically to conserve threatened, endangered, or culturally important wildlife, harbor the last viable populations of those species. For example, Mongolia established the Great Gobi Strictly Protected Area to conserve wild Bactrian camels and Gobi bears (*Ursus arctos gobiensis*), Sharga Nature Reserve for protection of the Mongolian saiga antelope (*Saiga tatarica mongolica*), Ikh Nart Nature Reserve to protect argali sheep, and Nomrog Strictly Protected Area to conserve a unique subspecies of moose (*Alces alces cameloides*) having nonpalmate antlers (like elk antlers). Without the protected areas, several of these and other species would likely disappear. As such, the growing network of protected areas in Mongolia bodes well for the flora and fauna of Central Asia, but only if accompanied by more active and effective conservation commitments. We remain optimistic that Mongolia will honor its culture and long history of conservation by working to protect and restore its natural heritage.

Parks: The Best Option for Wildlife Protection in Australia

MARTIN TAYLOR

AUSTRALIA IS A LAND LIKE NO OTHER, home to more biological riches than many other places on Earth. Its geographic isolation across 80 million years since the breakup of Gondwana has meant that most of Australia's animals and plants remain unique, without close relatives anywhere else. Australia and New Guinea are the only places on Earth where all three major divisions of mammals are present: the egg-laying monotremes (platypus and echidna), the marsupials, and the placental mammals. Of the 17 megadiverse countries, which together harbor the majority of Earth's species, Australia ranks at the top for vertebrate diversity and fifth for vascular plant diversity.[1] At least 130,000 different species of native animals and plants, nearly 8 percent of all life on Earth, are found in Australia,[2] along with two globally recognized biodiversity "hot spots"—the Southwest Australia plant diversity hot spot and the Great Barrier Reef.[3] Australia's rich biodiversity has very real economic value. In addition to the ecological benefits like clean water and clean air, which can be hard to put a dollar value on, nature-oriented visitors from overseas bring in over AU$19 billion a year, putting nature tourism among the country's top export earners.[4]

The greatest challenge to Australian biodiversity began in 1788 with the arrival of Europeans who, over the succeeding two centuries, converted the richest habitats to pastures, crops, mines, roads, and townships. Non-native species like cattle, sheep, cats, foxes, rabbits, and many weeds were introduced as well, transforming ecosystems even in the absence of land conversion. Land-based pollution, overfishing, and climate change have also transformed marine habitats, to the point that Australia's most famous protected area, the Great Barrier Reef Marine Park, has now lost half its coral cover in just a few decades.[5]

Today, 55 animals and 42 plant species are already extinct and 1,700 species are listed as threatened with extinction.[6] Of Australia's 57 species of kangaroos and allies, seven are extinct and 16 are listed as threatened with extinction. Two of the only three species of wombats are also listed as threatened, as is the koala.

Investment in protected areas

Until recently the only mechanism effective at stopping destruction and degradation of wildlife habitat was to buy land and put it in a national park or equivalent protected area, or—in the case of the oceans—declare a marine national park.

Progress in expanding Australia's protected area system, however, has been slow because governments have run hot and cold on investment in new protected areas, even if it just means converting areas of land or sea that the government already owns.

Buying land on the open market in order to protect it should be a more attractive option than imposing environmental regulations, because it is voluntary. Nonetheless, even the voluntary sale of agricultural properties with the aim of creating new national parks has been opposed by some rural interests.[7]

Governments seem to have been more willing to impose legislated protection for wildlife. Wildlife laws, however, have proven ineffective at stopping land clearing. Land clearing was brought under control only after public protests forced state governments to tighten vegetation legislation in key states in 2005–2006. But such legislation has proven to be less secure than expected. In Queensland, the state with the lion's share of national land clearing, a newly elected government in 2013 partially reversed a 2006 ban on large-scale clearing and removed protection for forests in an advanced stage of regrowth, even if they are endangered.[8]

The most dramatic advances in Australian protected areas over the past decade have been marine. These advances followed campaigns by broad alliances of conservation groups. In 2004 national parks grew from below 5 percent to over 33 percent of the Great Barrier Reef. The Australian Government also allocated AU$217.7 million to a structural adjustment package for affected fisheries and related business.[9] Then in 2012, a vast system of marine reserves was established across all Australian waters, raising the level of national park protection from below 2 percent to nearly 14 percent, nested within marine parks that grew from 7 percent in 2002 to 36.4 percent in 2012.

On land, there have also been major advances in protected areas. After a campaign by conservation groups led by WWF (World Wide Fund for Nature), the Australian government in 2008 announced a fivefold increase in funding—to AU$180 million over five years—for protected area purchase grants. Grants were offered on a very favorable 2:1 funding basis to suitable proponents—including state or local governments, private or indigenous groups—who made proposals meeting national strategic goals. This did not include the cost of managing protected areas in perpetuity, which is borne by the proponents and usually exceeds land purchase costs by a considerable margin.[10] Funding for Indigenous Protected Areas also increased markedly, and in the past four years Australia has seen over 15 million hectares (37 million acres) of indigenous lands brought under protected area agreements, bringing tangible benefits for conservation and for the health and well-being of indigenous communities.[11]

Even at these high-water marks for protected area investment, however, protected area investment still represented less than 8 percent of all federal government conservation spending.[12] Most Australian government conservation funding goes toward short-term conservation activities. Surveys of farmers show an increase of about 2 million hectares (nearly 5 million acres) treated with conservation activities such as excluding or reducing livestock, removing pests and weeds, foregoing clearing or restoring native vegetation. Although such activities are surely beneficial for biodiversity, in the absence of protected area agreements on the areas treated (also known as conservation covenants or easements), there is uncertainty as to whether those benefits will endure. A protected area, whether a national park or private land covenant, requires not only appropriate conservation activities but a permanent change in land (or sea) use. Only about 3–4 percent of farms in the survey had conservation covenants, while another 6–7 percent of farms had short-term conservation agreements. [13] Despite the increase in activities noted above, the total estimated area under all such conservation agreements decreased from 2007 to 2010.[14]

Wavering support

Protected areas have long been regarded without question as the primary conservation tool. Despite these major recent advances in protected area investments and outcomes in Australia, government support has wavered.

The security of the vast new system of marine national parks is now uncertain, after a new Australian Government took power in 2013 announcing revision of the zoning of the marine parks to accommodate recreational fishing, although retaining overall marine park boundaries.[15] In 2013, the federal government also terminated the terrestrial protected area purchase grants program after having given it a substantial boost in the previous five-year period.[16]

Wavering government support is linked to a growing criticism of the protected areas approach to conservation.

Critics variously contend that parks: are too expensive and insufficient to prevent biodiversity loss; do not really stop biodiversity loss from happening; are poorly managed; or are superfluous because they are mostly on residual land—land considered either too rugged or too unproductive for other uses and so, never at risk of loss anyway.[17] Finally, it has been claimed that with climate change moving species about, parks are all in the wrong places.

With all this bad press, it is small wonder governments have wavered in their support for protected areas. But what does the evidence say?

"Too expensive and insufficient to prevent biodiversity loss." It is often assumed that protected areas are the most expensive way to secure conservation outcomes. In theory, securing conservation agreements with existing landholders should be more cost-effective than buying them out to create a national park.[18] Remarkably, short-term activity-oriented grants may actually be more costly than simple land purchase grants. The federal government protected area purchase grants program has cost the government on average only AU$44.40 per hectare purchased,[19] while a stewardship program operated by the same department has cost more, on average, for short-term contracts than it would cost to buy equivalent properties in the same area.[20] Surprisingly, the federal government terminated the purchase grants program and boosted the stewardship program.[21]

The criticism that protected areas are insufficient to protect biodiversity is a self-fulfilling prophecy.[22] There is nothing intrinsic to protected areas, which means they are inevitably insufficient to save biodiversity. Sufficiency depends on how much investment is put into them. This is not to say that protected areas should be the only approach taken to conservation. Effective conservation requires not just protected areas but also improved resource use practices that minimize environmental impacts in the wider landscape or seascape.

"Paper parks." The "paper parks" idea is a long-standing criticism of protected areas mostly in the developing world, where financing of enforcement is often inadequate and parks are subject to incursions by loggers and ranchers. Hence, it is argued, such parks are parks only on paper, with little real world consequence for biodiversity conservation.[23] Some studies do suggest that community-managed fisheries have greater effectiveness than national parks in conserving fish stocks, largely due to high levels of community buy-in. However, most studies fail to support the paper parks criticism, showing genuine and substantial impacts of parks in halting habitat loss.[24]

Highly protected areas (national parks and some private reserves) are linked to stabilization of threatened species populations in Australia, while other approaches—including "multiple use" protected areas, recovery actions, and natural resource management activities—are not.[25] Some threatened species now occur only in national parks or private sanctuaries, having been lost in the wider unprotected and converted landscape. For example, wild populations of the bilby (*Macrotis lagotis*), the bridled nail-tail wallaby (*Onychogalea fraenata*), and the northern hairy-nosed wombat (*Lasiorhinus krefftii*) in the state of Queensland are now found only in national parks (Diamantina, Taunton, and Epping Forest National Parks, respectively), which were created specifically to save the last remaining wild populations of these endangered species.

One of Australia's most well-known biologists, Professor Tim Flannery, recently wrote an article entitled, "The Future for Biodiversity Conservation Isn't More National Parks,"[26] pointing to the documented decline of native mammals in Kakadu National Park as a rationale. Flannery did not mention other evidence showing that native wildlife, even if declining on Kakadu, is still doing better there than on neighboring grazing lands.[27] It is unclear, however, how the mammal decline problem supports a "no more national parks" position. It would seem rather to indicate a need for better management of national parks to deal with persistent threats to native wildlife.[28]

Nonetheless, there are legitimate concerns over the security of some protected area types. In some Australian states, entire commercial livestock properties are designated as protected areas under International Union for Conservation of Nature (IUCN) management category VI, despite no part of a property being closed to stock. It is unclear in such cases if these areas conform to IUCN guidelines that natural resource use in category VI be low-level, nonindustrial, and compatible with the primary purpose of nature conservation.[29] This is not to dismiss the genuine efforts by many farmers to reduce environmental impacts of their livestock or farming operations. But there should be a way of recognizing their important contribution to conservation without trying to shoehorn them into a protected area category.

The reverse problem may also occur. Private conservancies have taken on pastoral leases on state land, which they manage as protected areas, free of livestock grazing. Despite their best intentions, the properties remain pastoral leases under the law, because there is no legal means of declaring protected areas over such leases, and doing so in any case requires the consent of the state governments who are the landlords.

A final issue is that many non–national park protected areas are not protected from mining; they must contend with state mining laws that allow mining virtually everywhere except in national parks (except in a few cases where specific legislation has excluded mining).[30] Bimblebox Nature Refuge in central Queensland, for example, was purchased with a federal government grant to become a private protected area, and was declared a nature refuge under state legislation. However, its existence is now threatened by a large coal mine because state laws allow nature refuges to be mined.[31]

Even the historically high level of security of national parks has begun to erode. In Australia, national parks are mostly owned and managed by state governments. The federal government operates only a handful of national parks (Kakadu, Uluru, and Booderee). In recent years, some state governments have allowed commercial livestock, logging, hunting, high-impact recreation, and tourist developments in what previously were considered inviolate sanctuaries for nature.[32]

The examples above suggest that any ineffectiveness of parks and protected areas likely stems from weaknesses in government protected area policy. If governments want protected areas to be more effective at doing their job of protecting wildlife, then they need to tighten policy so that designation as a protected area confers genuine and permanent protection for wildlife habitats.

"Poorly managed." National Parks are often criticized as "locked-up," most recently by the Australian prime minister, Tony Abbott, saying: "We have quite enough National Parks, we have quite enough locked-up forests already. In fact, in an important respect, we have too much locked-up forest."[33]

"Locked-up," in this context, means "closed to commercial exploitation." A counterview is that a new national park unlocks land usually under exclusive private commercial use for the enjoyment of the public.[34] A common corollary of the "locked-up" position is that national parks are, almost by definition, poorly or "passively" managed. One critic described a national park as a "toxic ecological volcano, spewing out fire, kangaroos, weed seeds, and feral animals such as wild dogs into the surrounding countryside."[35]

By contrast, some critics allege, areas under extractive or consumptive use such as logging and livestock are "actively managed," and as a result they don't suffer from these problems and may therefore offer a better option for conservation. Quoting Australia's prime minister again: "When I look out tonight at an audience of people who work with timber, who work in forests, I don't see people who are environmental bandits, I see people who are the ultimate conservationists."[36]

Wildfires, kangaroos, and native animals like dingoes[37] are considered desirable in Australian protected areas in natural balance. Farmers understandably have a different view. Fires are a risk for farm buildings and infrastructure, dingoes may attack livestock, and kangaroos eat the grass. There is a fundamental and perhaps unbridgeable conflict of values and interests between consumptive and conservation uses. This is why protected areas are so critical for effective conservation. A current debate concerns whether "land sparing" or "land sharing" is the best approach to conservation. Land sparing means protected areas, and this includes sparing habitat patches on farms and ranches through appropriate covenants. Land sharing means conservation is achieved without protected areas by improved management of farms and ranches. Evidence suggests that "land sparing" is more effective for conservation.[38] But this does not mean we need to convert whole productive farms to protected areas. Rather, the whole-of-landscape approach recognizes an appropriate mix of protected areas, including high conservation value habitats protected by covenants on farms, and high environmental standards for farm practices elsewhere in the landscape, or for fishing in the marine environment.[39]

Excessive fire and invasive species can be harmful for biodiversity and are the dominant threats that occur on protected areas. Is there any evidence, as suggested by some critics, that national parks are especially burdened with such problems in comparison to neighboring grazing and forestry land? Are national parks "badly run zoos" as one critic claims?[40] Most wildfires start outside parks and burn into parks, not the other way around, and parks agencies have very well-funded fire, weed, and pest management programs, dispelling the "passive management" criticism.[41] A comparative study of northern national parks with other nearby tenures concluded that measurably higher biodiversity within parks can be attributed to the park management regime, finding that intrinsic differences are not due to accidents of location.[42]

This does not mean that management of protected areas is, by definition, ideal. To be effective there must be ongoing investment in management of ongoing threats. How to pay for good management is a constant question raised by governments. There has been discussion of payments for ecosystem services, with carbon storage being the one most well developed at present.[43] Protected areas secure the provision of services like clean water and clear air, and they harbor useful species like pollinators and wild genetic resources.[44] Although Australia is not known for its domesticated crops, it does have macadamia nuts. Only 3 percent of the range of wild macadamias is in protected areas, despite this representing the narrow genetic base of a AU$500-million-per-year global industry.[45] Northern Australian protected areas also turn out to harbor wild rice species that may hold the key to overcoming rice diseases.[46]

Ecosystem services can be hard to cost, but one service is not. National parks attract over AU$19 billion in foreign exchange every year into Australia as spending by international nature-oriented visitors, in addition to spending by domestic visitors. Governments already have a source of revenue for expanding and maintaining the fundamental asset of the nature tourism industry, the national parks system, in the form of taxes on spending by nature-oriented tourists and visitors. Such taxes end up in general revenue, however, and are not explicitly linked to or turned back into building and maintaining the parks as a basic asset of the nature tourism industry.[47]

"Mostly on residual land." Parks historically have been confined to so-called residual lands, residual in the sense of being "left over"—either too rugged or too unproductive and thus undesirable for agriculture, mining, forestry, or development. Since such areas were always at little risk of loss anyway, it is argued, then spending money to protect such land is "money

for nothing."[48] A corollary is that it is precisely the most agriculturally productive areas that need to be protected, because these are likely the richest and most favorable habitats for wildlife.[49]

Patterns of actual land use change do not support the residual land hypothesis very well. Only 20 percent of the land brought into highly protected status in Australia in the period 2005–2012 came from land mapped as having minimal use in 1992. The majority of additions to protected areas came from commercial livestock grazing land.[50] Also, it is by no means necessary that rugged, low-productivity land is inferior in biodiversity value. Indeed one emerging imperative to allow ecosystem adaptation to climate change is to protect steep altitudinal gradients and ecotones, since it is precisely along such steep gradients that whole ecosystems will be able to shift rapidly in response to a warming climate, whereas along the low gradients of plains and basins it may be impossible to reach a favorable climatic space within typical dispersal distances in time to track a rapidly changing climate.[51]

"All in the wrong places." Protected areas are bound to lose their wildlife as animals and plants attempt to shift range in response to climate change. Reserve systems clearly need to be designed based not only on where native species are found now but on where they *will* be, and on the pathways needed to get there.[52] But does this mean that current protected areas are "in the wrong places" for climate change? Recent assessments have found that the classic ecological representation principle of protected area design is robust to climate change. Although in a future climate many ecosystem and species currently present will be lost from a given protected area, other ecosystems and species will be gained, as they shift in response to climate change. Management will, however, have to be more accepting of biotic change than in the past.[53] Other studies have identified refugial areas, areas providing stable long-term habitat for many species despite climate change, and these are now being used by some agencies to plan future protected area purchases.[54] Australian state and territory governments have jointly adopted a national strategy for strategic growth of protected areas which recognizes climate change refugia as a priority resource for protection.[55]

Parks—the best option for wildlife protection in Australia

National parks and other highly protected areas provide the best option for wildlife protection in Australia. Inclusion of habitat in protected areas has been shown to promote threatened species recovery when little else does. Protected areas are a cost-effective, highly leveraged, and voluntary mechanism of conservation. Strategic acquisition and establishment of new protected areas should be the top-priority conservation investment in Australia.

Protected areas still need to be well managed to be effective. This requires ongoing investment in management of pervasive threats like inappropriate fire, weeds, and pests. When considering how to fund protected area growth and management, governments should value the ecosystem services they provide, in particular the tax revenue already obtained from spending by visitors attracted to Australia's incomparable protected areas and the wildlife they protect.

Effective conservation also requires a whole of landscape or seascape approach, ensuring that protected areas are complemented by resource uses that meet high environmental standards in the wider landscape or seascape.

Nongovernment and less strictly protected areas represent a growing component of the national system of protected areas in Australia. Security of protection is uncertain in some cases and could be greatly improved by government policy reform, to guarantee adherence to IUCN protected area standards and guidelines. Conservation covenants on private land could become the dominant type of protected area in Australia and also provide the best vehicle for a whole of landscape approach. Governments would do well to prioritize their conservation funding toward securing and maintaining enduring conservation agreements that integrate protected area covenants and high environmental performance standards for agriculture.

Australia's wildlife is unique and loved worldwide. A more focused and well-funded campaign of protected area expansion on public and private land is urgently needed to be sure Australia's wallabies, possums, wombats, and koalas survive both the past legacy of land use conversion and the coming storms of climate change.

AFTERWORD

DOUGLAS R. TOMPKINS

THE TWISTS AND TURNS in the road of most everyone's destiny seem to me to be random and totally unpredictable, at least as I look back on my own formation. As a twelve-year-old kid living in a rural environment on a back road four miles from a village of 600 people, I was invited to go rock climbing with a woman friend of my parents. One seemingly insignificant decision to go that day changed the trajectory of my life forever.

Once I got to the climbing area I immediately caught on to the athletics of rock climbing and that was it, I was hooked. As it turned out, I was being introduced to what might be called "the Nature Tradition," which is populated by conservation heroes such as John Muir, Bob Marshall, David Brower, and Arne Naess—people whose love for wild nature had been honed in the mountains. And so the course of my life as a conservationist began, although at the time I had no perspective on where I might be headed or what the factors were that pointed me there—toward a life dedicated to environmental activism and helping create new national parks.

Rock climbing and mountaineering eventually led me to found The North Face, now perhaps the leading outdoor clothing and equipment supplier in the world (something I could never have imagined before that day when the name first occurred to me as I worked my way, down on my knees with a chain saw, along the length of a fallen tree while working for a landscaping company at Lake Tahoe in California). After nearly ten years of building up The North Face, I sold it and started the Esprit company in San Francisco along with my former wife, Susie Tompkins, and another friend of ours. Those years in business distracted me from activism, although I spent at least four or five months each year somewhere in the world on climbing expeditions, white-water kayaking, or ski racing. Mountain sports took me to some of the wildest, most remote places on Earth and deepened my appreciation for wild nature. While I got to see many of the last great places on Earth—landscapes where beauty and diversity still flourished—international travel opened my eyes to the fact that everywhere nature was being whittled away by techno-industrial expansion. Essentially every place not formally protected (and some of those ostensibly "protected areas" too) were at risk of being destroyed by economic and population growth.

In the mid-1980s, after making a pointed analysis of the clothing industry and the role our own business had in furthering fashion-related consumerism, it became apparent to me that we were simply producing stuff that no one really needed. It was an exercise both in producing things that were unnecessary but also in creating, through clever advertising, consumer desires that had not existed before. It was, in fact, nothing more than needless consumption only adding to the ever-expanding ecological crisis that we all were ensnared in. Slowly, over time, I realized that I had to change my life and work toward reversing rather than exacerbating the crisis.

Incidentally, with the Esprit company at that time we were doing some interesting things in the then budding field of "sustainability" and corporate social responsibility; those initiatives turned out to be way ahead of their time. But my interest in these kinds of "green business" measures soon faded. All profit-oriented corporations, as much their owners may try to make them responsible, are stuck in their own ditch of contradictions. Ultimately it was too paradoxical to reconcile running a successful company with my motivation to help nature stave off the very impacts of commerce. I could not see anything better to do than to direct my energy toward full-time conservation, and I sold my interests in our businesses.

Since then people have often asked me why I threw in the towel completely on the business world despite having been for years and years working with a great group of people, many of whom had grown to be close friends. At the time, perhaps, I had less perspective, but in looking back it has become clear to me that the primary motivation behind the kind of large-scale conservation work that my wife, Kristine Tompkins, and I are engaged in—creating parklands, supporting environmental activism, restoring degraded landscapes, and establishing organic farms based on agroecology principles—is simply that we *worry about the future.*

This nagging sense of insecurity can feel constant, fed by the undoing of both nature and culture that we see going on around us day by day. Anyone who opens their eyes to look at the present state of the world will see the scars of overdevelopment in a thousand forms—industrial forestry clear-cuts that seem like war zones, industrial agriculture monocultures displacing natural habitat, industrial aquaculture fouling coastlines, urban sprawl and transport networks fragmenting landscapes, toxic waste sites, expanding oil and gas fields, the devastation caused by tar sands exploitation in Alberta, and so on.

Besides worrying about the future, I cannot stand to see beauty defiled, and things done badly. Aesthetics have always figured into my thinking as a guiding principle. The imposition of human artifacts into the landscape can either appear harmonious, if done thoughtfully, or be a disjunctive to our sense of beauty if executed badly. The saying "If it looks bad, it is bad, and if it looks good, it (*most likely*) is good" has become my foundation for any quick analysis of whether a landscape is healthy or not.

After leaving the business world, I knew that I needed to do more homework—real and substantive scholarship—to better inform my activism and conservation work. I read voraciously. If there is one thing I recommend to everyone who seeks to be a more effective conservationist or environmentalist, it is to sit down and read, and I mean read books, not "tweets." This requires time and discipline and, of course, the desire to consider the deep systemic questions confronting civilization. Digging into these worldview issues, the deep epistemological roots that undergird the "Myth of Progress," to understand how industrial growth based on megatechnologies is accelerating the extinction crisis (and climate change) is the first step toward developing effective strategies to reverse what some are calling the "Mother of All Crises." After all, with the richness and diversity of life and even Earth's atmospheric chemistry now being wrecked by overdevelopment associated with the Human Project, it's clear that activists have no time to waste on ineffective tactics and half measures.

I often argue with my friends in the social justice movement that *nature has to come first* if we hope to have even *the possibility* for building a healthy and equitable society. The glories of civilization will be totally irrelevant on a dead planet. For that reason, I put achieving social justice behind that of protecting nature, although it need be only a step behind and at the shoulder of the global environmental movement. As laudable and as important as social justice is, nature's laws are immutable and human aspirations can never be realized over the long term unless we have a healthy ecosphere.

Thus, within my circle of colleagues and thinkers whom I most respect are what I call The Wild Bunch—those philosophers, thinkers, writers, and activists focused on preserving *wildness*. Unless that intrinsic quality is present and ubiquitous in our human development schemes, we are doomed to failure. Without an explicit focus on maintaining wildness (and therefore the health and integrity of ecosystems), human activity typically degrades nature and exacerbates the extinction crisis, leading to an impoverishment of the very planet on which we depend to realize all of humanity's aspirations. If our species is causing other species to go extinct, then we can say for certain our culture is not "sustainable" and our activities not ethical. Thus I personally use *biodiversity health* as the ultimate metric to measure the real "March of Progress." I know of no other measure that is as fundamental as this. If someone has a better metric, I would love to know what it is.

Integrating that consciousness of what *wildness* means and that it is essential to inform virtually every action we take—from the most mundane and routine actions of our daily lives to how we collectively regulate the behavior of civilization itself—is a crucial first step on the path toward achieving "sustainability" on Earth. The growth of the environmental movement is evidence that this kind of thinking has begun slowly sinking into the body politic of humanity in the broad sense. I maintain that the environmental movement and its twin, the conservation movement, are unstoppable in the long run. Will the environmental movement be able to resist the forces of the global economy and development in the near term? Perhaps not; there is plenty of evidence to suggest it is losing the battle quite decisively at present, but in my view the movement is unstoppable in the long run. No one who is working for the health of wild nature, and therefore the health of humanity, should question whether they are on the right path. Win or lose, what could be better than dedicating one's life to trying to stop the advance of the biodiversity crisis, and then reverse it? It is righteous work, in simple terms.

There are both practical and ethical reasons for taking up a position along the long front of environmentalism. The practical part is simply the many benefits for reversing the ecological crisis that flow to us as individuals, and to society as a whole. Natural beauty, productive and healthy agriculture, clean water and air, healthy forests, abundant fish in the oceans, and more. Without these things humanity will suffer.

From an ethical position, it is a matter of simply accepting that we are bound *to share the planet with other creatures*. This is essentially a "religious" point of view. In practice it means that through the diffuse labyrinths of human economic activity, our moral stance dictates that we must not diminish the ecosphere in richness and diversity, quality or function. Although we know we will make honest mistakes, we need to acculturate society to this fundamental principle. It is no different than the simple mandate that says "we do not kill another human being" to say that we do not "kill" biodiversity or stifle the unfolding of evolution itself.

It is a hard reality to understand that the present global extinction crisis stems directly from human overdevelopment and overshoot. Yet until we understand that, and until we "get religion," civilization is destined for the dustbin of history.

Thus my wife, Kris, and I are dedicating our time and resources toward efforts to arrest the extinction crisis, and we have chosen to work on the formation of new national parks. Along with dedicated conservation colleagues (for park making is a collaborative activity), we have helped conserve well over 2 million acres and have worked with the Argentine and Chilean national park systems to expand or create anew five national parks thus far. We hope to more than double that number of new national parks before our conservation work is done.

Land conservation is at the top of the many strategies we must employ to help put the world back in balance, and national parks are the gold standard of conservation in these days of severe ecological crisis. In almost all countries, national parks represent the best-protected landscapes under that particular society's national laws. Although the statutes vary, the regulations vary, the funding and management standards by national governments vary—overall, national parks are the strongest and most broadly supported type of conservation designation.

Now with nearly a century and a half since the first parks were created, the world has seen an impressive growth in national park systems. We see that citizens in country after country around the world value their national parks and, in many instances, are actively working to expand their park systems.

Although national parks are not a panacea to reverse the ecological crisis, they are a crucial and proven conservation strategy that needs to be continued and expanded. The benefits are many and great. In simple terms, national parks and other strictly protected natural areas can be the anchors in large-scale, interconnected systems of conservation lands, which are frequently referred to as "wildlands networks" or "wildways." Protecting such systems is the central task of conservation. Only in sufficiently large, protected landscapes may evolutionary processes continue to unfold normally, sustaining the full diversity of life and the essence of wildness discussed in both this book and its companion, *Keeping the Wild* (Island Press 2014).[1] This is the life spirit that gives birth to evolution itself. Wildness is the breath and heartbeat of Nature herself. When one understands this, it becomes a lot easier to devise strategies and adjust habits and behaviors that will lead to *biological* sustainability, which is the foundation of any true "sustainability."

Land and marine conservation, ecological restoration and rewilding, activism, and the reform of agriculture are the cornerstones of a strategy to help get the world back in balance, the climate stabilized, and a future in which we share the planet with all the other creatures, the results of four billion years of evolution. Upon reflection it seems so simple, but in practice we have a great challenge ahead of us. The question is: Are you ready to do your part? Everyone is capable of taking up their position across that long front, to use their energy, political influence, financial or other resources, and talents of all kinds to be part of a global movement for ecological and cultural health. All will be useful. There is important and meaningful work to be done. To change everything, everyone is needed.

ACKNOWLEDGMENTS

Book making, like park making, is a group activity. *Protecting the Wild* exists due to the labors of many individuals, first and foremost to the writers whose works appear herein. We are grateful for their contributions, both to conservation and to this volume, and to various reviewers of individual chapters including the ever-helpful and erudite Curt Meine.

Protecting the Wild, and its companion, *Keeping the Wild* (Island Press 2014), grew out of a meeting of conservationists sponsored by the Weeden Foundation in 2012. Organized by Michael Soulé and Don Weeden, the participants considered the way that "new environmentalists" or "eco-pragmatists" have been seeking to reframe the primary goal of conservation away from preventing human-caused extinctions and toward the support of human economic aspirations, achieved in part through corporate partnerships.

All conservationists agree that a diversity of methods and strategies is necessary to advance conservation in the 21st century. But an approach that deemphasizes protected areas as a conservation tool (especially national parks and wilderness areas) and instead stresses better management of humanized landscapes is insufficient and flawed, in our view. Thus the need for *Protecting the Wild* and *Keeping the Wild*.

Book designer Kevin Cross, proofreader/indexer Leonard Rosenbaum, and copyeditor extraordinaire Mary Elder Jacobsen were superb collaborators. We also thank David Miller, Julie Marshall, Maureen Gately, and the entire Island Press team, our publishing partners.

Finally, we acknowledge the extraordinary places around the globe whose beauty, wildness, and diversity lives on due to the work of earlier conservationists. We are grateful for those parks, wilderness areas, and wildlife refuges, and for the people who saved them as wild islands of hope for the future.

—TOM BUTLER, EILEEN CRIST, AND GEORGE WUERTHNER

CONTRIBUTORS

SUKH AMGALANBAATAR is associated with the Institute of Biology at the Mongolian Academy of Sciences in Ulaanbaatar. He serves as Executive Director of the Argali Research Center, is the Ikh Nart Nature Reserve Director, and works with the Denver Zoo Mongolia Program. He has worked for decades on many conservation initiatives in Mongolia, focusing on argali sheep and protected areas management. He holds a PhD.

VICTORIA J. BAKKER is an assistant researcher and professor in the Department of Ecology at Montana State University. She earned a PhD from University of California, Davis, with a focus on movement behavior and habitat relations of squirrel populations in response to logging in southeastern Alaska.

ROBERT BALDWIN is a conservation biologist and associate professor at Clemson University whose research focuses on design of conservation and management plans based on field-based and GIS analyses of human-environment interactions. He has traveled and taught widely in field programs throughout the eastern United States and Canada.

PAUL BEIER is Regents' Professor in the School of Forestry at Northern Arizona University. His research interests include conservation biology and wildlife ecology. He has specialized in science-based design of wildlife corridors, which he actively works to conserve. He is a founding member and current president of SC Wildlands.

MARC BEKOFF is Professor Emeritus of Ecology and Evolutionary Biology at the University of Colorado, Boulder, and cofounder with Jane Goodall of Ethologists for the Ethical Treatment of Animals. He has edited a number of encyclopedias, written more than a thousand articles, and authored many books, including *Ignoring Nature No More: The Case for Compassionate Conservation* and, most recently, *Rewilding Our Hearts: Building Pathways of Compassion and Coexistence.*

ELIZABETH L. BENNETT is the Vice President for Species Conservation at the Wildlife Conservation Society. She has researched management of hunting and wildlife trade, strategic planning for wildlife conservation, and the ecology of primates in Peninsular Malaysia. Born in the United Kingdom, she worked on a range of conservation issues for many years in Malaysia, worked to address wildlife trade in Central Africa and China, and published extensively on topics including hunting in tropical forests and illegal wildlife trade.

TOM BUTLER, a Vermont-based conservation activist and writer, is the board president of the Northeast Wilderness Trust, and he directs the Foundation for Deep Ecology's publishing program. A coeditor of, and contributor to, *Keeping the Wild: Against the Domestication of Earth,* his books include *Wildlands Philanthropy, Plundering Appalachia,* and *ENERGY: Overdevelopment and the Delusion of Endless Growth.*

TIM CARO is a professor at the University of California, Davis. He conducts basic and applied research, and development work in Tanzania, where he focuses on how anthropogenic forces affect large mammal populations in protected areas. Currently he is identifying wildlife corridors in Tanzania and examining the impacts of roads through African protected areas. He is the author of five books including *Behavioral Ecology and Conservation Biology, Antipredator Defenses in Birds and Mammals,* and *Cheetahs of the Serengeti Plains.*

EILEEN CRIST teaches in the Department of Science and Technology in Society at Virginia Tech, where she is advisor for the undergraduate program Humanities, Science, and Environment. A coeditor of, and contributor to, *Keeping the Wild: Against the Domestication of Earth*, she is author of *Images of Animals: Anthropomorphism and Animal Mind* and coeditor of *Gaia in Turmoil* and *Life on the Brink: Environmentalists Confront Overpopulation.*

CARLOS CUEVAS, a forestry engineer and ecologist, is recognized for his key role toward establishing more than 2 million acres of private and public protected areas, terrestrial and marine, in Chilean Patagonia, equivalent to 3 percent of all protected lands and waters established in Chile since 1907. Working closely with Douglas and Kristine Tompkins for twenty years, Cuevas has assisted in the creation of the Tictoc-Melimoyu Marine Protected Area, Corcovado National Park, Yendegaia National Park, Pumalín Nature Sanctuary, and the Valle Chacabuco Park—the future Patagonia National Park.

CORY R. DAVIS is a Research Associate in the University of Montana's College of Forestry and Conservation. He has studied the effects of forest fragmentation on avian demography and the effects of land-use changes on protected areas.

JOHN DAVIS cofounded *Wild Earth* journal and The Wildlands Project (now Wildlands Network) with luminary conservation friends nearly a quarter century ago. He later served as Biodiversity Program Officer at the Foundation for Deep Ecology, then as Conservation Director of the Adirondack Council, before leaving office work to trek the Atlantic/Appalachian/Adirondack and Spine of the Continent wildways outlined in Dave Foreman's book *Rewilding North America*. Now the Wildways Advocate for Wildlands Network and volunteer land steward in the Split Rock Wildway, Davis is the author of *Big, Wild, and Connected*, published in 2013 by Island Press.

DOMINICK A. DELLASALA is cofounder and President and Chief Scientist of the Geos Institute in Ashland, Oregon, and President of the Society for Conservation Biology, North America Section. He is the author of *Temperate and Boreal Rainforests of the World: Ecology and Conservation* and has also published extensively in periodicals, on topics including forest and fire ecology, landscape ecology, conservation biology, and endangered species management.

DANIEL F. DOAK is a professor in the Environmental Studies Program at University of Colorado, Boulder, and also holds the Colorado Chair in Environmental Studies. A population and community ecologist and conservation biologist, Doak conducts research on the ecology and management of rare species and habitats, biodiversity protection and management, population and community ecology, and the effects of climate change on ecological systems.

ANDREW P. DOBSON is a professor in the Department of Ecology and Evolutionary Biology at Princeton University. Dobson's current research focuses on the ecology of infectious disease and its role in conservation. He has worked with projects to conserve elephants in East Africa, carnivores in the Serengeti, parasites in food-webs, and finches in the backyards of New England. He earned a PhD from the University of Oxford, where his work involved developing mathematical models of climate change's impact on bird populations.

MARC DOUROJEANNI is a consultant and Professor Emeritus at of the National Agrarian University of La Molina, Lima, Peru. He has written extensively and has a broad background in the areas of forestry, wildlife, and parks. He served as first Chief of the Environment Division of the Inter-American Development Bank and later as Principal Environmental Advisor of the IDB, based in Brazil. Dourojeanni is the founder of Pronaturaleza, the largest Peruvian environmental NGO.

BROCK EVANS is a lawyer and an environmentalist. Current president of the Endangered Species Coalition, he has served as director (Washington, D.C., office) and Northwest representative of the Sierra Club, which awarded him the John Muir Award. He has lectured widely and written extensively, including his recently released *Fight & Win: Brock Evans's Strategies for the New Eco-Warrior*. A graduate of the University of Michigan Law School, Evans was a Fellow of the Institute of Politics at Harvard University's Kennedy School of Government.

KATHLEEN H. FITZGERALD is Vice President of Conservation Strategy for the African Wildlife Foundation in Nairobi, Kenya, where she has worked for seven years. She cofounded and was Executive Director of the Northeast Wilderness Trust in the United States. Fitzgerald has more than twenty years of experience in large landscape conservation, having developed community conservancies, secured wildlife corridors, and helped establish REDD+ projects in Africa. She holds a Master's in Botany from the Field Naturalist Program at the University of Vermont.

JOHN FRANCIS is the author of *Planetwalker: 22 Years of Walking; 17 Years of Silence*, which details his rejection of motorized-vehicle use and long-term commitments to walking and a vow of silence—all motivated by his experience as a young-adult volunteer struggling to clean up after and save wildlife harmed by a 1971 oil spill in San Francisco Bay. Francis founded Planetwalk and was named the first national Geographic Education Fellow.

CURTIS FREESE lectures, writes, and consults on conservation issues and is adjunct professor in Sustainability Studies at the University of Massachusetts-Dartmouth. He has worked on biodiversity and wildlands research and conservation in marine and terrestrial ecosystems throughout much of North America and Latin America, as well as in Africa and the Arctic. A recipient of the George B. Rabb Conservation Award, Freese holds a PhD in ecology from Johns Hopkins University.

BRUCE EVAN GOLDSTEIN is an associate professor of environmental design and environmental studies at University of Colorado Boulder. He is the editor of *Collaborative Resilience: Moving Through Crisis to Opportunity*. Goldstein has a number of projects under way, including a study of the Locally Managed Marine Areas Network in the South Pacific.

JANE GOODALL is a British primatologist, ethologist, and conservationist. Goodall is well-known for the long-term, ongoing study of wild chimpanzees in Gombe National Park, Tanzania. Founder of the Jane Goodall Institute and the Roots & Shoots program for youth, now in over 130 countries, she has worked extensively on environmental and animal welfare issues. She has written numerous books, appeared in many wildlife documentaries and been honored in many countries.

BENJAMIN HALE is an associate professor of philosophy and environmental studies at the University of Colorado, Boulder. Hale is coeditor of the journal *Ethics, Policy & Environment* and is Vice President of the International Society for Environmental Ethics.

KARSTEN HEUER is President of the Yellowstone to Yukon Conservation Initiative (Y2Y), working to connect and protect habitat over a 2,200-mile-long mountain corridor so people and nature can thrive. A wildlife biologist, explorer, writer, and filmmaker, he has produced award-winning books and films, including *Walking the Big Wild*, which chronicles his 2,200-mile Yellowstone to Yukon hike. Heuer is a Fellow of the Royal Canadian Geographical Society.

MICHAEL J. KELLETT is the cofounder and executive director of RESTORE: The North Woods. He has thirty years of experience in advocacy for national parks, public lands, and endangered wildlife. In 1994 he developed the original proposal for a 3.2-million-acre Maine Woods National Park and Preserve. He also works with the Utah-based Glen Canyon Institute, to restore Glen Canyon and a free-flowing Colorado River and to upgrade Glen Canyon National Recreation Area to an expanded National Park. He has visited more than 245 U.S. National Park System units, 80 national forests, and dozens of national wildlife refuges and wilderness areas across America.

HELEN KOPNINA is a coordinator for the Sustainable Business program at The Hague University of Applied Sciences, the Netherlands. Her research areas include environmental education, environmental social sciences, environmental anthropology, conservation, and education for sustainable societies. She has published numerous books, including *Environmental Anthropology: Future Directions*, coedited with Eleanor Shoreman-Ouimet. Kopnina holds a PhD from Cambridge University.

HARVEY LOCKE, a conservationist, writer, speaker, and photographer, is recognized as a global leader in the field of parks and wilderness and large landscape conservation. He is a founder of the Yellowstone to Yukon Conservation Initiative, with the goal of creating a continuous corridor for wildlife from Yellowstone National Park in the United States to northern Canada's Yukon Territory. In 1999 Locke was named one of Canada's leaders for the twenty-first century by *Time* magazine, Canada. In 2013 he received the J. B. Harkin Award for Conservation form the Canadian Parks and Wilderness Society and in 2014 he received the Fred M. Packard International Parks Merit Award from IUCN at the World Parks Congress.

ROEL LOPEZ is Director of the Texas A&M Institute of Renewable Natural Resources and a professor in the Department Wildlife and Fisheries Sciences at Texas A&M University. His focuses include wildlife management, military-related sustainable ranges initiatives, and natural resource management.

DOUGLAS J. MCCAULEY is an assistant professor in the Department of Ecology, Evolution and Marine Biology at the University of California, Santa Barbara, where his lab research focuses on understanding how community structure influences ecosystem dynamics, determining how ecosystems are interactively and energetically coupled to one another, and quantifying how humans perturb these dynamics and shape patterns of biodiversity.

GEORGE MONBIOT, an English writer known for his environmental and political activism, is a regular columnist for *The Guardian*. He is in the process of setting up a new organization called Rewilding Britain. With many titles to his credit, Monbiot's most recent book, *Feral: Searching for Enchantment on the Frontiers of Rewilding*, discusses the large-scale restoration of ecosystems: rewilding.

REED F. NOSS is Provost's Distinguished Research Professor at the University of Central Florida. His research examines the application of science to species-level and ecosystem-level conservation planning, restoration, and management. Current focuses include southern grasslands and the effects of development on bird communities. Noss has served as editor-in-chief of *Conservation Biology* and president of the Society for Conservation Biology. He holds a Master's in ecology and a PhD in wildlife ecology.

KATARZYNA NOWAK is a Junior Research Fellow at Durham University, England, and a Research Associate at the University of the Free State, Qwaqwa, South Africa. Her interests include threatened species and the influence of human-dominated landscapes, as well as species diet, conservation status, and distribution. Nowak holds a PhD in Biological Anthropology from the University of Cambridge.

MIKHAIL PALTSYN graduated from Moscow State University, has lived in the Russian Altai Mountains, and has worked for conservation of endangered species of Altai-Sayan Ecoregion, primarily the snow leopard and Altai argali, assessing their population status in Russia and adjacent Mongolia, and coordinating extensive conservation projects on their behalf. He is working toward a PhD in conservation biology, and one of his ongoing projects, with WWF, considers the conservation of big cats in Russia.

SPENCER R. PHILLIPS is a natural resource economist and founder of Key-Log Economics, LLC, which brings economic information to land use, ecosystem management, and community development decisions and crafts policy and market solutions to foster sustainable connections between community, economic, and ecosystem health. He is also adjunct faculty at the University of Virginia and Goucher College, lecturing in ecological economics, natural resource policy, and spatial analysis for public policy. He holds an M.S. and Ph.D. in agricultural and applied economics.

BARBARA AND CHRISTOPH PROMBERGER have spent most of their professional lives in the Romanian Carpathians. They are currently developing a wilderness reserve with full protection for all its components, with the aim of not just protecting the last remnants of pristine nature but of also restoring degraded areas and managed forests back to their original state. The Prombergers have helped develop a wolf management plan in Germany; a large carnivore research project on wolves, bears, and lynx in Romania; and conservation proposals for several areas in Turkey, among numerous conservation efforts.

RICHARD P. READING is the Vice President for Conservation and founder of the Department of Conservation Biology at the Denver Zoological Foundation. An adjunct professor at the University of Denver and Senior Research Professor at the University of Colorado, Denver, Reading holds a PhD in wildlife ecology and is a prolific author of scholarly and popular articles. He has worked on conservation projects across the globe, with a major research focus on developing interdisciplinary approaches to conservation.

CONRAD REINING is the Associate Director of the Arts and Sciences Development Office at Dartmouth College. As Eastern Program Director for the Wildlands Network, he coordinated conservation efforts toward developing a transborder network of linked conservation areas in the Northern Appalachians of the northeastern United States and southeastern Canada.

CHRISTOF SCHENCK holds a PhD in Biology/Zoology from the Ludwig-Maximilian-University, Munich, Germany. He is the president of Help for Threatened Wildlife and Executive Director of the Frankfurt Zoological Society in Germany, where he oversees conservation projects worldwide. Schenck previously led FZS's Giant Otter Project in Peru, which he launched with his wife, biologist Elke Staib. He is a member of the IUCN's Otter Specialist Group.

TUVDENDORJ SELENGE is the Executive Director of the Mongolian Conservation Coalition. Selenge has worked with a number of different conservation and international aid organizations to conserve Mongolia's wildlife and natural areas for over twenty years. Much of her work has focused on improving management of protected areas.

ANTHONY R. E. SINCLAIR, a Professor Emeritus at the University of British Columbia and former Director of the Beaty Biodiversity Research Centre at UBC, Sinclair has conducted research on the Serengeti of Tanzania for more than forty years. His ecological research investigating the role of biodiversity in ecosystem functions extends around the world to Africa, Australia, New Zealand, and Canada. In 2013 The Wildlife Society awarded Sinclair the Aldo Leopold medal.

GARY TABOR is founder and Executive Director of the Center for Large Landscape Conservation. In 2013 he won an Australian–American Fulbright Professional Scholarship in Climate Change and Clean Energy. A conservation scientist and wildlife veterinarian, Tabor is a cofounder of the Yellowstone to Yukon Conservation Initiative.

MARTIN TAYLOR is a conservation scientist with WWF-Australia and a member of the IUCN World Commission on Protected Areas. Taylor's published work provides important analyses of the effectiveness of the Endangered Species Act in the United States and of the effectiveness of protected areas and other conservation actions for threatened species in Australia. He has served as the conservation scientist with the Center for Biological Diversity in Arizona, as an invited delegate to the Scientific Committee of the International Whaling Commission and as an NGO observer at CITES.

JOHN TERBORGH is a James B. Duke Professor of Environmental Science at Duke University, where he is also Codirector of the Center for Tropical Conservation. He has operated the Cocha Cashu Biological Station in Manu National Park in Peru since 1973. A 1992 MacArthur Fellow, Terborgh holds a PhD in plant physiology from Harvard University and has written extensively, including the books *Diversity and the Tropical Rain Forest, Requiem for Nature,* and *Making Parks Work: Strategies for Preserving Tropical Nature.*

DOUGLAS R. TOMPKINS is a wilderness advocate, mountaineer, organic farmer, and conservationist. For more than two decades, he has worked alongside his wife, Kristine Tompkins, to restore degraded farms and to establish large-scale protected areas, including new national parks in Argentina and Chile. Through a family foundation, Tompkins supports environmental activism in North and South America and has published numerous conservation activism-related books and a series of photo-format books focused on parklands, the most recent of which is *Iberá: The Great Wetlands of Argentina.*

STEPHEN C. TROMBULAK, a conservation biologist and landscape ecologist, is a professor of Environmental and Biosphere Studies and also Director of Sciences at Middlebury College, Vermont. He currently directs two primary research programs—one examining forest-dwelling beetles and one looking at landscape-level wildlife connectivity in the Northern Appalachians.

EMILY WAKILD teaches Latin American and environmental history at Boise State University, Idaho, where she is an associate professor. She holds a PhD in History. Her book *Revolutionary Parks: Conservation, Social Justice, and Mexico's National Parks, 1910–1940,* received numerous awards. With a grant from the National Science Foundation, Wakild is writing a comparative history of transnational conservation and scientific research in Amazonian and Patagonian South America.

GANCHIMEG WINGARD is the Mongolia Program Director for the Denver Zoological Foundation. She holds a Master's in environmental science from Charles University in Prague, Czech Republic, and a Master's in wildlife ecology from the University of Montana. She has worked for the Mongolian Ministry for Nature and Environment and on conservation in Mongolia for more than twenty years.

GEORGE WUERTHNER is the ecological projects director for the Foundation for Deep Ecology. He has visited and photographed hundreds of national park units in the United States, including all Alaskan park units, and even more wilderness areas, to gain first-hand knowledge of their ecology, and to see natural landscapes that operate with a minimum of human influence. A coeditor of, and contributor to, *Keeping the Wild: Against the Domestication of Earth*, he has published 36 books on a wide variety of topics including national parks, natural history, wilderness areas, and environmental issues.

NOTES

INTRODUCTION

1. Frank Graham Jr. describes the park's birth, the passage of the "forever wild" clause at the 1894 New York state constitutional convention, and the subsequent defense of the Adirondack Forest Preserve's constitutional protections in his classic book, *The Adirondack Park: A Political History* (New York: Alfred A. Knopf, 1978).

2. The land use changes, geology, wildlife status, and many other facets of Adirondack Park ecology and history are wonderfully illuminated in J. Jenkins, *The Adirondack Atlas: A Geographic Portrait of the Adirondack Park* (New York: Wildlife Conservation Society, 2004). The recovery of otter, black bear, beaver, white-tailed deer, and other native species from their greatly reduced nineteenth-century populations is another example that habitat conservation and wildlife protection laws can be extremely effective.

3. See D. Duncan, *Seed of the Future: Yosemite and the Evolution of the National Park Idea* (San Francisco: Yosemite Conservancy, 2013).

4. See passengerpigeon.org for information about events marking the 100th anniversary of passenger pigeon's extinction.

5. James Morton Turner describes the development of that wilderness bill campaign, its eventual success, and the way it influenced subsequent history in his brilliant book *The Promise of Wilderness: American Environmental Politics Since 1964* (Seattle: University of Washington Press, 2012).

6. See E. Zahniser, *Where Wilderness Preservation Began: Adirondack Writings of Howard Zahniser* (Utica, NY: North Country Books, 1992).

7. D. Gibson, pers. comm., 2014. Conservation activist and historian David Gibson, a long-time friend of the Schaefer and Zahniser families, cofounded Adirondack Wild: Friends of the Forest Preserve (adirondackwild.org).

8. D. Foreman, "Wilderness: From Scenery to Nature" in *Wild Earth: Wild Ideas for a World Out of Balance,* ed. T. Butler (Minneapolis: Milkweed Editions, 2002).

9. L. Savoy, "Wilderness and Civil Rights 50 Years Later: Recognizing the Ties of Race and Place," *Huffington Post* (9-3-14), http://www.huffingtonpost.com/lauret-savoy/wilderness-and-civil-righ_b_5760902.html.

10. B. Coetzee, K. Gaston, and S. Chown, "Local Scale Comparisons of Biodiversity as a Test for Global Protected Area Ecological Performance: A Meta-Analysis," *PLoS ONE* 9, no. 8 (2014): e105824, doi:10.1371/journal.pone.0105824.

11. G. Wuerthner, E. Crist, and T. Butler, eds. (Washington, D.C.: Island Press, 2014).

12. Birthing new national parks is a collaborative activity, but Argentine biologist and conservationist Sofia Heinonen deserves especial commendation for the successful creation of Impenetrable National Park. She worked tirelessly to align the politics and private funding needed, the majority of which came in the form of a major grant from Conservation Land Trust–Argentina, a foundation established by Douglas and Kristine Tompkins.

13. *Protecting the Wild* focuses on terrestrial protected areas due to space and thematic constraints. The editors fully recognize, however, that Earth is mostly a blue planet, and no conservation agenda that seeks to fully protect the wild can ignore the pressing need for a global system of marine protected areas, anchored by strictly protected marine wilderness areas.

HARVEY LOCKE

1. M. L. Parry, O. F. Canziani, J. P. Palutikof, P. J. van der Linden, and C. E. Hanson, eds., *Climate Change 2007: Impacts, Adaptation and Vulnerability* (Cambridge, UK: Cambridge University Press, 2007).

2. J. Zalasiewicz, M. Williams, A. Haywood, and M. Ellis, "The Anthropocene: A New Epoch of Geological Time?" *Philosophical Transactions of Royal Society* 369, no. 1938 (2011): 835–41.

3. World Commission on Environment and Development, *Our Common Future* (Oxford: Oxford University Press, 1987), pp. 22, 147, 166.

4. Union of Concerned Scientists. "World Scientists' Warning to Humanity" (Cambridge, MA: Union of Concerned Scientists, 1992). www.ucsusa.org/about/1992-world-scientists.html.

5. Union of Concerned Scientists. "World Scientists' Warning to Humanity."

6. World Commission on Environment and Development, *Our Common Future* (Oxford: Oxford University Press, 1987), pp. 22, 147, 166.

7. United Nations Conference on Environment and Development (UNCED), Rio de Janeiro, June 3–14, 1992. http://www.un.org/geninfo/bp/enviro.html.

8. See the Convention on Biological Diversity, Article 1 and Article 2, link to full text at http://www.cbd.int/doc/legal/cbd-en.pdf.

9. See Article 8 of the Convention on Biological Diversity, link to full text at http://www.cbd.int/doc/legal/cbd-en.pdf.

10. SCBD. *Decisions Adopted by the Conference of the Parties to the Convention on Biological Diversity at Its Sixth Meeting*, UNEP/CBD/COP/6/20 (Montreal, CN: Secretariat to the Convention on Biological Diversity 2002), p. 319.

11. SCBD. *Global Biodiversity Outlook 3* (Montreal, CN: Secretariat to the Convention on Biological Diversity, 2010a).

12. SCBD. *Decisions Adopted by the Conference of the Parties to the Convention on Biological Diversity at Its Tenth Meeting*, UNEP/CBD/COP/10/27, (Montreal, CN: Secretariat to the Convention on Biological Diversity, 2010b), p. 119.

13. M. Soulé and M. A. Sanjayan, "Conservation Targets: Do They Help?" *Science* 279, no. 5359 (1998): 2060–61.

14. R. F. Noss and A. Y. Cooperrider, *Saving Nature's Legacy: Protecting and Restoring Biodiversity* (Washington, D.C.: Island Press, 1994).

15. E. O. Wilson, *The Future of Life* (New York: Random House, 2003). See also http://www.smithsonianmag.com/science-nature/can-world-really-set-aside-half-planet-wildlife-180952379/?no-ist (2014).

16. J. W. Terborgh, "Reserves: How Much Is Enough and How Do We Get There from Here?" in *Companion to Principles of Conservation Biology*, 3rd ed., ed. M. J. Groom, G. K. Meffe, and C. R. Carroll (Sunderland, MA: Sinauer Press, 2006).

17. R. L. Pressey, R. M. Cowling, and M. Rouget, "Formulating Conservation Targets for Biodiversity Pattern and Process in the Cape Floristic Region, South Africa," *Biological Conservation* 112 (2003): 99–127.

18. L. K. Svancara et al., "Policy-driven versus Evidence-based Conservation: A Review of Political Targets and Biological Needs," *BioScience* 55, no. 11 (2005): 989–95.

19. Boreal Scientists' Letter, May 14, 2007. See the Ottawa, ON, Boreal Songbird Initiative website at www.borealbirds.org for a link to the letter dated May 14, 2007; for a direct link see http://www.borealbirds.org/sites/default/files/pubs/ScienceLetter-English.pdf.

20. A. S. L. Rodrigues and K. J. Gaston, "How Large Do Reserve Networks Need to Be?" *Ecology Letters* 4 (2001): 602–9.

21. The Nature Conservancy of Canada. *Canadian Rockies Ecoregional Assessment, Version 2.0* (Ontario, CAN: Nature Conservancy of Canada, 2004), science. natureconservancy.ca/initiatives/blueprints/canrockies_w.php.

22. H. Norwegian, "Dehcho First Nations, Canada," in *Protecting Wild Nature on Native Lands*, ed. J. Cajeune, V. Martin, and T. Tanner (Boulder, CO: WILD Foundation, 2005).

23. R. F. Noss et al., "Bolder Thinking for Conservation," *Conservation Biology* 26, no. 1 (2012): 1–4.

24. See Article 2 of the Convention on Biological Diversity, link to the full text at http://www.cbd.int/doc/legal/cbd-en.pdf.

25. N. Dudley and S. Stolton, eds., *Defining Protected Areas: An International Conference in Almeria, Spain* (Gland, CH: IUCN, 2008).

26. N. Dudley, ed., *IUCN Guidelines for Applying Protected Area Management Categories* (Gland, CH: IUCN, 2008). https://www.iucn.org/about/work/programmes/gpap_home/gpap_capacity2/gpap_pub/gpap_catpub/.

27. For the list of "IUCN Protected Areas Categories System" and detailed summaries of categories, see the IUCN Web site, http://www.iucn.org/about/work/programmes/gpap_home/gpap_quality/gpap_pacategories/.

28. N. Dudley, ed., *IUCN Guidelines for Applying Protected Area Management Categories*; H. Locke and B. Mackey, "The Nature of the Climate," *International Journal of Wilderness* 15, no. 2 (2009): 7–13; N. E. Heller and E. Zavaleta, "Biodiversity Management in the Face of Climate Change: A Review of 22 Years of Recommendations," *Biological Conservation* 142 (2009): 14–32; G. Worboys, W. Francis, and M. Lockwood, eds., *Connectivity Conservation Management: A*

Global Guide (London: Earthscan, 2010); *Nature* editorial, "Think Big," *Nature* 469 (2011): 131, doi:10.1038/469131a; R. F. Noss et al., "Bolder Thinking for Conservation," *Conservation Biology* 26, no. 1 (2012): 1–4.

29. J. A. Hodgson, C. D. Thomas, B. A. Wintle, and A. Moilanen, "Climate Change, Connectivity and Conservation Decision Making: Back to Basics," *Journal of Applied Ecology* 46, no. 5 (2009): 964–69.

30. Royal Government of Bhutan, Ministry of Agriculture, Department of Forest, Nature Conservation Division NCD/Admin (02)/2009/595, November 30, 2009.

31. For example, see G. Harman, "El Mensage de Mérida: Climate Change Isn't All about Stuffing Our Collective Tailpipe; Restoring Oceans of Wilderness Is Just as Vital to Saving the Planet," *San Antonio Current* (9 Dec. 2009), http://www2.sacurrent.com/news/story.asp?id=70751.

32. See http://natureneedshalf.org/boulder-colorado/.

33. Capital Regional District. *Regional Parks Strategic Plan 2012–21,* https://www.crd.bc.ca/docs/default-source/parks-pdf/regional-parks-strategic-plan-2012-21.pdf?sfvrsn=0.

34. Royal Government of Bhutan, Ministry of Agriculture, Department of Forest, Nature Conservation Division NCD/ Admin (02)/ 2009/595, November 30, 2009 and http://natureneedshalf.org/bhutan/.

35. IUCN. *Half of Seychelles Has Become Protected* (Gland, CH: IUCN, 2013), http://www.iucn.org/about/union/secretariat/offices/esaro/_news/?7922/Half-of-Seychelles-islands-become-protected.

36. For more information on Natura 2000, see the website at http://www.natura.org.

37. IUCN Red List. *The IUCN Red List of Threatened Species,* 2013, http://www.iucnredlist.org.

38. V. G. Martin, "Nature Needs Half," *Sanctuary Asia*, December 2010, pp. 80–81.

39. J. Lear, *Radical Hope: Ethics in the Face of Cultural Devastation* (Cambridge, MA: Harvard University Press, 2006).

40. P. Kareiva, R. Lalasz, and M. Marvier, "Conservation in the Anthropocene: Beyond Solitude and Fragility," *Breakthrough Journal*, Fall 2011, pp. 29–37.

41. H. Locke, "Postmodernism and the Attempted Hijacking of Conservation" in *Keeping the Wild,* ed. George Wuerthner, Eileen Crist, and Tom Butler (Washington, D.C.: Island Press, 2014), pp. 146–61.

42. H. Locke, "Nature Answers Man," *Policy Options* (Montreal, QC: Institute for Research on Public Policy, September–October 2013), pp. 1–6.

REED NOSS ET AL.

1. M. R. W. Rands et al., "Biodiversity Conservation: Challenges Beyond 2010," *Science* 329 (2010): 1298–1303.

2. C. Perrings et al., "Ecosystem Services for 2020," *Science* 330 (2010): 323–24.

3. Convention on Biological Diversity, *Strategic Plan for Biodiversity 2011–2020 and the Aichi Targets* (Montreal, Canada: Secretariat of the Convention on Biological Diversity, 2010), http://www. cbd.int/doc/strategic-plan/2011–2020/Aichi-Targets-EN.pdf (accessed April 2011).

4. R. F. Noss and A. Y. Cooperrider, *Saving Nature's Legacy: Protecting and Restoring Biodiversity* (Washington, D.C.: Island Press, 1994).

5. R. A. Croker, *Pioneer Ecologist: The Life and Work of Victor Ernest Shelford 1877–1968* (Washington, D.C.: Smithsonian Institution Press, 1991).

6. Brundtland Commission, *Our Common Future: Report of the World Commission on Environment and Development* (Oxford, U.K.: Oxford University Press, 1987).

7. Millennium Ecosystem Assessment, *Current State and Trends Assessment,* Millennium Assessment Report, 2005. Available from http://www.maweb.org/en/ (accessed April 2011).

8. M. Parry, O. Canziani, J. Palutikof, P. van der Linden, and C. Hanson, eds., *Climate Change 2007: Impacts, Adaptation and Vulnerability* (Cambridge, UK: Cambridge University Press, Intergovernmental Panel on Climate Change, Working Group 2, 2007).

9. International Union for Conservation of Nature (IUCN). *IUCN Red List of Threatened Species, Version 2010.1* (Gland, Switzerland: IUCN, 2010). Available from http://www.iucnredlist.org/ (accessed April 2011).

10. R. F. Noss, "Protected Areas: How Much Is Enough?" in *National Parks and Protected Areas: Their Role in Environmental Protection,* ed. R. G. Wright (Cambridge, MA: Blackwell, 1996), pp. 91–120.

11. L. K. Svancara, R. Brannon, J. M. Scott, C. R. Groves, R. F. Noss, and R. L. Pressey, "Policy-Driven vs. Evidence-Based Conservation: A Review of Political Targets and Biological Needs," *Biological Sciences* 55 (2005): 989–95.

12. H. Andrén, "Effects of Habitat Fragmentation on Birds and Mammals in Landscapes with Different Proportions of Suitable Habitat: A Review," *Oikos* 71 (1994): 355–66.

13. J. Berger, "The Longest Mile: How to Sustain Long Distance Migration in Mammals," *Conservation Biology* 18 (2004): 320–32.

14. J. F. Franklin and D. B. Lindenmayer, "Importance of Matrix Habitats in Maintaining Biological Diversity," *Proceedings of the National Academy of Sciences* 106 (2009): 349–50.

15. New South Wales Government, *Great Eastern Ranges Initiative* (Sydney: New South Wales Government, 2010). Available from http://www. environment.nsw. gov.au/ger/index.htm (accessed April 2011).

16. Yellowstone to Yukon Conservation Initiative, *Yellowstone to Yukon: A Blueprint for Wildlife Conservation* (Canmore, Alberta: Yellowstone to Yukon Conservation Initiative, 2010). Available from http://www.y2y.net/data/1/rec_docs/675_A_Blueprint_for_ Wildlife_Conservation_reduced.pdf (accessed April 2011).

17. W. Jetz, D. S. Wilcove, and A. P. Dobson, "Projected Impacts of Climate and Land-Use Change on the Global Diversity of Birds," *PLoS Biology* (2007). doi:10.1371/journal.pbio0050157.

18. D. E. Bunker, F. DeClerck, J. C. Bradford, R. K. Colwell, I. Perfecto, O. L. Phillips, M. Sankaran, and S. Naeem, "Species Loss and Above-ground Carbon Storage in a Tropical Forest," *Science* 310 (2005): 1029–31.

19. Rands et al., "Biodiversity Conservation: Challenges Beyond 2010," 1298–1303.

20. Happy Planet Index, *The Happy Planet Index: Version 2.0* (London: Happy Planet Index, 2010). Available from http://www.happyplanetindex.org/ (accessed April 2011).

21. M. E. Soulé and J. Terborgh, eds., *Continental Conservation: Scientific Foundations of Regional Reserve Networks* (Washington, D.C.: Island Press, 1999).

22. R. A. Croker, *Pioneer Ecologist: The Life and Work of Victor Ernest Shelford 1877–1968.*

DANIEL F. DOAK ET AL.

1. P. Kareiva, M. Marvier, and R. Lalasz, "Conservation in the Anthropocene: Beyond Solitude and Fragility," *Breakthrough Journal* (Winter 2011), http://thebreakthrough.org/index.php/journal/past-issues/issue-2/conservation-in-the-anthropocene/; P. Kareiva and M. Marvier, "What Is Conservation Science?" *Bioscience* 62 (2012): 962–69; M. Marvier, "The Value of Nature Revisited," *Front Ecol Environ* 10 (2012): 227.

2. P. Kareiva, M. Marvier, and R. Lalasz, "Conservation in the Anthropocene: Beyond Solitude and Fragility," *Breakthrough Journal* (Winter 2011), http://thebreakthrough.org/index.php/journal/past-issues/issue-2/conservation-in-the-anthropocene/; P. Kareiva and M. Marvier, "What Is Conservation Science?" *Bioscience* 62 (2012): 962–69; P. Kareiva et al., "Domesticated Nature: Shaping Landscapes and Ecosystems for Human Welfare," *Science* 316 (2007): 1866–69; P. Kareiva and M. Marvier, "Conservation for the People," *Sci Am* 297 (2007): 50–57.

3. See Supplemental Table 1 in D. F. Doak, V. J. Bakker, B. E. Goldstein, and B. Hale, "What Is the Future of Conservation?," *Trends in Ecology and Evolution* 29 (2013): 77–81; see also L. Naughton-Treves et al., "The Role of Protected Areas in Conserving Biodiversity and Sustaining Local Livelihoods," *Annual Review of Environment & Resources* 30 (2005): 219-C-211, and see C. Campagna and T. Fernandez, "A Comparative Analysis of the Vision and Mission Statements of International Environmental Organisations," *Environmental Values* 16 (2007): 369–98.

4. P. Kareiva, M. Marvier, and R. Lalasz, "Conservation in the Anthropocene: Beyond Solitude and Fragility," *Breakthrough Journal* (Winter 2011), http://thebreakthrough.org/index.php/journal/past-issues/issue-2/conservation-in-the-anthropocene/.

5. P. Kareiva and M. Marvier, "What Is Conservation Science?" *Bioscience* 62 (2012): 962–69.

6. P. Kareiva, M. Marvier, and R. Lalasz, "Conservation in the Anthropocene: Beyond Solitude and Fragility," *Breakthrough Journal* (Winter 2011), http://thebreakthrough.org/index.php/journal/past-issues/issue-2/conservation-in-the-anthropocene/; P. Kareiva and M. Marvier, "What Is Conservation Science?" *Bioscience* 62 (2012): 962–69.

7. P. Kareiva, M. Marvier, and R. Lalasz, "Conservation in the Anthropocene: Beyond Solitude and Fragility," *Breakthrough Journal* (Winter 2011), http://thebreakthrough.org/index.php/journal/past-issues/issue-2/conservation-in-the-anthropocene/.

8. Ibid.

9. Ibid.

10. M. Marvier and H. Wong, "Resurrecting the Conservation Movement," *Journal of Environmental Studies and Sciences* 2 (2012): 291–95.

11. P. Kareiva, quoted in T. Dunkel, "Can We Move beyond Man vs. Nature?" *Nature Conservancy Magazine* (2011), 32–45.

12. Ibid.

13. P. Kareiva, M. Marvier, and R. Lalasz, "Conservation in the Anthropocene: Beyond Solitude and Fragility," *Breakthrough Journal* (Winter 2011), http://thebreakthrough.org/index.php/journal/past-issues/issue-2/conservation-in-the-anthropocene/.

14. See M. Soulé, "The 'New Conservation,'" *Conserv. Biol.* 27 (2013), 895–97; K. Suckling, "Conservation for the Real World," *Breakthrough Journal* (2012), http://thebreakthrough.org/journal/debates/conservation-in-the-anthropocene-a-breakthrough-debate/conservation-for-the-real-world; R. Hilborn, "Marine Parks Are Fishy," *Breakthrough Journal* (2012), http://thebreakthrough.org/journal/debates/conservation-in-the-anthropocene-a-breakthrough-debate/marine-parks-are-fishy; P. Robbins, "Corporate Partners Can Be Bad News," *Breakthrough Journal* (2012), http://thebreakthrough.org/journal/debates/conservation-in-the-anthropocene-a-breakthrough-debate/corporate-partners-can-be-bad-news; B. Martinez and L. Hayward, "The Wrong Conservation Message," *Breakthrough Journal* (2012), http://thebreakthrough.org/journal/debates/conservation-in-the-anthropocene-a-breakthrough-debate/the-wrong-conservation-message; and T. Caro et al., "Conservation in the Anthropocene," *Conserv. Biol.* 26 (2012): 185–88. See also Supplemental Tables 2–3 in D. F. Doak, V. J. Bakker, B. E. Goldstein, and B. Hale, "What Is the Future of Conservation?," *Trends in Ecology and Evolution* 29 (2013): 77–81.

15. C. Campagna and T. Fernandez, "A Comparative Analysis of the Vision and Mission Statements of International Environmental Organisations," *Environmental Values* 16 (2007): 369–98; G. Pinchot, *The Fight for Conservation* (New York: Doubleday, Page & Company, 1910); F. D. Krupp, "New Environmentalism Factors in Economic Needs," *The Wall Street Journal* 20 November 1986; G. A. Barton, *Empire Forestry and the Origins of Environmentalism: Cambridge Studies in Historical Geography* (Cambridge, MA: Cambridge University Press, 2002).

16. G. Pinchot, *The Fight for Conservation* (New York: Doubleday, Page & Company, 1910).

17. FOREST EUROPE UNECE and FAO. *State of Europe's Forests 2011; Status and Trends in Sustainable Forest Management in Europe.* Ministerial Conference on the Protection of Forests in Europe (2011).

18. But see P. M. Kareiva, "QnAs with Peter M. Kareiva," *Proc Natl Acad Sci USA* 109 (2012): 10127.

19. T. Caro et al., "Conservation in the Anthropocene," *Conserv. Biol.* 26 (2012): 185–88.

20. W. Cronon, "The Trouble with Wilderness or, Getting Back to the Wrong Nature," *Environmental History* 1 (1996): 7–28.

21. P. Kareiva and M. Marvier, "What Is Conservation Science?" *Bioscience* 62 (2012): 962–69.

22. See Supplemental Table 2 in D. F. Doak, V. J. Bakker, B. E. Goldstein, and B. Hale, "What Is the Future of Conservation?," *Trends in Ecology and Evolution* 29 (2013): 77–81.

23. A. S. L. Rodrigues, "Are Global Conservation Efforts Successful? *Science* 313 (2006): 1051–52; M. Hoffmann et al., "The Changing Fates of the World's Mammals," *Philosophical Transactions of the Royal Society B-Biological Sciences* 366 (2011): 2598–610; M. Hoffmann et al., "The Impact of Conservation on the Status of the World's Vertebrates," *Science* 330 (2010): 1503–09; S. Chape et al., "Measuring the Extent and Effectiveness of Protected Areas as an Indicator for Meeting Global Biodiversity Targets," *Philosophical Transactions: Biological Sciences* 360(2005): 443–55.

24. S. P. Hays, *Conservation and the Gospel of Efficiency: The Progressive Conservation Movement, 1890–1920* (Cambridge, MA: Harvard University Press, 1959); S. P. Hays and B. D. Hays, *Beauty, Health, and Permanence: Environmental Politics in the United States, 1955–1985* (Cambridge, MA: Cambridge University Press, 1987).

25. B. Worm et al., "Rebuilding Global Fisheries," *Science* 325 (2009): 578–85; D. Pauly et al., "Fishing Down Marine Food Webs," *Science* 279 (1998): 860–63.

26. P. Kareiva and M. Marvier, "Conservation for the People," *Sci Am* 297 (2007): 50–57.

27. B. J. Cardinale et al., "Biodiversity Loss and Its Impact on Humanity," *Nature* 486 (2012): 59–67; F. Ang and S. Van Passel, "Beyond the Environmentalist's Paradox and the Debate on Weak versus Strong Sustainability," *Bioscience* 62 (2012): 251–59.

28. P. Kareiva and M. Marvier, "Conservation for the People," *Sci Am* 297 (2007): 50–57.

29. See Supplemental Table 3 in D. F. Doak, V. J. Bakker, B. E. Goldstein, and B. Hale, "What Is the Future of Conservation?," *Trends in Ecology and Evolution* 29 (2013): 77–81.

30. T. Dunkel, "Can We Move beyond Man vs. Nature?" *Nature Conservancy Magazine* (2011), 32–45.

31. M. Chapin, *Conservation Refugees: The Hundred-Year Conflict between Global Conservation and Native Peoples* (Cambridge, MA: MIT Press, 2009).

32. L. Naughton-Treves et al., "The Role of Protected Areas in Conserving Biodiversity and Sustaining Local Livelihoods," *Annual Review of Environment & Resources* 30 (2005): 219-C-211; W. M. Adams et al., "Biodiversity Conservation and the Eradication of Poverty," *Science* 306 (2004): 1146–49.

33. L. Naughton-Treves et al., "The Role of Protected Areas in Conserving Biodiversity and Sustaining Local Livelihoods," *Annual Review of Environment & Resources* 30 (2005): 219-C-211.

34. See, for example, K. S. Andam et al., "Protected Areas Reduced Poverty in Costa Rica and Thailand," *Proceedings of the National Academy of Sciences* 107 (2010): 9996–10001.

35. D. Roe et al., "Linking Biodiversity Conservation and Poverty Reduction: De-polarizing the Conservation–Poverty Debate," *Conservation Letters* 6 (2013): 162–71.

36. W. M. Adams et al., "Biodiversity Conservation and the Eradication of Poverty," *Science* 306 (2004): 1146–49.

37. S. Sawyer and E. T. Gomez, *The Politics of Resource Extraction: Indigenous Peoples, Multinational Corporations and the State* (New York: Palgrave Macmillan, 2012).

38. J. G. Robinson, "Common and Conflicting Interests in the Engagements between Conservation Organizations and Corporations," *Conserv. Biol.* 26 (2012): 967–77; J. G. Frynas, "Corporate Social Responsibility or Government Regulation? Evidence on Oil Spill Prevention," *Ecology and Society* 17, no. 4 (2012): 4, http://dx.doi.org/10.5751/ES-05073-170404; http://www.ecologyandsociety.org/vol17/iss4/art4/.

39. Statement of 500 indigenous groups at Rio+20 UN Conference on Sustainable Development. KARI-OCA. KARI-OCA 2 declaration. http://indigenous4motherearthrioplus20.org/kari-oca-2-declaration/. "The 'Green Economy' promises to eradicate poverty but in fact will only favor and respond to multinational enterprises and capitalism. It is a continuation of a global economy based upon fossil fuels, the destruction of the environment by exploiting nature through extractive industries such as mining, oil exploration and production, intensive mono-culture agriculture, and other capitalist investments. All of these efforts are directed toward profit and the accumulation of capital by the few. The Green Economy is nothing more than capitalism of nature; a perverse attempt by corporations, extractive industries and governments to cash in on Creation by privatizing, commodifying, and selling off the Sacred and all forms of life and the sky, including the air we breathe, the water we drink and all the genes, plants, traditional seeds, trees, animals, fish, biological and cultural diversity, ecosystems and traditional knowledge that make life on Earth possible and enjoyable."

40. For example, see J. W. Bolderdijk et al., "Comparing the Effectiveness of Monetary versus Moral Motives in Environmental Campaigning," *Nature Clim. Change* (2012); and see D. McKenzie-Mohr, *Fostering Sustainable Behavior: An Introduction to Community-Based Social Marketing*, 3rd ed. (British Columbia: New Society Publishers, 2011).

41. M. Chapin, *Conservation Refugees: The Hundred-Year Conflict between Global Conservation and Native Peoples* (Cambridge, MA: MIT Press, 2009).

42. S. R. Kellert, *Birthright: People and Nature in the Modern World* (New Haven, CT: Yale University Press, 2012); T. Doyle and S. MacGregor, eds., *Environmental Movements around the World: Shades of Green in Politics and Culture* (Westport, CT: Praeger, 2013); F. Berkes, *Sacred Ecology: Traditional Ecological Knowledge and Resource Management* (London: Taylor & Francis, 1999).

43. M. Marvier and H. Wong, "Resurrecting the Conservation Movement," *Journal of Environmental Studies and Sciences* 2 (2012): 291–95; J. R. Farmer et al., "Motivations Influencing the Adoption of Conservation Easements," *Conserv. Biol.* 25 (2011): 827–34.

44. M. Bonta and C. Jordan, "Diversifying the Conservation Movement" in *Diversity and the Future of the U.S. Environmental Movement*, ed. E. Enderle (New Haven: Yale School of Forestry & Environmental Studies Publication Series, 2007), pp. 13–34; http://www.uvm.edu/sustain/webfm_send/351; M. Perez, "Poll: Latino Voters Support Conservation," *Associated Press California Health Report*, 30 October 2012; J. Zogby, "After Sandy, Poll Shows GOP Faces Growing Environmental Divide with Voters," *Forbes* (2012), http://www.forbes.com/sites/johnzogby/2012/11/14/after-sandy-poll-shows-gop-faces-growing-environmental-divide-with-voters/.

45. J. M. McPherson, *For Cause and Comrades: Why Men Fought in the Civil War* (Oxford: Oxford University Press, 1997).

46. P. Hawken, *Blessed Unrest: How the Largest Social Movement in History Is Restoring Grace, Justice, and Beauty to the World* (New York: Viking Press, 2007).

47. P. Kareiva, M. Marvier, and R. Lalasz, "Conservation in the Anthropocene: Beyond Solitude and Fragility," *Breakthrough Journal* (Winter 2011), http://thebreakthrough.org/index.php/journal/past-issues/issue-2/conservation-in-the-anthropocene/; P. Kareiva and M. Marvier, "What Is Conservation Science?" *Bioscience* 62 (2012): 962–69.

48. See Appendix 3 in D. F. Doak, V. J. Bakker, B. E. Goldstein, and B. Hale, "What Is the Future of Conservation?," *Trends in Ecology and Evolution* 29 (2013): 77–81, available online at http://dx.doi.org/10.1016/j.tree.2013.10.013. (See http://www.cell.com/trends/ecology-evolution/abstract/S0169-5347(13)00262-0?_returnUR L=http%3A%2F%2Flinkinghub.elsevier.com%2Fretrieve%2Fpii%2FS016953471 3002620%3Fshowall%3Dtrue.)

DOUGLAS J. McCAULEY

1. G. C. Daily, *Nature's Services* (Washington, D.C.: Island Press, 1997).

2. P. Kareiva, R. Lalasz, and M. Marvier, "Conservation in the Anthropocene: Beyond Solitude and Fragility," *Breakthrough Journal*, Fall 2011, p. 1.

3. T. H. Ricketts, G. C. Daily, P. R. Ehrlich, and C. D. Michener, "Economic Value of Tropical Forest to Coffee Production," *Proceedings of the National Academy of Sciences of the United States of America* 101 (2004): 12579–82.

4. R. Costanza, R. dArge, R. de Groot, et al., "The Value of the World's Ecosystem Services and Natural Capital," *Nature* 387 (1997): 253–60.

5. R. Costanza, R. de Groot, P. Sutton, et al., "Changes in the Global Value of Ecosystem Services," *Global Environmental Change* 26 (2014): 152–58.

6. B. Hayward, *From the Mountain to the Tap: How Land Use and Water Management Can Work for the Rural Poor* (United Kingdom: NR International, 2005); available at www.frp.uk.com/ assets/Water_book.pdf.

7. R. Woodroffe, S. Thirgood, and A. Rabinowitz, eds., *People and Wildlife: Conflict or Co-existence?* (New York: Cambridge Univ. Press, 2005).

8. E. Willott, "Restoring Nature, Without Mosquitoes? *Restoration Ecology* 12, no. 2 (2004): 147–53.

9. E. O. Wilson, *The Diversity of Life* (Cambridge, MA: Belknap Press of Harvard Univ. Press, 1992).

10. J. Terborgh, *Requiem for Nature* (Washington, D.C.: Island Press, 1999).

EMILY WAKILD

1. E. Wakild, *Revolutionary Parks: Conservation, Social Justice, and the Mexican Revolution, 1910–1940* (Tucson: University of Arizona Press, 2011).

2. P. Kareiva, R. Lalasz, and M. Marvier, "Conservation in the Anthropocene: Beyond Solitude and Fragility" *Breakthrough Journal* 2 (Fall 2011): 29–37, (quotes from pp. 31 and 33).

3. D. Brockington, R. Duffy, and J. Igoe, *Nature Unbound: Conservation, Capitalism and the Future of Protected Areas* (London: Earthscan, 2008), p. 149.

4. For instance, R. Neumann, *Imposing Wilderness: Struggles over Livelihood and Nature Preservation in Africa* (Berkeley: University of California Press, 2002); P. West, *Conservation Is Our Government Now: The Politics of Ecology in Papua New Guinea* (Durham, NC: Duke University Press, 2006).

5. M. Chapin, "A Challenge to Conservationists," *World Watch Magazine* (Nov. 2004): 17–29, (quotes from pp. 26 and 29, emphasis mine).

6. M. Dowie, *Conservation Refugees: The Hundred-Year Conflict between Global Conservation and Native Peoples* (Cambridge, MA: MIT Press, 2009), p. 266.

7. E. Marris, *Rambunctious Garden: Saving Nature in a Post-Wild World* (New York: Bloomsbury, 2011).

8. R. MacArthur and E. O. Wilson, *Island Biogeography* (Princeton, NJ: Princeton University Press, 1967). See also D. Quammen, *The Song of the Dodo: Island Biogeography in an Age of Extinctions* (New York: Scribner, 1997).

9. On the unnecessary constrictions placed by false dichotomies, see T. Lovejoy, "Glimpses of Conservation Biology, Act II," *Conservation Biology* 20, no. 3 (2006): 711–12.

10. For an introduction to some of these trends, see S. W. Miller, *An Environmental History of Latin America* (Cambridge, UK: Cambridge University Press, 2007) and W. Dean, *With Broadax and Firebrand: The Destruction of the Brazilian Atlantic Forest* (Berkeley: University of California Press, 1997).

11. M. J. Dourojeanni, *Crónica forestal del Perú* (Lima, Peru: Editorial San Marcos and Universidad Nacional Agraria, La Molina, 2009), p. 259–66.

12. R. ELizalde MacClure, *La sobrevivencia de Chile: La conservación de sus recursos naturales renovables* (Santiago, Chile: Servicio Agrícola y Ganadero Ministerio de Agricultura. Santiago de Chile: El Escudo, 1970).

13. M. Buchinger, "Special Latin American Issue," *The Nature Conservancy News* 1, no. 1 (May 1965), (Denver Public Library, Conservation Collection); M. Buchinger, "Conservation in Latin America," *BioScience* 15, no. 1 (1965): 32–7 and "International Cooperation in Natural Area Preservation," *BioScience* 18, no. 5 (1968): 388–92.

14. G. H. Shepard, K. Rummenhoeller, J. Ohl-Shacherer, and D. W. Yu, "Trouble in Paradise: Indigenous Populations, Anthropological Policies, and Biodiversity Conservation in Manu National Park, Peru," *Journal of Sustainable Forestry* 29 (2010): 252–301.

15. See the film, *Amazon Gold*, 2012, directed by Reuben Aaronson.

16. Oral History Interview, author with Manuel Ríos Rodriguez, Lima Peru, July 3, 2013.

17. E. Wakild, "Parables of Chapultepec: Urban Parks, National Landscapes, and Contradictory Conservation in Modern Mexico" in *A Land between Waters: Environmental Histories of Modern Mexico*, ed. C. R. Boyer (Tucson: University of Arizona, 2012): 192–217.

18. E. Ortiz, "Una joya del mundo en el Perú," *El Comercio,* Lima, 26 May 2013.

HELEN KOPNINA

1. See E. Garland, "The Elephant in the Room: Confronting the Colonial Character of Wildlife Conservation in Africa," *African Studies Review* 51, no. 3 (2008): 74; and G. Holmes, "The Rich, the Powerful and the Endangered: Conservation Elites in the Dominican Republic," *Antipode* 42, no. 3 (2010): 624–46, respectively.

2. Associated Press in New Delhi. "Indian State to Let Forest Guards Shoot Poachers on Sight," *The Guardian*, 23 May 2012, http://www.guardian.co.uk/environment/2012/may/23/indian-state-forest-guards-poachers.

3. A. Belford, "Save the Tigers, Shoot the Humans," *The Global Mail,* 21 August 2012, http://www.theglobalmail.org/feature/save-the-tigers-shoot-the-humans/348/.

4. J. Walston, J. G. Robinson, E. L. Bennett, U. Breitenmoser, G. A. B. da Fonseca, et al., "Bringing the Tiger Back from the Brink—The Six Percent Solution," *PLoS Biol.* 8, no. 9 (2010): e1000485, doi:10.1371/journal.pbio.1000485.

5. Y. V. Jhala, Q. Qureshi, R. Gopal, and P. R. Sinha, eds., "Status of the Tigers, Co-predators, and Prey in India, 2010," National Tiger Conservation Authority, Government of India, New Delhi, and Wildlife Institute of India, Dehradun, 2011. TR 2011/003 pp-302; K. Nowell and X. Ling, "Taming the Tiger Trade: China's Markets for Wild and Captive Tiger Products Since the 1993 Domestic Trade Ban" (Hong Kong: TRAFFIC East Asia, 2007); K. U. Karanth, J. M. Goodrich, S. Vaidyanathan, G. V. Reddy, "Landscape-scale, Ecology-based Management of Wild Tiger Population" (Washington, D.C.: Global Tiger Initiative, World Bank, and Wildlife Conservation Society, 2010).

6. T. Chaunduri, "Learning to Protect: Environmental Education in a South Indian Tiger Reserve," in *Anthropology of Environmental Education,* ed. H. Kopnina (New York: Nova Science Publishers, 2012); S. H. S. Narain, M. G. Panwar, V. Thapar, and S. Singh, *Joining the Dots: The Report of the Tiger Task Force* (Delhi, India: The Ministry of Environment and Forests, Government of India, 2005).

7. J. Walston et al., "Bringing the Tiger Back from the Brink—The Six Percent Solution," *PLoS Biol.* 8, no. 9 (2010).

8. N. Sahgal, *Indira Gandhi: Her Road to Power* (New York: Frederick Ungar, 1982).

9. D. G. Miquelle, M. Yu, D. A. Dunishenko, D. A. Zvyaginstsev, A. Darensky et al., "A Monitoring Program for the Amur Tiger: Twelve-Year Report, 1998–2009," (2009), p. 54. In accordance with the Russian National Strategy for Tiger Conservation, a cooperative project conducted by representatives of numerous organizations; for complete list of individuals and institutions involved with this report, please see: http://www.21stcenturytiger.org/assets/21tiger/docs/Russia_Tiger_Monitoring_ReportNov2009.pdf.

10. "On September 25th, Vladivostok and Panda Celebrated Tiger Day for the 12th Time," WWF (26 September 2011), accessed January 8, 2012, http://www.wwf.ru/resources/news/article/eng/874226/09/2011.

11. J. Walston et al., "Bringing the Tiger Back from the Brink—The Six Percent Solution," *PLoS Biol.* 8, no. 9 (2010).

12. "Russia President Putin Encounters Sochi Leopard Cubs," *BBC News Europe,* February 4, 2014, http://www.bbc.com/news/world-europe-26038480.

13. "Russian Protests: Putin's People," *The Economist* (21 Jan. 2012), pp. 28–29.

14. R. Eckersley, "The State and Access to Environmental Justice: From Liberal Democracy to Ecological Democracy," Keynote Speech presented at the Access to Environmental Justice Conference of the Environmental Defender's Office, Western Australia (20 February 2004), http://www.edowa.org.au/files/presentations/EDO_AEJ_RobynEckersley.pdf; J. Barry, B. Minteer, and B. T. Pepperman, eds., "Vulnerability and Virtue: Democracy, Dependency and Ecological Stewardship," *Democracy and the Claims of Nature* (Lanham, MD: Rowman & Littlefield, 2002), 133–52; H. Ward, "Liberal Democracy and Sustainability," *Environmental Politics* 17, no. 3 (2008): 386–409.

15. J. S. Dryzek, "Ecology and Discursive Democracy: Beyond Liberal Capitalism and the Administrative State," *Capitalism, Nature, Socialism* 3, no. 2 (1992):18–42; R. Leakey and V. Morell, *Wildlife Wars: My Fight to Save Africa's Natural Treasures* (New York: St. Martin's Press, 2001).

16. P. R. Wilshusen, S. R. Brechin, L. Fortwangler, and P. C. West, "Reinventing a Square Wheel: Critique of a Resurgent 'Protection Paradigm' in International Biodiversity Conservation," *Society and Natural Resources* 15 (2002): 17–40.

17. D. Western, *Natural Connections: Perspectives in Community-based Conservation* (Washington, D.C.: Island Press, 1994).

18. D. R. Craig, L. Yung, W. T. Borrie, "'Blackfeet Belong to the Mountains': Hope, Loss, and Blackfeet Claims to Glacier National Park, Montana," *Conservation and Society* 10, no. 3 (2012): 232–42.

19. N. Heann, "Who's Got the Money Now?: Conservation-Development Meets the *Nueva Ruralidad* in Southern Mexico" in *Environmental Anthropology Today,* ed. H. Kopnina and E. Shoreman (New York: Routledge Press, 2011).

20. S. Goldenberg, "Solomon Islands Villagers Kill 900 Dolphins in Conservation Dispute," *Guardian,* 24 January 2013, http://www.guardian.co.uk/environment/2013/jan/24/solomon-islands-villagers-kill-900-dolphins.

21. W. Catton, "Destructive Momentum: Can an Enlightened Environmental Movement Overcome It?" in *Life on the Brink: Environmentalists Confront Overpopulation,* ed. P. Cafaro and E. Crist (Athens, GA: University of Georgia Press, 2012), 123–29.

22. R. Paehlke, F. Fischer, and M. Black, eds., "Environmental Challenges to Democratic Practice," in *Greening Environmental Policy: The Politics of a Sustainable Future* (London: Paul Chapman Publishing, 1996).

23. H. Kopnina, "Environmental Justice and Biospheric Egalitarianism: Reflecting on a Normative-philosophical View of Human-nature Relationship," *The Earth Perspectives* 1, no. 8 (2014). http://www.earth-perspectives.com/content/1/1/8.

24. N. Carter, *The Politics of the Environment: Ideas, Activism, Policy* (New York: Cambridge University Press, 2007).

25. R. Lidskog and I. Elander, "Addressing Climate Change Democratically: Multi-level Governance, Transnational Networks and Governmental Structures," *Sustainable Development* 18, no. 1 (2010): 32–41.

26. B. Baxter, *A Theory of Ecological Justice* (New York: Routledge Research in Environmental Politics, 2005).

27. M. Bookchin, "Social Ecology Versus Deep Ecology: A Challenge for the Ecology Movement," Anarchy Archives. [First published in *Green Perspectives: Newsletter of the Green Program Project*, nos. 4–5 (Summer 1987), according to the Anarchy Archives website, which indicates that quotation marks originally appeared around the term *deep ecology* in the *Green Perspectives* article but were removed from the online posting linked here.], http://dwardmac.pitzer.edu/Anarchist_Archives/bookchin/socecovdeepeco.html; G. Wenzel, *Animal Rights, Human Rights: Ecology, Economy and Ideology in the Canadian Arctic* (London: Belhaven Press, 1991); C. Zerner, "Toward a Broader Vision of Justice and Nature Conservation," in *People, Plants and Justice: The Politics of Nature Conservation* (New York: Columbia University Press, 2000); P. West, "Translation, Value, and Space: Theorizing an Ethnographic and Engaged Environmental Anthropology," *American Anthropologist* 107, no. 4 (2006): 632–42; J. Igoe, "Rereading Conservation Critique: A Response to Redford," *Oryx* 45, no. 3 (2011): 333–34.

28. See, for example, R. Fletcher, *Romancing the Wild: Cultural Dimensions of Ecotourism* (Durham, NC: Duke University Press, 2014).

29. D. Brockington, *Fortress Conservation: The Preservation of the Mkomazi Game Reserve, Tanzania* (Bloomington and Indianapolis: Indiana University Press, 2002).

30. V. Strang, in a paper sent to the author, based on Strang's presentation at Notes for Plenary Debate—IUAES World Anthropology Conference, Manchester, UK, August 5–10, 2013. Motion: "Justice for People Must Come Before Justice for the Environment," http://www.youtube.com/watch?v=oldnYTYMx-k.

31. Ibid.

32. T. Turner, "The Role of Indigenous Peoples in the Environmental Crisis: The Example of the Kayapó of the Brazilian Amazon," *Perspectives Biol. Med.* 36, no. 3 (1993): 526–47.

33. W. D. Newmark, N. L. Leonard, H. I. Sariko, and D.-G. M. Gamassa, "Conservation Attitudes of Local People Living Adjacent to Five Protected Areas in Tanzania," *Biological Conservation* 63 (1993):177–83; M. Infield and A. Namara, "Community Attitudes and Behaviour Towards Conservation: An Assessment of a Community Conservation Programme Around Lake Mburo

National Park, Uganda," *Oryx* 35 (2001): 48–60; T. Trusty, "From Ecosystem Services to Unfulfilled Expectations: Factors Influencing Attitudes Toward the Madidi Protected Area," in *Environmental Anthropology Today*, ed. H. Kopnina and E. Shoreman-Ouimet (New York and Oxford: Routledge, 2011).

34. J. Desmond, "Requiem for Roadkill: Death and Denial on America's Roads," in *Environmental Anthropology: Future Trends,* ed. H. Kopnina and E. Shoreman-Ouimet (New York and Oxford: Routledge, 2013), 46–58.

35. V. Strang, in a paper sent to the author, based on Strang's presentation at Notes for Plenary Debate—IUAES World Anthropology Conference, Manchester, UK, August 5–10, 2013. Motion: "Justice for People Must Come Before Justice for the Environment," http://www.youtube.com/watch?v=oldnYTYMx-k.

36. P. Singer, *Animal Liberation: A New Ethics for Our Treatment of Animals* (New York: New York Review/Random House, 1975); P. Taylor, *Respect for Nature: A Theory of Environmental Ethics* (Princeton: Princeton University Press, 1986); L. Ferry, *The New Ecological Order* (Chicago, IL: University of Chicago Press, 1995); T. Regan, *Animal Rights, Human Wrongs: An Introduction to Moral Philosophy* (Lanham, MD: Rowman & Littlefield, 2003), pp. 63–64, 89.

37. A. Naess, "The Shallow and the Deep: Long-range Ecology Movement: A Summary," *Inquiry* 16 (1973): 95–99.

38. F. Mathews, *The Ecological Self* (London: Routledge, 1994).

39. P. Kareiva, R. Lalasz, and M. Marvier, "Conservation in the Anthropocene: Beyond Solitude and Fragility," *Breakthrough Journal,* Fall 2011, pp. 29–27; E. Marris, *Rambunctious Garden: Saving Nature in a Post-Wild World* (New York: Bloomsbury, 2011).

40. E. Crist, "Abundant Earth and Population," in *Life on the Brink: Environmentalists Confront Overpopulation,* ed. P. Cafaro and E. Crist (Athens, GA: University of Georgia Press, 2012), 141–53; M. Bekoff, *Ignoring Nature No More: The Case for Compassionate Conservation* (Chicago: University of Chicago Press, 2013); H. Kopnina, "Forsaking Nature? Contesting 'Biodiversity' Through Competing Discourses of Sustainability," *Journal of Education for Sustainable Development* 7, no. 1 (2013): 47–59.

41. M. Osava, "The Unsustainable Political Deficiencies of Environmentalism," *IPS,* Inter Press Service News Agency, December 27, 2011, accessed January 9, 2012, http://ipsnews.net/news.asp?idnews=106317.

42. R. Stevenson, "Tensions and Transitions in Policy Discourse: Recontextualizing a Decontextualized EE/ESD Debate," *Environmental Education Research* 12, no. 3–4 (2006): 277–90.

43. J. S. Dryzek, "Democracy and Earth System Governance," (paper presented at the Amsterdam Conference on the Human Dimensions of Global Environmental Change, The Netherlands, December 2–4, 2009).

44. R. Routley, "Is There a Need for a New, an Environmental Ethic?" in *Proc. 15th World Congr. Philos.* (Manchester, NH: Sophia, 1973), pp. 205–10; A. Dobson and D. Bell, eds., *Environmental Citizenship* (Cambridge, MA: MIT Press, 2005).

45. J. S. Dryzek, "Ecology and Discursive Democracy: Beyond Liberal Capitalism and the Administrative State," *Capitalism, Nature, Socialism* 3, no. 2 (1992): 18–42;

J. S. Dryzek, "Democracy and Earth System Governance," (paper presented at the Amsterdam Conference on the Human Dimensions of Global Environmental Change, The Netherlands, December 2–4, 2009); R. Eckersley, "Green Justice, the State and Democracy" (paper presented at the Environmental Justice: Global Ethics for the 21st Century Conference at Melbourne University, 1997); D. Foreman, "Putting the Earth First," in *Debating the Earth: The Environmental Politics Reader,* ed. J. S. Dryzek and D. Schlosberg (Oxford: Oxford University Press, 1998), 358–64; J. Terborgh, *Requiem for Nature* (Washington, D.C.: Island Press/Shearwater Books, 1999); J. F. Oates, *Myth and Reality in the Rain Forest: How Conservation Strategies Are Failing in West Africa* (Oakland: University of California Press, 1999); A. Dobson and D. Bell, eds., *Environmental Citizenship* (Cambridge, MA: MIT Press, 2005); M. Saward, "Authorisation and Authenticity: Representation and the Unelected" in *Journal of Political Philosophy* 17 (2009): 1–22.

46. J. O'Neill, "Who Speaks for Nature?" in *How Nature Speaks: The Dynamics of the Human Ecological Condition,* ed. Y. Haila and C. Dyke (Durham, NC: Duke University Press Books, 2006).

47. D. R. Liddick, *Eco-Terrorism: Radical Environmental and Animal Liberation Movements* (Westport, CT: Praeger Publishers, 2006).

48. For further reading on tiger conservation and recovery issues, see E. Dinerstein et al., *Setting Priorities for the Conservation and Recovery of Wild Tigers, 2005–2015: A User's Guide* (Washington, D.C., and New York: WWF, WCS, Smithsonian, and NFWF-STF, 2006); http://www.panthera.org/node/52, Tigers Forever, a joint Program of Panthera and the Wildlife Conservation Society [accessed previously, 19 December 2011, at http://www.panthera.org/tigers_forever.html]; "Building a Future for Wild Tigers," The World Bank (2012), accessed December 1, 2013, http://web.worldbank.org/tigers. See http://web.worldbank.org/WBSITE/EXTERNAL/NEWS/0,,contentMDK:21796122~pagePK:64257043~piPK:437376~theSitePK:4607,00.html.

49. M. Bekoff, *Ignoring Nature No More: The Case for Compassionate Conservation* (Chicago: University of Chicago Press, 2013).

50. V. Strang, Notes for Plenary Debate—IUAES World Anthropology Conference, Manchester, UK, August 5–10, 2013. Motion: "Justice for People Must Come Before Justice for the Environment," http://www.youtube.com/watch?v=oldnYTYMx-k.

ANTHONY R. E. SINCLAIR

1. M. Shellenberger and T. Nordhaus, "Introduction" in *Love Your Monsters: Post-environmentalism and the Anthropocene,* ed. M. Shellenberger and T. Nordhaus (Washington, D.C.: Breakthrough Institute, 2011), pp. 5–7; see as well P. Kareiva, R. Lalasz, and M. Marvier, "Conservation in the Anthropocene: Beyond Solitude and Fragility" in *Love Your Monsters: Post-environmentalism and the Anthropocene,* pp. 26–36.

2. The IUCN categories of protection are given in Wright, R. G., and Mattson, D. J. 1996. The origin and purpose of National Parks and Protected Areas. *National Parks and Protected Areas: Their Role in Environmental Protection,* ed. R. G.

Wright (Oxford: Blackwell Science), pp. 3–14; A. R. E. Sinclair, "Integrating Conservation in Human and Natural Ecosystems" in *Serengeti III: Human Impacts on Ecosystem Dynamics*, ed. A. R. E. Sinclair, C. Packer, S. A. R. Mduma, and J. M. Fryxell (Chicago: University of Chicago Press, 2008), 471–95.

3. Origin of Yellowstone National Park, D. Houston, personal communication; also S. T. Olliff, P. Schullery, G. E. Plumb, and L. H. Whittlesey, "Understanding the Past: The History of Wildlife and Resource Management in the Greater Yellowstone Area" in *Yellowstone's Wildlife in Transition*, ed. P. J. White, R. A. Garrott, and G. E. Plumb (Cambridge, MA: Harvard University Press, 2013), pp. 10–28.

4. Origin of Kruger National Park, N. Owen-Smith, personal communication; also J. Carruthers, *The Kruger National Park: A Social and Political History* (Pietermaritzburg, South Africa: University of Natal Press, 1995).

5. The case for protected areas is given in *National Parks and Protected Areas: Their Role in Environmental Protection*, ed. R. G. Wright (Oxford: Blackwell Science, 1996); J. G. Nelson and R. Serafin, eds., *National Parks and Protected Areas: Keystones to Conservation and Sustainable Development* (New York: Springer-Verlag, 1997); J. Terborgh, C. V. Schaik, L. Davenport, and M. Rao, eds., *Making Parks Work: Strategies for Preserving Tropical Nature* (Washington, D.C.: Island Press, 2002); S. Stolton and N. Dudley, eds., *Arguments for Protected Areas: Multiple Benefits for Conservation and Use* (Washington, D.C.: Earthscan, 2010).

6. L. Cantú-Salazar and K. J. Gaston, "Very Large Protected Areas and Their Contribution to Terrestrial Biological Conservation," *BioScience* 60 (2010): 808–18.

7. How Serengeti National Park provides protection is given in A. R. E. Sinclair, K. Metzger, J. M. Fryxell, and S. A. R. Mduma, eds., *Serengeti IV: Sustaining Biodiversity in a Coupled Human-Natural System* (Chicago: Chicago University Press, 2014).

8. J. G. C. Hopcraft, R. M. Holdo, E. Mwangomo, et al., "Why Are Wildebeest the Most Abundant Herbivore in the Serengeti Ecosystem?" in A. R. E. Sinclair, K. Metzger, J. M. Fryxell, and S. A. R. Mduma, eds., *Serengeti IV: Sustaining Biodiversity in a Coupled Human-Natural System* (Chicago: Chicago University Press, 2014).

9. K. L. Metzger, A. R. E. Sinclair, S. Macfarlane, M. B. Coughenour, and J. Ding, "Scales of Change in the Greater Serengeti Ecosystem" in *Serengeti IV: Sustaining Biodiversity in a Coupled Human-Natural System*, ed. A. R. E. Sinclair, K. Metzger, J. M. Fryxell, and S. A. R. Mduma (Chicago: Chicago University Press, 2014).

10. A. E. Byrom, W. A. Ruscoe, A. K. Nkwabi, et al., "Small Mammal Diversity and Population Dynamics in the Greater Serengeti Ecosystem" in *Serengeti IV: Sustaining Biodiversity in a Coupled Human-Natural System*, ed. A. R. E. Sinclair, K. Metzger, J. M. Fryxell, and S. A. R. Mduma (Chicago: Chicago University Press, 2014).

11. *Serengeti IV: Sustaining Biodiversity in a Coupled Human-Natural System*, ed. A. R. E. Sinclair, K. Metzger, J. M. Fryxell, and S. A. R. Mduma (Chicago: Chicago University Press, 2014)

12. M. E. Craft, K. Hampson, J. O. Ogutu, and S. M. Durant, "Carnivore Communities in the Greater Serengeti Ecosystem" in *Serengeti IV: Sustaining Biodiversity in a Coupled Human-Natural System,* ed. A. R. E. Sinclair, K. Metzger, J. M. Fryxell, and S. A. R. Mduma (Chicago: Chicago University Press, 2014).

13. Ibid.

14. H. G. Tingvold, R. Fyumagwa, C. Bech, L. F. Baardsen, H. Rosenlund, and E. Røskaft, "Determining Adrenocortical Activity as a Measure of Stress in African Elephants (*Loxodonta africana*) in Relation to Human Activities in Serengeti Ecosystem," *African Journal of Ecology* (2013), doi:10.1111/aje.12069.

15. A. R. E. Sinclair, "Integrating Conservation in Human and Natural Systems" in *Serengeti III: Human Impacts on Ecosystem Dynamics,* ed. A. R. E. Sinclair, C. Packer, S. A. R. Mduma, and J. M. Fryxell (Chicago: University of Chicago Press, 2008), pp. 471–95.

16. A. R. E. Sinclair, D. S. Hik, O. J. Schmitz, G. G. E. Scudder, D. H. Turpin, and N. C. Larter, "Biodiversity and the Need for Habitat Renewal," *Ecological Applications* 5 (1995): 579–87.

17. D. Craigie et al., "Large Mammal Population Declines in Africa's Protected Areas," *Biological Conservation* 143 (2010): 2221–28.

18. Loss of species from protected areas, and from African parks in particular, has been documented in W. D. Newmark, "Isolation of African Protected Areas," *Frontiers in Ecology and Environment* 6 (2008): 321–28; W. D. Newmark, "Insularization of Tanzanian Parks and the Local Extinction of Large Mammals," *Conservation Biology* 10 (1996): 1549–56; "Extinction of Mammal Populations in Western North American National Parks," *Conservation Biology* 9 (1995): 512–26; W. D. Newmark, "The Role and Design of Wildlife Corridors with Examples from Tanzania," *Ambio* 12 (1993): 500, 504; W. D. Newmark, "A Land Bridge Island Perspective on Mammalian Extinctions in Western North American Parks," *Nature* 325 (1987): 430, 432.

19. W. F. Laurance and 215 other authors, "Averting Biodiversity Collapse in Tropical Forest Protected Areas," *Nature* 489 (2012): 290–94.

20. D. H. Janzen, "No Park Is an Island: Increase in Interference from Outside as Park Size Decreases," *Oikos* 41 (1983): 402–10; D. Lindenmayer, B. J. F. Franklin, and J. Fischer, "General Management Principles and a Checklist of Strategies to Guide Forest Biodiversity Conservation," *Biological Conservation* 131 (2006): 433–45.

21. C. R. Peters et al., "Paleoecology of the Serengeti-Mara Ecosystem" in *Serengeti III: Human Impacts on Ecosystem Dynamics,* ed. A. R. E. Sinclair, C. Packer, S. A. R. Mduma, and J. M. Fryxell (Chicago: University of Chicago Press, 2008), pp. 47–94.

22. A Site of Special Scientific Interest (SSSI) is deemed to be one of England's most important for wildlife or geology. SSSIs represent amongst others areas of wetland, chalkland rivers, meadows high in flowering plant diversity, and peat bogs as examples. There are over 4,100 SSSIs in England, covering around 8 percent of the country's land area. Some 70 percent of these sites (by area) are internationally important for their wildlife and designated as Special Areas of

Conservation (SACs), Special Protection Areas (SPAs) or Ramsar sites. More information can be found at www.naturalengland.org.uk/ourwork/conservation/designations/sssi/default.aspx.

23. Problems with the implementation of community-based conservation are illustrated by C. A. Harvey plus 11 other authors "Integrating Agricultural Landscapes with Biodiversity Conservation in the Mesoamerican Hotspot," *Conservation Biology* 22 (2008): 8–15; S. A. Bhagwat, K. J. Willis, H. J. B. Birks, and R. J. Whittaker, "Agroforestry: A Refuge for Tropical Biodiversity?" *Trends in Ecology and Evolution* 23 (2008): 261–67; R. L. Chazdon plus 10 other authors, "Beyond Reserves: A Research Agenda for Conserving Biodiversity in Human-Modified Tropical Landscapes," *Biotropica* 41 (2009): 142–53.

24. Ibid.

25. M. P. Wells and T. O. McShane, "Integrating Protected Area Management with Local Needs and Aspirations," *Ambio* 33 (2004): 513–19; C. A. Garcia et al., "Biodiversity Conservation in Agricultural Landscapes: Challenges and Opportunities of Coffee Agroforests in the Western Ghats, India," *Conservation Biology* 24 (2009): 479–88.

26. T. Lybbert and C. B. Barrett, "Does Resource Commercialization Induce Local Conservation? A Cautionary Tale from Southwestern Morocco," *Society and Natural Resources* 17 (2004): 413–30; T. O. McShane and M. Wells, eds., *Getting Biodiversity Projects to Work: Towards More Effective Conservation and Development* (New York: Columbia University Press, 2004).

27. J. Murombedzi, "Devolving the Expropriation of Nature: The 'Devolution' of Wildlife Management in Southern Africa" in *Decolonizing Nature,* ed. W. M. Adams and M. Mulligan (London: Earthscan, 2003), 135–51.

28. Examples of community-based conservation in Africa: D. Hulme, and M. Murphree, eds., *African Wildlife and Livelihoods* (Oxford: James Currey, 2001): B. Child, ed., *Parks in Transition* (London: Earthscan, 2004).

29. E. J. Milner-Gulland et al., "Dramatic Decline in Saiga Antelope Populations," *Oryx* 35 (2001): 340–45.

30. T. Lybbert and C. B. Barrett, "Does Resource Commercialization Induce Local Conservation? A Cautionary Tale from Southwestern Morocco," *Society and Natural Resources* 17 (2004): 413–30; T. O. McShane and M. Wells, eds., *Getting Biodiversity Projects to Work: Towards More Effective Conservation and Development* (New York: Columbia University Press, 2004); T. Holmern, E. Roskaft, J. Mbaruka, S. Y. Mkama, and J. Muya, "Uneconomical Game Cropping in a Community-based Conservation Project Outside the Serengeti National Park, Tanzania," *Oryx* 36 (2002): 364–72.

31. L. Emerton, "The Nature of Benefits and the Benefits of Nature" in *African Wildlife and Livelihoods,* ed. D. Hulme and M. Murphree (Oxford: James Currey, 2001); I. Bond, "CAMPFIRE and the Incentives for Institutional Change," also in *African Wildlife and Livelihoods,* pp. 227–43.

32. P. F. Donald, R. E. Green, and M. F. Heath, "Agricultural Intensification and the Collapse of Europe's Farmland Bird Populations," *Proceedings of the Royal Society, B.* 268 (2001): 25–29; R. D. Gregory, D. G. Noble, and J. Custance, "The State of

Play of Farmland Birds: Population Trends and Conservation Status of Lowland Farmland Birds in the United Kingdom," *Ibis* 146, Supp. 2 (2004): 1–13.

33. See citations for W. D. Newmark in endnote 18; P. Scholte, "Immigration, a Potential Time-Bomb under the Integration of Conservation and Development," *Ambio* 32 (2003): 58–64; P. Scholte and W. T. De Groot, "From Debate to Insight: Three Models of Immigration to Protected Areas," *Conservation Biology* 24 (2009): 630–32.

34. M. Shellenberger and T. Nordhaus, "Introduction" in *Love Your Monsters: Post-environmentalism and the Anthropocene*, ed. M. Shellenberger and T. Nordhaus (Washington, D.C.: Breakthrough Institute, 2011), pp. 5–7; see as well P. Kareiva, R. Lalasz, and M. Marvier, "Conservation in the Anthropocene: Beyond Solitude and Fragility" in *Love Your Monsters: Post-environmentalism and the Anthropocene*, pp. 26–36; M. Rosenzweig, *Win-Win Ecology: How Earth's Species Can Survive in the Midst of Human Enterprise* (Oxford: Oxford University Press, 2003) ; P. Kareiva and M. Marvier, "What Is Conservation Science?" *BioScience* 62 (2012): 962–69.

35. M. Shellenberger and T. Nordhaus, "Introduction" in *Love Your Monsters: Post-environmentalism and the Anthropocene,* ed. M. Shellenberger and T. Nordhaus (Washington, D.C.: Breakthrough Institute, 2011), pp. 5–7; see as well P. Kareiva, R. Lalasz, and M. Marvier, "Conservation in the Anthropocene: Beyond Solitude and Fragility" in *Love Your Monsters: Post-environmentalism and the Anthropocene,* pp. 26–36; see chapters by E. Ellis, "The Planet of No Return: Human Resilience on an Artificial Earth" and M. Sagoff, "The Rise and Fall of Ecological Economics: A Cautionary Tale" in *Love Your Monsters: Post-environmentalism and the Anthropocene,* ed. M. Shellenberger and T. Nordhaus (Washington, D.C.: Breakthrough Institute, 2011), pp. 37–65.

36. M. Shellenberger and T. Nordhaus, "Introduction" in *Love Your Monsters: Post-environmentalism and the Anthropocene,* ed. M. Shellenberger and T. Nordhaus (Washington, D.C.: Breakthrough Institute, 2011), pp. 5–7; see as well P. Kareiva, R. Lalasz, and M. Marvier, "Conservation in the Anthropocene: Beyond Solitude and Fragility" in *Love Your Monsters: Post-environmentalism and the Anthropocene,* pp. 26–36.

37. M. Rosenzweig, *Win-Win Ecology: How Earth's Species Can Survive in the Midst of Human Enterprise* (Oxford: Oxford University Press, 2003).

38. P. F. Donald, R. E. Green, and M. F. Heath, "Agricultural Intensification and the Collapse of Europe's Farmland Bird Populations," *Proceedings of the Royal Society, B.* 268 (2001): 25–29; R. D. Gregory, D. G. Noble, and J. Custance, "The State of Play of Farmland Birds: Population Trends and Conservation Status of Lowland Farmland Birds in the United Kingdom," *Ibis* 146, Supp. 2 (2004): 1–13; For declines in ecosystem processes see J. C. Biesmeijer et al., "Parallel Declines in Pollinators and Insect-pollinated Plants in Britain and the Netherlands," *Science* 313 (2006): 351–54; K. J. Gaston and R. A. Fuller, "Commonness, Population Depletion and Conservation Biology," *Trends in Ecology and Evolution* 25 (2008): 372–80; B. J. Cardinale et al., "Biodiversity Loss and Its Impact on Humanity," *Nature* 486 (2012): 59–67; K. J. Gaston, "Valuing Common Species," *Science* 327 (2010): 154–55.

39. Salinization of Australia: A. M. Grieve, "Salinity and Waterlogging in the Murray-Darling Basin," *Search* 18 (1987): 72–74; D. J. McFarlane, R. J. George, and P. Farrington, "Changes in the Hydrologic Cycle" in *Reintegrating Fragmented Landscapes,* ed. R. J. Hobbs and D. A. Saunders (New York: Springer-Verlag, 1993), pp. 147–86.

40. B. Smith, "Creating a Buzz in India: Enhancing the Relationship between People and Pollinators in Eastern India," DEFRA Darwin Initiative Project (No. 019-24), *Gamewise* (Autumn/Winter 2012), 20–21.

41. T. H. Ricketts et al., "Landscape Effects on Crop Pollination Services: Are There General Patterns?" *Ecology Letters* 11 (2008): 499–515.

42. S. Thirgood, R. Woodroffe, and A. Rabinowitz, "The Impact of Human-Wildlife Conflict on Human Lives and Livelihoods" in *People and Wildlife: Conflict or Coexistence?* ed. R. Woodroffe, S. Thirgood, and A. Rabinowitz (Cambridge: Cambridge University Press, 2005), pp. 49–71.

43. S. Thirgood, R. Woodroffe, and A. Rabinowitz, "The Impact of Human-Wildlife Conflict on Human Lives and Livelihoods" in *People and Wildlife: Conflict or Coexistence?* ed. R. Woodroffe, S. Thirgood, and A. Rabinowitz (Cambridge, UK: Cambridge University Press, 2005), pp. 49–71; A. R. E. Sinclair, D. Ludwig, and C. Clark, "Conservation in the Real World," *Science* 289 (2000): 1875; A. Balmford and T. Whitten, "Who Should Pay for Tropical Conservation, and How Should the Costs Be Met? *Oryx* 37 (2003): 238–50; P. J. Nyhus, S. A. Osofsky, P. Ferraro, F. Madden, and H. Fischer, "Bearing the Costs of Human-Wildlife Conflict: The Challenges of Compensation Schemes" in *People and Wildlife: Conflict or Coexistence?* ed. R. Woodroffe, S. Thirgood, and A. Rabinowitz (Cambridge, UK: Cambridge University Press, 2005), pp. 107–21; R. Woodroffe, S. Thirgood, and A. Rabinowitz, "The Future of Co-existence: Resolving Human-Wildlife Conflicts in a Changing World" in *People and Wildlife: Conflict or Coexistence?* ed. R. Woodroffe, S. Thirgood, and A. Rabinowitz (Cambridge, UK: Cambridge University Press, 2005) pp. 388–405.

44. M. Shellenberger and T. Nordhaus, "Introduction" in *Love Your Monsters: Post-environmentalism and the Anthropocene,* ed. M. Shellenberger and T. Nordhaus (Washington, D.C.: Breakthrough Institute, 2011), pp. 5–7; see as well P. Kareiva, R. Lalasz, and M. Marvier, "Conservation in the Anthropocene: Beyond Solitude and Fragility" in *Love Your Monsters: Post-environmentalism and the Anthropocene,* pp. 26–36.

45. W. M. Adams, "When Nature Won't Stay Still: Conservation, Equilibrium and Control" in *Decolonizing Nature: Strategies for Conservation in a Post-colonial Era,* ed. W. M. Adams and M. Mulligan (London: Earthscan, 2003), pp. 221–46.

46. Wright, R.G., and Mattson, D.J. 1996. "The Origin and Purpose of National Parks and Protected Areas" in *National Parks and Protected Areas: Their Role in Environmental Protection,* ed. R. G. Wright (Oxford: Blackwell Science, 1996), pp. 3–14; K. L. Jope and J. C. Dunstan, "Ecosystem-Based Management: Natural Processes and Systems Theory" in *National Parks and Protected Areas: Their Role in Environmental Protection,* ed. R. G. Wright (Oxford: Blackwell Science, 1996), pp. 45–62.

EILEEN CRIST

1. M. Oliver, "Waste Land: An Elegy," *Orion* 22 (September/October 2003).

2. B. McKibben, *Eaarth: Making a Life on a Tough New Planet* (New York: Times Books, 2010), 2. For a brief up-to-date summary of humanity's global ecological footprint see D. A. DellaSala, "Global Change," *Reference Module in Earth Systems and Environmental Sciences* (Elsevier 11 Sept. 2013), doi:10.1016/B978-0-12-409548-9.05355-0.

3. D. Brower, *Let the Mountains Talk, Let the Rivers Run* (Gabriola Island: New Society Publishers, 2000), 17.

4. E. O. Wilson, *A Window on Eternity: A Biologist's Walk through Gorongosa National Park* (New York: Simon & Schuster, 2014), 132.

5. T. Birch, "The Incarceration of Wildness: Wilderness Areas as Prisons," in *Deep Ecology for the 21st Century,* ed. G. Sessions (Boston: Shambhala Publications, 1995), 339–55, 351.

6. While 13 represents the official approximate percentage of land protected worldwide, this inclusive estimate masks the fact that only about 6 percent of it is *strictly* protected from human use. D. Brockington et al., "Conservation, Human Rights, and Poverty Reduction," *Conservation Biology* 20, no. 1 (2006): 250–52, (p. 250). The IUCN's classification of Protected Areas divides them into six types, ranging from biodiversity-focused objectives like wilderness protection (strictly protected), to those incorporating human uses like "sustainable natural resource management." For global data and trends regarding protected areas, see UNEP's World Conservation Monitoring Centre, http://www.unep-wcmc.org/.

7. D. Quammen, "Hallowed Ground: Nothing Is Ever Safe," *National Geographic* (October 2006).

8. Jack Turner makes this argument cogently in his essay "The Wild and the Self," in *The Rediscovery of the Wild*, ed. P. Kahn and P. Hasbach (Cambridge, MA: MIT Press, 2013), 27–50.

9. See T. Steinberg, *Down to Earth: Nature's Role in American History* (New York: Oxford University Press, 2002); P. Shabekoff, *A Fierce Green Fire: The American Environmental Movement* (Washington, D.C.: Island Press, 2003).

10. H. Thoreau, *Walden or, Life in the Woods* (New York: Vintage Books, 1991), 239.

11. T. Birch, "The Incarceration of Wildness," 339.

12. R. Manning, *Rewilding the West: Restoration in a Prairie Landscape.* (Berkeley: University of California Press, 2009), p. 6.

13. "Protection of freshwater biodiversity," they note, "is perhaps the ultimate conservation challenge because, to be fully effective, it requires control over the upstream drainage network, the surrounding land, the riparian zone, and—in the case of migrating aquatic fauna—downstream reaches. Such prerequisites are hardly ever met..." D. Dudgeon et al., "Freshwater Biodiversity: Importance, Threats, Status and Conservation Challenges," *Biol. Rev.* 81 (2006): 163–82, (p. 176); Stuart Pimm and his colleagues make the same point. "The Biodiversity of Species and their Rates of Extinction, Distribution, and Protection," *Science* (30 May 2014): 1246752-1-10, (p. 6).

14. S. Pimm et al., "The Biodiversity of Species and Their Rates of Extinction, Distribution, and Protection," *Science,* p. 5.

15. In many parts of the world, "protected areas support the last populations of many species." C. Hambler and S. Canney, *Conservation* (Cambridge, UK: Cambridge University Press, Second Edition, 2013), 199.

16. See D. Wilcove, *No Way Home: The Decline of the World's Great Animal Migrations.* (Washington, D.C.: Island Press, 2008).

17. "Why," asked John Muir, "are Big Tree groves always found on well watered spots? Simply because Big Trees give rise to streams. It is a mistake to suppose that the water is the cause of the groves being there. On the contrary, the groves are the cause of the water being there." See J. Muir, *Our National Parks* (San Francisco: Sierra Club Books, 1909), p. 243.

18. See B. Czech, "The Imperative of Steady State Economics for Wild Animal Welfare," in *Ignoring Nature No More: The Case for Compassionate Conservation,* ed. M. Bekoff (Chicago: Chicago University Press, 2013), 179.

19. Climate change calls for "the careful design of dynamic conservation systems that operate on a landscape scale." L. Hannah et al., "Conservation of Biodiversity in a Changing Climate," *Conservation Biology* 16, no. 1 (2002): 264–68, (p. 265). Conservation biologists Camille Parmesan and John Matthews also emphasize the importance of "the design of new reserves to allow for shifts in distributions of…species." In C. Parmesan and J. Matthews, "Biological Impacts of Climate Change," Chapter 10, *Principles of Conservation Biology,* 3d edition, ed. M. Groom et al. (Sunderland, MA: Sinauer Associates, Inc., 2005), 333–74.

20. C. Thomas et al., "Protected Areas Facilitate Species' Range Expansions," *PNAS* 109 (28 August 2012): 14063–68. See also, "Think Big," Editorial. *Nature* (13 January 2011), 131; A. Johnston et al., "Observed and Predicted Effects of Climate Change on Species Abundance in Protected Areas," *Nature Climate Change* 3 (December 2013): 1055–61.

21. J. Miller, "Biodiversity Conservation and the Extinction of Experience," *Trends in Ecology & Evolution* 20 (August 2005): 430–34.

22. J. Waldman, "The Natural World Vanishes: How Species Cease to Matter," *Yale Environment 360* (8 April 2010).

23. See G. Monbiot, "For More Wonder, Rewild the World," TED Global 2013; G. Monbiot, *Feral: Searching for Enchantment on the Frontiers of Rewilding.* (London: Allen Lane, 2013).

24. Emphasizing strictly protected areas for preventing extinctions in no way disparages the critical importance of protecting biodiversity, and caring for landscapes, outside such areas. For elaborations of this point, see P. Ehrlich and R. Pringle, "Where Does Biodiversity Go from Here? A Grim Business-as-Usual Forecast and a Hopeful Portfolio of Partial Solutions," *PNAS* (12 August 2008): 11579–86; W. F. Laurance et al., "Averting Biodiversity Collapse in Tropical Forest Protected Areas," Letter to *Nature,* 489, (13 September 2012): 290–94.

25. Wilson, *A Window on Eternity,* 137–38. The exception is indigenous peoples who preserve their traditional lifestyles and population densities.

26. See M. Wells and T. McShane, "Integrating Protected Area Management with Local Needs and Aspirations," *Ambio* 33, 8 (December 2004): 513–19; A. Agrawal and K. Redford, "Poverty, Development, and Biodiversity Conservation: Shooting in the Dark?" Working Paper no. 26, March 2006, Wildlife Conservation Society. S. Sanderson and K. Redford, "Contested Relationships between Biodiversity Conservation and Poverty Alleviation," *Oryx* 37, 4 (2003): 389–90; D. Doak et al., "What Is the Future of Conservation?" *Trends in Ecology and Evolution,* 2013.

27. P. Ehrlich and R. Pringle, "Where Does Biodiversity Go from Here?" *PNAS,* p. 11582.

28. For examples, see D. Quammen, "Hallowed Ground: Nothing is Ever Safe." See also, B. Taylor, "Dangerous Territory: The Contested Space Between Imperial Conservation and Environmental Justice," *RCC Perspectives (special issue),* eds. C. Mauch and L. Robin, Rachel Carson Center, 2014.

29. F. Berkes, "Rethinking Community-Based Conservation," *Conservation Biology* 18, no. 3 (June 2004): 621–30.

30. On the positive effects of natural surroundings on mental and physical health, see N. Schultz, "Nurturing Nature," *New Scientist* (6 November 2010): 35–37.

31. C. Fraser, *Rewilding the World: Dispatches from the Conservation Revolution* (New York: Picador, 2009).

32. P. Ehrlich and R. Pringle, "Where Does Biodiversity Go from Here?" *PNAS.*

33. C. Hambler and S. Canney, *Conservation,* 317. See also K. MacKinnon, "Are We Really Getting Conservation So Badly Wrong?" *PLoS Biol* 9, no. 1 (2011) [Accessed June 6, 2014], http://www.plosbiology.org/article/info%3Adoi%2F10.1371%2Fjournal.pbio.1001010.

34. E. O. Wilson, *A Window on Eternity,* 141.

35. Langdon Winner coined "technological somnambulism." "Technology as Forms of Life," in *Philosophy of Technology,* ed. D. Kaplan (Oxford: Rowman & Littlefield, 2004), 103–13.

36. T. Birch, "The Incarceration of Wildness," 351.

37. L. Krall, "Resistance," in *Keeping the Wild: Against the Domestication of Earth,* ed. G. Wuerthner, E. Crist, and T. Butler (Washington, D.C.: Island Press, 2014), 205–10.

38. For a well-crafted response to the claim that wilderness advocacy is misanthropic, see P. Keeling, "Wilderness, People, and the False Charge of Misanthropy," *Environmental Ethics* 35 (Winter 2013): 387–405.

39. Wilderness defenders are not opposed to indigenous people's presence in wild nature. See H. Locke and P. Dearden, "Rethinking Protected Area Categories and the New Paradigm," *Environmental Conservation* 32, no. 1 (2005): 1–10. As Daniel Doak and colleagues point out, "indigenous groups and conservationists have…frequently formed alliances to protect lands and counter extractive industries." "What Is the Future of Conservation?" *Trends in Ecology & Evolution* 29 (2013).

40. In agreement with Paul Keeling, "standing up for wilderness against human control and domination of all the land involves a form of antagonism—namely, active opposition to that domination—by definition. But it is a mistake to confuse that opposition with hating humans." P. Keeling, "Wilderness, People, and the False Charge of Misanthropy," 404.

41. A. Naess, "Self-Realization: An Ecological Approach to Being in the World," in *Deep Ecology for the 21st Century*, ed. G. Sessions (Boston: Shambhala Publications, 1995), 225–39.

42. David Johns elaborates this point in his essay "With Friends Like These Wilderness and Biodiversity Do Not Need Enemies," in *Keeping the Wild: Against the Domestication of Earth*, ed. G. Wuerthner, E. Crist, and T. Butler (Washington, D.C.: Island Press, 2014), 31–44.

43. Wilderness is "entirely an invention of past and present cultures, or a socially constructed abstraction," in the words of Robert McCullough. "The Nature of History Preserved; or, The Trouble with Green Bridges" in *Reconstructing Conservation: Finding Common Ground*, ed. B. Minteer and R. Manning (Washington, D.C.: Island Press, 2003), 33–42, (p. 33).

44. Here I echo Tom Butler's points in "'Natural Capital' Is a Bankrupt Metaphor," a response essay to The Nature Conservancy's CEO Mark Tercek's "Money Talks—So Let's Give Nature a Voice." See http://www.earthisland.org/journal/index.php/eij/article/whats_a_tree_worth/.

45. D. Peterson, "Talking about Bushmeat," in *Ignoring Nature No More: The Case for Compassionate Conservation*, ed. M. Bekoff, 72.

46. D. Brower, *Let the Mountains Talk, Let the Rivers Run*, 46; for scientific arguments in support of enlarging and interconnecting nature reserves, see M. Soulé and J. Terborgh, eds., *Continental Conservation: Scientific Foundations of Regional Reserve Networks* (Washington, D.C.: Island Press, 1999).

47. T. Birch, "The Incarceration of Wildness," 349, emphasis original.

48. T. Birch, "The Incarceration of Wildness," 350.

49. As journalist Mike Pflanz writes, "the illegal trade in wildlife… and body parts has never been more lucrative." M. Pflanz, "The Ivory Police," *The Christian Science Monitor* (2 March 2014): 26. A trained military response against poachers armed with sophisticated weapons and backed by criminal cartels is called for. See Damien Mander's International Anti-Poaching Foundation work and TED talk (http://www.iapf.org/en/about/blog/entry/modern-warrior-damien-mander-at-tedxsydney).

50. E. O. Wilson, *A Window on Eternity*, 132. On the movement to conserve half the world, visit: http://natureneedshalf.org/home/.

51. D. Brockington, *Fortress Conservation: The Preservation of the Mkomazi Game Reserve* (Bloomington: Indiana University Press, 2002); M. Dowie, "Conservation Refugees: When Protecting Nature Means Kicking People Out," *Orion* (November/December 2005); M. Dowie, "The Hidden Cost of Paradise," *Stanford Social Innovation Review* (Spring 2006): 31–38.

52. A. Agrawal, K. Redford, and E. Fearn, "Conservation and Human Displacement," in *State of the Wild* 2008–2009, ed. E. Fearn (Washington, D.C.: Island Press, 2008), 201. See also D. Wilkie et al., "Parks and People: Assessing the Human Welfare Effects of Establishing Protected Areas for Biodiversity Conservation," *Conservation Biology* 20, no. 1 (2006): 247–49.

53. C. Hambler and S. Canney, *Conservation*, 3338; K. Redford, M. Levy, E. Sanderson, and A. de Sherbinin, "What Is the Role for Conservation Organizations in Poverty Alleviation in the World's Wild Places?" *Oryx* 42, no. 4 (2008): 516–28.

54. See for example, P. Kareiva and M. Marvier, "Conservation for the People," *Scientific American* 294, no. 4 (October 2007): 50–57; P. Kareiva, R. Lalasz, and M. Marvier, "Conservation in the Anthropocene: Beyond Solitude and Fragility," *Breakthrough Journal*, Fall 2011, pp. 29–37. For some responses to so-called people-centered conservation, see S. Sanderson and K. Redford, "Contested Relationships Between Biodiversity Conservation and Poverty Alleviation"; S. Sanderson and K. Redford, "The Defense of Conservation Is Not an Attack on the Poor," *Oryx* 38, no. 2 (2004): 146–47; H. Locke and P. Dearden "Rethinking Protected Areas Categories and the New Paradigm"; Agrawal et al., "Conservation and Human Displacement"; M. E. Hannibal, "Sleeping with the Enemy," *Huffington Post*, 2 June 2014, http://www.huffingtonpost.com/mary-ellen-hannibal/sleeping-with-the-enemy_1_b_5423950.html.

55. Thaddeus Miller and his colleagues describe social conservationists as those "who advocate various forms of sustainable use and privilege conservation-oriented development and welfare-oriented goals such as poverty alleviation and social justice." T. Miller et al., "The New Conservation Debate: The View from Practical Ethics," *Biological Conservation* 144 (2011): 948–57.

56. P. Stokowski, "Community Values in Conservation," *Reconstructing Conservation*, ed. B. Minteer and R. Manning, 292, emphasis added.

57. For an argument of why social justice cannot be built on a colonized Earth, see my "Ptolemaic Environmentalism," in *Keeping the Wild: Against the Domestication of Earth*, ed. G. Wuerthner, E. Crist, and T. Butler (Washington, D.C.: Island Press, 2014), 16–30.

58. On the deluded mainstream plan to pursue "sufficient economic growth for everyone to become rich" (in William Rees's words), see W. Rees, "Avoiding Collapse: An Agenda for Sustainable Degrowth and Relocalizing the Economy," *Canadian Centre for Policy Alternatives*, (June 2014): 1–20.

59. M. Shellenberg and T. Nordhaus, "Evolve: The Case for Modernization as the Road to Salvation," in *Love Your Monsters: Postenvironmentalism and the Anthropocene* (Oakland, CA: The Breakthrough Institute, 2011 PDF e-book).

60. What Michael Pollan calls the industrial food chain's "journey of forgetting" applies to the entire gamut of modern material culture, which is always sourced from the natural world (without gratitude) and often at the cost of human impoverishment (with little compunction). M. Pollan, *The Omnivore's Dilemma* (New York: Penguin Press, 2006), 10.

CHRISTOF SCHENCK

1. Brothers Grimm, "Little Red Riding Hood," *Grimms' Fairy Tales: The Complete Fairy Tales of the Brothers Grimm,* http://www.grimmstories.com/en/grimm_fairy-tales/little_red_cap.

2. See the discussion of etymology on the "Wilderness" page on the Wikipedia website, http://de.wikipedia.org/wiki/Wildnis.

3. See the entries for "wilderness," "wildnis," "wildlife," and other words having "wild" as their root on the web page "German Dictionary by Jacob Grimm and Wilhelm Grimm," Berlin-Brandenburg Academy of Science and Humanities— Göttingen Academy of Sciences and Humanities (© 1998–2014 by Trier Center for Digital Humanities / Competence Centre for Electronic Processing and Publication in the Humanities at the University of Trier, http://woerterbuchnetz.de/cgi-bin/WBNetz/wbgui_py?sigle=DWB&mode=Vernetzung&hitlist=&patternlist=&lemid=GW21254.

4. See "Population in Germany," *The Statistica Portal,* on the Statistica website, http://de.statista.com/statistik/faktenbuch/338/a/laender/deutschland/bevoelkerung-in-deutschland/.

5. See the discussion of "road network" on Wikipedia, http://de.wikipedia.org/wiki/Stra%C3%9Fennetz.

6. See the website page "Land Use—What Is It?" (October 21, 2013), http://www.bmub.bund.de/themen/strategien-bilanzen-gesetze/nachhaltige-entwicklung/strategie-und-umsetzung/reduzierung-des-flaechenverbrauchs/.

7. See the discussion of "Natura 2000" on Wikipedia, http://de.wikipedia.org/wiki/Natura_2000.

8. *Convention on Biological Diversity,* United Nations 1992, http://www.cbd.int/doc/legal/cbd-en.pdf.

9. United Nations, "We Can End Poverty," *Millenium Development Goals and Beyond 2015,* http://www.un.org/millenniumgoals/environ.shtml.

10. For further details related to IUCN categories, see the website for the International Union for Conservation of Nature, in particular: http://www.iucn.org/about/work/programmes/gpap_home/gpap_quality/gpap_pacategories/gpap_pacategory2/, and https://portals.iucn.org/library/efiles/html/PAPS-016/4.%20Applying%20the%20categories.html.

11. See the discussion on bark beetles, website for the "National Park Service, Bayerischer Wald," http://www.nationalpark-bayerischer-wald.de/nationalpark/management/waldmanagement/borkenkaefer/bk_bekaempfung.htm; and see further discussion under "Bavarian Forest National Park," http://de.wikipedia.org/wiki/Nationalpark_Bayerischer_Wald.

12. See the website of the Brandenburg Wilderness Foundation, http://www.stiftung-nlb.de/.

13. *National Strategy on Biological Diversity* (August 2007), http://www.bmub.bund.de/service/publikationen/downloads/details/artikel/bmu-brochure-national-strategy-on-biological-diversity/?tx_ttnews%255BbackPid%255D=918.

14. See the "National Parks" section on the website for the Bundesamt für Naturschutz (BFN), or "Academy for Nature Conservation," http://www.bfn.de/0308_nlp.html.

15. Wild Europe, "EC Presidency Conference on Wilderness and Large Natural Habitat Areas," under *Wilderness and Large Natural Areas,* on website of Wild Europe (2014), http://www.wildeurope.org/index.php/about-us/prague-conference.

16. Ibid.

17. Wild Europe, "Wilderness Benefits for EU Strategy," under *Wilderness and Large Natural Areas,* on website of Wild Europe (2014), http://www.wildeurope.org/index.php/benefits/benefits-for-eu-bio-strategy.

18. "Message from Prague: An Agenda for Europe's Wild Areas," Summary of the Conference on Wilderness and Large Natural Habitat Areas, Prague, Czech Republic, May 27–28, 2009, p. 1, http://cmsdata.iucn.org/downloads/090528_final_prague_message.pdf.

19. "Our Common Future, Chapter 2: Towards Sustainable Development" (from A/42/427, Our Common Future: Report of the World Commision on Environment and Development), *UN Documents: Gathering a Body of Global Agreements,* http://www.un-documents.net/ocf-02.htm.

20. Brothers Grimm, "Little Red Riding Hood," *Grimms' Fairy Tales: The Complete Fairy Tales of the Brothers Grimm,* http://www.grimmstories.com/en/grimm_fairy-tales/little_red_cap.

GEORGE MONBIOT

1. See the "Pais Dinogad" page, http://www.cs.ox.ac.uk/people/geraint.jones/rhydychen.org/about.welsh/pais-dinogad.html.

2. D. A. Hetherington, T. C. Lord, and R. M. Jacob, "New Evidence for the Occurrence of Eurasian Lynx (Lynx lynx) in Medieval Britain," *Journal of Quaternary Science* 21, no. 1 (2006): 3–8, doi:10.1002/jqs.960.

3. D. Hetherington, "The Lynx" in *Extinctions and Invasions: A Social History of British Fauna,* ed. T. O'Connor and N. Sykes (Oxford, UK: Windgather Press, 2010).

4. O. Rackham, *The History of the Countryside* (London: J. M. Dent & Sons, 1986).

5. C. Roberts, *The Unnatural History of the Sea* (London: Gaia Books, 2007).

6. H. Van Lavieren, "Can No-take Fishery Reserves Help Protect Our Oceans?" on the website *Our World,* United Nations University (February 2012), http://ourworld.unu.edu/en/can-no-take-fisheries-help-protect-our-oceans/.

7. D. Hetherington, "The Lynx in Britain's Past, Present and Future," *ECOS* 27, no.1 (2006): 66–74.

8. D. Hetherington et al., "A Potential Habitat Network for the Eurasian Lynx (*Lynx lynx*) in Scotland," *Mammal Review* 38, no. 4 (2008): 285–303.

9. Rewilding Europe, "Making Europe a Wilder Place," 2012 brochure, http://www.rewildingeurope.com/assets/uploads/Downloads/Rewilding-Europe-Brochure-2012.pdf.

10. See, respectively, the website for Trees for Life at http://www.treesforlife.org.uk/ and for Knepp Castle Estate at http://www.knepp.co.uk/.

JOHN DAVIS

1. R. Noss, *Forgotten Grasslands of the South* (Washington, D.C.: Island Press, 2012).

2. D. Foreman, *Rewilding North America: A Vision for Conservation in the 21st Century* (Washington, D.C.: Island Press, 2004).

3. For more on Rewilding Europe, see the foundation's website, http://www. rewildingeurope.com/.

HARVEY LOCKE AND KARSTEN HEUER

1. G. Catlin, 1844 *Letters and Notes in the Manners, Customs, and Conditions of the North American Indians* (1844), 2 Vols. (London; repr., New York: Dover, 1973) 1: pp. 261–62.

2. H. Locke, "Civil Society and Protected Areas: Lessons from Canada," *The George Wright Forum* 26, no. 2 (2009).

3. See the website for Highway Wilding, Wildlife Monitoring and Research Collaborative in the Canadian Rocky Mountains, http://highwaywilding.org/.

4. *H. Locke and W. Francis,* "Strategic Acquisition and Management of Small Parcels of Private Lands in Key Areas to Address Habitat Fragmentation at the Scale of the Yellowstone to Yukon Region," *Ecological Restoration* 30, no. 4 (December 2012): 293–95.

5. Nature Editorial, "Think Big," *Nature* 469, no. 131 (Jan. 2011), doi:10.1038/469131a.

6. For further reading, see also: C. Chester, *Conservation across Borders: Biodiversity in an Interdependent World* (Washington, D.C.: Island Press, 2006); N. E. Heller and E. Zavaleta, "Biodiversity Management in the Face of Climate Change: A Review of 22 years of Recommendations," *Biological Conservation* 142 (2009): 14–32; J. A. Hodgson, C. D. Thomas, B. A. Wintle, and A. Moilanen, "Climate Change, Connectivity and Conservation Decision Making: Back to Basics," *Journal of Applied Ecology* 46, no. 5 (2009): 964–69, doi:10.1111/j.1365-2664.2009.01695.x; W. Konstant, H. Locke, and J. Hanna, "Waterton-Glacier International Peace Park: The First of Its Kind" in *Transboundary Conservation: A New Vision for Protected Areas*, ed. R. A. Mettermeier et al. (Mexico: Cemex-Agrupacion Sierra Madre-Conservation International, 2005); H. Locke, "Preserving the Wild Heart of North America: The Wildlands Project and the Yellowstone to Yukon Biodiversity Strategy," *Borealis* 15 (1994): 18; H. Locke, "The Need and Opportunity for Landscape Scale Conservation in the Yellowstone to Yukon Region: A Vision for the 21st Century," in *Greater Yellowstone Public Lands: A Century of Discovery, Hard Lessons, and Bright Prospects, Proceedings of the 8th Biennial Scientific Conference on the Greater Yellowstone Ecosystem,* ed. A. Wondrak-Biel (Wyoming: Yellowstone Center for Resources, Yellowstone National Park, 2006), pp. 99–108, http://www. nps.gov/yell/naturescience/8thconferenceproceedings.htm; H. Locke, "Civil Society and Protected Areas: Lessons from Canada," *The George Wright Forum* 26, no. 2, (2009); H. Locke, "Transboundary Cooperation to Achieve Wilderness Protection and Large Landscape Conservation," *Park Science* 28, no. 3 (Winter 2011–2012); H. Locke, ed., *Yellowstone to Yukon: The Journey of Wildlife and Art* (Golden, CO: Fulcrum Press, 2012); H. Locke and M. McKinney, "Flathead Valley

Flashpoint," *Water without Borders: Canada, the U.S. and Transboundary Water,* ed. E. S. Norman, A. Cohen, and K. Bakker (Toronto: University of Toronto Press, 2013); National Park Service, "A Call to Action: Preparing for a Second Century of Stewardship and Engagement" (Washington, D.C.: National Park Service, 2011), http://www.nps.gov/CallToAction; W. Newmark, "A Land Bridge Island Perspective on Mammalian Extinctions in Western North American National Parks," *Nature* 325 (1987): 430–32; Parks Canada Agency, *Unimpaired for Future Generations? Protecting Ecological Integrity with Canada's National Parks,* 2 Vols. (Ottawa, Ontario, Canada: Report of the Panel on the Ecological Integrity of Canada's National Parks, 2000); K. Salazar, T. J. Vilsak, L. P. Jackson, and N. H. Sutley "America's Great Outdoors: A Promise to Future Generations" (Washington, D.C.: U.S. Government Printing Office, 2011), http://americasgreatoutdoors.gov/report; M. Soulé and J. Terborgh, *Continental Conservation: Scientific Foundations of Regional Reserve Networks* (Washington, D.C.: The Wildlands Project and Island Press, 1999); G. Worboys, W. L. Francis, and M. Lockwood, eds., *Connectivity Conservation Management: A Global Guide* (London: Earthscan, 2010).

GEORGE WUERTHNER

1. L. C. Cramton, *Early History of Yellowstone National Park and Its Relation to National Park Policies* (Ann Arbor: University of Michigan Library, 1932).

2. National Parks Worldwide, http://nationalparksworldwide.com/.

3. G. Wuerthner, *Yellowstone: A Visitor's Companion* (Harrisburg, PA: Stackpole Books, 1992), pp. 24–31.

4. E. Marris, *Rambunctious Garden: Saving Nature in a Post–Wild World* (New York: Bloomsbury, 2011), pp. 18–25.

5. G. Wuerthner, *Yellowstone: A Visitor's Companion,* p. 4.

6. R. Bartlett, *Yellowstone: A Wilderness Besieged* (Tucson: University of Arizona Press, 1985), pp. 12–73.

7. M. D. Spence, *Dispossessing the Wilderness: Indian Removal and the Making of the National Parks* (New York: Oxford University Press, 1999).

8. A. L. Haines, *Yellowstone National Park: Its Exploration and Establishment* (Washington, D.C.: National Park Service, U.S. Dept. of the Interior, 1974).

9. G. Black, *Empires of Shadows: The Epic Story of Yellowstone* (New York: St. Martin's Press, 2012), pp. 109–10.

10. "Three Gorges Dam," on the website of International Rivers, http://www.internationalrivers.org/campaigns/three-gorges-dam.

11. G. Wuerthner, "The Yellowstone Fires of 1988: A Living Wilderness" in *Wildfire: A Century of Failed Forest Policy* (Covelo, CA: Island Press, 2006), pp. 46–70.

12. T. R. Vale, "Fire and Native People: Natural or Humanized Landscape?" in *Wildfire: A Century of Failed Forest Policy,* ed. George Wuerthner (Covelo, CA: Island Press, 2006), pp. 13–16.

13. W. Ludlow, *Report of a Reconnaissance from Carroll, Montana Territory to Yellowstone National Park Made in the Summer of 1875* (Washington, D.C.: U.S. Government Printing Office, 1875).

14. W. E. Strong, *A Trip to the Yellowstone National Park in July, August and September 1875* (Norman, OK: University of Oklahoma Press, 1968).

15. R. B. Keiter, *To Conserve Unimpaired: The Evolution of the National Park Idea* (Covelo, CA: Island Press, 2013), p. 204.

16. L. C. Cramton, *Early History of Yellowstone National Park and Its Relation to National Park Policies* (Ann Arbor: University of Michigan Library, 1932).

17. A. Murie, *Fauna of the National Parks of the United States: Ecology of the Coyote in Yellowstone,* National Park Fauna Series 40 (Washington, D.C.: U.S. Government Printing Office, 1940).

18. A. S. Leopold, S. A. Cain, C. A. Cottam, I. N. Gabrielson, T. L. Kimball, *Wildlife Management in the National Parks: The Leopold Report,* 1963, http://www.nps.gov/history/history/online_books/leopold/leopold.htm.

19. J. D. Varley and P. Schullery, *Freshwater Wilderness: Yellowstone Fishes and their World* (Wyoming: Yellowstone Library and Museum Association, 1983), pp. 100–107.

20. R. F. Noss et al., "A Multicriteria Assessment of the Irreparability and Vulnerability of Sites in the Greater Yellowstone Ecosystem," *Conservation Biology* 16, no. 4 (2002): 895–908.

21. Yellowstone to Yukon Conservation Initiative, http://y2y.net/.

MARC BEKOFF

1. M. Bekoff, ed., *Ignoring Nature No More: The Case for Compassionate Conservation* (Chicago: University of Chicago Press, 2013).

2. M. Bekoff, *Rewilding Our Hearts: Building Pathways of Compassion and Coexistence* (Novato, CA: New World Library, 2014).

3. For more on the Centre for Compassionate Conservation, see the link on the UTS (University of Technology, Sydney) website, http://www.uts.edu.au/research-and-teaching/our-research/centre-compassionate-conservation.

4. M. Bekoff, *Rewilding Our Hearts: Building Pathways of Compassion and Coexistence.*

5. M. Bekoff, *The Emotional Lives of Animals* (Novato, CA: New World Library, 2007); M. Bekoff, *Why Dogs Hump and Bees Get Depressed: The Fascinating Science of Animal Intelligence, Emotions, Friendship, and Conservation* (Novato, CA: New World Library, 2013).

6. M. Bekoff, "First Do No Harm," *New Scientist* (28 August 2010), pp. 24–25, http://www.newscientist.com/article/mg20727750.100-conservation-and-compassion-first-do-no-harm.html#.U3DtyMbacVs.

7. M. Bekoff, *Minding Animals: Emotions, Awareness, and Heart* (New York: Oxford University Press, 2002).

8. See the website for Animals Asia, https://www.animalsasia.org/us/.

9. P. Shipman, *The Animal Connection: A New Perspective on What Makes Us Human* (New York: W. W. Norton & Co., 2011).

10. T. T. Williams, *Finding Beauty in a Broken World* (New York: Pantheon, 2008).

11. M. Soulé and R. Noss, "Rewilding and Biodiversity: Complementary Goals for Continental Conservation," *Wild Earth* (Fall 1998), pp. 15, 18–28.

12. See the website for The Rewilding Institute, http://rewilding.org/rewildit/.

13. See the Rewilding Institute, http://rewilding.org/rewildit/.

14. A. Balmford and R. M. Cowling, "Fusion or Failure: The Future of Conservation Biology," *Conservation Biology* 3 (June 2006): 692–95, doi:10.1111/j.1523-1739.2006.00434.x.

15. P. W. Schultz, "Conservation Means Behavior," *Conservation Biology* 25 (November 2011): 1080–83.

16. M. Bekoff, *Rewilding Our Hearts: Building Pathways of Compassion and Coexistence.*

SPENCER R. PHILLIPS

1. R. F. Kennedy Jr., *Humankind* (Podcast), Produced by David Freudberg, retrieved October 14, 2014, from http://www.humanmedia.org/catalog/program.php?products_id=31.

2. J. Muir, in *John of the Mountains: The Unpublished Journals of John Muir*, ed. W. M. Hanna (Madison, WI: University of Wisconsin Press), p. 138.

3. The Wilderness Society, *9 Surprising Reasons for Kids to Get Outside This Summer*, Retrieved July 12, 2014 from http://wilderness.org/blog/9-surprising-reasons-kids-get-outside-summer.

4. A. Coumo. Press Release: "Governor Cuomo Announces Conservation Easement of Adirondack Site Where Federal Wilderness Act Was Penned," Albany, NY, September 10, 2014, retrieved from https://www.governor.ny.gov/press/09102014-easement-wilderness-act.

5. Proverbs 14:12 and 16:25 (New American Standard Bible).

6. Deuteronomy 1:30–32, as translated in E. H. Peterson, *The Message*, retrieved from Bible Gateway website Oct. 12, 2014, https://www.biblegateway.com/.

7. Deuteronomy 8:2, as translated in E. H. Peterson, *The Message.*

8. See Leviticus 16:21-22.

9. Luke 3:4 (New Revised Standard Version [NRSV]).

10. Matthew 3:1–2 (NRSV).

11. Matthew 4:2–11, as translated in E. H. Peterson, *The Message*, retrieved from Bible Gateway website Oct. 12, 2014, https://www.biblegateway.com/.

12. Luke 22:42 (NRSV).

13. Matthew 5:3, as translated in E. H. Peterson, *The Message*, retrieved from Bible Gateway website Oct. 12, 2014, https://www.biblegateway.com/, 12 Oct. 2014.

14. C. Solomon, "Rethinking the Wild: The Wilderness Act Is Facing a Midlife Crisis," *New York Times*, 5 July 2014, http://www.nytimes.com/2014/07/06/opinion/sunday/the-wilderness-act-is-facing-a-midlife-crisis.html?_r=0.

15. Wilderness Society founder Harvey Broome said of the wilderness, "Here are bits of eternity, which have a preciousness beyond all accounting." See the Harvey Broome page on the website of The Wilderness Society [accessed October 12, 2014], http://wilderness.org/bios/founders/harvey-broome.

16. C. Solomon, "Rethinking the Wild," *New York Times.*

17. Never mind that this seems to be exactly the intention of redistricting, voter ID laws, and other measures taken in several states, but that's another conversation.

18. R. Marshall, "The Problem of the Wilderness," *Scientific Monthly* 30, no. 2 (February 1930): 141–48. [Author's emphasis on "freedom."] Note that Marshall singles out the *freedom* of the wilderness as that attribute in need of defense.

19. C. Solomon, "Rethinking the Wild," *New York Times.*

20. I should emphasize that such activities to protect property, restore or maintain natural conditions, or enhance recreational safety may be appropriate and effective outside of wilderness. It is okay to have gardens and climbing gyms, just not everywhere.

TIM CARO

1. J. Terborgh, C. van Schaik, L. Davenport, and M. Rao, eds., *Making Parks Work: Strategies for Preserving Tropical Nature* (Washington, D.C.: Island Press, 2002).

2. E. Marris, *Rambunctious Garden: Saving Nature in a Post-Wild World* (New York: Bloomsbury, 2011); P. Kareiva, R. Lalasz, and M. Marvier, "Conservation in the Anthropocene: Beyond Solitude and Fragility" in *Love Your Monsters: Post-environmentalism and the Anthropocene*, ed. M. Shellenberger and T. Nordhaus (Washington, D.C.: Breakthrough Institute, 2011), pp. 26–36.

3. T. Caro, J. Darwin, T. Forrester, C. Ledoux-Boom, and C. Wells, "Conservation in the Anthropocene," *Conservation Biology* 26 (2011): 185–88.

4. Katavi-Rukwa Ecosystem Management Plan, unpublished report (United Republic of Tanzania, Ministry of Tourism and Natural Resources, Tanzania National Parks, 2002).

5. N. Burgess et al., *Terrestrial Ecoregions of Africa and Madagascar: A Conservation Assessment* (Washington, D.C.: Island Press, World Wildlife Fund, 2004).

6. T. Banda, M. W. Schwartz, and T. Caro, "Woody Vegetation Structure and Composition along a Protection Gradient in a Miombo Ecosystem of Western Tanzania," *Forest Ecology and Management* 230 (2006): 179–85; T. Banda et al., "The Woodland Vegetation of the Katavi-Rukwa Ecosystem in Western Tanzania," *Forest Ecology and Management* 255 (2008): 3382–95.

7. T. Caro, "Densities of Mammals in Partially Protected Areas: The Katavi Ecosystem of Western Tanzania," *Journal of Applied Ecology* 36 (1999a): 205–17; T. Caro, "Abundance and Distribution of Mammals in Katavi National Park, Tanzania," *African Journal of Ecology* 37 (1999b): 305–13; T. Caro, "Umbrella Species: Critique and Lessons from East Africa," *Animal Conservation* 6 (2003): 171–81.

8. For definitions, see T. Caro, T. A. Gardner, C. J. Stoner, E. Fitzherbert, and T. R. B. Davenport, "Assessing the Effectiveness of Protected Areas: Paradoxes Call for Pluralism in Evaluating Conservation Performance," *Diversity and Distributions* 15 (2009a): 178–82.

9. M. Waltert, B. Meyer, and C. Kiffner, "Habitat Availability, Hunting or Poaching: What Affects Distribution and Density of Large Mammals in Western Tanzania Woodlands? *African Journal of Ecology* 47 (2009): 737–46.

10. P. Mgawe, M. Borgerhoff Mulder, T. Caro, and S. J. Seel, *Historia ya Kabila la Wapimbwe* (Dar es Salaam: Mkuki ya Nyota, 2012a).

11. M. Borgerhoff Mulder, T. Caro, and O. A. Msago, "The Role of Research in Evaluating Conservation Strategies in Tanzania: The Case of the Katavi-Rukwa Ecosystem," *Conservation Biology* 21 (2007): 647–58.

12. P. Mgawe, M. Borgerhoff Mulder, T. Caro, A. Martin, and C. Kiffner, "Factors Affecting Bushmeat Consumption in the Katavi-Rukwa Ecosystem of Tanzania," *Tropical Conservation Science* 5 (2012b): 446–62.

13. T. Caro, "Densities of Mammals in Partially Protected Areas: The Katavi Ecosystem of Western Tanzania"; T. Caro, "Umbrella Species: Critique and Lessons from East Africa."

14. T. Caro, "Densities of Mammals in Partially Protected Areas: The Katavi Ecosystem of Western Tanzania."

15. A. Martin, T. Caro, and M. Borgerhoff Mulder, "Bushmeat Consumption in Western Tanzania: A Comparative Analysis from the Same Ecosystem," *Tropical Conservation Science* 5 (2012): 351–62; A. Martin and T. Caro, "Illegal Hunting in the Katavi-Rukwa Ecosystem," *African Journal of Ecology* 51 (2013): 172–75.

16. T. Caro et al., "Consequences of Different Forms of Conservation for Large Mammals in Tanzania: Preliminary Analyses," *African Journal of Ecology* 36 (1998): 303–20.

17. T. Gardner, T. Caro, E. Fitzherbert, T. Banda, and P. Lalbhai, "Conservation Value of Multiple-Use Areas in East Africa," *Conservation Biology* 21 (2007): 1516–25.

18. W. F. Laurance et al., "Averting Biodiversity Collapse in Tropical Forest Protected Areas," *Nature* 489 (2012): 290–94.

19. T. Caro and P. Scholte, "When Protection Falters," *African Journal of Ecology* 45 (2007): 233–35; D. Western, S. Russell, and I. Cuthill, "The Status of Wildlife in Protected Areas Compared to Non-protected Areas of Kenya," *PLoS ONE* 4, no. 7 (2009): e6140; I. D. Craigie et al., "Large Mammal Population Declines in Africa's Protected Areas," *Biological Conservation* 143 (2010): 2221–28.

20. C. Stoner et al., "Changes in Herbivore Populations across Large Areas of Tanzania," *African Journal of Ecology* 45 (2007a): 202–15.

21. C. Stoner, T. Caro, S. Mduma, C. Mlingwa, G. Sabuni, and M. Borner, "Assessment of Effectiveness of Protection Strategies in Tanzania Based on a Decade of Survey Data for Large Herbivores," *Conservation Biology* 21 (2007b): 635–46.

22. J. O. Ogutu, N. Owen-Smith, H.-P. Piepho, and M. Y. Said, "Continuing Wildlife Population Declines and Range Contraction in the Mara Region of Kenya During 1977–2009," *Journal of Zoology* 285 (2011): 99–109.

23. D. Roe, F. Nelson, and C. Sandbook, eds., *Community Management of Natural Resources in Africa: Impacts, Experiences and Future Directions* (London: International Institute of the Environment and Development, 2009).

24. See, for example, K. S. Andam, P. J. Ferraro, A. Pfaff, G. A. Sanchez-Azofeifa, and J. A. Robalino, "Measuring the Effectiveness of Protected Area Networks in Reducing Deforestation," *Proceedings of the National Academy of Sciences* 105 (2008): 16089–94; and see also, for example, J. S. Brooks, K. A. Weylan, and M. Borgerhoff Mulder, "How National Context, Project Design, and Local Community Characteristics Influence Success in Community-Based Conservation Projects," *Proceedings of the National Academy of Sciences* 109 (2012): 21265–70.

25. A. Agrawal and C. C. Gibson, "Enchantment and Disenchantment: The Role of Community in Natural Resource Conservation," *World Development* 27 (1999): 629–49; E. Ostrom, "A Diagnostic Approach for Going beyond Panaceas," *Proceedings of the National Academy of Sciences* 25 (2007): 15181–87.

26. A. S. L. Rodrigues et al., "Effectiveness of the Global Protected Area Network in Representing Species Diversity," *Nature* 428 (2004): 640–43; A. Beresford, G. Buchanan, P. Donald, S. Butchart, L. Fishpool, and C. Rondinini, "Poor Overlap between the Distribution of Protected Areas and Globally Threatened Birds in Africa," *Animal Conservation* 14 (2011): 99–107; S. H. Butchart et al., "Protecting Important Sites for Biodiversity Contributes to Meeting Global Conservation Targets," *PLoS ONE* 7 (2012): e32529; C. N. Jenkins, S. L. Pimm, and L. N. Joppa, "Global Patterns of Terrestrial Vertebrate Diversity and Conservation," *Proceedings of the National Academy of Sciences* 110 (2013): E2602–E2610.

27. W. F. Laurance, "When Bigger Is Better: The Need for Amazonian Mega-Reserves," *Trends in Ecology and Evolution* 20 (2005): 645–48; C. A. Peres, "Why We Need Megareserves in Amazonia," *Conservation Biology* 19 (2005): 728–33.

28. UNESCO, task force on: "Criteria and Guidelines for the Choice and Establishment of Biosphere Reserves"—Final Report (Paris: UNESCO, MAB report series, 1974); R. F. Noss, "A Regional Landscape Approach to Maintain Diversity," *BioScience* 33 (1983): 700–06.

29. F. Nelson, N. Rugemeleza, and W. A. Rodgers, "The Evolution and Reform of Tanzanian Wildlife Management," *Conservation and Society* 5 (2007): 232–61.

30. D. A. Rudnick et al., "The Role of Landscape Connectivity in Planning and Implementing Conservation and Restoration Priorities," *Issues in Ecology* 16 (2012): 1–20.

31. C. W. Epps, S. K. Wasser, J. L. Keim, B. M. Mutayoba, and J. S. Brashares, "Quantifying Past and Present Connectivity Illuminates a Rapidly Changing Landscape for the African Elephant," *Molecular Ecology* 22 (2013): 1574–88.

32. T. Jones, T. Caro, and T. R. B. Davenport, "Wildlife Corridors in Tanzania" (Arusha, Tanzania: Tanzania Wildlife Research Institute—TAWIRI, 2009), 60.

33. T. Caro, T. Jones, and T. R. B. Davenport, "Realities of Documenting Wildlife Corridors in Tropical Countries," *Biological Conservation* 142 (2009b): 2807–811.

34. T. T. Struhsaker, "Strategies for Conserving Forest National Parks in Africa with a Case Study from Uganda" in *Making Parks Work: Strategies for Preserving Tropical Nature*, ed. J. Terborgh, C. van Schaik, L. Davenport, and M. Rao (Washington, D.C.: Island Press, 2002), pp. 97–111.

35. T. Caro and J. Riggio, "The Big 5 and Conservation," *Animal Conservation* 16 (2013): 261–62.

36. E. Di Minin, I. Fraser, R. Slotow, and D. C. MacMillan, "Understanding Heterogeneous Preference of Tourists for Big Game Species: Implications for Conservation and Management," *Animal Conservation* 16 (2013): 249–58.

KATHLEEN H. FITZGERALD

1. For more on Julius K. Nyerere, his views on wildlife conservation, and this quote from the *Arusha Manifesto*, see the Julius Nyerere website, http://www.juliusnyerere.info/index.php/nyerere/about/category/nyerere_philosophy/.

2. In 2007, 13 rhino were killed in South Africa. Over 1,000 rhino were killed in South Africa in 2013. This represents a 7,692 percent increase. The total rhino population in Africa is less than 25,000. African Wildlife Foundation: Elephant, Rhino Strategies document, 2014. See also rhino poaching statistics from Save the Rhino, http://www.savetherhino.org/rhino_info/poaching_statistics, accessed 24 November 2014.

3. Ibid.

4. African Wildlife Foundation: African Ape Initiative Strategy, 2013. Campbell, G., J. Junker, C. Boesch and H. Kuhl. 2012. Global A.P.E.S. status report: A report with information from the A.P.E.S. Project. UNEP/UNESCO/GRASP/Council 2/7.

5. H. Van Rensburg, "Africa Is Rising Fast," *Forbes* (November 2012).

6. See the website for Congo Basin Forest Partnership, http://pfbc-cbfp.org/Stateoftheforest.html.

7. BBC, "Deforestation 'Faster in Africa'," *BBC News*, 26 May 2009, http://news.bbc.co.uk/2/hi/africa/8066871.stm.

8. "Dwindling Space for Africa's Great Apes," provided by Max Planck Society on the Phys.Org website, 26 September 2012, http://phys.org/news/2012-09-dwindling-space-africa-great-apes.html.

9. International Institute for Environment and Development. Land Grab Briefing. September 2013.

10. World Bank, *Where Is the Wealth of Nations? Measuring Capital for the 21st Century* (Washington, D.C.: World Bank, 2006) http://siteresources.worldbank.org/INTEEI/214578-1110886258964/20748034/All.pdf

11. *State of Biodiversity in Africa 2010*, United Nations Biodiversity Program.

12. N. Dudley, ed., *Guidelines for Applying Protected Area Management Categories* (Gland, Switzerland: IUCN, 2008).

13. P. Udoto, "Wildlife as a Lifeline to Kenya's Economy: Making Memorable Visitor Experiences," *The George Wright Forum* 29, no. 1 (2012): 51–58.

14. *South Africa Tourism Annual Report* 2012, http://www.southafrica.net/uploads/files/2012_Annual_Report_v9_03092013.pdf.

15. D. J. McGahey et al., "Investigating Climate Change Vulnerability and Planning for Adaptation: Learning from a Study of Climate Change Impacts on the Mountain Gorilla in the Albertine Rift," *Natural Science* 5 (2013): 10–17.

16. International Panel on Climate Change, 2007 Report summary for policy makers.

17. W. D Newmark, "Isolation of African protected areas," *Frontiers in Ecology and the Environment* 6 (2008): 321–328; http://dx.doi.org/10.1890/070003.

18. W. Richard, S. Fynn, and M. C. Bonyongo, "Functional Conservation Areas and the Future of Africa's Wildlife, *African Journal of Ecology*, 49 (2010): 175–88.

19. K. H. Fitzgerald, "Community Payment for Ecosystem Services in the Amboseli Ecosystem: Leasing Land for Livelihoods and Wildlife," Technical Paper Series, African Wildlife Foundation (September 2013), available at http://www.awf.org/about/resources/books-and-papers.

20. N. Dudley, ed., *Guidelines for Applying Protected Area Management Categories* (Gland, Switzerland: IUCN, 2008).

21. J. Hutton, W. M. Adams, and C. James, "Back to the Barriers: Changing Narratives in Biodiversity Conservation," *Forum for Development Studies* 32, no. 2 (2005; published online 28 Jan. 2011): 341–70, doi:10.1080/08039410.2005.9666319, available at http://www.tandfonline.com/doi/abs/10.1080/08039410.2005.9666319#preview.

22. See the website of the Namibian Association of CBNRM (Community-Based Natural Resource Management) Support Organisations, http://www.nacso.org.na/index.php.

23. Krug, W. Private Supply of Protected Land in Southern Africa: A Review of Markets, Approaches, Barriers and Issues. World Bank/OECD International Workshop on Market Creation for Biodiversity Products and Services Paris. 2001.

24. Zimbabwe National Environmental Policy, 2003.

25. J. Elliot, H. Gibbons, D. King, A. King, and T. Lemenager. Exploring Environmental Complementarity between Type of Protected Areas in Kenya (2014), available at http://www.afd.fr/webdav/shared/PUBLICATIONS/RECHERCHE/Scientifiques/Focales/19-VA-Focales.pdf.

26. *The Value of the Ethiopian Protected Area System: Message to Policy Makers* (Ethiopia Wildlife Conservation Authority, December 2010), http://www.cbd.int/financial/values/ethiopia-valueprotectedareas.pdf.

ELIZABETH L. BENNETT

1. IUCN/SSC. *Strategic Planning for Species Conservation: A Handbook, Version 1.0* (Gland, Switzerland: IUCN Species Survival Commission, 2008).

2. E. Sanderson, J. Forrest, C. Loucks, J. Ginsberg, and E. Dinerstein, *Setting Priorities for the Conservation and Recovery of Wild Tigers: 2005–2015: The Technical Assessment* (New York and Washington, D.C.: Wildlife Conservation Society, WWF, Smithsonian and National Fish and Wildlife Foundation—Save the Tiger Fund, 2006); J. F. Oates et al., *Regional Action Plan for the Conservation of the Cross River Gorilla* (*Gorilla* gorilla diehli) (Arlington, VA: IUCN/Species Survival Commission Primate Specialist Group and Conservation International, 2007).

3. R. E. Bodmer and P. E. Puertas, "Community-based Co-management of Wildlife in the Peruvian Amazon" in *Hunting for Sustainability in Tropical Forests,* ed. J. G. Robinson and E. L. Bennett (New York: Columbia University Press, 2000), pp. 395–409.; J. G. Robinson and K. H. Redford, "Jack of All Trades, Master of None: Inherent Contradictions Among ICD Approaches" in *Getting Biodiversity*

Projects to Work: Towards More Effective Conservation and Development, ed. T. O. McShane and M. P. Wells (New York: Columbia University Press, 2004) pp. 10–34; C. M. Hill, "Working with Communities to Achieve Conservation Goals" in *Wildlife and Society: The Science of Human Dimensions,* ed. M. J. Manfredo, J. J. Vaske, P. J. Brown, D. D. Decker, and E. A. Duke (Washington, D.C.: Island Press, 2009), pp. 117–128.

4. J. G. Robinson, "Recognizing Differences and Establishing Clear-eyed Partnerships: A Response to Vermeulen and Sheil," *Oryx* 41 (2007): 443–44; R. Nasi et al., *Conservation and Use of Wildlife-Based Resources: The Bushmeat Crisis,* Technical Series no. 33 (Secretariat of the Convention on Biological Diversity, Montreal, and Center for International Forestry Research, Bogor, Indonesia, 2008); J. G. Robinson and H. Queiroz, "Márcio Ayres: New Approaches to the Conservation and Management of Protected Areas in Amazonia" in *The Amazon Várzea: The Decade Past and the Decade Ahead,* ed. M. Pinedo-Vasquez, M. L. Ruffino, R. R. Sears, E. S. Brondizio, and C. Padoch (New York: Springer Verlag and New York Botanical Garden Press, 2011).

5. J. M. Hutton and N. Leader-Williams, "Sustainable Use and Incentive-Driven Conservation: Realigning Human and Conservation Interests," *Oryx* 37 (2003): 215–26.

6. T. Milliken, R. W. Burns, and L. Sangalakula, *The Elephant Trade Information System (ETIS) and the Illicit Trade in Ivory,* Report to the 15th Meeting of the CITES Conference of the Parties, CoP 15, Doc. 44.1 Annex (2009b), http://www. cites.org/common/cop/15/doc/E15-44-01A.pdf [accessed 20 March 2010].

7. T. Milliken, R. W. Burns, and L. Sangalakula, *The Elephant Trade Information System (ETIS) and the Illicit Trade in Ivory,* Report to the 15th Meeting of the CITES Conference of the Parties, CoP 15, Doc. 44.1 Annex (2009b).

8. TRAFFIC, *South African Delegates Visit Viet Nam to Address Illegal Rhino Horn Trade* (2010a), http://www.traffic.org/home/2010/10/20/south-african-delegates-visit-viet-nam-to-address-illegal-rh.html [accessed 3 December 2010].

9. E. J. Milner-Gullard et al., "Dramatic Declines in Saiga Antelope Population," *Oryx* 35 (2001): 340–45; L. Li, Y. Zhou, and E. L. Bennett, *Report of a Survey on Saiga Horn in Markets in China* (2007), Report to the 14th Meeting of the CITES Conference of the Parties, CoP14 Inf 14, http://www.cites.org/common/cop/14/inf/E14i-14.pdf [accessed 20 March 2010].

10. E. Sanderson et al., *Setting Priorities for the Conservation and Recovery of Wild Tigers: 2005–2015: The Technical Assessment.*

11. J. Walston et al., "Bringing the Tiger Back from the Brink—The Six Percent Solution," *PLoS Biology* 8, no. 9 (2010): e1000485, doi:10.1371/journal. pbio.1000485.

12. A. Johnson, personal communication.

13. F. M. Ali, *India Tiger Park "Has No Tigers,"* BBC News, 2009, http://news.bbc. co.uk/2/hi/south_asia/8150382.stm [accessed 20 March 2010].

14. M. E. Zimmerman, "The Black Market for Wildlife: Combating Transnational Organized Crime in the Illegal Wildlife Trade," *Vanderbilt Journal of Transnational Law* 36 (2003): 1657–89; E. L. Bennett, "Social Dimensions of

Managing Hunting in Tropical Forests" in *Wildlife and Society: The Science of Human Dimensions,* ed. M. J. Manfredo, J. J. Vaske, P. J. Brown, D. D. Decker, and E. A. Duke (Washington, D.C.: Island Press, 2009) pp. 289–300; T. Milliken, R. H. Emslie, and B. Talukdar, *African and Asian Rhinoceroses—Status, Conservation, and Trade,* A report from the IUCN Species Survival Commission African and Asian Rhino Specialist Groups and TRAFFIC to the CITES Secretariat pursuant to Resolution Conf. 9.14 (Rev. CoP14) and Decision 14.89. Report to the 15th Meeting of the CITES Conference of the Parties, CoP 15 Doc. 45.1 (Rev1) Annex, (2009a), http://www.cites.org/eng/cop/15/doc/E15-45-01A.pdf [accessed 20 March 2010]; B. Christy, "Asia's Wildlife Trade: The Kingpin," *National Geographic* (January 2010), http://ngm.nationalgeographic.com/2010/01/asian-wildlife/christy-text/1 [accessed 20 March 2010]; CITES Secretariat, *Monitoring of Illegal Hunting in Elephant Range states.* Report to the 15th Meeting of the Conference of the Parties (2010a), CoP 15 Doc. 44.2, http://www.cites.org/eng/cop/15/doc/E15-44-02.pdf [accessed 20 March 2010].

15. Anon., *Vietnam Seizes Thousands of Smuggled Pangolins* (2008a), http://www.earthtimes.org/articles/news/189494,vietnam-seizes-thousands-of-smuggled-pangolins.html [accessed 20 March 2010]; S. K. Wasser et al., "Combating the Illegal Trade in African Elephant Ivory with DNA Forensics," *Conservation Biology,* 22 (2008): 1065–71; S. Guynup, "On the Ground: Pangolins in Peril," *Defenders Magazine,* (Winter 2010), http://www.defenders.org/newsroom/defenders_magazine/winter_2010/on_the_ground_pangolins_in_peril.php [accessed 3 December 2010]; A. Kramer, "At Russia-China Border, Bear Paws Sell Best," *New York Times* (30 June 2010), http://www.nytimes.com/2010/06/30/world/asia/30animals.html [accessed 3 December 2010].

16. B. Davies, *Black Market: Inside the Endangered Species Trade in Asia* (San Rafael, CA: Earth Aware Editions, 2005); World Bank, *Going, Going, Gone... The Illegal Trade in Wildlife in East and South-east Asia* (Washington, D.C.: World Bank, Environment and Social Development Department, East Asia and Pacific Region, 2005); B. Christy, "Asia's Wildlife Trade: The Kingpin," *National Geographic* (January 2010), http://ngm.nationalgeographic.com/2010/01/asian-wildlife/christy-text/1 [accessed 20 March 2010].

17. TRAFFIC, *What's Driving the Wildlife Trade? A Review of Expert Opinion on Economic and Social Drivers of the Wildlife Trade and Trade Control Efforts in Cambodia, Indonesia, Lao PDR and Vietnam* (Washington, D.C.: East Asia and Pacific Region Sustainable Development Department, World Bank, 2008).

18. T. Milliken, R. H. Emslie, and B. Talukdar, *African and Asian Rhinoceroses— Status, Conservation, and Trade*; T. Milliken, R. W. Burns, and L. Sangalakula, *The Elephant Trade Information System (ETIS) and the Illicit Trade in Ivory,* Report to the 15th Meeting of the CITES Conference of the Parties, CoP 15, Doc. 44.1 Annex (2009b).

19. CITES Secretariat, *Monitoring of Illegal Trade in Ivory and Other Elephant Specimens,* Report to the 15th Meeting of the Conference of the Parties, CoP 15 Doc 44.1 (Rev. 1) (2010b), http://www.cites.org/eng/cop/15/doc/E15-44-01.pdf [accessed 20 March 2010].

20. T. Milliken, R. W. Burns, and L. Sangalakula, *The Elephant Trade Information System (ETIS) and the Illicit Trade in Ivory*, Report to the 15th Meeting of the CITES Conference of the Parties, CoP 15, Doc. 44.1 Annex (2009b).

21. Anon., *Wild Animal Breeding Law Sparks Controversy* (2008b), http://english. vietnamnet.vn/social/2008/06/787765/ [accessed 20 March 2010].

22. Anon., *Huge Seizure of Tiger Skins, Bear Paws and Saiga Horns in Russian Far East* (2007), http://www.wildlifeextra.com/go/news/russia-tiger-skins. html&template=news_archive_item#cr [accessed 20 March 2010].

23. TRAFFIC, *Major Ivory Seizure in Thailand* (2010b), http://www.traffic.org/home/ 2010/2/27/major-ivory-seizure-in-thailand.html [accessed 3 December 2010].

24. Anon., *Hai Phong Customs Investigates Ivory Smuggling* (2009b), http://english. vietnamnet.vn/social/2009/03/838942/ [accessed 20 March 2010].

25. T. Milliken, R. H. Emslie, and B. Talukdar, *African and Asian Rhinoceroses— Status, Conservation, and Trade.*

26. T. Milliken, R. W. Burns, and L. Sangalakula, *The Elephant Trade Information System (ETIS) and the Illicit Trade in Ivory*, Report to the 15th Meeting of the CITES Conference of the Parties, CoP 15, Doc. 44.1 Annex (2009b).

27. M. D. Madhusudan and K. U. Karanth, "Hunting for an Answer: Is Local Hunting Compatible with Large Mammal Conservation in India?" in *Hunting for Sustainability in Tropical Forests*, ed. J. G. Robinson and E. L. Bennett (New York: Columbia University Press, 2000), pp. 339–355; T. Milliken, R. W. Burns, and L. Sangalakula, *The Elephant Trade Information System (ETIS) and the Illicit Trade in Ivory*, Report to the 15th Meeting of the CITES Conference of the Parties, CoP 15, Doc. 44.1 Annex (2009b).

28. CITES Secretariat, *Rhinoceroses*. Report to the 15th Meeting of the Conference of the Parties, CoP 15 Doc 45.1 (Rev. 1) (2010c), http://www.cites.org/eng/cop/15/ doc/E15-45-01.pdf [accessed 20 March 2010].

29. E. L. Bennett, "Social Dimensions of Managing Hunting in Tropical Forests" in *Wildlife and Society: The Science of Human Dimensions.*

30. Ibid.

31. B. Christy, "Asia's Wildlife Trade: The Kingpin," *National Geographic* (January 2010), http://ngm.nationalgeographic.com/2010/01/asian-wildlife/christy-text/1 [accessed 20 March 2010].

32. T. Milliken, R. H. Emslie, and B. Talukdar, *African and Asian Rhinoceroses— Status, Conservation, and Trade.*

33. Interpol, *Powerful Alliance to Fight Wildlife Crime Comes into Effect* (2010), http://www.interpol.int/Public/ICPO/PressReleases/PR2010/PR098.asp [accessed 3 December 2010].

MICHAEL J. KELLETT

1. C. L. Shafer, "The Unspoken Option to Help Safeguard America's National Parks: An Examination of Expanding U.S. National Park Boundaries by Annexing Adjacent Federal Lands," *Columbia Journal of Environmental Law* 35, no. 1 (2010): 57–124.

2. R. Noss et al., "Bolder Thinking for Conservation," *Conservation Biology* 26, no. 1 (2012).

3. R. W. Dietz and B. Czech, "Conservation Deficits for the Continental United States: An Ecosystem Gap Analysis," *Conservation Biology* 19, no. 5 (October 2005): 1478–87; J. M. Scott, F. W. Davis, R. G. McGhie, R. G. Wright, C. Groves, and J. Estes, "Nature Reserves: Do They Capture the Full Range of America's Biological Diversity?" *Ecological Applications* 11, no. 4 (2001): 999–1007.

4. T. H. Ricketts, E. Dinerstein, D. M. Olson, C. J. Loucks, et al., *Terrestrial Ecoregions of North America: A Conservation Assessment,* World Wildlife Fund Ecoregions Assessments (Washington, D.C.: Island Press, 1999).

5. R. F. Noss, E. T. LaRoe III, and J. M. Scott, *Endangered Ecosystems of the United States: A Preliminary Assessment of Loss and Degradation,* National Biological Service Biological Report 28 (Washington, D.C.: National Biological Service, 1995).

6. B. Babbitt, "A River Runs Against It: America's Evolving View of Dams," *Open Spaces Quarterly* 1, no. 4 (2001): 11–15.

7. R. A. Abell, D. M. Olson, E. Dinerstein, P. T. Hurley, et al., *Freshwater Ecoregions of North America: A Conservation Assessment,* World Wildlife Fund (Washington, D.C.: Island Press, 2000).

8. S. J. Zegre and A. Hereford, *National River Data Inventory and Database Plan,* prepared by Downstream Strategies for the National Park Service (Morgantown, WV: NPS, 2012).

9. National Park Service, *The Wild and Scenic Rivers Act, Yosemite National Park: Merced Wild & Scenic River Plan* (Yosemite, CA: NPS, January 2013).

10. D. Owen, "The Disappointing History of the National Marine Sanctuaries Act," *NYU Environmental Law Journal* 11, no. 3 (2003).

11. D. A. DellaSala, *Why Forests Need to Be Enlisted in Climate Change Actions* (Ashland, OR: Geos Institute, 2013).

12. Secretariat of the Convention on Biological Diversity, Strategic Plan for Biodiversity 2011–2020 and the Aichi Targets: "Living in Harmony with Nature" (Montreal, Canada: Convention on Biological Diversity and United Nations Environmental Program).

13. *The National Park Service Organic Act,* 16 U.S.C. § 1 (1916).

14. National Park Service, *Management Policies 2006* (Washington, D.C.: NPS, 2006), p. 11.

15. National Parks Conservation Association, "New Infographic Shows Why Budget Cuts Must End to Protect National Parks and Economies Nationwide," (Washington, DC: NPCA, 2013, http://www.npca.org/news/media-center/press-releases/2013/new-infographic-shows-why.html (Accessed 13 February 2014).

16. Hart Research Associates and North Star Opinion Research, "Strong Bipartisan Support For National Parks," Findings from a National Survey Conducted on Behalf of The National Parks Conservation Association and National Park Hospitality Association (Washington, DC: NPCA, 2012), p. 10

17. T. Power, *The Economic Benefits of the Proposed Maine Woods National Park and Preserve* (Hallowell, ME: RESTORE: The North Woods, 2001).

18. National Park Service, *2012 National Park Visitor Spending Effects: Economic Contributions to Local Communities, States, and the Nation,* Natural Resource Report NPS/NRSS/EQD/NRR—2014/765 (Fort Collins, CO: NPS 2014).

19. L. Koontz and B. Meldrum, *Effects of the October 2013 Government Shutdown on National Park Service Visitor Spending in Gateway Communities,* Natural Resource Report NPS/EQD/NRSS/NRR—2014/761 (Washington, D.C.: National Park Service, February 2014).

20. Public Opinion Strategies and Fairbank, Maslin, Maulin, Metz & Associates, Conservation in the West Poll, Governance of Conservation, Sponsored by Colorado College (Colorado Springs, CO: CC, 2014).

21. National Park Service, "News Release: Despite Economic Downturn, Americans and Foreign Visitors Flocked to Our National Parks in 2009," 23 February 2010 http://home.nps.gov/news/release.htm?id=966 (Accessed 25 February 2014)

22. See National Park Service, "The National Parks: Shaping the System" (Washington, D.C.: NPS, 2005).

23. See G. Nicklas and K. Proescholdt, "Keeping the Wild in Wilderness: Minimizing Non-Conforming Uses in the National Wilderness Preservation System" (Wilderness Watch, April 2005).

24. See "Wilderness Acreage by Agency," on the Wilderness Statistics Reports page on the website of Wilderness.net, http://www.wilderness.net/NWPS/chartResults?chart type=acreagebyagency and Wilderness.net, Number of Wilderness Units by Agency, http://www.wilderness.net/NWPS/chartResults?chartType=UnitsByAgency).

25. U.S. Forest Service, *Fiscal Year 2014 Budget Overview* (Washington, D.C.: U.S. Department of Agriculture, 2013).

26. R. Voss, *Taxpayer Losses from Logging Our National Forests,* The John Muir Project of Earth Island Institute (Cedar Ridge, CA: JMP, 2005), pp. 1–2.

27. U.S. Department of the Interior, *Fiscal Year 2014 Budget Justifications: Bureau of Land Management* (Washington, D.C.: USDI, 2013).

28. K. Moskowitz and C. Romaniello, *Assessing the Full Cost of the Federal Grazing Program,* prepared for the Center for Biological Diversity (Tucson, AZ: CBD, October 2002).

29. U.S. Department of the Interior, *Fiscal Year 2014 Budget Justifications: Fish and Wildlife Service* (Washington, D.C.: USDI, 2013).

30. K. and S. Berman, *Mandates, Economic Impacts, and Local Concerns: Who Should Manage Mount St. Helens?,* Environmental Law Clinic, University of Washington School of Law, for the National Parks Conservation Association (Seattle, WA: ELC, 2008).

31. See H. S. Hampton, "Opposition to National Parks," *Journal of Forest History* 25, no. 1 (January 1981): 36–45.

CURTIS H. FREESE

1. L. Coad et al., "The Ecological Representativeness of the Global Protected Areas Estate in 2009: Progress Towards the CBD 2010 Target" (UNEP-WCMC, WWF-US and ECI, University of Oxford, 2009).

2. S. D. Fuhlendorf et al., "Conservation of Pattern and Process: Developing an Alternative Paradigm of Rangeland Management," *Rangeland Ecology and Management* 65 (2012): 579–89; F. B. Sampson, F. L. Knopf, and W. Ostlie, "Great Plains Ecosystems: Past, Present and Future," *Wildlife Society Bulletin* 32, no. 1 (2004): 6–15.

3. CEC and TNC, *North American Central Grasslands Priority Conservation Areas: Technical Report and Documentation,* ed. J. W. Karl and J. Hoth, (Montreal, Quebec: Commission for Environmental Cooperation and The Nature Conservancy, 2005).

4. My comments are particularly focused on west-central and south-central semi-arid prairies, a region of 450 million acres as defined in E. F. Wiken, F. J. Nava, and G. Griffith, *North American Terrestrial Ecoregions—Level III* (Montreal, Canada: Commission for Environmental Cooperation, 2011).

5. M. P. Gutmann, W. J. Parton, G. Cunfer, and I. C. Burke, "Population and Environment in the U.S. Great Plains" in *Population, Land Use, and Environment: Research Directions,* ed. B. Entwisle and P. C. Stern (Washington, D.C.: National Academies Press, 2005), pp. 84–105.

6. G. Cunfer, "The New Deal's Land Utilization Program in the Great Plains," *Great Plains Quarterly* 21 (2001): 193–210.

7. CEC and TNC, *North American Central Grasslands Priority Conservation Areas.*

8. M. P. Gutmann et al., "Population and Environment in the U.S. Great Plains."

9. Sampson et al., "Great Plains Ecosystems"; CEC and TNC, *North American Central Grasslands Priority Conservation Areas.*

10. North American Bird Conservation Initiative, "State of the Birds, United States of America, 2009," http://www.stateofthebirds.org/pdf_files/State_of_the_Birds_2009.pdf.

11. R. C. Anderson, "Evolution and Origin of the Central Grassland of North America: Climate, Fire, and Mammalian Grazers," *Journal of the Torrey Botanical Society* 133 (2006): 626–47.

12. CEC and TNC, *North American Central Grasslands Priority Conservation Areas.*

13. D. Smith et al., *Yellowstone Wolf Project: Annual Report, 2010*: YCR-2011-06, (National Park Service, Yellowstone National Park, Yellowstone Center for Resources, Yellowstone National Park, Wyoming, 2011); N. Webb, E. Merrill, and J. Allen, *Density, Demography, and Functional Response of a Harvested Wolf Population in West-Central Alberta, Canada: Management Summary* (Calgary: Department of Biological Sciences, University of Alberta, 2009).

14 A. S. Laliberte and W. J. Ripple, "Wildlife Encounters by Lewis and Clark: A Spatial Analysis Between Native Americans and Wildlife," *BioScience* 53 (2003): 994–1003.

15. Fuhlendorf et al., "Conservation of Pattern and Process: Developing an Alternative Paradigm of Rangeland Management," p. 580.

16. R. F. Limb et al., "Pyric-Herbivory and Cattle Performance in Grassland Ecosystems," *Rangeland Ecology and Management* 64, no. 6 (2011): 659–63.

17. K. M. Havstad et al., "Ecological Services to and from Rangelands of the United States," *Ecological Economics* 64 (2007): 261–68.

18. D. E. Popper and F. J. Popper, "The Great Plains: From Dust to Dust," *Planning* 53 (December 1987): 12–18; M. P. Gutmann et al., "Population and Environment in the U.S. Great Plains."

19. N. M. Hodur, D. A. Bangsund, R. C. Coon, and F. L. Leistritz, *Changing Land Ownership Patterns in the Northern Great Plains* (Fargo, ND: Department of Agribusiness and Applied Economics, North Dakota State University, 2012).

20. R. Skaggs, "Ecosystem Services and Western U.S. Rangelands," *Choices* 23, no. 2 (2008): 37–41.

21. The Nature Conservancy, "Places We Protect," http://www.nature.org/ ourinitiatives/regions/northamerica/unitedstates/nebraska/placesweprotect/ switzer.xml (accessed September 11, 2014).

22. Turner Enterprises, Inc., "Turner Ranches," http://www.tedturner.com/turner-ranches/ (accessed September 11, 2014).

23. M. G. Sorice, U. P. Kreuter, B. P. Wilcox, and W. E. Fox, "Classifying Land-Ownership Motivations in Central Texas, USA: A First Step in Understanding Drivers of Large-Scale Land Cover Change," *Journal of Arid Environments* 80 (2012): 56–64.

24. American Prairie Reserve, http://www.americanprairie.org/ (accessed September 11, 2014).

25. Nature Conservancy Canada, http://www.natureconservancy.ca/en/ (accessed September 11, 2014); The Nature Conservancy, http://www.nature.org/ ourinitiatives/regions/northamerica/index.htm (accessed September 11, 2014).

26. Indian Land Tenure Foundation, http://www.iltf.org/land-issues (accessed September 11, 2014).

27. Badlands National Park, National Park Service, U.S. Department of the Interior and Oglala Sioux Tribe Parks and Recreation Authority, and Oglala Sioux Tribe, *South Unit Badlands National Park Final General Management Plan and Environmental Impact Statement, April 2012.*

MARC J. DOUROJEANNI

1. A. G. Bruner, R. Gullison, E. Rice, and G. A. B. da Fonseca, "Effectiveness of Parks in Protecting Tropical Biodiversity," *Science* 291, no. 5501 (2001): 125–28; D. Nepstad et al., "Inhibition of Amazon Deforestation and Fire by Parks and Indigenous Lands," *Conservation Biology* 20, no. 1 (2006): 65–73.

2. A. Veríssimo, M. Vedoveto Rolla, and S. de M. Futada, *Protected Areas in the Brazilian Amazon: Challenges and Opportunities* (Belém, Brazil: Imazon, 2011), p. 96; C. Nolte, A. Agrawal, K. M. Silvius, and B. S. Soares-Filho, "Governance Regime and Location Influence Avoided Deforestation Success of Protected Areas in the Brazilian Amazon," *PNAS* Early Edition (2012): 6, www.pnas.org/ cgi/doi/10.1073/pnas.1214786110.

3. M. Galvin and T. Haller, eds., *People, Protected Areas and Global Change: Participatory Conservation in Latin America, Africa, Asia and Perspectives,* Swiss National Centre of Competence in Research (NCCR) North-South, University of Bern, Vol. 3 (Bern: Geogra-Bernensia, 2008), p. 560; L. Porter-Bolland et

al., "Community Managed Forests and Forest Protected Areas: An Assessment of Their Conservation Effectiveness across the Tropics," *Forest Ecology and Management* 268 (2012): 6–17.

4. A. C. Diegues, *O Mito Moderno da Natureza Intocada* (Sao Paulo: Hucitec, 2005), p. 169; J. Santilli, *Socioambientalismo e Novos Direitos* (São Paulo: Peiropolis, 2005), p. 303.

5. H. Portugués and P. Huerta, *Mapa de deforestación de la Amazonía peruana 2000* (Lima: PROCLIM/CONAM, 2005), p. 99.

6. CDC/UNALM, *Diagnóstico sobre el estado de la conservación de los bosques a nivel nacional y de las regiones de costa: Estudio para el Programa de Inversiones del Programa Nacional de Conservación de Bosques* (Lima: Centro de Datos para la Conservación/Universidad Nacional Agraria de La Molina y Fundación para el Desarrollo Agrario, 2011), p. 21.

7. CDC/UNALM, ibid.; FDA (Fundación para el Desarrollo Agrario), *Programa de inversión "Programa Nacional de Conservación de Bosques en los Departamentos de Amazonas, Lambayeque, Loreto, Madre de Dios, Piura, San Martín, Tumbes y Ucayali" (PNCB–PI)*, (Realizado por La Fundación para el Desarrollo Agrario con financiamiento de JICA), (Lima: Ministerio del Ambiente, Programa Nacional de Conservación de Bosques, 2011), p. 271, maps and graphics.

8. CDC/UNALM, ibid.

9. H. Portugués and P. Huerta, *Mapa de deforestación de la Amazonía peruana 2000* (Lima: PROCLIM/CONAM, 2005), p. 99.

10. FDA (Fundación para el Desarrollo Agrario), *Programa de inversión "Programa Nacional de Conservación de Bosques en los Departamentos de Amazonas, Lambayeque, Loreto, Madre de Dios, Piura, San Martín, Tumbes y Ucayali" (PNCB–PI)*, (Realizado por La Fundación para el Desarrollo Agrario con financiamiento de JICA), (Lima: Ministerio del Ambiente, Programa Nacional de Conservación de Bosques, 2011), p. 271, map and graphics.

11. F. Rodríguez, M. Rodríguez, and P. Vásquez, *Realidad y perspectivas: La Reserva Nacional Pacaya-Samiria* (Lima: ProNaturaleza, 1995), p. 60.

12. CDC/UNALM, *Diagnóstico sobre el estado de la conservación de los bosques a nivel nacional y de las regiones de costa: Estudio para el Programa de Inversiones del Programa Nacional de Conservación de Bosques* (Lima: Centro de Datos para la Conservación/Universidad Nacional Agraria de La Molina y Fundación para el Desarrollo Agrario, 2011), p. 21.

13. Ibid.

14. P. J. C. Oliveira et al., "Land-Use Allocation Protects the Peruvian Amazon," *Science* 317, no. 5842 (2007): 1233–36.

15. H. G. Lund, *What Is a Degraded Forest?* White Paper prepared for FAO (Rome: UN Food and Agriculture Organization, 2009), p. 42.

16. G. P. Asner, D. E. Knapp, E. N. Broadbent, P. J. C. Oliveira, M. Keller, and J. N. Silva, "Selective Logging in the Brazilian Amazon," *Science* 310, no. 5747 (2005): 480–82.

17. C. A. Peres, "Evaluating the Impact and Sustainability of Subsistence Hunting at Multiple Amazonian Sites" in *Hunting for Sustainability in Tropical Forests,*

342 | NOTES TO PAGES 221–223

ed. J. G. Robinson and E. L. Bennett (New York: Columbia Univ. Press, 2000); C. A. Peres et al., "Demographic Threats to the Sustainability of Brazil Nuts Exploitation," *Science* 302, no. 5653 (2003): 2112–14.

18. H. G. Lund, *What Is a Degraded Forest?* White Paper prepared for FAO (Rome: UN Food and Agriculture Organization, 2009), p. 42; C. Souza Jr. and D. Roberts, "Mapping Forest Degradation in the Amazon Region with Ikonos Images," *International Journal of Remote Sensing* 26 (2005): 425–29.

19. INRENA, *Plan Maestro de la Reserva Nacional Pacaya-Samiria,* Instituto Nacional de Recursos Naturales, (Iquitos, Perú: Ministerio de Agricultura, 2000), p. 151.

20. M. J. Dourojeanni and C. Ponce, *Los Parques Nacionales del Perú* (Madrid, España: Instituto de la Caza Fotográfica (INCAFO), 1978—Colección La Naturaleza en Iberoamerica), p. 224.

21. A. Veríssimo, M. Vedoveto Rolla, and S. de M. Futada, *Protected Areas in the Brazilian Amazon: Challenges and Opportunities* (Belém, Brazil: Imazon, 2011), p. 96; C. Nolte, A. Agrawal, K. M. Silvius, and B. S. Soares-Filho, "Governance Regime and Location Influence Avoided Deforestation Success of Protected Areas in the Brazilian Amazon," *PNAS* Early Edition (2012): 6, http://www.pnas.org/cgi/doi/10.1073/pnas.1214786110.

22. M. J. Dourojeanni and R. E. Quiroga, *Gestión de áreas protegidas para la conservación de la biodiversidad. Evidencias de Brasil, Honduras y Perú* (Washington, D.C.: Banco Interamericano de Desarrollo, Departamento de Desarrollo Sostenible, 2006), p. 116.

23. G. Faleiros, "A escolha de Chico Mendes," *O Eco,* 8 December 2006, http://www.oeco.org.br/reportagens/1815-oeco_19953; "Resex Chico Mendes tem 10 mil cabeças de gado," http://terramagazine.terra.com.br/blogdaamazonia/blog.

24. M. J. Dourojeanni and R. E. Quiroga, *Gestión de áreas protegidas para la conservación de la biodiversidad. Evidencias de Brasil, Honduras y Perú* (Washington, D.C.: Banco Interamericano de Desarrollo, Departamento de Desarrollo Sostenible, 2006), p. 116.

25. See the following links: http://www.dpz.es/prensa/2012/12/notas/np121204-1.asp; http://elblogdejoaquinventura.blogspot.com.br/2013/01/el-presupuesto-de-ordesa-y-monte.html; http://www.chistabinos.es/PNac_Posets%2017%20 SEP%20SAN%20JUAN%20PLAN-GISTAIN.pdf; http://noticias.terra.es/ciencia/el-presupuesto-para-parques-nacionales-se-reduce-un-412-para-2013,159b38e 21721a310VgnVCM4000009bcceb0aRCRD.html; http://www.rondasomontano.com/revista/53796/; http://www.parquenatural.com/blog/ver/cabo-de-gata-nijar-recibe-el-2010-con-cerca-de-1-millon-de-euros.

26. CDC/UNALM, *Diagnóstico sobre el estado de la conservación de los bosques a nivel nacional y de las regiones de costa: Estudio para el Programa de Inversiones del Programa Nacional de Conservación de Bosques* (Lima: Centro de Datos para la Conservación/Universidad Nacional Agraria de La Molina y Fundación para el Desarrollo Agrario, 2011), p. 21.

27. See the following links: http://www.dpz.es/prensa/2012/12/notas/np121204-1.asp; http://elblogdejoaquinventura.blogspot.com.br/2013/01/el-presupuesto-de-ordesa-y-monte.html; http://www.chistabinos.es/PNac_Posets%2017%20

SEP%20SAN%20JUAN%20PLAN-GISTAIN.pdf; http://noticias.terra.es/ciencia/el-presupuesto-para-parques-nacionales-se-reduce-un-412-para-2013,159b38e21721a310VgnVCM4000009bcceb0aRCRD.html; http://www.rondasomontano.com/revista/53796/; http://www.parquenatural.com/blog/ver/cabo-de-gata-nijar-recibe-el-2010-con-cerca-de-1-millon-de-euros.

28. M. Dowie, "Conservation Refugees: When Protecting Nature Means Kicking People Out," *Orion* online, (November/December 2005), http://www.orionmagazine.org/index.php/articles/article/161/; J. Fairhead, M. Leach, and I. Scoones, "Green Grabbing: A New Appropriation of Nature?" *Journal of Peasant Studies* 39, no. 2 (2011): 237–61; A. White, A. Khare, and A. Molnar, "Who Owns, Who Conserves and Why It Matters," *Forest Trends* (2005): 16–20.

29. M. Allegretti, "The Social Construction of Public Policies: Chico Mendes and the *Seringueiros* Movement," *Desenvolvimento e Meio Ambiente*, Editora UFPR 18 (2008): 39–59.

30. M. T. Pádua, "Análise Crítica da Nova Lei do Sistema de Unidades de Conservação da Natureza do Brasil," *Revista de Direito Ambiental*, São Paulo 21 (Jan.–March 2001); M. T. Pádua, "Protegidas?" *O Eco* (9 Dec. 2004); M. T. Pádua, "O truque das categorias," *O Eco* (21 Sept. 2005).

31. I. Camara, "Para que servem as APAs?" *O Globo*, Rio de Janeiro (5 Dec. 2000); M. T. Pádua, "Áreas de proteção ambiental" in *Direito Ambiental das áreas Protegidas*, coord. A. B. H. Benjamim (São Paulo: Ed. Forense Universitaria, 2005), pp. 425–33.

32. A. C. Diegues, *O Mito Moderno da Natureza Intocada* (Sao Paulo: Hucitec, 2005), p. 169; J. Santilli, *Socioambientalismo e Novos Direitos* (São Paulo: Peiropolis, 2005), p. 303; J. Barborak, 1997 "Mitos e realidades da concepção atual de áreas protegidas na América Latina" in *Anais Congresso Brasileiro de Unidades de Conservação, 15–23 de Novembro de 1997*, Vol. 1 (Curitiba, Paraná, 1997), pp. 39–47.

33. This national park is located in the Cerrado biome, limiting with the biome of the Amazon.

34. M. J. Dourojeanni and M. T. Pádua, *Biodiversidade, A Hora Decisiva*, 2nd ed. (Curitiba: Universidade Federal do Paraná, 2007), p. 282.

35. J. C. Magalhães, "Rondônia revoga proteção a florestas," *Folha de São Paulo*, 10 August 2010.

36. A. Ribeiro, "O negocio que salvou a floresta," Época/Negócios, Feveiro 2012, pp. 102–06.

37. M. J. Dourojeanni and M. T. Pádua, *Biodiversidade, A Hora Decisiva*, 2nd ed. (Curitiba: Universidade Federal do Paraná, 2007), p. 282; M. J. Dourojeanni, *Amazonia Probable y Deseable: Ensayo sobre el Presente y el Futuro de la Amazonia* (Lima: Universidad Inca Garcilaso de la Vega, Textos Universitarios, 2011), p. 273. C. Nolte, A. Agrawal, K. M. Silvius, and B. S. Soares-Filho, "Governance Regime and Location Influence Avoided Deforestation Success of Protected Areas in the Brazilian Amazon," *PNAS* Early Edition (2012): 6, www.pnas.org/cgi/doi/10.1073/pnas.1214786110; C. A. Peres, "Conservation in Sustainable-Use Tropical Forest Reserves," *Conservation Biology* 25, no. 6 (2011): 1124–29.

38. The Pampa Galeras National Reserve was created in 1967; Pacaya-Samiria in 1968; and another dozen reserves before that by Chico Mendes in Brazil. The concept of communal reserves, which inspired the extractive reserves in Brazil, was launched by Peruvian environmentalists in the 1970s.

39. J. Terborgh and C. P. van Schaik, "Minimizing Species Loss: The Imperative of Protection" in *Last Stand: Protected Areas and the Defense of Tropical Biodiversity*, ed. R. Kramer, C. P. van Schaik, and J. Johnson (New York: Oxford University Press, 1997), pp. 15–35; L. Gibson et al., "Primary Forests Are Irreplaceable for Sustaining Tropical Biodiversity," *Nature* 478 (2011): 378–81.

BARBARA AND CHRISTOPH PROMBERGER

1. "Urwälder in den Karpaten Rumäniens" Dietmar Gross BN + HSS – Seminar: Alte Bäume – Zentren der Artenvielfalt 2008.

2. G. F. Borlea, "Romania," in United Nations FAO Forestry Department's *Issues and Opportunities in the Evolution of Private Forestry and Forestry Extension in Several Countries with Economies in Transition in Central and Eastern Europe* (Rome: Food and Agriculture Organization of the United Nations, Forestry Department, 1997), in FAO Corporate Document Repository, http://www.fao.org/docrep/w7170e/w7170e0f.htm.

3. "Urwälder in den Karpaten Rumäniens" Dietmar Gross BN + HSS – Seminar: Alte Bäume – Zentren der Artenvielfalt 2008.

MIKHAIL PALTSYN

1. D. M. Olson and E. Dinerstein, "The Global 200: Priority Ecoregions for Global Conservation," *Annals of the Missouri Botanical Garden* 89 (2002): 199–224.

2. Millenium Ecosystem Assessment, *Subglobal Assessment Report: Altai-Sayan Ecoregion*, 2005, retrieved November 2011, from http://www.maweb.org/en/SGA.AltaiSayan.aspx. K. N. Kupriyanov, *Biodiversity of the Altai-Sayan Ecoregion*, 2003. Kemerovo: WWF-Russia. UNDP-GEF 2007. *Biodiversity of the Altai-Sayan Ecoregion. Web database.* Accessed December 19, 2013. http://www.bioaltai-sayan.ru/regnum/eng/index.htm.

3. WWF, *Altai-Sayan Ecoregional Conservation Strategy*, 2012.

4. Ibid.

5. J. Krause et al., "The Complete Mitochondrial DNA Genome of an Unknown Hominin from Southern Siberia," *Nature* 464, no. 7290 (2010): 894–97, doi:10.1038/nature08976, PMID 20336068.

6. UNESCO World Heritage Convention, *World Heritage List* 2012, retrieved May 2012, http://whc.unesco.org/en/list.

7. WWF, *Altai-Sayan Ecoregional Conservation Strategy*, 2012.

8. P. Batima, *Climate Change Vulnerability and Adaptation in the Livestock Sector of Mongolia*, Final Report Submitted to Assessments of Impacts and Adaptations to Climate Change (AIACC), Project no. AS 06, 2006; A. O. Kokorin, ed., *Assessment Report: Climate Change and Its Impact on Ecosystems, Population and Economy of the Russian Portion of the Altai-Sayan Ecoregion* (Moscow: WWF-Russia, 2011), p. 152.

9. M. MacDonald, Report on the development of a map for the Altai-Sayan Ecoregion (Arnhem: Mott MacDonald, 2012).

10. WWF, *Altai-Sayan Ecoregional Conservation Strategy*, 2012.

11. Ibid.

12. Mongolian Society for Range Management, *Warm Welcome to the Steppes of Mongolia*, brochure for the participants of the International VIII Rangeland Congress XXI International Grassland Congress Post Tour in Mongolia, 2009.

13. WWF, *Altai-Sayan Ecoregional Conservation Strategy*, 2012.

14. Ibid.

15. T. Erdenechuluun, *Wood Supply in Mongolia: The Legal and Illegal Economies* (Washington, D.C.: World Bank, Mongolia Discussion Papers, East Asia and Pacific Environment and Social Development Department, 2006).

16. A. Shishikin et al., *Fire Danger Mitigation: A Strategy for Protected Areas of the Altai-Sayan Ecoregion* (Krasnoyarsk: UNDP, 2012).

17. A. Brukhanov, *Environmental Assessment of Siberia Forests: Alarming Results* (WWF-Russia, 2009).

18. D. P. Mallon, "Saiga tatarica," IUCN Red List 2008, on IUCN website, retrieved November 2011, http://www.iucnredlist.org/apps/redlist/details/19832/0; M. Yu. Paltsyn, S. V. Spitsyn, A. N. Kuksin, et al., *Conservation of Altai Argali in Transboundary Area of Russia and Mongolia* (Krasnoyarsk: UNDP, 2011) [in Russian]; M. Yu. Paltsyn, S. V. Spitsyn, S.V. Istomov, and A. N. Kuksin, *Conservation of Snow Leopard in Russia* (Krasnoyarsk: UNDP, 2012); I. V. Karyakin et al., *Distribution and Population Status of the Saker Falcon* (Falco cherrug) *in Russia and Kazakhstan Based on Results of Surveys in 2005–2012* (Russian Raptor Research and Conservation Network, 2012); S. N. Lineytsev, T. V. Yashina, Yu. N. Kalinkin, A. N. Kuksin, E. S. Ankipovich, *Assessment of Musk Deer* (Moschus moschyiferus) *Abundance in Key Conservation Areas of UNDP/ GEF Project: Biodiversity Conservation in the Russian Portion of the Altai-Sayan Ecoregion*. Research Report, 2008; J. Batbold, N. Batsaikhan, K. Tsytsulina, and G. Sukhchuluun, *Marmota sibirica*, IUCN 2012, IUCN Red List of Threatened Species, Version 2012.2. <www.iucnredlist.org>. Downloaded on 26 April 2013.

19. S. N. Lineytsev, T. V. Yashina, Yu. N. Kalinkin, A. N. Kuksin, E. S. Ankipovich, *Assessment of Musk Deer* (Moschus moschyiferus) *Abundance in Key Conservation Areas of UNDP/GEF Project: Biodiversity Conservation in the Russian Portion of the Altai-Sayan Ecoregion* Research Report, 2008.

20. A. A. Vasilchenko and S. G. Babina, "Current Status of the Forest Reindeer (*Rangifer tarandus valentinae*) in Protected Areas of Altai-Sayan Ecoregion" in *Biodiversity Monitoring in Protected Areas*, Proceedings of inter-regional conference, May 17–20, 2010 (Barnaul: ARKTIKA, 2010) p. 130 [in Russian].

21. I. V. Karyakin et al., *Distribution and Population Status of the Saker Falcon* (Falco cherrug) *in Russia and Kazakhstan Based on Results of Surveys in 2005–2012* (Russian Raptor Research and Conservation Network, 2012).

22. M. Yu. Paltsyn, S. V. Spitsyn, S. V. Istomov, and A. N. Kuksin, *Conservation of Snow Leopard in Russia* (Krasnoyarsk: UNDP, 2012).

23. UNESCO World Heritage Convention 2012, *World Heritage List*. Retrieved May 2012 from http://whc.unesco.org/en/list.

24. *Strategy for Conservation of Snow Leopard in the Russian Federation*. Approved by the Ministry of Natural Resources and Environment of the Russian Federation, Decree of August 18, 2014, #23-r.

25. WWF, *Altai-Sayan Ecoregional Conservation Strategy*, 2012.

RICHARD P. READING ET AL.

1. R. P. Reading, D. J. Bedunah, and S. Amgalanbaatar "Conserving Mongolia's Grasslands with Challenges, Opportunities, and Lessons for America's Great Plains," *Great Plains Research* 20, no. 1 (2010): 85–108. Website of The World Bank, see Data page for Mongolia. http://data.worldbank.org/country/mongolia. Accessed 9 June 2013.

2. P. W. Germeraad and Z. Enebisch, *The Mongolian Landscape Tradition: A Key to Progress; Nomadic Traditions and Their Contemporary Role in Landscape Planning and Management in Mongolia* (Schiedam, Netherlands: Germeraad and Enebisch, BGS, 1996); M. Rossabi, "Mongolia in the 1990s: From Commissars to Capitalists," *Occasional Papers of the Open Society in Central Eurasia* 2 (1997): 1–16.

3. B. Chimed-Ochir, "Protected Area of Mongolia in Past, Present and Future," in *Proceedings of the Second Conference on National Parks and Protected Areas of East Asia: Mobilizing Community Support for National Parks and Protected Areas in East Asia*, Kushiro, Hokkaido, Japan, June 30–July 5, 1996 (Tokyo, Japan: Japanese Organizing Committee for the Second Conference on National Parks and Protected Areas of East Asia, 1997), pp. 51–55; R. P. Reading, H. Mix, B. Lhagvasuren, and N. Tseveenmyadag, "The Commercial Harvest of Wildlife in Dornod Aimag, Mongolia," *Journal of Wildlife Management* 62 (1998): 59–71; R. P. Reading, M. Johnstad, S. Amgalanbaatar, Z. Batjargal, and H. Mix, "Expanding Mongolia's System of Protected Areas," *Natural Areas Journal* 19 (1999): 211–22; R. P. Reading, D. J. Bedunah, and S. Amgalanbaatar, "Conserving Biodiversity on Mongolian Rangelands: Implications for Protected Area Development and Pastoral Uses," in *Rangelands of Central Asia: Proceedings of the Conference on Transformations, Issues, and Future Challenges*, comp. D. J. Bedunah, E. D. MacArthur, and M. Fernandez-Gimenez. (Rocky Mountain Research Station, Fort Collins, CO: U.S. Department of Agriculture, Forest Service, RMRS-P-39, 2006), 1–17.

4. A. Namkhai and D. Myagmarsuren, *Protected Areas of Mongolia* (Ulaanbaatar, Mongolia: Mongolian Ministry for Nature and Environment, 2012).

5. C. Finch, *Mongolia's Wild Heritage: Biological Diversity, Protected Areas, and Conservation in the Land of Chingis Khaan* (Boulder, CO: Avery Press, 1996); P. W. Germeraad and Z. Enebisch, *The Mongolian Landscape Tradition: A Key to Progress; Nomadic Traditions and Their Contemporary Role in Landscape Planning and Management in Mongolia*.

6. P. W. Germeraad and Z. Enebisch, *The Mongolian Landscape Tradition: A Key to Progress; Nomadic Traditions and Their Contemporary Role in Landscape Planning and Management in Mongolia*; B. Chimed-Ochir, "Protected Area of Mongolia in Past, Present and Future."

7. B. Chimed-Ochir, "Protected Area of Mongolia in Past, Present and Future."

8. C. Finch, *Mongolia's Wild Heritage: Biological Diversity, Protected Areas, and Conservation in the Land of Chingis Khaan.*

9. R. P. Reading, M. Johnstad, S. Amgalanbaatar, Z. Batjargal, and H. Mix, "Expanding Mongolia's System of Protected Areas," *Natural Areas Journal* 19 (1999): 211–22.

10. R. P. Reading, D. J. Bedunah, and S. Amgalanbaatar "Conserving Mongolia's Grasslands with Challenges, Opportunities, and Lessons for America's Great Plains," *Great Plains Research* 20, no. 1 (2010): 85–108.

11. N. Enkhtsetseg, *Assessment on Implementation Stats of Phase First of the National Program on Protected Areas in Mongolia* (Ulaanbaatar, Mongolia, WWF Mongolia Programme, 2009), 71.

12. N. Enkhtsetseg, *Assessment on Implementation Stats of Phase First of the National Program on Protected Areas in Mongolia* (Ulaanbaatar, Mongolia, WWF Mongolia Programme, 2009), 71.

13. W. B. Henwood, "Toward a Strategy for the Conservation and Protection of the World's Temperate Grasslands," *Great Plains Research* 20 (2010): 121–34.

14. N. Enkhtsetseg, *Assessment on Implementation Stats of Phase First of the National Program on Protected Areas in Mongolia* (Ulaanbaatar, Mongolia, WWF Mongolia Programme, 2009), 71.

15. R. P. Reading, D. J. Bedunah, and S. Amgalanbaatar, "Conserving Biodiversity on Mongolian Rangelands: Implications for Protected Area Development and Pastoral Uses," in *Rangelands of Central Asia: Proceedings of the Conference on Transformations, Issues, and Future Challenges*, comp. D. J. Bedunah, E. D. MacArthur, and M. Fernandez-Gimenez. (Rocky Mountain Research Station, Fort Collins, CO: U.S. Department of Agriculture, Forest Service, RMRS-P-39, 2006), 1–17; R. P. Reading, D. J. Bedunah, and S. Amgalanbaatar "Conserving Mongolia's Grasslands with Challenges, Opportunities, and Lessons for America's Great Plains," *Great Plains Research* 20, no. 1 (2010): 85–108.

16. Ibid.

17. R. P. Reading, H. Mix, B. Lhagvasuren, and N. Tseveenmyadag, "The Commercial Harvest of Wildlife in Dornod Aimag, Mongolia," *Journal of Wildlife Management* 62 (1998): 59–71; P. Zahler et al., "Illegal and Unsustainable Wildlife Hunting and Trade in Mongolia," *Mongolian Journal of Biological Sciences* 2 (2004): 23–32; J. R. Wingard and P. Zahler, *Silent Steppe: The Illegal Wildlife Trade Crisis in Mongolia*, Mongolia Discussion Papers, East Asia and Pacific Environment and Social Development Department (Washington, D.C.: World Bank, 2006).

18. E. L. Clark et al, "Mongolian Red List of Mammals," *Regional Red List Series,* Vol. 1. (London: Zoological Society of London, 2006).

19. P. Zahler et al, "Illegal and Unsustainable Wildlife Hunting and Trade in Mongolia."

20. R. P. Reading, D. J. Bedunah, and S. Amgalanbaatar, "Conserving Biodiversity on Mongolian Rangelands: Implications for Protected Area Development and

Pastoral Uses," in *Rangelands of Central Asia: Proceedings of the Conference on Transformations, Issues, and Future Challenges,* comp. D. J. Bedunah, E. D. MacArthur, and M. Fernandez-Gimenez. (Rocky Mountain Research Station, Fort Collins, CO: U.S. Department of Agriculture, Forest Service, RMRS-P-39, 2006), 1–17; R. P. Reading, D. J. Bedunah, and S. Amgalanbaatar "Conserving Mongolia's Grasslands with Challenges, Opportunities, and Lessons for America's Great Plains," *Great Plains Research* 20, no. 1 (2010): 85–108.

21. B. Chimed-Ochir, "Protected Area of Mongolia in Past, Present and Future."

22. M. Fernández-Giménez, "The Role of Ecological Perception in Indigenous Resource Management: A Case Study from the Mongolian Forest-steppe," *Nomadic Peoples* 33 (1993): 31–46; P. W. Germeraad and Z. Enebisch, *The Mongolian Landscape Tradition: A Key to Progress; Nomadic Traditions and Their Contemporary Role in Landscape Planning and Management in Mongolia.*

23. T. Potanski, "Decollectivisation of the Mongolian Pastoral Economy (1991–92): Some Economic and Social Consequences," *Nomadic Peoples* 33 (1993): 123–35; N. Honhold, *Livestock Population and Productivity and the Human Population of Mongolia, 1930 to 1994* (Ulaanbaatar, Mongolia: Ministry of Food and Agriculture, 1995); P. W. Germeraad and Z. Enebisch, *The Mongolian Landscape Tradition: A Key to Progress; Nomadic Traditions and Their Contemporary Role in Landscape Planning and Management in Mongolia.*

24. P. W. Germeraad and Z. Enebisch, *The Mongolian Landscape Tradition: A Key to Progress; Nomadic Traditions and Their Contemporary Role in Landscape Planning and Management in Mongolia.*

25. R. P. Reading, D. J. Bedunah, and S. Amgalanbaatar "Conserving Mongolia's Grasslands with Challenges, Opportunities, and Lessons for America's Great Plains," *Great Plains Research* 20, no. 1 (2010): 85–108.

26. R. P. Reading, D. J. Bedunah, and S. Amgalanbaatar "Conserving Mongolia's Grasslands with Challenges, Opportunities, and Lessons for America's Great Plains," *Great Plains Research* 20, no. 1 (2010): 85–108.

MARTIN TAYLOR

1. J. Williams et al., *Biodiversity Theme Report, Australia State of the Environment Report 2001* (Canberra: Australian Government, 2001).

2. A. D. Chapman, *Numbers of Living Species in Australia and the World,* 2nd ed. (Canberra, AU: Australian Biological Resources Study, 2009).

3. R. A. Mittermeier, N. Myers, and J. B. Thomsen, "Biodiversity Hotspots and Major Tropical Wilderness Areas: Approaches to Setting Conservation Priorities," *Conservation Biology* 12 (1998): 516–20.

4. Tourism Research Australia. *Snapshots 2009: Nature Tourism in Australia* (Canberra, AU: Australian Government, 2009); M. F. J. Taylor, S. Eber, and P. Toni, *Changing Land Use to Save Australian Wildlife* (Sydney: WWF-Australia, 2014).

5. G. De'ath, K. E. Fabricius, H. Sweatman, and M. Puotinen, "The 27-year Decline of Coral Cover on the Great Barrier Reef and Its Causes," *Proceedings of the National Academy of Sciences* 109, no. 44 (2012): 17995–9.

6. See www.environment.gov.au/biodiversity. This does not include other species listed only on state and territory threatened species lists.

7. For example, the purchases of Yanga sheep station, in southern New South Wales, and Toorale station, in the north of the same state, to become new national parks, were opposed by some rural interests, http://www.abc.net.au/news/2005-09-07/opposition-wants-govt-to-stop-yanga-station/2098208; http://www.abc.net.au/worldtoday/content/2008/s2368107.htm.

8. M. F. J. Taylor, "Bushland at Risk of Renewed Clearing in Queensland" (Sydney: WWF-Australia, 10 May 2013).

9. J. Gunn, G. Fraser, and B. Kimball, *Review of the Great Barrier Reef Marine Park Structural Adjustment Package* (Canberra: Australian Government, 2010), http://www.environment.gov.au/resource/review-great-barrier-reef-marine-park-structural-adjustment-package.

10. M. F. J. Taylor, J. A. Fitzsimons, and P. S. Sattler, *Building Nature's Safety Net 2014: A decade of protected area achievements in Australia* (Sydney: WWF-Australia, 2014).

11. Indigenous Protected Areas (Australian Government website), http://www.environment.gov.au/indigenous/ipa/.

12. Ibid.

13. See Figure 8 in M. Barson, J. Mewett, and J. Paplinska, "Trends in On Farm Biodiversity Management in Australia's Agricultural Industries: Caring for Our Country Sustainable Practices Fact Sheet 5," Department of Agriculture, Fisheries and Forestry, Canberra, ACT, August 2012, http://nrmonline.nrm.gov.au/downloads/mql:2865/PDF.

14. Ibid., see Figure 9.

15. G. Hunt and R. Colbeck, *Supporting Recreational Fishing While Protecting Our Marine Parks,* Australian Government media release, 14 Dec. 2013, http://www.environment.gov.au/minister/hunt/2013/mr20131214.html.

16. *Caring for Our Country: An Outline for the Future 2013–2018* (Canberra: Australian Government, 2013), http://www.nrm.gov.au/about/caring/review/pubs/c4oc-outline-future.pdf.

17. P. J. Ferraro and S. K. Pattanayak, "Money for Nothing? A Call for Empirical Evaluation of Biodiversity Conservation Investments," *PLoS Biol* 4 (2006) e105, doi:10.1371/journal.pbio.0040105.

18. V. Adams, R. L. Pressey and N. Stoeckl, "Estimating Land and Conservation Management Costs: The First Step in Designing a Stewardship Program for the Northern Territory," *Biological Conservation* 148 (2012): 44–53.

19. M. F. J. Taylor, J. A. Fitzsimons, and P. S. Sattler, *Building Nature's Safety Net 2014: A decade of protected area achievements in Australia* (Sydney: WWF-Australia, 2014).

20. Department of Sustainability, Environment, Water, Population and Communities, *Review of the Environmental Stewardship Program* (Canberra: Australian Government, 2010). http://www.nrm.gov.au/resources/publications/stewardship/esp-review.html.

21. *Caring for Our Country: An Outline for the Future 2013–2018* (Canberra: Australian Government, 2013), http://www.nrm.gov.au/about/caring/review/pubs/c4oc-outline-future.pdf.

22. C. Mora and P. F. Sale, "Ongoing Global Biodiversity Loss and the Need to Move Beyond Protected Areas: A Review of the Technical and Practical Shortcomings of Protected Areas on Land and Sea," *Marine Ecology Progress Series* 434 (2011): 251–66.

23. S. Schwartzman, A. Moreira, and D. Nepstad, "Rethinking Tropical Forest Conservation: Perils in Parks," *Conservation Biology* 15 (2000): 1351–57.

24. T. R. McClanahan, M. J. Marnane, J. E. Cinner, and W. E. Kiene, "A Comparison of Marine Protected Areas and Alternative Approaches to Coral-Reef Management," *Current Biology* 16, no. 14 (2006): 1408–13; A. G. Bruner, R. E. Gullison, R. E. Rice, and G. A. da Fonseca, "Effectiveness of Parks in Protecting Tropical Biodiversity, *Science* 291, no. 5501 (2001): 125–28.

25. M. F. Taylor et al., "What Works for Threatened Species Recovery? An Empirical Evaluation for Australia," *Biodiversity and Conservation* 20, no. 4 (2011): 767–77; M. C. Bottrill et al., "Does Recovery Planning Improve the Status of Threatened Species?" *Biological Conservation* 144, no. 5 (2011): 1595–1601.

26. T. Flannery, "The Future for Biodiversity Conservation Isn't More National Parks," *The Conversation* (29 Nov. 2012), https://theconversation.com/the-future-for-biodiversity-conservation-isnt-more-national-parks-11027. See also response by D. Bowman, "Biodiversity Crisis Demands Bolder Thinking than Bagging National Parks," *The Conversation* (29 Nov. 2012), https://theconversation.com/biodiversity-crisis-demands-bolder-thinking-than-bagging-national-parks-11022.

27. J. C. Woinarski, J. Green, A. Fisher, M. Ensbey, and B. Mackey, "The Effectiveness of Conservation Reserves: Land Tenure Impacts upon Biodiversity across Extensive Natural Landscapes in the Tropical Savannahs of the Northern Territory," *Land* 2, no. 1 (2013): 20–36.

28. B. Murphy, C. Trauernicht, and D. Bowman, "Scientists and National Park Managers Are Failing Northern Australia's Vanishing Mammals," *The Conversation* (20 Dec. 2012), http://theconversation.com/scientists-and-national-park-managers-are-failing-northern-australias-vanishing-mammals-10089.

29. N. Dudley, *Guidelines for Applying Protected Area Management Categories*, (Gland, Switzerland: IUCN, 2010).

30. V. Adams and K. Moon, "Security and Equity of Conservation Covenants: Contradictions of Private Protected Area Policies in Australia," *Land Use Policy* 30 (2013): 114–19; J. Irving, "Arkaroola—Creating a New Type of Protected Area," in *Innovation for 21st Century Conservation*, ed. P. Figgis, J. Fitzsimons, and J. Irving (Sydney, AU: Australian Committee for IUCN, 2012), pp. 88–93, http://aciucn.org.au/wp-content/uploads/2013/05/Innovation_for_21st_century_conservation_low.pdf.

31. L. Burton, "Queensland Nature Refuge a Casualty of Mining," *ABC Rural News* 23 Dec 2013, http://www.abc.net.au/news/2013-12-23/bimblebox-nature-reserve/5172742.

32. C. Booth, "Park Attack," *Wildlife Australia* 50 (2013): 22–6, http://www.wildlife. org.au/magazine/editions/2013/autumn/parkattack.pdf.

33. T. Abbott, "Address to the 2014 Forestworks Dinner" (transcript of address presented by Australian prime minister Tony Abbott), in Canberra, Australia, 4 March 2014, https://www.pm.gov.au/media/2014-03-04/address-2014-forestworks-dinner-canberra.

34. M. Hockings, M. Maron, and M. Barnes, "National Parks Are the Least Locked Up Land There Is," *The Conversation* (17 June 2013), http://theconversation.com/national-parks-are-the-least-locked-up-land-there-is-15138.

35. M. Duffy, "Carr's Green Legacy Is a Black Mark," *Sydney Morning Herald*, 30 July 2005.

36. T. Abbott, "Address to the 2014 Forestworks Dinner," cited above.

37. Although a relatively recent arrival, the Asian dog, or dingo, is now considered a native species. It is the largest remaining terrestrial carnivore and plays a critical role in food web stability. See W. J. Ripple et al., "Status and Ecological Effects of the World's Largest Carnivores," *Science* 343, no. 6167 (2014), doi:10.1126/science.1241484.

38. B. Phalan et al., "Reconciling Food Production and Biodiversity Conservation: Land Sharing and Land Sparing Compared," *Science* 333 (2011): 1289–91.

39. M. F. J. Taylor, S. Eber, and P. Toni, *Changing Land Use to Save Australian Wildlife* (Sydney: WWF-Australia, 2014).

40. P. Bridgewater, "National Parks Need to Embrace Global Change," *The Conversation* (15 July 2013), http://theconversation.com/national-parks-need-to-embrace-global-change-15599.

41. Standing Committee on Environment, Communications, Information Technology and the Arts. *Conserving Australia: Australia's National Parks, Conservation Reserves and Marine Protected Areas* (Canberra, AU: Australian Senate, 2007), http://www.aph.gov.au/~/media/wopapub/senate/committee/ecita_ctte/completed_inquiries/2004-07/nationalparks/report/report.ashx.

42. J. C. Woinarski et al., "The Effectiveness of Conservation Reserves: Land Tenure Impacts upon Biodiversity across Extensive Natural Landscapes in the Tropical Savannahs of the Northern Territory," *Land* 2, no. 1 (2013): 20–36.

43. *Payments for Ecosystem Services; Getting Started: A Primer* (Forest Trends, The Katoomba Group, and United Nations Environment Programme, 2008).

44. N. Dudley and S. Stolton, *Arguments for Protected Areas : Multiple Benefits for Conservation and Use* (IUCN, 2010), http://www.iucn.org/about/work/programmes/gpap_home/gpap_solutions/gpap_arguments/?11476/Arguments-for-protected-areas--Multiple-benefits-for-Conservation-and-Use.

45. B. Williams, "Future of Nut Trees in Balance," *News Ltd,* online edition, 1 June 2010.

46. C. McKilliop, "Wild Rice Key to Global Food Security," *ABC Rural* online edition 13 June 2014.

47. This should not be misconstrued as support for tourism development of national parks nor of the view that national parks need tourism to survive. Careless or excessive tourism development of parks can serve only to undermine their primary conservation purpose, and ultimately undermine the very value they represent to the tourism industry itself. See S. Beeton, "Is Nature-based Tourism Development Really What Our National Parks Need?" *The Conversation* (25 Sept. 2012), http://theconversation.com/is-nature-based-tourism-development-really-what-our-national-parks-need-9090 and also S. Moore et al., "Our National Parks Need Visitors to Survive," *The Conversation* (7 Aug. 2013), http://theconversation.com/our-national-parks-need-visitors-to-survive-15867.

48. P. J. Ferraro and S. K. Pattanayak, "Money for Nothing? A Call for Empirical Evaluation of Biodiversity Conservation Investments," *PLoS Biol* 4, no. 4 (2006).

49. I. Craigie et al., "Terrestrial Protected Areas of Australia" in *Austral Ark: The State of Wildlife in Australia and New Zealand,* ed. A. Stow, N. Mclean, and G. I. Holwell (Cambridge, UK: Cambridge University Press, forthcoming).

50. M. F. J. Taylor, S. Eber, and P. Toni, *Changing Land Use to Save Australian Wildlife* (Sydney: WWF-Australia, 2014).

51. R. L. Pressey et al., "Conservation Planning in a Changing World," *Trends in Ecology and Evolution* 22, no. 11 (2007): 583–92.

52. M. B. Araújo et al., "Would Climate Change Drive Species Out of Reserves? An Assessment of Existing Reserve-selection Methods," *Global Change Biology* 10, no. 9 (2004): 1618–26.

53. M. Dunlop et al., *The Implications of Climate Change for Biodiversity Conservation and the National Reserve System: Final Synthesis* (Canberra, AU: CSIRO, 2012); R. Maggini et al., Protecting and Restoring Habitat to Help Australia's Threatened Species Adapt to Climate Change (Gold Coast, AU: National Climate Change Adaptation Research Facility, 2013), 54.

54. A. E. Reside et al., *Climate Change Refugia for Terrestrial Biodiversity: Defining Areas that Promote Species Persistence and Ecosystem Resilience in the Face of Global Climate Change* (Gold Coast, AU: National Climate Change Adaptation Research Facility, 2013). http://www.nccarf.edu.au/publications/climate-change-refugia-terrestrial-biodiversity.

55. National Reserve System Task Group. *Strategy for Australia's National Reserve System 2009–2030* (Canberra, AU: Australian Government, 2009), http://www.environment.gov.au/node/21198.

AFTERWORD

1. See G. Wuerthner, E. Crist, and T. Butler, eds., *Keeping the Wild: Against the Domestication of Earth* (Washington, D.C.: Island Press, 2014).

INDEX

ABOUT ISLAND PRESS

Since 1984, the nonprofit organization Island Press has been stimulating, shaping, and communicating ideas that are essential for solving environmental problems worldwide. With more than 800 titles in print and some 40 new releases each year, we are the nation's leading publisher on environmental issues. We identify innovative thinkers and emerging trends in the environmental field. We work with world-renowned experts and authors to develop cross-disciplinary solutions to environmental challenges.

Island Press designs and executes educational campaigns in conjunction with our authors to communicate their critical messages in print, in person, and online using the latest technologies, innovative programs, and the media. Our goal is to reach targeted audiences—scientists, policymakers, environmental advocates, urban planners, the media, and concerned citizens—with information that can be used to create the framework for long-term ecological health and human well-being.

Island Press gratefully acknowledges major support of our work by The Agua Fund, The Andrew W. Mellon Foundation, Betsy & Jesse Fink Foundation, The Bobolink Foundation, The Curtis and Edith Munson Foundation, Forrest C. and Frances H. Lattner Foundation, G.O. Forward Fund of the Saint Paul Foundation, Gordon and Betty Moore Foundation, The Kresge Foundation, The Margaret A. Cargill Foundation, New Mexico Water Initiative, a project of Hanuman Foundation, The Overbrook Foundation, The S.D. Bechtel, Jr. Foundation, The Summit Charitable Foundation, Inc., V. Kann Rasmussen Foundation, The Wallace Alexander Gerbode Foundation, and other generous supporters.

The opinions expressed in this book are those of the author(s) and do not necessarily reflect the views of our supporters.